PEN

THE LOST WORLD

Company director, musician, o︴ ,
music critic, cricket fan, glo︴ ⌐rapner—all in
one—Kumar Prasad Mukherji ︴ ⌐u an interesting life. His very
first recital on All India Radio was on the national hook-up and his
very first book in Bengali, written at the age of sixty-five, received
the coveted Rabindranath Tagore Award. In his late seventies now,
he leads a retired life teaching and writing on music and cricket.

The Lost World of
Hindustani Music

KUMAR PRASAD MUKHERJI

PENGUIN BOOKS

PENGUIN BOOKS
Published by the Penguin Group
Penguin Books India Pvt. Ltd, 11 Community Centre, Panchsheel Park,
New Delhi 110 017, India
Penguin Group (USA) Inc., 375 Hudson Street, New York, New York 10014, USA
Penguin Group (Canada), 90 Eglinton Avenue East, Suite 700, Toronto,
Ontario, M4P 2Y3, Canada (a division of Pearson Penguin Canada Inc.)
Penguin Books Ltd, 80 Strand, London WC2R 0RL, England
Penguin Ireland, 25 St Stephen's Green, Dublin 2, Ireland
(a division of Penguin Books Ltd)
Penguin Group (Australia), 250 Camberwell Road, Camberwell,
Victoria 3124, Australia (a division of Pearson Australia Group Pty Ltd)
Penguin Group (NZ), cnr Airborne and Rosedale Roads, Albany,
Auckland 1310, New Zealand (a division of Pearson New Zealand Ltd)
Penguin Group (South Africa) (Pty) Ltd, 24 Sturdee Avenue, Rosebank,
Johannesburg 2196, South Africa

Penguin Books Ltd, Registered Offices: 80 Strand, London WC2R 0RL, England

First published by Penguin Books India 2006

Copyright © Kumar Prasad Mukherji 2006

10 9 8 7 6 5 4 3 2

ISBN-13: 9780143061991   ISBN-10: 0143061992

Typeset in *Goudy Old Style* by SÜRYA, New Delhi
Printed at Anubha Printers, Noida

To my kid sister Srobona

Contents

1

Early Years

I was for that time lifted above earth
And possest joys not promised in my birth
                              —Neville Cardus
                              in *Second Innings*

This is a book on music. To be precise it is a book on
Hindustani music and musicians. It also attempts to
narrate and analyze the history of creativity in Hindustani
music, mainly khayal and thumri, about the cross-fertilization
of influences among gharanas. This, I feel, might perhaps be
of interest to scholars who are genuinely interested in the
evolution and stylistic patterns of our vocal music as well as
to lay listeners of the older generation. I shall be happy, if in
the process, I can recapture a past that I regard with deep
nostalgia, the colourful musical atmosphere of a dying feudal
age, when budding musicians still in their teens—such as I—
looked up to the great ustads as beings who walked the earth
who were scarcely mortal. The patrons, of course, were the
zamindars, nawabs, rajas and maharajas, some of whom were
sworn disciples of their court musicians—attesting to their
relationship with the gandabandh tied around their wrists.

It will be my endeavour not to present myself consciously
in this book, except to some extent in this introductory
chapter, as has been my custom in my writings in Bengali. At
the same time, since this is also the story of my deep personal

involvement with music, I cannot help lapsing into autobiography. I can only assure my readers of authenticity, even though I may have allowed my imagination some play in the course of half a century spent in gathering source material from ustads, *samajhdars* and dedicated listeners.

If I have had a difficulty, it has lain in recapturing the glories of bygone days of ustads and tawayefs in a language, not my mother tongue, a language that is inimical to the flowery expressions of the court musicians of the nineteenth and early twentieth century. If Ernest Bramah, who wrote the *Kai Lung* series in high-flown Mandarin Chinese, knew Urdu and belonged to this wonderful era, he might have made a better job of it. 'O thou of handsome mien, is it for this unworthy servant of thine to question thy noble parentage?' Words to this effect may not sound inappropriate in Mandarin Chinese or Urdu but do not lend themselves easily to the language of traders and empire-builders learnt second-hand by a boy in an Indian school seven decades ago.

My father's influence on me, stoutly resisted when I was growing up, was a subtle one. A formidable intellectual and even more formidable parent, he is recognized as one of the founder-fathers of Indian sociology, which he taught along with economics in the University of Lucknow where he was quite an institution and was affectionately known as D.P. He occupied no less an important position in Bengali literature as a novelist in the tradition of 'stream of consciousness'. A brilliant essayist and an intrepid free thinker, his correspondence with Rabindranath Tagore on music came out in the form of a book as far back as 1938.

All this, however, did not qualify him to bring up his only child. A typical example: when I was six I once begged to be taken to the zoo. My father promptly said, 'Don't be silly. Are you a baby? You should come with me to the museum.' He took me to the section in the Calcutta Museum where some excellent specimens of Gandhar and Bharhut sculptures remain to this day. But the huge skeleton of a whale and an Egyptian mummy were not adequate compensation for my acute disappointment. Later in life, in any city I found myself in, I would make a beeline for the zoo—be it Mysore, Singapore, Jakarta, Sydney, London or San Diego.

Human memory is highly selective. It tends to reject unpleasant incidents and store all that is good to remember. I find it a bit odd that I cannot, at this age, recall what I did on Friday last week, but can sing hundreds of compositions, which I learnt decades ago.

Memories of my childhood in Lucknow are sweet. The spacious lawns, the rose-scented gardens, the shafts of light through the tall silver oaks on the dewy grass on a wintry morning, the distant sound of bugles from the Police Lines— these kaleidoscopic images can be recalled at will seventy years later. And not merely images. I can recall the intense pleasure of the closeness and warmth of my mother's body when she sat me down near the fireplace and fed me puri gobi with green peas and my favourite bread pudding when I could not have been more than three or four years old. Even now, when I open an old book, I search for the familiar smell of my father's library where stale cigarette smoke and the emanations from the yellow leaves of old books mingled into a delectable masculine scent.

And what a beautiful city the Lucknow of my childhood was! Chattar Manzil on the banks of the Gomti river, the old Imambara, the Roomi Darwaza, they all looked so tall and majestic. The zoological gardens in Benarsi Bagh were full of blossoming seasonal flowers, the guavas plucked from the trees in Secunderabagh were pink inside and tasted so sweet. The Urdu they spoke in Lucknow had an exclusive accent and even ordinary people like the tongawallas and the men who came every morning to sell fish or vegetables in push carts were ever so courteous, their words redolent of the traditional sophistication of the city—these are not memories which grew exaggerated through distance in time. I know because I went back to spend my college and university days in Lucknow after schooling in Calcutta. When I visited

Lucknow for the last time in 1978 I swore not to return. I was horrified to see the rapidity and thoroughness with which they were destroying the serene beauty bestowed on this city by the Nawabs of Oudh and the British. It is the same with Calcutta, and with Darjeeling, once upon a time the queen of hill stations.

Henry Clemenceau, when he was no longer the Prime Minister of France, once came to Delhi, mercifully long before the Birla Temple was built, and spent the day looking at the ancient monuments and tombs. When he returned to the Viceregal Lodge, through the spacious highway between the North and South block, he laughed and said, 'What wonderful ruins these will make!' Today the same buildings appear dignified and noble compared to the PWD architecture of the post-Independence era.

I feel sometimes, as a nation, and I speak for Pakistan and Bangladesh as well, we have no sense of beauty and have done our best to forget what foreigners through the centuries— the Pathans, the Mughals and the British—tried to teach us. Like an alchemist gone mad, we have enthusiastically reversed the process of turning lead into solid gold.

I remember the day His Majesty George V died and the Union Jack was flown at half-mast in the Police Lines. My only Anglo-Indian friend, Theodore Roy, who came to play with us, said, 'I am sorry the king is dead.' I said, 'Well, I am not one bit sorry and you can go to hell with your king emperor.' Not being satisfied with this seditious statement, I persuaded, in a fit of patriotism, my other companions to boycott Theo. This has remained my sole contribution towards the cause of Indian Independence.

I can also remember the day Italy declared war on Abyssinia. The children from the neighbouring quarters of university professors who played with bows and arrows would take sides. While my sympathy was with poor Abyssinia, two of my close friends would always side with fascist Italy. One of them, to whom I shall always be grateful for my musical education and sharing of musical experiences, grew up into a mild-mannered singer who became an alchoholic and died even before he reached sixty. Putuda, as I called him, was one of the very few genuine disciples of Ustad Amir Khan. The other surviving soldier of the Italian army turned out to be an introvert in a perpetual temper. He had impeccable academic credentials, which he hardly put to use. He leads a retired life in Delhi.

That happy childhood, when one experienced the innocent and unfettered joy of living, did not last long. After a very brief experiment in a so-called public school meant for children of rich taluqdars, I was despatched to Calcutta along with my mother to live with my uncles. The younger of the two, a professor of history (his children and their spouses are all academicians—I am the black sheep of the family) and a memorable hypochondriac, lived to a ripe old age without suffering any ailments known to medical science except chronic dyspepsia, which might have been brought about by ceaseless worries about his own state of health rather than sinful food habits. He and his wife bestowed on me their unbounded affection and did their best to spoil me with chocolates, clothes and books both in Bengali and English.

I was introduced at a tender age to R.M. Ballantyne's adventure stories, Rider Haggard, Jonathan Swift as well as Bengali writers like Hemendra Kumar Roy whom all my friends considered the maestro of all writers and would have cheerfully have given hairs from their heads to for an autograph. My uncle believed in discipline too, however, and I grew up in the midst of a series of dos and don'ts. He was paranoid about infections and imaginary catastrophies that might befall his nephew and it was my mother's strong common sense that saved me from becoming a namby-pamby, house-bound child.

My father's intention of sending me to an Indian school in Calcutta was to ensure that I did not lose touch with my mother tongue and Sanskrit, which was a wise move. I learnt English the proper way by reading the classics and not the kind of chi-chi English that boys in Anglo-Indian schools learnt to speak and write. I also did not acquire their indifference to their mother tongues, Hindi or Bengali, and never lost touch in later life with Indian and specifically Bengali culture. The masters in the Indian school to which I went were poor but hard-working, and one or two of them were endowed with imagination. One in particular, who was born into affluence and took up teaching history and English in the school as a hobby, was a cousin of mine. He introduced us to Conan Doyle, Stevenson, the science fiction of H.G. Wells, and finally Dickens, all before I reached thirteen, because he thought, and rightly so, that these authors wrote the best English. In the process our dormant imaginations were fired by those masters of prose.

In Calcutta I was simultaneously initiated into the basics of Hindustani music by our neighbour Rabindra Lal Roy, who taught me sa-re-ga-ma, two dhamars and a Lakshan geet in Yaman Kalyan. He was no performer but was capable of original thinking and after stints in Visva-Bharati in Santiniketan, and in Patna, ended up as chairman, department of music, University of Delhi. He was my first guru and I am grateful to him for reasons that I shall presently come to. The two disciples of his who made the grade are his daughter Malabika Kanan and myself. She did it through years of talim and hard work whereas my journey into the world of Hindustani music was accidental.

I must confess I found the daily exercise of the basics a dreadful bore at the age of eight or nine. Those were the days of K.L. Saigal, Pankaj Mullick and Kananbala whose film songs, composed by R.C. Boral of New Theatres, I loved to distraction. My friends in school were not musical although my Putuda was. In fact, he had already started taking lessons from Tarapada Chakraborty, the first Bengali singer, in my opinion, of proper khayal. He was a man of remarkable talent but little or no talim. His voice was deep, flexible and melodious and he had the ability to create atmosphere with his favourite ragas of Yaman, Puriya, Shudh Kalyan, Chhayanat and Darbari. It was much later that I fell under his spell.

During my early training under Rabindra Lal Roy, which did not last more than a year and a half, I was, at fifteen, incapable of appreciating classical music though I was forced to listen to a lot of it largely because of my father.

Once he took study leave for eight months and came to Calcutta. There was a procession of musicians and his literary friends to the house every day. Everybody who was anybody in the local world of music came to sing or play over the weekends. There was Radhika Mohan Moitra, who looked every inch the handsome young zamindar of Bengali novels, which he was. He was learning sarod at that time from Mohammed Amir Khan and was a regular visitor to the house. So was Kumar Sachin Deb Burman who was learning from Bhishma Deb Chatterjee. His Bengali khayals and semi-classical songs were a rage in Calcutta before he drifted to Bollywood. Bhishma Deb was easily the most famous Bengali musician at that time. He had learnt from Ustad Badal Khan who was from Sonepat, now in Haryana, but for some mysterious reason was labelled as a great sarangi-player from Agra. No sarangi-player can give a vocalist his gayaki. Bhishma Deb invented a style of his own that resembled no school of singing before or after. The cognoscenti of Calcutta who had heard him at his peak swore he was potentially no inferior to the luminaries of his time. Unfortunately, he never got his due in the select circles in UP, Delhi, Lahore or Bombay. But he made an impression in Allahabad at the prestigious All India Conference held every year through the auspices of Dakshina Ranjan Bhattacharya, the vice-chancellor of the university and a great connoisseur of music.

Those days, there being no good hotels in Allahabad, the artistes were lodged in tents erected specially for the occasion in the university campus. One morning, Bhishma Deb was practising inside his tent when Habibuddin, the famous tabla-player whose abrasive nature was a byword, was out on his morning walk. He enquired from Bhishma Deb's elder brother, Taradas, who was standing outside the tent, who the singer was. Upon being informed that the virtuoso was no less than

Bhishma Deb, the 'Royal Bengal Tiger', Habibuddin told Tarababu, 'Excellent! Tell him the rifle from the Meerut gun factory has arrived and will meet him tomorrow in the mehfil.'

Tarapadababu, who sang once in our house, was a self-taught musician of phenomenal talent with a remarkable gift of imitation. Every three or four years he changed his musical colours like a chameleon. I have known people who had heard him imitate Narayan Rao Vyas in the earliest phase of his musical career. He heard Pandit Omkarnath Thakur at a conference in Muzaffarpur and came under his spell for a while—until he heard Abdul Karim Khan in 1936. He promptly switched over to Kirana gayaki. Next year, he was bowled over by Ustad Faiyaz Khan and, predictably, introduced the nom tom alap, rhythmic bol-bant and bol-taans into his gayaki. He ultimately settled down in a style that could be best described as Abdul Faiyaz Karim Khan, the vistar in Kirana and the rest à la Faiyaz Khan of Agra. Curiously enough, he had a natural propensity for the flexible bahlawa with long meends of the Gwalior gayaki. No one knows to which ustad he was indebted for this facet of his style.

It is true Tarapadababu became a formal disciple of Acharya Girija Shankar Chakraborty but that was during Girijababu's declining years, when he was unable to perform in public due to poor health, or to teach properly. In Girijababu's younger days Calcutta offered the biggest market for ustads and tawayefs. While a fair number of tawayefs settled down in Calcutta to cater to the pleasure of the babus, few of the ustads from the north or west did. Two of those who did were Taj Khan and Ali Baksh Khan who were court musicians of the Nawab Wajid Ali Shah of Oudh, exiled to Metiabruz, in Calcutta. Others were Ustad Badal Khan who lived and died in Calcutta well past his hundred years, the legendary Maujuddin Khan, another self-taught scintillating singer of khayal and thumris, a lot of second-raters like Ustad Mehendi Hussain Khan and Ashfaq Hussain Khan of Rampur, Zamiruddin Khan, Keshav Dhekne of Gwalior gharana and

Ramesh Thakur, brother of Pandit Omkar Nath. Pandit Dilip Chandra Vedi stayed for three years and taught Kananbala. Ustad Maseed Khan and his son Keramatulla Khan, the well-known tabla-player, chose Calcutta as their home.

Jnan Prakash Ghosh was Maseed Khan's premier disciple. That is why Calcutta's tabla-players have achieved world-renown today. Among those who spent parts of their lives in this city are Ustad Muzaffar Khan of Delhi, Ustad Amir Khan and, of course, Ustad Bade Ghulam Ali Khan. The styles of the last two in recent years had the biggest impact on Calcutta vocalists and quite a few Bengali musicians without any direct talim have tried to blend the styles of these two ustads with results that often are little short of disastrous.

Girijababu was the last of the Bengali vocalists who had more than adequate talim from famous Muslim ustads. He learnt dhrupad from Radhika Mohan Goswami; the doyen of Betia gharana, though legitimately he belonged to the Vishnupur gharana by birth. Thereafter, like quite a few contemporary musicians of Calcutta, he took talim from Ustad Badal Khan, the sarangi-player. Then he heard Muzaffar Khan and followed him to Delhi. Khansaheb's original talim was from Ali Baksh Khan of the court of the exiled Nawab of Oudh in Calcutta, but he subsequently moved to Delhi for a while. He was related to Ustad Faiyaz Khan on his father's side and as such, belonged legitimately to the Rangila gharana of Agra, though his style was somewhat different. According to Raja Deba Prasad Garg of Mahishadal, whom Muzaffar Khan taught for some time, he was the natural father of Zohrabai Agrewali, possibly the most accomplished female musician of her time. Most of her discs were cut as far back as the first quarter of the twentieth century but they have not dated one bit.

Girijababu, not satisfied with the limited talim from the peripatetic Muzaffar Khan, went from Delhi to Rampur. There he became a formal disciple of the great Inayet Hussain Khan, khayalia and composer who had married the daughter of the legendary Ustad Haddu Khan of Gwalior gharana. Sadat Ali Khan, better known as Nawab Chhamman of the Rampur dynasty, also gave a few dhrupad bandishes as well as thumri compositions to Girijababu. But his reputation as a thumri singer was mainly due to his close association with Bhaiyya Saheb Ganpat Rao, the guru of Moijuddin Khan, whose name I have mentioned earlier and about whom I propose to write in greater detail.

All this, however, did not enable Girijababu to gain any worthwhile standing outside Bengal. He will always be remembered as an acharya, a teacher of teachers, and to him goes the credit of spreading a love of classical music among the gentry in Calcutta. Before him it was unthinkable for a girl from a good family to be initiated into any music other than kirtan and the songs of Tagore, Atul Prasad and Nazrul Islam. Khayal and thumri were associated with tawayefs and baijis, in other words, 'bad women'.

Deba Prasad Garg tells a story about Muzaffar Khan and Tarapada Chakraborty. At one of the music festivals, which for some strange reason we in India call music conferences, Tarapadababu accompanied the ustad to the hall. He was billed at around eight in the evening, immediately before Muzaffar Khan's recital. Instead of waiting in the green room, the ustad decided to listen to the young artiste. Within minutes, the ustad turned to Deba Prasad and said, 'Sounds like this lad is a follower of Abdul Karim'. As his recital proceeded, the ustad gradually lapsed into silence. When it was over, he had tears in his eyes. He was so overwhelmed; he would not get up and prepare for his own performance. He kept saying, 'No one should sing after this, certainly not me. This is glorious music. I have never heard anything like this.' Deba Prasad tried to persuade him, as did the organizers and other local artistes, but Khansaheb appeared adamant.

People had come in large numbers to hear the guru of Acharya Girija Shankar, and the man behind the show, Bhupen Ghosh of Pathuriaghata, was extremely worried. At his behest and the combined entreaties of other senior artistes, Tarapadababu did what he was told. He went and fell at the feet of Muzaffar Khan and said, 'You are my guru's guru, my ustad's ustad, my music is not worth a *khota* paisa to your rupee. If I am the cause of your not singing this evening, I shall go home and kill myself.' Khansaheb relented, took the stage and sang a gorgeous khayal in Adana.

Dilip Kumar Roy of Pondicherry and my father did their best to persuade Tarapadababu to go to Sawai Gandharv in Bombay to take formal talim and authentic bandishes from him, since it was he who was heading the Kirana school after the death of Ustad Abdul Karim Khan. Gangubai Hangal, Firoz Dastur and Bhimsen Joshi went to him and prospered. Tarapadababu's adamant refusal, I think, has been a great loss to music.

I must have been nine when I heard three of the greatest musicians of the century, precisely the three who, according to my friend Ustad Vilayet Khan the sitar-player, had the greatest impact on his music. The first was Ustad Abdul Karim Khan, the founder of Kirana khayal gayaki. This was his second visit to Calcutta. On an earlier occasion, when he came to the city, he was hardly known. Since then, his records, especially the Bhairavi thumri *Jamuna Ke Teer* and *Piya Bin Nahi Aawat Chain* in Jhinjhoti had created a sensation. All the artistes flocked to the University Institute Hall. All I remember was that Khansaheb was sitting with his mouth open, the tanpuras were playing, the accompanists were not sitting idle either, but no sound was emanating from Abdul Karim Khan's mouth. I kept on asking my father the reason for this mysterious phenomenon and all he said was 'Hush! Keep quiet. I'll tell you later.'

Later, indeed much later, I realized Khansaheb was singing Basant and as he was lingering on the sa, the tonic in the upper octave and his voice had mingled with the finely tuned tanpuras and the shadaj of the harmonium so well that it created the illusion that he had lost his voice. Many people since have talked to me about this swarasiddhi, this man who had attained the pinnacle of purity, and the mesmerizing quality of his sur. Firoz Dastur also told me of a similar experience.

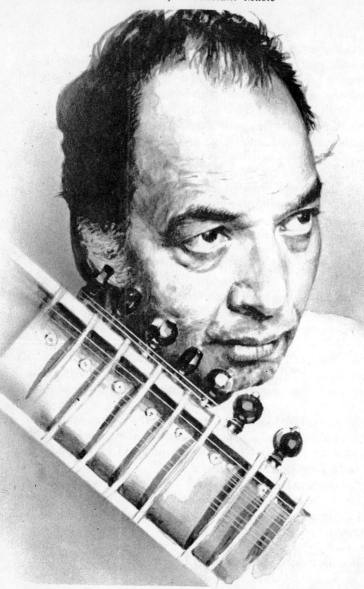

Ustad Vilayet Khan

The same year I heard Ustad Faiyaz Khan at a private soiree. Ustad Hafiz Ali Khan, better known today as Amjad Ali Khan's father, played Todi on the sarod and it was the renowned vocalist Bhishma Deb Chatterjee who accompanied him on the tabla. During the jhala at its fastest he would massage his left biceps occasionally with his right hand, smiling all the while, while the left hand was busy with the *bayan*, thereby affording my friends and me much merriment. Faiyaz Khan followed this with a long alaap in Jaunpuri and his khayal *'Phulwan ki gendanwa maika na maro'*. I remember nothing except the full-throated pukars, the higher notes in the upper octave surcharged with emotion, which actually brought tears to the eyes of some.

Possibly at about the same time, I heard Ustad Inayet Khan, Vilayet's father, on the surbahar. The peculiar notes emanating from his instrument in the ati mandra saptak were comical to my ears but I liked his drut gat on the sitar without any idea of what he was playing. I was too young to appreciate all this wonderful music but unconsciously I had allowed the grace of great art to touch me.

Film music pursued me through the years till I was fifteen. I passed my matriculation at the age of thirteen from Calcutta University and returned to Lucknow. I used to cycle a couple of miles from the university campus through Daliganj, over the iron bridge which commanded a lovely view of the Imambara and the ancient buildings of old Lucknow, to Government Jubilee Intermediate College. I wore my newly-acquired long trousers and a sola hat, which was much favoured by the British during summers in India. The rice-eating Bengali boy invited the usual ragging from the older boys but it did not last long, partly because of my prowess on the soccer field and my singing of songs from popular films. Also, my ability to swear in more than one language with fervour and passion. Urdu was added in no time to the repertoire, establishing my standing with the boys.

My rival was a handsome, mild-mannered boy called Suresh Mathur who was a devout worshipper of Pankaj

Mallick, whose film song *Piya Milan Ko Jana* was a hit in the early Forties. Suresh would practise every day by singing into an empty earthen pot, the kind used for cooking rice, in order to lend depth and timbre to his voice. He cherished a secret vanity and thought his voice resembled that of Pankaj Mallick. The sola hat replaced the earthen pot in college, during the off periods when we had quite a soiree in one of the vacant classrooms. Years later I met Suresh in the Dehra Dun Club, when he had become a handsome briefless lawyer inclined to overindulgence at the expense of an English widow twice his age who would occasionally hiss at him if he looked twice at a younger woman.

Gradually, I acquired a few friends who lived on the other side of the river in the city. They initiated me into raga sangeet once again. One of them could whistle small pieces like 'Phulawale kanth' in Bahar, 'Bolre papihara' in Miyan Malhar or 'Bajubandh khul khul jaye' in Bhairavi. His elder brother played the sarod. It was in their house in 1942 that I heard S.C.R. Bhat sing Miyan Malhar, supported by K.G. Ginde, and Dinkar Kaikini with whom I became friends years later and sang jugalbandi together for a while in conferences. I heard Sakhawat Ali Khan, a member of the Keramatulla Kaokab Khan dynasty, on sarod, and his son Iliyas Khan on sitar. That night, more than any other specific occasion that I can remember, helped me to shed my earlier skin and opened the gates to the magic world to which I belonged by birthright. My juvenile wanderings had ceased at the age of fifteen and classical music welcomed me back with open arms.

At this point of time a strange thing happened to me. Rabindra Lal Roy's *Rag Nirnaya* fell into my hands. The book is really 'Bhatkhande Made Easy'. His five volumes contain descriptions of all the ragas to be found together with vistar, the thaats, arohis and avarohis. As I turned the pages I would become familiar with three or four ragas a day. In due course I would compose bandishes, the words of which were weak and some times comically inappropriate although the structure was grammatically correct. As I sang those ragas I had the feeling I had known most of them always. I would diligently go through the fortnightly *Indian Listener* and listen to all the artistes—major, minor, even obscure ones—every day on the radio. One evening I heard Kamod on the sarod by Ustad Alauddin Khan, father of Ali Akbar and guru of Ravi Shankar. I promptly composed a bandish and started singing it. As far as I can remember the composition vaguely resembled the well-known *Ka Re Jane Na Doongee* in teentaal.

This awakening was very strange and may be of psychological interest to some but I have not come across anyone to whom a similar thing has happened. Those who believe in that kind of thing might say that this *sanskaar* is from a *purvajanma*, or previous birth. Those who swear by the Montessori method of teaching infants might talk of unconscious absorption in one's childhood. I have heard from my mother that I was surrounded by reproductions of famous Renaissance paintings and prints of French impressionists when I was an infant, and gramophone records of Zohrabai, Piara Sahab, Moijuddin Khan, Abdul Karim, Faiyaz Khan and others were constantly played by my father. Maybe some of that entered my unconscious and hibernated all those years, only to come out and totally envelop me at the age of fifteen.

All this did not do much good to my studies and I barely missed first class in my intermediate final. In my fifteenth year I entered university and was persuaded by my father to take honours in economics, against my wishes. At home at the age of fifteen I was saddled with books on Marxism apart from Kropotkin, Trotsky, Lenin and Sidney and Beatrice Webb's works. My father, who called himself a Marxologist (not Marxist), was determined to make me follow in his footsteps, a project at which he failed miserably, as usual. My other subjects, which I loved, were history, Sanskrit and English literature. That was the time I made friends with Mahesh Varma, A.K. Saran and Parimal Dasgupta— three very fine minds. Saran in particular, a great mind today, had an intellect much superior to ours. Unfortunately, my friends could not share my passion for music, not being musical themselves, as was the case with two successive girlfriends I acquired in my four years in college.

We were all very precocious for our age and liked monkeying around with ideas, words and phrases. Our essays were full of recondite allusions and we spent hours in the library, in advance, on a subject to be taught by the professor a day or two later, only to be able to put awkward questions to him. The undergraduate days were full of fun. We did not wear our intellectual airs awkwardly because we could also laugh at ourselves. Nonetheless, that was the age when plumes needed be displayed and we did that with a flourish.

Two of my college friends, Hemchand Joshi and P.N. Chinchore, were good singers to whom I owe a lot. Chinchore had finished doing his Sangeet Visharad and was in the sixth year in the Marris Music College. I would sit with him on the lawns of the university and ask him to sing what he had learnt the previous day. It would take me no more than a quarter of an hour to acquire the compositions and may be another half an hour to learn by heart the features and the movements of the new raga. This was easy because I would be able to absorb the raga in its totality and not in phrases. Later, I would be able to analyze the composition and develop and adorn the phrases while singing it. I have retained this habit in my old age when I make my students appreciate that the development of a raga is not in progressive notes only. It is the phrases which constitute the anatomy of the raga, and unless these are appropriately highlighted, the raga-bhava cannot be established. With age, my power of absorption and retention have, however, been steadily on the decline, which is inevitable—like losing one's hair and teeth—but nonetheless, tragic.

Although I sang all the time, in the bathroom, on a bike or with likeminded aspiring musicians in neighbouring hostels, I never practised at home. Once, however, I borrowed a tanpura and was singing in my bedroom. My father overheard

me. Next day a teacher, a gentleman in a frayed sherwani
and cap, Abdur Rahman Akhtar, was engaged to teach me.
He was an occasional radio artiste and very proud of it. I
learnt a couple of compositions in Behag and Bhairav and
there ended my formal lessons from an ustad—to be resumed
thirty years later. I realized, as possibly did Abdur
Rahmansaheb, that I was not cut out for memorizing
stereotyped lessons like the paltas, or combination of notes,
that constituted part of the preliminary talim of every disciple.
Looking back, I feel my singing was no worse than his. I was
essentially more imaginative and had a natural flair for taans,
though being unaccustomed to rigorous practice, my notes
naturally were not as pure as his.

I lived intensely, for the next four years till I left
university, in three distinct worlds. There was the world of
books and passionate debates with friends who jumped at
every opportunity to argue on any subject till midnight.
There were friends on the cricket field, tennis lawns and the
rowing club. I loved cricket passionately but was never very
good at it. Even now I could not agree more with Julius
Rebeiro, the ex-police commissioner of Bombay, whose idea
of happiness is to watch Tendulkar batting on TV, with no
fear of the telephone ringing.

And not the least of the three worlds was my world of
music. I spent much time listening to minor ustads of
Lucknow hoping to come by some bandishes by flattering
their vanity. There were visiting ustads, some of them big
names who would appear in charity concerts specially convened
for the war fund in the Forties. There were, of course, private
soirees in the houses of the wealthy, and in Lucknow there
was no dearth of them. They called themselves rajas and
nawabs and competed with one another in offering patronage
to ustads and tawayefs of repute. It was not difficult to obtain
access to these jalsas since every brick in the University
College buildings owed its existence to the landowners of
Oudh and their children came to the university as a matter
of course. The BA degree held snob value for the progeny of

the landed gentry, although some of them never pursued their studies beyond the portals of the Colvin Taluqdar School.

One of my musical friends, Maulana Mohammed Hussain, lived in Hewett Hostel, the famous sanctuary of the kunwar sahibs, the offspring of taluqdars, and talented sportsmen. One remembers Ghaus Mohammad, India's number one tennis-player, who had made up his mind to reside permanently in the university, ostensibly studying for finals in BA. Also (Babu) Kunwar Digvijay Singh, the brilliant centre-forward who captained India's hockey team to victory in the Olympics six years after I left the university. The typical resident of Hewett Hostel maintained a big wardrobe, half a dozen pairs of hand-made shoes, expensive hats and gloves in winter. One might have found a single rose in an empty bottle of gin on the writing table, and yesterday's newspaper, but hardly any books, pencils or writing pads. I do not yet know how Mohammed Hussain managed to qualify for the residentship of this elite hostel. Dressed in an achkan and a velvet cap, and a chain-smoker, Mohammed Hussain's conversation was punctuated with an abundance of witty obscenities, the like of which was rare those days in the student community of Lucknow.

There are some people who jog religiously in the morning, live on balanced diets, never forget to have their nightcaps of Horlicks or Complan, yet suffer from indifferent health for years and years. The same could be said about Mohammed Hussain's music. Nonetheless, he pursued his riyaz with unabated enthusiasm and endlessly supplied cups of tea and cheap cigarettes to friends who cared to listen to him. I was one of them, mainly so I could practise during my off periods in his room. Another close musical friend was N.K.P. Salve, a highly erratic bowler of the leg spin and googlies, who, later in life, became the president of the Board of Cricket Control in India and a member of Indira Gandhi's Cabinet.

I knew Mohammed Hussain was from the state of Rampur but I was certainly not prepared to find the court musician and guru of the Nawab Raza Ali Khan of Rampur, Ustad Mushtaq Hussain Khan, with his tin trunk and *razai* and his eldest son Ishtiaq Hussain, in a ten-by-twenty room of the Hewett Hostel. The same afternoon I heard Shuddh Sarang from him. It was a rare experience. Normally, his singing was fidgety and erratic and would appear to some as somewhat lacking in aesthetic sense, but he was a great ustad whose stock of compositions seemed unlimited. That afternoon, however, he was more composed than usual and concentrated on the vistar for over half an hour. His favourite saying was, 'You get electricity only when negative and positive wires are joined together. That is how you get sur.' I must say it was the first time I realized what years of sadhana, or dedicated practice, can do for one's music, something that I have never been able to experience in all my life for a variety of reasons.

Ustad Mushtaq Hussain Khan used to come to Lucknow, a few hours' journey from Rampur, twice a month for his radio programmes. One evening he turned to me and asked me whether I sang at all. To my answer in the negative he turned to Mohammed Hussain and said, 'This friend of yours sits here for hours to listen to my music, his daads, appreciative noises, are made also at the right times, why does he not learn to sing?' Maulana Mohammed Hussain, with a twinkle in his eyes, said, 'But, Ustad, he sings quite regularly and he sings quite well. *Kyun, bhai, kuchh sunaiye Khan Sahab ko,* why don't you sing for Khan Sahab?' I must have been very nervous but I managed to sing Behag for half an hour. The composition I sang, *Balam re morey man ke,* was one I had learnt from Abdur Rahman Akhtar. At the end of it, the ustad asked me from whom I had been taking my lessons.

'From no one in particular, *main to sun sun ke thora sa ga leta hoon.*' (This was a lie of which I feel ashamed even now. However, it was not a blatant lie, since what I sang, except for the composition, was not the product of Abdur Rahman Khan's lessons. Nonetheless, one must acknowledge one's debts to whoever gives one even a single bandish, as the great Ustad Vilayet Hussain Khan of Agra gharana mentions in his book *Sangeet Sansmaran.*)

Ustad Mushtaq Hussain Khan absolutely refused to believe what I said. 'How can it be?' he said to his son Ishtiaq Hussain, 'This lad is singing in tune and taal, his treatment of Behag also shows some understanding. How can a boy of this age sing for half an hour without talim?' He was genuinely mystified because such things do not happen in the households of ustads where boys are initiated at the age of five or six and the average budding shagird is not usually a bright specimen. To cut a long story short, I was taken on as a disciple the following afternoon on payment of a thali of sweets and fifty-one rupees, a not inconsiderable sum those days for a seventeen-year-old dependent on his mother for an extra bit of pocket money.

I got very little out of Khansaheb, my second guru, except three or four vilambit compositions, some tips on how to practise heavy taans with shuddh akar and plenty of opportunities to listen to him. Even now I retain traces of his Gwalior gayaki in the midst of my Agra presentation. The result is not unsatisfactory, considering the Agra gharana imported khayal from Gwalior roughly three hundred years ago and therefore there is no inherent conflict between the two.

A few months later, the most important event of my musical life occurred. It must have been in the month of December in 1944. I once again heard Ustad Faiyaz Khan, the undisputed monarch after the death of Abdul Karim Khan, and according to most of my elders whose opinion I valued, the musician of the century. By now my receptivity had reached a higher level of sophistication and my critical faculty was aroused. Khansaheb's music was like a blow to the solar plexus that made me forget all that I had heard before. His regal personality, the timbre of his extraordinarily rich voice, his total command over the medium and the ragadari overwhelmed me. It was Yaman he sang followed by Darbari and Suha Kanhra. For weeks I could hear his voice and the phrases inside my head, and then onwards, whatever I sang was Faiyaz Khan's. I sat glued to the radio whenever he sang from Delhi or Bombay. Baroda had not yet acquired a station with transmitting facilities and that is where he lived as the court musician of the Gaekwads.

Within eight months Ustad Faiyaz Khan came again to Lucknow. He was the last to sing at three in the morning in the conference, which began with Bismillah Khan's shehnai and young Ali Akbaı Khan's sarod recital. This time it was the early morning raga Lalit, his favourite, followed by Todi and Bhairavi thumri. What I felt was not mere joy or ecstasy but something that shook me to the very core of my musical being, something that was an invasion of my soul. It was relatively simpler music compared to that of Bade Ghulam Ali Khan or Amir Khan, whom I heard later. But it was the simplicity of classicism, which deals with fundamentals. Years later, K.G. Ginde, possibly the last of the erudite singers from the past, and a clone of Pandit Shrikrishna Ratanjankar, told me, 'You and I would know how difficult it is to sing the so-called simple music of Faiyaz Khan.'

At about the same time S.K. Choubey, a disciple of Ustad Faiyaz Khan who taught English literature in the Lucknow Christian College, took me to Khansaheb in the Empire Hotel in Kaisarbagh and said, 'Khan Sahab, this is the son of Professor Mukherji, he imitates you a lot, *aap ka bahut nakal karta hai.*' God knows what Faiyaz Khan thought when he looked at the seventeen-year-old boy before him. In a tone of grave courtesy, as if I were an artiste of some consequence, he requested me to sing for him saying, '*Phir hum logon ko kuchh sunaiye.*' I shudder at the thought of the cheek of young Mukherji, who, without any ado, pulled out the harmonium, fixed the sur and pancham and sang Khansaheb's 78 RPM record *More Mandara* in Jayjaiwanti.

I sang from A to Z, leaving out nothing, not even his halaq taans beginning from the Gandhar in taar saptak and the tehais. All present, mainly Khansaheb's shagirds, were in gales of merriment but Khansaheb did not permit himself even a smile. Instead he took the same pitch and started his *alaap* in Jayjaiwanti. Someone from his entourage quickly tuned the tanpuras and the tabla. I remember with great pride that he asked me to accompany him and corrected me on one or two points. Three decades later, in my very first broadcast on radio, which was on national hook-up, I remembered every phrase and every nuance of his recital that evening. My first commercial cassette also contained the same Jayjaiwanti. When I sang in the Baroda palace before a large distinguished audience, which included Ghulam Rasool Khan, Faiyaz Khan's lifelong companion and harmonium-player, I again chose the same raga as a tribute to the memory of the brief talim I received from the great man way back in 1945.

Thanks to P.N. Chinchore I had quite a few opportunities to listen to his guru and my father's friend Shrikrishna Ratanjankar, at that time principal of the Marris Music College of Lucknow. He had combined Ustad Mushtaq Hussain's gayaki with that of Faiyaz Khan and evolved a style that was a delight for the connoisseur. He was also a composer of great merit and unquestionably the most cerebral musician of his star-studded era. I swear I have not come across anyone in my entire life whose delineation and ability to invent new phrases of a raga could match Ratanjankar's. He was truly a musician's musician who spent the better part of his life on spreading Bhatkhandeji's system of teaching music on a pittance of a hundred rupees a month.

All this made my father sit up and take serious notice of my extra-curricular activities. He called me one morning to his library and told me quietly that in his opinion music and studies did not go together. At least he himself had failed to combine the two. It was, therefore, in the fitness of things that I made a choice. In his considered opinion I should pursue my studies with undivided attention till I obtained my master's degree. He added, however, that if I was really devoted to music with the kind of passion that would induce me to disregard his advice, I could no doubt go ahead, but that would be unfortunate. It must be remembered that in the pre-Independence era in India, music offered precious few openings for jobs that provided a decent living, unless one could really go to the top of one's profession. I am not unhappy I listened to his advice. At the same time, I succeeded in later life in combining music with a career in industrial management in government more successfully than my father could have imagined. Although my achievements in life are small compared to those of the late Professor D.P. Mukherji, they all came after his death. In fact, the blossoming of my personality after the shadow of my formidable father's presence was removed is a textbook case for psychologists.

I had two bad years after I passed out of the university when I got involved in commerce. It was a soulless occupation in a British mercantile firm where the intellectual development of an average fellow saheb, white or brown, was that of a retarded adolescent. I breathed a sigh of relief when I got out of the maze of balance sheets and cocktails and drifted into government service, though Kanpur, my first posting, offered a dreary contrast to the glamorous Calcutta of the late Forties.

I got precious little music to listen to except over an occasional weekend at Lucknow, only forty-eight miles away. However, my head assistant in office was a Sangeet Visharad from Marris College and I got some opportunities to practise in his house and soon collected a small group of friends who could be persuaded to listen to me. Two tabla-players were recruited from the office staff. One specialized in simple vilambit ektaal and the other in drut teentaal and neither could play anything else.

With great dexterity and through the kindness of Bhagwan Sahay, the chief secretary, I manoeuvred a posting as the UP government's liaison officer in Calcutta. During the next ten years, as I changed postings, I had little or no practice but was not ever completely out of touch with Indian classical music. Thanks to Satyajit Ray and a few others I developed a keen taste for European music. It all started with a trip to the Mozart music festival at Lucerne in the summer of 1956 when my father was seriously ill in Zurich. The music of

Haydn, Bach and Beethoven followed and there was no end to listening to records day and night. I spent nearly a fortune on music systems and LPs. Indian classical music would come to my ears in notations but European music to me had an emotional appeal. I consider myself fortunate to be able to respond to both varieties intellectually and emotionally, a blessing that I have not been able to share with many.

One was T.C. Satyanath, Sat to his many friends in Calcutta. To him goes the credit of initiating the cream of the fashionable mercantile society into Indian classical music much before Vijay Kichlu embarked on that project. Satyanath had an extremely good ear for classical music, European, Karnatak or north Indian, and he would occasionally accompany me on the violin during my infrequent practising sessions. Later in life, when I was touring west and south India with Pandit V.G. Jog, then my constant travelling companion and accompanist in musical soirees, I met Satyanath in Cochin. There, as the vice-chairman of a well-known tea firm, he was living in a perpetual alcoholic haze. I told him if I ever wrote my autobiography I would call it *From T.C. Satyanath to V.G. Jog.* He looked at me critically and said, 'Better call it *Fallen Hairs.*'

I did not own a tanpura till 1959 when I was in my thirty-second year. Dulal Chakraborty, a senior tabla-player known to me for many years, persuaded me to buy one for twenty-five rupees. A tabla and bayan cost another twenty-five. He extracted a promise, which I tried my best to keep in spite of tours and tremendous pressure of building up an alternate career. I had got married a couple of years earlier and my wife, who loved music and had a natural flair for singing in tune, never pursued music seriously. During my practice sessions she would invariably leave the house, until she could reconcile herself to my singing quite a few months later. It did not take me long to get into my stride and curiously enough, I started singing in public in a big way within four or five years. In spite of the fact I had not taken talim from any ustad for a sufficient length of time, my presentation, as I look back, was technically and grammatically correct. The style was Agra, nay, typically that of Faiyaz Khan.

My first major recital fifteen years after the demise of my idol was attended by Ustad Ata Hussain Khan, brother-in-law and premier disciple of Ustad Faiyaz Khan. At the end of it, when I went to him to pay my respects, he asked me whether I had ever received talim from the great man. He was astonished to hear that I had not, and that I had not heard him in person more than half a dozen times. He looked at me quizzically; he was almost blind then, and said, '*Jisko jaisa chahoge usko waysa paoge* (You will perceive Him the way you want Him).'

It was not for another seven years that I went for formal talim from Ata Hussain Khan. He was a better teacher than a performer, unlike Latafat Hussain Khan who was exactly the opposite. Between the two of them, I received sustained talim for fourteen years, which increased my knowledge, but to be truthful, did not appreciably enrich my gayaki. Neither was my total presentation much different at the end of it. Meanwhile, I had started getting regular bookings in conferences in Calcutta and outside. One of the reasons, of course, was that being a public servant I did not demand any fees. But that alone did not account for my getting respectable billing, sometimes with Ravi Kichlu in a duo, mostly alone, on the last evening of a festival just before somebody like Ustad Ali Akbar or Ustad Vilayet Hussain Khan came on. In 1972, Ustad Latafat Khan, a nephew and disciple of Ustad Faiyaz Khan, heard me in Bombay and told V.G. Jog that I had more of Faiyaz Khan in me than anybody of Khansaheb's clan.

So did Yunus Hussain, another Agra gharana pandit of my generation. Deba Prasad Garg, Raja of Mahishadal, who worshipped Faiyaz Khan and learnt from him for a number of years, heard a radio recital of mine and wrote to me saying that for a few minutes he was in a state of confusion trying to make out whether it was an old recording of the last days of Khansaheb from the All India Radio archives. He was of the opinion that my inflexions, tonal quality and expressions were closer to Faiyaz Khan's than anybody else's. Shafi Ahmed Khan, the seniormost surviving ustad of the Agra gharana, currently attached to the ITC Sangeet Research Academy, says Faiyaz Khan's gayaki has been faithfully imitated and absorbed by Asad Ali Khan, Sohan Singh and myself. But the first two had received talim from Faiyaz Khan. I had not. Neither have I heard more than ten per cent of what other members of his gharana had the good fortune to hear. Dinkar Kaikini, who partnered me in duo recitals for some time in Calcutta, Delhi and Bombay, calls me the *Ekalavya shishya* of Faiyaz Khan, quoting the parallel from the *Mahabharata* in which the youth Ekalavya, denied lessons in archery by guru Dronacharya, worshipped his idol and practised incessantly till he became the equal of, if not a greater warrior than, Arjuna. I find this to be one of the strangest things that has happened to me and I state, I trust without immodesty, the facts as they are.

Obviously it is not the quality of the music that stands comparison but the surprising affinity with my idol which had struck everybody who heard me in my prime or have listened to my commercial CDs of the Seventies and Eighties. It is like somebody from another country resembling a person not connected by blood ties so closely that he is taken as a brother or a son. G.K. Chesterton once remarked that fact was indeed stranger than fiction because fiction is a product of the human mind. Life offers facts or events that may well be outside the scope of human imagination and are therefore strange to us.

A passing remembrance of my role as the music critic of *The Statesman*, Calcutta, off and on for fifteen years, may not be out of place here. Those were busy years indeed. Apart from a demanding job in a senior position in a large government undertaking, I had my own riyaz and recitals in Calcutta as well as in other cities. There had been occasions when I carried a change of clothes for a public recital to office where I would finish a meeting barely in time to go to Mahajati Sadan, Kalamandir or Rabindra Sadan. Oddly enough, it did not affect my voice or the quality of the recital. (Obviously, with age, I stopped taking that kind of risk.) Added to all this came long hours of listening to indifferent music, punctuated of course by some very rewarding recitals from the greats on occasion. Bade Ghulam Ali and Amir Khan were alive then and maestros of sitar and sarod based in America would pay their annual visits. The remuneration for my reviews in *The Statesman* was negligible and copy had to be submitted the day following the recital. Heaven knows why I accepted the assignment when my living did not depend on it and criticism, even when justified, was never taken kindly by artistes. What they failed to realize was that a critic's business was to evaluate a particular performance and had little to do with the standing of the artiste. Also, even great artistes cannot guarantee consistency.

I remember my father saying once that a critic should bear in mind that the performer is trying to give his best, sometimes under adverse conditions, and should therefore be given necessary licence. I admit the truth of it as a performer but big artistes sometimes create conditions themselves that are not conducive to good recitals, especially if they accept too many successive bookings in different parts of the country. Singing or playing at midnight with a plane ticket for an early-morning flight in the pocket does not always contribute to quality performance. In such circumstances, the honest critic cannot afford to be a respector of persons.

It did not take me long to be branded as a difficult critic. I was kind to the young and up-and-coming talents. But the seniors did not escape lightly. Looking back, I feel I was always honest, and, by and large, a fair critic. Many artistes, mainly the reputed ones, however did not think so. I rubbed Amjad Ali Khan the wrong way by mentioning that alaap in his case was a warming-up process for display of his technical virtuosity and jet-propelled jhala. This indeed was so before

he matured, when I was the first to write about a Behag he
played in a conference organized by me, which I felt was
better than any Behag I had ever heard on sarod, even by his
father Ustad Hafiz Ali Khan. The report ended with the
sentence: 'It was a superb recital, supremely balanced in
conception and executed with charm, virtuosity and an
intimate touch, all his own. The Piloo and the synthetic
Bhatiali dhun that followed were good in their own rights but
the Behag haunted me throughout the night.' One cannot
say I was miserly with praise where it was due.

Turning to the seniors, here is one on Kumar Gandharva:

'Kumar Gandharva owes his second visit in recent
years to the Calcutta Music Circle. Years ago in the
late Thirties, at the age of nine, he took Calcutta by
storm with his imitation of Abdul Karim Khan.
Shades of it are still noticeable in the manner he hits
the top notes which can still move some women to
tears. Meanwhile, he has acquired a lot of soul and
is rapidly making a bid for the position occupied by
the late Pujya Pandit Omkarnath Thakur. But the
late Panditji, whose voice production and mannerisms
are copied by Kumar Gandharva, would have scarcely
taken liberties with Behag and Gaud Malhar in this
fashion. Ga re ga sa re with nyas on rekab, almost in
the manner of Shudh Kalyan in Behag, or the ni dha
ni phrase of Miyan Malhar grafted on Gaud Malhar,
would indicate a total disregard for grammar and
tradition. It even shook his boyhood friend V.G. Jog
accompanying him on the violin. Abdul Karim Khan
often took liberties with a raga, though not of this
magnitude, but according to most critics of his time,
whatever he sang was music. Most of us are not
fanatical purists, but a radical departure from the
tenets of classical music can be condoned sometimes
if the total effect is rewarding. He merely succeeded
in boring us in the end. Let this be a reminder that

talent, however exceptional, is no substitute for genius.'

On Bhimsen Joshi, thirty years away from the savant that he is today:

'Years ago, Bhimsen represented Kirana ably, if not brilliantly. Today he is our leading singer with a style which is predominantly Kirana with shades of Alladiya Khan's gayaki under a veneer of Marathi Natya Sangeet. In the intervening years his repertoire has steadily refused to grow but he has worked hard on giving his music a polish and bloom, which are the envy of all vocalists. His voice production, pukars, the vigour of his taans and the soulful quality of his music combine to build up an atmosphere which no one after the death of Bade Ghulam Ali and Amir Khan is capable of doing. Meanwhile, his antics on the stage have tended to give his recital an audio-visual appeal which certainly gives the average uninitiated listener his money's worth. He has also forsaken the discipline necessary for preparation of a recital expected from a musician of his standing.

That coming to sing straight from the airport to a major conference with a return plane ticket for the early morning flight in one's pocket is not quite the best way of doing it was proved when he started his Chhaya. The voice was tired and he kept failing to hit some of the notes accurately for half an hour, for reasons which, to quite a few of us who were close to him, were understandable. He went through the motions like one who was reciting a dull passage from memory. Everything was there except the touch, which has made Bhimsen Joshi what he is today.

I was intrigued by the strong emphasis on the nishad as an ascendant note in Chhaya. I have heard this raga from Ustad Faiyaz Khan, Ustad Bade Ghulam Ali Khan and Ustad Mushtaq Hussain Khan of

Rampur, the home of Chhaya or Chhayanat. And of course from Ratanjankar who knew the precise structure of a raga better than anyone else. To me phrases like pa ni re and pa ni sa ga re bring memories of Hansadhwani and Khem Kalyan far too vividly to allow me to enjoy my Chhaya in peace.'

There I was, leaping like a monkey from tree to tree, out of reach of the artistes, quite unconscious of the effect of my acrobatics, until I criticized Ravi Shankar in my column. All hell broke loose the following morning. Panditji was not yet the icon he is today but well on his way to becoming a holy cow in the eyes of a large number of Bengalis. Jnan Prakash Ghosh, who was sitting next to me during the recital and was in total agreement with me on the points of criticism, later wrote a letter to the editor. Apparently, the music critic had attacked the great cultural ambassador without reason and he should be well advised to keep his inky paws off the darling of Bengal. When confronted, he said the spoken word was one thing but to put it in print for public consumption was another, as if the integrity of the music critic does not amount to much. Others, who had not attended the recital, branded me as 'Vilayet's man' until within a fortnight I had to point out in my column that successive use of chromatic notes, the two gandhars and two nishads in raga Jog played by Vilayet is foreign to our classical music except in meends.

There was only Ali Akbar Khan left, whose 'man' I had to be. I find in my file a column I wrote on Ustad Ali Akbar Khan, which must have finally put the seal on this widely-held opinion: (A few others continued to hold mixed views while the private thoughts of the loyal supporters of some of the victims bordered on the homicidal.)

'Once in a while, in every sphere of life, one comes across a phenomenon like Ali Akbar Khan, who changes the entire process of thinking and the course of activity with which he is associated by sheer genius. Even those who are no admirers of the

Alauddin dynasty are bound to admit in their heart of hearts that a complete evaluation of instrumental music in northern India has been largely due to members of the school, particularly Ali Akbar and his brother-in-law Ravi Shankar. By making this statement I am not belittling the immense contribution of the followers of the Imdad Khani gharana, who have contributed to this change. They have, and Ali Akbar in particular, made it impossible for a whole generation to play bad sarod or sitar, just as Tagore has made it difficult for Bengalis to write bad poetry.

All this does not necessarily give Ali Akbar's own sarod-playing immunity from criticism. The entire 1965–66 season I was obliged to follow him from conference to conference like a desperate and obstinate gambler chasing a 'system' in the fond hope that he would finally reward my patience at long odds. I would usually catch him in the early hours of the morning playing with a plane ticket in his pocket. Occasionally, he would rush straight from the airport to a late-evening recital far too fatigued to concentrate on the atmosphere of the raga and would take refuge behind layakari and jhala at the speed of sound. I continued to maintain, however, that on his day he was capable of producing music beyond the reach and comprehension of other instrumentalists.

The Parichaya group gave him the opportunity of making his first major appearance at Rabindra Sadan. He had been away for nearly a year as custodian of our music abroad, which everyone knows, is now a major item of export. To his apprehensive admirers, who worried that the process of acclimatization might yet not be complete, he sprang a surprise by giving a scintillating recital. Commencing with alaap, jod and jhala in Shree, he followed it up

with a gat in Gaurimanjari. The fluency which
marked his superb alaap made one forget that Shree
was an *audav sampurna* raga. The character of the
raga was established within minutes with the all-
pervading sound of the rekhab and the striking
meend from rekhab to pancham and back. The jod
and jhala made one marvel at the difficult phrasing
of the layakari. Above all, he handled both Shree
and Gaurimanjari with the ease and facility which
lesser instrumentalists would display in handling, say,
Kafi or Bhairavi. Virtuosity blended superbly with
emotion in his *baaj*. It was easily the best music I
heard this season or am likely to hear for a long
time.'

So on and so forth. I finally gave up the job after fifteen years
of attending festivals and soirees, which would leave me
ragged and limp at the end of the season. In between I
resigned once because of the ruthless hand of the sub-editor
which often made my column look like it had come out of
a slaughterhouse. I was persuaded to go back by the new
editor Nihal Singh on condition my copy would remain
unmutilated, a pleasure I enjoyed with my morning cup of tea
for the remaining years. Increasing responsibilities in office
coupled with a perceptible fall in the quality of music, which
I was forced to listen to year in and year out, made my mind
up to quit. I must have written thousands and thousands of
words and I was apt to repeat myself. On occasions I was also
inclined to make my critical faculty subservient to premeditated
clever phrases, a habit that an honest critic should guard
himself against.

As a performer I was being left out because I could not
cover my own recitals in my column in the premier daily of
Calcutta. Reporting of musical events in other English papers
and vernacular dailies and weeklies was of indifferent quality
and I could not but care little for their criticisms or eulogies
about me. One reviewer who later matured into a formidable

critic and always preferred to use the bludgeon rather than the rapier was very green then and sometimes made incorrect observations of a technical nature and tendentious assessments about one or two artistes which, after years, he privately admitted to be wrong. Finally, even though I had a limited social life, my circle also included musicians, and my column created some embarrassment for both my wife and myself. Music criticism in India is a highly sensitive subject. Most musicians do not read English and those of recent days, who do, are not familiar with literary English. So they depend on their admirers, and things get exaggerated and misunderstood at second or third hand. The critic, unless he is also an equally famous performer, is not held in the kind of esteem that exists in Europe and America. All this finally made me hand over my job to Buddhadeb Dasgupta, the well-known sarod player, who did the balancing act on the trapeze with such rare skill that he continued for several years without offending anybody!

To go back to my music, with passing years—that is, more than fifty years after the death of Ustad Faiyaz Khan— I find my style has changed somewhat with the development of my own musical personality. In the last ten years I have done a project on gharanas under the aegis of the Ford Foundation for the Sangeet Research Academy, Calcutta, and have listened to thousands of hours of recordings of masters, old and new. I have tried to analyze the different gayakis with illustrations from such recordings. I have over the years benefitted immensely from the company of *vidvans*, people who are capable of using their analytical faculty apart from their knowledge, starting with my father, Shrikrishna Ratanjankar and his disciples such as S.C.R. Bhat, K.G. Ginde, Dinkar Kaikini, Sumati Mutatkar, Babbanrao Haldankar and Dr M.R. Gautam of the Agra gharana, all of whom have helped me to go deeper into the subject of Hindustani music.

Above all, I have been listening carefully to the greats of instrumental music: Ustad Ali Akbar Khan, Ustad Vilayet

Hussain Khan and Pandit Ravi Shankar, not to mention Nikhil Banerjee. All this, particularly their alaaps, have had some influence on my gayaki. It is unfortunate, however, as Ram Asrey Jha of Allahabad says, 'When I was young I did not know what real music was. When I began to get an inkling of it I found I was already an old man and the greats had departed for the other world.' That is good enough reason for me to embark on this book, which I propose to call *The Lost World of Hindustani Music*. In fact it is really my lost world.

2

The Birth of Khayal

Lucknow was still a beautiful city of gardens in my college days in the Forties, especially the University campus. Like those in summer in England, the gardens there were a riot of colours in the winter sunshine under a blue sky. Members of the staff of the university, attired in spotless cream flannels and silk shirts, would play tennis in the evening on manicured lawns. Their spouses, one or two of them British memsahibs, delicately sipped tea from bone-china cups at garden parties. Wartime petrol rationing had made the sight of the motorcar scarce, there were bicycles galore. From the chief secretary of the UP government down to the meanest clerks in the secretariat, who incidentally sported Chinese silk jackets and white drill trousers in summer and tweeds in winter, but not neckties, which symbolized the difference in class, people were cycling everywhere. We, as well as the girl students, did the same. The Shia Muslim and the Hindu Khatri girls were very fair of complexion, and when droves of them came out of the hostels on their bikes they looked like creatures from fairy tales to our adolescent eyes.

The languages in which we conversed were English and Hindustani, in which Hindi and Urdu coexisted happily. The Sanskritized Hindi favoured today in the 'cow belt' of India was virtually unknown then. So was the highly Persianised Urdu of the country on the other side of the border. Lucknow Urdu, in comparison with that of Delhi, which city the aristocratic Lucknowite considered an overgrown village, was

more refined and spoken with an accent, which, like the
Oxonian's, was exclusive and elitist. He would have been
truly horrified to hear the Urdu telecast by Pakistan TV in
a strong Punjabi accent today. I shall always remember the
mournful countenance of the Raja of Salanpur whose brother
opted for the newly-born West Pakistan consisting of Punjab,
the North-Western Frontier Provinces, Sindh and Baluchistan,
which, he truly believed, was the land of barbarians.

Lucknow cuisine was also different. Biryani, it was
generally thought, was not fit for the discerning palate. It was
eaten by Delhiwalas. The Lucknowite favoured pulao, thirty-
six kinds of which were in existence then. The kebabs,
especially kakori kebabs, used to melt in the mouth. The
poultry for the mussallam and a memorable dish called
chicken handi would be fed small balls made of kesar (saffron)
and the milk for the sheermal bread would be from a cow
that had devoured tons of rose petals. But the cuisine, which
the affluent Muslim and the Hindu Kayasth of old Lucknow
favoured, was singularly unimaginative when it came to
desserts. As a Bengali I can afford to act superior about dishes
of fish, vegetables and sweets though it is common knowledge
that the Bengali cook makes a mess of meat dishes. What I
occasionally ate at garden parties of the minor potentates to
the accompaniment of chaitis, kajris and ghazals by lesser-
known Lucknow tawayefs were balai, shahi tukra, kheer and
mangoes, preceded of course by glorious kebabs. Right from
the days of the first Mughal emperor Babar, Muslims were
fascinated by the mango and cultivated numerous varieties.

Before I get down to more serious matters I must share a
story narrated by my father which is more eloquent of the
Lucknow of my childhood than any I can readily think of.
Every year, in the white *baradari* built by the Nawab of Oudh,
an exhibition of mangoes would take place. There were of
course the delicate Safedas and Dussehris from the adjacent
Malihabad district, the Langdas from Benaras, the slightly
oversweet Chausas from Aligarh, even Fazlis, Himsagars,
Kohitoors and Ranis from north Bengal. Once, the British

governor who inaugurated the numaish, was obviously from the Bombay cadre of the Indian Civil Service. In his opening speech he expressed his happiness to be in the midst of all these wonderful varieties of the mango fruit but regretted the absence of the Alfonso of Bombay, which was his great favourite. When His Excellency departed from the *baradari*, the old Nawab of Chaulakha buttonholed my father and said, 'Tell me, Professor Saheb, what kind of a gentleman is this governor who, while he is our *mehman*, our honoured guest, actually praises a fruit from Bombay and not from our own Avadh? Anyway, *Bambai to suna hai ajab jagha hai jahan biwi apne miyan ko tum keh ke pukarti hai* (Bombay, one hears, is a strange place where a wife actually addresses her husband as *tum* in public)!'

The Lucknow society of my youth was totally free from communal sentiment; nor can the older citizens remember any riots between Hindus and Muslims, though minor fracases between Shias and Sunnis were not unknown. Those who champion the two-nation theory are not aware of the nature of Indian culture, which has always been an amalgam of Hindu, Muslim, Buddhist and Christian cultures, the signs of which are evident in food habits, clothes, art, architecture and most so in music. Here you have Hindus singing *Karim Rahim* and Muslims beginning their dhrupad alaaps with *Hari Om Anantanarayan*. Khayals and thumris feature mostly the Radha Krishna theme. Hari dhamar and thumri would now be anathema to Muslims in our neighbouring Islamic states but not to Indian musicians—whether Shias or Sunnis. The last Nawab of Lucknow, Wajid Ali Shah, used to perform Raasleela in the role of Krishna with the ladies of his harem, and composed bandishes in praise of him. I take pride in the fact that it is the same city that was responsible for the birth of khayal in its present form, which is roughly three hundred years old.

Khayal, I repeat, as it is sung now, owes its existence to sources not earlier than the early eighteenth century. The birth of khayal, in its earlier form, is mistakenly attributed to

Amir Khusrau in the thirteenth century. According to Thakur Jaidev Singh, an outstanding scholar of music and philosophy, it took place many centuries ago. 'I maintain,' he writes, 'that the so-called khayal style of musical composition is only a natural development of sadharan geeti which used the exquisite features of all the styles. It is this sadharan geeti with the predominant use of Bhinna in it that became the khayal. There is definite proof that such styles of musical compositions have been in existence in Indian music at least from the seventh or eighth century AD. The sadharani style of composition with its generous and plentiful use of gamaks became our khayal composition. Khayal exploited all the famous features without bothering about their names—khatka, murki, meend, kamp, aandolan—everything was beautifully woven into its structure. When Amir Khusrau in the thirteenth century heard the ornate style, or rupak alapti, full of so many embellishments, he could not think of designating this music of creative imagination better than by the word khayal. Khayal was imported neither from Arabia nor Persia. There was a certain style of musical composition and a certain style of rendering already prevalent in Indian music. Khayal was only a natural development of that style. Neither did Amir Khusrau invent it nor Sharqui, king of Jaunpur (fifteenth century) although each of them may have lent a hand in its development.' (*Commemoration volume of Dr. S.N. Ratanjankar—1961*)[1]

Badshah Jalaluddin Akbar's (1556-1605) minister Abul Fazal writes in his *Aain-e-Akbari*:

'The prevalent geet in Jaunpur is called chutkala. Songs composed in the languages of Tailang and Karnatak in southern India are called dhoru. Geet sung in Bengal is known as bangla. What is sung in Delhi is called qaul and tarana. Amir Khusrau started qaul and tarana which are derived from the Persian style of singing of two musicians of his time called Dahalvi Samoot and Tatar, and Khusrau mixed the Persian saut and naksh with Hindustani music.'

Rajyeshwar Mitra, who has translated the above passage from Persian into Bengali in his book *Mughal Bharater Sangeet Chinta*, is of the opinion that the anecdotes, which credit the origin of khayal to Khusrau, an important figure in Alauddin Khilji's court, are obviously products of the sycophantic imagination of his followers. The truth, he says, is Amir Khusrau was not a great admirer of Hindustani music.[1] He was the son of a Turkish father and his mother belonged to Hindustan. Khusrau was not proud of being labelled a Hindustani and his desire to import Persian music was to denigrate the music of Hindustan in the court of Alauddin Khilji. Khusrau was a scholar of the Persian language but it is debatable whether he had comparable knowledge of Persian music. He interacted regularly with Persian travellers and heard a lot of Persian music prevalent in Hindustan at that time. The ragas that he created show an attempt to blend Persian tunes with Hindustani ones and could not have been of a high order because they have not stood the test of time. *Qaul* and qawaali prospered because of their poetic quality. However, there is no doubt that he had tried to liberate the traditional Hindustani music shackled by the shastrakars and the grammarians and showed a new path which, in the hands of the Muslim Sufis, developed into a form of considerable aesthetic appeal.

Amir Khusrau himself mentions in a *quata* that he is the poet of poets and an ustad:

> 'My poems run into three volumes and my musical compositions, if they are put together, would also run into another three volumes.'

Ziauddin Barni, in his *Tarikh-e-Firozshahi*, writes that a poet like Khusrau would not be born again before the last trumpet (*qayamat*) and that he considered himself fortunate to have received the affection of Khusrau and Nizammuddin Aulia, his mentor, but he does not mention Khusrau's prowess as a singer or a musicologist, nor do any of his contemporaries, for that matter, attribute the birth of qawaali to Amir Khusrau.

On the other hand, evidence exists that qawaals existed as far back as Sultan Iltutamish's reign (1210-1235) and qawaali composers were mostly Sufis, beginning with Khwaja Moinuddin Chishti of Ajmer.

Two things emerge from the research of several historians and musicologists. Qawaali, which is a religious song in which more than one person joins in the chorus, prospered in the hands of the Muslim Sufis. The other conclusion one is entitled to draw is that khayal was born out of a marriage between sadharan geeti and qawaali. But no one knows about the earlier forms of khayal. The present-day musicologist, who is more interested in music as a performing art, rather than what it is in the dry pages of musical history—a lot of which is speculation—might agree with the author that khayal in its present form owes its existence to the later day Mughals as well as the Nawabs of Oudh, the capital of which was Faizabad, later Lucknow. Akbar the Great, the illiterate boy-king, grew up into a great statesman and a patron of the arts and had the legendary dhrupad singer Miyan Tansen in his court. Khayal, which was sung by the commoner in *desi* or *madhyadesi* languages, did not enter the durbar till the days of Shahjahan. Faqirullah, known originally as Saif Khan, a favourite of the emperor Aurangzeb (responsible for the imprisonment of his father, Emperor Shahjahan, and the assassination of his eldest brother, Dara Shikoh, which paved the way to the throne for Aurangzeb at the age of thirty-nine in 1658), was also a musician. In his book *Ragdarpan*, which he had requested Emperor Aurangzeb to release by reading out the *Khutba*, he makes derogatory remarks about Miyan Tansen, who belonged to Aurangzeb's great-grandfather's court, and actually calls him an *atayee*, i.e., one who has not had proper talim from an ustad and does not legitimately belong to the musician class. It is a term which, in my younger days, the Muslim ustads did not hesitate to apply to the budding Ravi Shankar. According to Faqirullah, dhrupad, during the reign of Man Singh Tomar of Gwalior, in the fifteenth century, was purer, and Tansen and his sycophants were responsible for its degeneration. The wonderful compositions of Raja Man Singh and Nayak Bakshu went into oblivion and were replaced by the compositions of Tansen and his progeny, the great favourites of the Emperor. Such observations have been made through the ages by the new against the old, which cannot, however, make us forget that ragas like Miyan ki Todi, Miyan ki Malhar and Darbari Kanhra, which are attributed to Miyan Tansen, could not have been the work of anyone other than a genius.

Whatever his opinion, Faqirullah has listed the top singers of Emperor Akbar's court, placing Miyan Tansen first, followed by Haji Sujan Khan, the dhrupad singer in Nauharbani and the founder of the Agra gharana. It is not likely that any of the following in Akbar's durbar ever sang khayal.

Miyan Tansen
Haji Sujan Khan
Surgiyan Khan
Chand Khan and Suraj Khan Fatehpuri
Miyan Chand and Rashid Mikha (disciples of Tansen)
Tantarang and Bilas Khan (sons of Tansen)
Ramdas Munthia
Daud Khan Dhadhi
Mohammad Khan Dhadhi
Madan Rai Dhadhi
Mulla Ashak Dhadhi
Khizr Khan and his brother Naubat Khan
Hussain Khan Patanni from Afghanistan
Bazbahadur, ruler of Malwa
Nayak Charju, creater of the raga Charju ki Malhar
Nayak Bhagwan
Surat Sen, favourite son of Miyan Tansen
Lala and Debi, brothers of Brahman Aqil
Sun Bachchi

They were all famous singers according to Faqirullah but not as knowledgeable as predecessors such as Nayak Bhanu, Nayak Pandui and Nayak Bakhshu. Those who were mere singers, however great they might have been, could not be called 'nayak' unless they were equally knowledgeable and well-acquainted with the shastras. They used to sing dhrupad sitting on chairs while their accompanists on the veena (been) and mridanga (pakhawaj) sat on the carpets. They could not only sing beautifully but were well versed in the theory of music and could quote extensively from *Manakatuhal* and *Sangeetratnakar* with explanations and commentaries. Those who had knowledge of the theory of music but were not singers of quality were called vidvans, or pandits (today every Hindu musician calls himself a pandit and every Muslim singer or instrumentalist, an ustad irrespective of their merit). In the eighth chapter of *Ragdarpan*, singers of merit, one reads, should have the following qualities. They must have a good voice, which should roam freely in all the three octaves. Their music must have aesthetic appeal. They must have full knowledge of application of graha, nyasaa, raganga, bhasha anga, kriya anga, all the alankars, full command over laya and must conform to the discipline of Shastriya Sangeet. They should have full understanding of Shuddha and Chhayalag prakars of ragas, and have good memory and full control of all kinds of gamaks, dhwani vikar and kaku-prayog. Above all, their music must be aesthetically pleasing. One wonders to what extent these demands on today's Indian musicians would be considered reasonable and how many musicians would qualify to adhere to these norms. Even in Faqirullah's time musicians were divided into two categories—uttam and adham. Those whose living depended on tuitions were not musicians but shikshakas. Those who were mere musicians and incapable or unwilling to give lessons to pupils were generally called ankars. Ranjaks were those who could delight their audiences quickly. Those who could sing ragas correctly and interpret their sentiments were known as bhavaks. The reader may note that the terms are in Sanskrit though *Ragdarpan* was written in Farsee, or Persian.

There are interesting examples of how musicians were

rewarded by their patrons, which, even by the standards of remuneration set by our famous musicians in the country and abroad today, would he considered fantastically lavish. Manuchchi & Bernier have mentioned some in their travel accounts. Abraham Eraly in his book *Great Mughals* describes the '*backsheesh*' of one crore rupees given to Miyan Tansen by the ruler of Batta. Emperor Jahangir, who succeeded his father Akbar and ruled for twenty-two years, was a pleasure-loving king, a hard drinker and passionately devoted to his beautiful begum Nurjahan, whom he married after getting her husband Sher Afghan assassinated. Once he got a flautist named Mohammad Naiyee weighed on a scale, and silver rupees equal to his weight were given to him along with an elephant to carry the money. Khan Khanan Abdur Rahim, an amir during the latter days of Akbar's reign, paid a Hindu musician one lakh rupees. Sultan Abul Hassan, of Golkonda in the south, captured and imprisoned in Daulatabad by Emperor Aurangzeb, once overheard a musician play and told his courtiers, 'Alas! I would have rewarded this man at least a lakh of rupees had I my kingdom today.' Aurangzeb, who was still in the Deccan at that time, got to hear it and sent a lakh of rupees to the Sultan.

Aurangzeb, the bigot that he was, followed the dictates of the Quran to the letter and appears in history as anti-Hindu and anti-music. But this is not entirely correct. From Akbar's time, princes had to go through a course of music and religious teachings along with archery, riding and martial arts, and this presumably was responsible for Aurangzeb's innate antipathy to classical music, possibly the same way some of us develop aversion to mathematics taught by unimaginative school masters. *Ragdarpan* was completed by Faqirullah in 1666. It was only after 1668 that the emperor made his distaste for music public. The same year the court musicians, Khushhal Khan, Bisram Khan, Rasbeen Khan and others, were told that they could come to the durbar as usual but no music would be permitted. Music in court was forbidden but the musicians were not sacked. In 1668, on

October 21, forty musicians were given sets of formal clothes and three thousand rupees each. When Bisram Khan died, his son Bhupat Khan was paid a sum of money for his father's last rites along with a new set of formal attire.

Ustad Alladiya Khan, the founder of the Jaipur school of khayal, was born into a family of dhrupad singers in 1855, and died at the age of ninety-one in 1946. No doubt he witnessed a lot of social and musical changes in his lifetime. In a short book of memoirs, which has been translated by Amlan Dasgupta and Urmila Bhirdikar, based on notes kept by the ustad's grandson Azizuddin, Alladiya Khan recounted quite a few incidents of the generosity of feudal patrons of the eighteenth and nineteenth centuries. The custom those days on auspicious occasions like weddings or birthdays of the feudal potentates was to arrange a whole night's session of music, which would start late in the evening with a tawayef's mujra followed by sitar, sursingar and rababs. Then would come the dhrupad singers and finally, khayalias.

Dhadhis would sing songs composed in praise of the feudal lords. Bahram Khan, predecessor of the Dagars, belonged to this community. Dhadhis were allotted seats with dhrupad and khayal singers, though later, when they took to playing tabla and the sarangi, they went down in the social hierarchy. Mirasis belonged to an even lower echelon and their womenfolk, unlike the others', would sing in public. The courtiers and invitees would sit in one corner facing the artiste and bags of silver coins would be thrown to him from time to time with cries of 'Marhaba', 'Subhan-Allah' and 'Kya baat, kya baat'. An ustad could expect anything up to twenty thousand rupees in a single evening. Alladiya Khan mentions a soiree in the house of Kishori Singh, brother of Maharaja Jaswant Singh of the state of Jodhpur in Rajputana, now called Rajasthan. The singer, Ustad Nasir Khan, was singing a song in Gaud Malhar, one of the ragas of the rainy season. A refrain in the song, which needed repetition, contained the words 'motiyana meha barase (drops of water are falling like pearls'). As the singer adorned this line with different phrases and alankaras, Kishori Singh ordered a tray of pearls, which he started throwing in handfuls to the singer. On another occasion he spent three lakhs of rupees, the equivalent of a month's pay to the army and police maintained by the state, on wrestlers, tawayefs and ustads in three days. Kishori Singhji was the commander-in-chief of the state forces. Soon after, when pay-day arrived, he went and locked himself up in his bedroom. A couple of days later, word went to the Maharaja, who naturally came over with the British attending physician, anxious about his brother's state. Kishori Singh's confession, with tears in his eyes, made the Maharaja breathe a sigh of relief. "Thank God you are all right! Why should a trivial thing like this get you down, my boy? Come and have breakfast now." That was all that the Maharaja had to say about three hundred thousand rupees of taxpayers' money (valued two hundred times, easily, in today's currency).

The Maharaja of Datia in Rajasthan had heard the famous dhrupad Dagarbani singers Shadi Khan and Murad Khan and invited them to his court. A bed of one-and-a-quarter lakh of silver rupees was made with silk carpets piled on top. This was the dais on which they were asked to sit and give their recital, at the end of which the entire money was given as baksheesh. An elephant was ordered by the Maharaja to carry them and the money to the guesthouse, at some distance from the palace. He bade them adieu with the parting words to Shadi Khan, 'O Ustad of Ustads! One has not come across a greater spinner of musical webs than the two of you but when you go home you will realise that your patron has a larger heart than the dais on which you sat today.' Shadi Khan thanked him profusely and mounted the elephant. On the way he threw away fistfuls of silver coins to the crowd following him. Word reached the Maharaja and a messenger was sent to call the twin ustads back. To the Maharaja's curious queries Shadi Khan said, 'My Lord, your charitable disposition and fame have reached the four corners of the earth and this servant of yours will remain indebted to you for life. But perhaps you also may not find a musician with feelings for the poor like the one who has the honour to stand before you.' The Maharaja was so impressed that he made a present of another ten thousand rupees to Shadi and Murad Khan.

The most touching story is that of Mantol Khan, an ancestor of Alladiya Khan, who lived in Atrauli, a small town known for its singers near Aligarh. Once, the Maharaja of Alwar, yet another native state in Rajasthan not far from Delhi, asked his courtiers, 'Tell me, friends, have you ever come across a musician who brings tears to the eyes of listeners, even such listeners as who are blasé and have heard the best in the country, like me?' Some in the Maharaja's court were quiet while others said, 'Maharaj, O king of kings! The best of musicians in the country are at your beck and call and there is no one that you have not heard and rewarded. It they have failed to move you, we think there is no one who can bring tears to your eyes.' However, one in the crowd of samajhdars said, 'Maharaj, in my humble opinion there is one Mantol Khan of Atrauli, who is capable of bringing tears to a listener with a heart of stone, but he is not likely to come and enjoy the unprecedented fortune in his life of singing before you. He does not stir out of his house, he wears saffron or black clothes and like a fakir he does not wear shoes or a cap. He cannot be tempted with rewards. After his last son Karim Baksh was born, he said to his wife, "Here is someone now who is going to look after you when he grows up. You do not need me any longer. My life is going to take a different direction. Allah will give you peace and your material needs will be taken care of." That boy has grown up into a fine singer and Mantol Khan did not see his wife's face again until her *janaza* came out for burial.'

The Maharaja's curiosity was aroused. He lost no time in sending a messenger with a persuasive tongue with sepoys to Atrauli. When the messenger knocked on the door of the shabby house of Mantol Khan and his son conveyed the invitation to his father, Khansaheb was annoyed. His music was not for sale. Besides, he had his own riyaz and his disciples to look after. The answer was a definite no. No amount of persuasion could shake his resolution to not stir out of his home.

Three years went by. There was a relay of messengers. One day, Karim Baksh summoned sufficient courage to ask his father to step out and look at the flowers in the garden. Mantol Khan was completely taken aback to see tents and sepoys outside his house and asked who they were and what they were doing there. On being told that they had been waiting for three years for him to change his mind, he was extremely annoyed that his own son could harbour such base thoughts that his father would succumb to the temptations of wealth and fame in return for his precious music, which he had dedicated to Allah. Karim Baksh, with great presence of mind, told his father that he did not want him to go to Alwar but that the Maharaja's men, whose patience had been exhausted, could arrest him and members of his family for ignoring the Maharaja's command. Poor Mantol Khan, of course, had no idea that the Maharaja's powers did not extend beyond his state to a town in British India. However, even sadhus do not like to entertain the idea of a life in prison. Mantol Khan finally agreed to visit Alwar, after a great deal of grumbling and prayers to the Almighty.

After the usual courtesies were exchanged between the ustad and his host, the recital was arranged in the durbar before a packed house. Even ladies assembled in large numbers behind the bamboo curtains. Mantol Khan's son was supposed to sing before the father, whose outrage had not yet subsided and who was not in the best mood for an important recital. However, the clever Karim Baksh, himself a fine singer, deliberately strayed from the set rules of the raga. After a while, Mantol Khan, who was listening, said loudly, 'No, no, that is not the way to sing this raga; what have I been teaching you all these years?' He promptly sat down beside his son and showed him how to tackle the raga. Slowly and gradually, he got into the mood and atmosphere of the raga and forgot the presence of the audience. He sang one raga after another for three hours with his eyes closed, tears flowing down his face. There was not a single dry eye in the court and the Maharaja was weak with uncontrollable sobbing. When the recital finally ended, the Maharaja of Alwar came down from his throne, grasped Mantol Khan's hands with both of his and said, 'Tell me, Ustad, how did you acquire such divine powers which would melt a heart of stone! Tell me what you wish. There is nothing that I possess which you cannot have. State your wish and you can have it.' All Mantol Khan had to say was, 'May it please your exalted highness, if you are really happy with my music and want to grant my prayer, kindly do not call me again.'

The reward he received he gave away in charity saying all he wished to leave behind were two tanpuras for his two sons.

To return to the great days of the Mughals. Khayal was resurrected and gradually found place in the durbar side by side with dhrupad during Shahjahan's reign (1627-1658). *Ragdarpan* makes special mention of Sheikh Bahauddin Barnawa who roamed all over India and was in the habit of fraternising with fakirs. He went to the south to sample Karnatak music and learnt the mridangam. When he returned to Delhi at the age of fifty, there was no one in Hindustan who was a better or more knowledgeable singer than Sheikh Bahauddin Barnawa. His compositions in dhrupad as well as in khayal were famous as was his skilful rendering of these.

Mastering the chutkalas of Jaunpur was not easy, but Sheikh Nasiruddin, a contemporary of Bahauddin, was equally adept at taranas and chutkalas, which he could render with the same skill as Sultan Sharqi of the fifteenth century according to knowledgeable critics. This book makes special mention of Lal Khan, who had learnt dhrupad from Miyan Tansen's son Bilas Khan and married his daughter and was awarded the title of Gunasamudra Khan. Other disciples of Bilas Khan, the creator of the morning raga Bilaskhani Todi, were Mishir Manjan Dhadhi and a famous *kalawant* of Gujarat named Bakhat Khan. There was Gun Khan who impressed Shuja, son of Shahjahan and the ruler of the Bihar Bengal Suba, so much with his versatile command over margee and desi sangeet, that Shuja took him away from Delhi. Equally if not more prominent was Idal Singh, grandson of Rajaram Saha, a Hindu singer who ruled Kharagpur district in Bihar. His knowledge of all branches of Hindustani music was comparable to that of Sultan Sharqi and even Amir Khusrau. Faqirullah further says that Idal Singh possessed a golden voice the like of which people had not heard. Lal Khan's son Khushhal Khan was the most famous singer of Faqirullah's time and found favour with Emperor Aurangzeb till 1668, when music was banned in the durbar.

What surprises me more than anything else is the description of ragas quoted by Faqirullah from the *Manakatuhal,* written or commanded to be composed by Raja Man Singh Tomar of Gwalior in the fifteenth century, during whose reign dhrupad flourished, and finds mention in the history of music for the first time in a clear and undisputed manner. If we do not accept Thakur Jaidev Singh's thesis of dhrupad and khayal being derived from *Ragalapti* and *Rupakalapti,* respectively, another thousand years back, we have to come to the conclusion that the birth of khayal in Amir Khusrau's time in the thirteenth century preceded dhrupad by a couple of hundred years. What is totally confusing is the description of ragas in *Manakatuhal.* I am giving only three examples out of the many quoted by Rajyeshwar Mitra in his introduction to his book mentioned earlier.

Raga Malkauns—it is an amalgam of Hindol, Basant, Jayjaiwanti, Pancham, Khat, Sarang and Sawani. This should be sung in the morning and in the spring season. How the same Malkauns in the pentatonic scale with komal gandhar, komal dhaivat and komal nishad came to be known as a midnight raga boggles one's imagination. However, Malkauns, as it is sung in the north, is still called Hindolam in Karnatak music.

Raga Basant is supposed to be a mixture of Sarang, Nat Malhar, Bilawal and Devgiri ragas. These today are shuddh swara ragas whereas the Basant, known a generation ago as Paraj Basant, has komal rishabh and komal dhaivat. Even Adi Basant sports a rishabh that is komal.

Raga Bhupali—mentioned as a mixture of Iman and Gunakri, or Gunkali—is a morning raga. Bhupali today, as everyone knows, has a simple sa re ga pa dha sa, all shuddh swaras in the pentatonic scale.

Both Malkauns and Bhupali as sung in India today are found in Chinese music.

No wonder Pandit Vishnu Narayan Bhatkhande threw up his hands after studying all the Sanskrit texts. Even if we allow the change from Kafi scale to Bilawal in north India (the earlier scale had the third and sixth minor notes, now the tempered scale consists of major and minor notes as in Europe) the description of ragas from the past makes no sense to us, though the names are the same.

A discussion on ragas and their origin may not be out of place here. There is little doubt that folk music is the basis of raga sangeet. To quote D.P. Mukherji, 'The historical fact about our classical music is that it was never above incorporating the folk, the regional even non-Indian types. Dhrupad, which is reputed to have been sung before Akbar, and which is so highbrow that nobody now listens to it, was in a sense the Agra-Gwalior style just as hori dhamar belonged to Mathura. Bengal gave Bangal Bhairav; Sindh, Sindhu; Surat, Surat; Gujarat, Gurjari Todi; Bihar, Bihari; Multan, Multani; Jaunpur, Jaunpuri Todi; and the hills gave Pahari, just as Turkey gave Turask Todi. All these raginis are shastric—not only the ragas but the rhythms as well; for example, hori dhamar of fourteen beats and punjabi theka of sixteen. This process of adaptation continued right up to the end of the eighteenth century, though in diminishing strength. Such features are nothing special to Indian music. They are mentioned because many people in India think that our ragas and raginis emanated from the gods and the rishis,' (Modern Indian Culture, second edition 1942, reprinted and published by Rupa & Co under the title *Indian Culture—a Sociological Study* in 2002.)

I think the features of the ragas stopped changing since we adopted the tempered scale, possibly with the advent of early Christian missionaries. If we take the scale of Bilawal, all seven major notes, and change the key step by step we get ragas like Kafi, Bhairavi, Iman, Khambaj, Asavari with shuddh rishabh which is very close to Jaunpuri Todi. Modulation or changing the scale of these ragas would breed others with minor changes here, and so on. There is a folk tune prevalent in the Himalayas, which goes like this—G G G R S, S S S D. P., D. S R G, G G G G R S. This is the original tune that gave birth to Pahari, Bhupali, Deshkar, Shuddh Kalyan, Jait Kalyan—all based on S R G P D S (sa re ga pa dha sa). Changing this scale would give birth to Malkauns, Durga, Dhani, Megh and even raga Marwa, which, however, consists of six notes. This pentatonic scale is to be found in China. Whether we got it from there or exported it along with Buddhism, is a matter of speculation. In Karnatak music most ragas owe their existence to either skipping of one or two notes in their scale, which still resembles the old Kafi scale, or by changing one major note to minor. Major ragas in the south, though under different names, are common to those in north and west India.

In my opinion, the basis of our ragas is murchhana, or modulation, not in the Indian sense of the term, but change of key as understood in European music. I am fully aware of the fact that ragas have also been created by eminent musicians from Miyan Tansen to Daraspiya (Mahboob Khan of Agra Atrauli Gharana), Ustad Alauddin Khan to Ravi Shankar, Ali Akbar Khan and Vilayet Khan, ragas which fall outside my thesis. I am talking of major ragas, the fundamental ones, which have stood the test of time.

To return to music under Mughal rule. Aurangzeb died at the age of 88, in the Deccan in 1707, fighting rebel forces. This led to the disintegration of the empire. Since the ban on music in the Delhi durbar in 1668, it not only lost imperial patronage but also that of feudal lords and wealthy courtiers of the emperor. Musicians left Delhi and sought refuge in neighbouring towns like Agra, Gwalior, Ambeta, Sonepat, Atrauli and even as far as Kairana, or Kirana, in today's Saharanpur district of UP. All these centres later gave birth to several gharanas, or schools, of dhrupad and khayal. The story goes that the musicians took out a 'burial procession of music' after the ban in Delhi. On hearing this, the Emperor had remarked, 'Ask them to dig the grave deep.'

Several successors to the throne came and went during the dark days of the Mughal Empire between 1707, the death of Aurangzeb, and the accession to the throne of Mohammad Shah Rangeela in 1719. He was not only a great patron of music but had in his court two famous musicians, Niyamat Khan and Firoz Khan, who composed bandishes in dhrupad and khayal under the pen names of Sadarang and Adarang. These are sung by all gharanas to this day. The musicians learnt Sanskrit and Brajbhasha from Azam Shah, one of the princes; khayal from Tattar, a noted qawaali singer, and dance from the *natuas* to understand and master the rhythmic patterns of the bols of pakhawaj. Most of Sadarang's dhrupads have later been sung as khayals like '*Sughar bana ban ao gao sab mil Bedarbakht piya piara*', composed by him on the occasion of the wedding of Bedarbakht, the son of prince Azam Shah.

Niyamat Khan, in particular, was a great favourite of the emperor, so much so that after a memorable recital of Khansaheb in the durbar, Mohammad Shah decided to honour him with the governorship of a province. The seat of the Gujarat governor was vacant and Niyamat Khan was ordered to take over, to the great consternation of the Wazir-e-azam, the prime minister. Not being in a position to contest the decision of His Majesty, he quietly approached Niyamat Khan with the suggestion that he should order his musical instruments in large quantities as these would not be available in Gujarat, which, as everybody knew, was a savage country. There was no harm in some delay. A week or two later, Niyamat Khan, who had been busy packing, duly turned up at the durbar. Noting the surprise on the Badshah's face, the

Wazir-e-azam whispered to him that some delay was inevitable since Niyamat Khan had to order a thousand tanpuras and an equal number of tablas and pakhawajes. It would be incumbent upon the new governor to introduce the courtly manners, the refined zaban (tongue) of Delhi and spread the great music of the Delhi durbar, of which the Badshah was so fond, among the uncultured Gujarati sardars. The music of Niyamat Khan could turn the fierce lion of Gir forest into a docile hound. One was sure the new governor would make the warring sardars equally docile by casting his spell on them. It worked. After all, Mohammad Shah had Mughal blood in him. The hint was taken and the earlier 'farmaan' was cancelled to the great relief of the prime minister.

This is the same Mohammad Shah during whose reign the Persian Nadir Shah invaded India. The Badshah was so obsessed with music and dance that he had little time for anything else. As a result, even with a larger army Mohammad Shah suffered a massive defeat. Not being content with victory, Nadir Shah's men plundered Delhi and massacred innocent civilians. Mohammad Shah, the emperor of the remnant of the one-time glorious Mughal empire, had to kneel before Nadir Shah and surrender his peacock throne along with ninety lakh rupees and an untold quantity of precious stones and jewellery.

Noted khayalias and composers that Niyamat and Firoz Khan were, no one knows in what style they sang. The policy of the puritanic Aurangzeb and the gradual disintegration of the Mughal Empire had led to poets and musicians seeking patronage in native states. Lucknow, which was the capital of a subah (province), began to grow in importance under the rule of Shia Nawabs. Among poets, the famous ones were Mir Taki Mir and Sauda. Musicians and courtesans flocked to the court of Faizabad, later shifted to Lucknow. A parallel stream of khayal singing evolved in the courts of Nawab Shuja-ud-Daula (1756–1775) and his son Asaf-ud-Daula (1775–1798) of Lucknow more or less at the same time as in Delhi. The most famous ustad to whom this style is attributed was Ghulam

Rasool. His son Ghulam Nabi was equally famous as the singer who had spent a number of years in Punjab among the camel drivers and imbibed the regional style of singing from them by listening to wedding and other songs. The sophisticated version of this taan-pradhan light classical music is now known as 'tappa' with which the pen name of Ghulam Nabi 'Shori Miyan' has become famous all over Hindustan.

Ghulam Rasool's disciples Shakkar Khan and Makkhan Khan, the two qawaal bachchas, were responsible for taking this form of khayal to Gwalior, the main gayaki from which other styles have evolved. It would be in the fitness of things to state that Gwalior is the parent Khayal gharana, which has given birth to Agra, Patiala, Jaipur, Kirana and other minor gharanas. The credit for this goes to Lucknow, the originator of this modern khayal gayaki with which we are familiar today.

A word about thumri, or the light classical variety that confines itself to a few light ragas like the Piloo, Kafi, Khamaj, Barwa, Zila, Gara, Bhairavi, etc., though I have heard thumris in one or two heavier ragas like the Desh, Bihag, Yaman and Jogiya as well. To quote D.P. Mukherji again, 'Dhrupad is defined in the texts as songs in praise of gods and kings. Gradually, the kings prevailed, and the gods were sung about outside the courts in desi fashion. By the sixteenth and early seventeenth centuries, when it became a courtly affair, music gained in sweetness and subtlety, but it lost its pristine simple vigour. Eventually it became vocal gymnastics until the romantics in provincial durbars started protesting. One such protest was thumri, which probably originated, certainly developed, in Lucknow. That protest also petered out into grossly sensual and mechanically repetitive expositions. Indian feudalism by then had completely isolated itself from the life of the people.' (ibid)

Popular belief is that thumri was created by Nawab Wajid Ali Shah of Lucknow. This myth is exploded by a single piece of evidence. Captain Willard, who was a bandmaster in the state of Banda in the United Provinces in the early nineteenth century, wrote in his book, *The Music of*

Hindusthan, that of all the musical forms which he had studied and listened to during his thirty-five years in India, thumri with its erotic appeal was the one he liked most. This book was published when Wajid Ali Shah was barely ten years old. Thakur Jaidev Singh, however traces the earliest form of thumri to the *Harivansh Puran* (around 200 AD) called *Chalitam nrityasahitam* sung along with dance that Lord Krishna learnt in the court of Devraj, the king of gods in Heaven. Be that as it may, musicologists headed by Peter Manuel (*The Evaluation of Modern Thumri*) are of the opinion that thumri in the form we know today, somewhat influenced by khayal, became an independent vocal form by the beginning of 1800. However the 'uchchaar', i.e., the musical pronunciation of thumri, is totally different from that of khayal. Its theme is invariably romantic and features Nayika-bhed in stereotype phrases. My own view is that teen taal ki thumri, also known as bol-bant ki thumri as distinct from the slower versions i.e. bol banao ki thumri, evolved out of kathak dance in Lucknow.

One of the best composers of this bol-bant ki thumri was Sanad Piya (Tawakkul Hussain of Rampur). Others were Kadar Piya, Lallan Piya and of course Kalka Bindadin of Lucknow, ancestors of the famous kathak dancer Birju Maharaj. Originally bol-bant ki thumri in drut teentaal was sung as an accompaniment to kathak dance before it was taken up seriously by vocalists at a later stage. Bol banao ki thumri (with its home in Benaras), sung at a much slower tempo culminated in *laggi* which consists of tabla played at a very fast rhythm. It was during *laggi* that abhinaya (acting or communication of the meaning of the words through gestures) was permitted. Bol-bant ki thumri also had gat nikaas, i.e., words uttered at a high speed imitating the bols of the gat or the composition of the instrumentalist. One of the well-known composers of this variety of thumri was Lallan Piya whose one thousand compositions were published by Naval Kishore Press, Lucknow, in early twentieth century. Some of these were known as Adhar-band thumris where the use of lips was not required. These songs did not contain words that contained *Pa Pha Ba Bha Ma,* since they cannot be uttered without the use of the lips.

Peter Manuel in his article 'Courtesans and Hindustani Music, Asian Review' is of the opinion that Hindustani music and the kathak dance style owe much to the tawayefs of Lucknow. As one who has spent one's formative years in pre-Independence Lucknow, I endorse this view. Thumri, not the elongated version in slower tempo favoured by the tawayefs of Benaras, but the drut bol-bant thumri in teentaal belonging to the Kalka Bindadin gharana, constitutes an important expressional element (bhav batlana and bol banana) of kathak. Thakur Jaidev Singh once mentioned two remarkable instances of abhinaya in two separate dance forms by two all-time greats. The first one was Achchhan Maharaj, father of Birju, of the Kalka Bindadin kathak dynasty. There was a phrase in the song 'Achaanak aan pare (he suddenly dropped in from nowhere') that he interpreted through abhinaya in eighteen different ways! The second one was when Thakursaheb was visiting Uday Shankar's Almora Centre. Uday Shankar's guru was Nambudiripad, a famous name in Kathakali, a dance form that traces its origin to the Japanese Kabuki and where expression, especially movement of the eyes, plays a dominant part. He showed how one eye could express gaiety and laughter while tears swelled in the other. Thakur Jaidev Singh was speechless at the end of the performance, which lasted ten whole minutes.

Abdul Halim Sharar, whose book *Lucknow, the Last Phase of Oriental Culture* was translated and edited by Fakhir Hussain and E.S. Harcourt, was strongly of the view that the morals, manners and distinctiveness of Lucknow culture were sustained by the courtesans and tawayefs. Thumri travelled with them to Calcutta, the biggest market and the then capital of India, via Benaras along with the exiled Nawab Wajid Ali Shah. But the babu culture of Bengal could not absorb or sustain, leave alone develop, this new genre despite the legendary Maujuddin, Gauhar Jaan, Janki Bai, Achchan Bai, Malka Jaan, Jaddan Bai and many others. More about this later.

3

Gwalior Gharana

Ustad Vilayet Hussain Khan of the Agra gharana, in his book *Sangeet Sansmaran,* has written that the Gwalior khayal gayaki owes its origin to Abdulla Khan and Qadir Baksh and that the latter had two sons Naththan Khan and Peer Baksh. My own researches, corroborated by the annals of the family of Krishna Rao Shankar Pandit, the last of the giants of this gharana, as well as the thesis of P.N. Chinchore on Rajabhaiya Poochwale, indicate that Naththan Khan and Peer Baksh were one and the same person. He was the son of Makkhan Khan the qawaal, disciple of Ghulam Rasool Khan of Lucknow. It is this Naththan Peer Baksh who taught Khuda Baksh of Agra and was solely responsible for exporting khayal to the Agra gharana, which had an unbroken tradition of dhrupad from the days of Haji Sujan Khan of the court of Emperor Akbar. Naththan Peer Baksh also taught his three grandsons Hassu, Haddu and Natthu Khan, big names in the world of Hindustani music in the nineteenth century. Qadir Baksh was the father of these three brothers.

Shakkar Khan was not only the disciple of Ghulam Rasool Khan of Lucknow, he was also his son-in-law. Shakkar and Makkhan, known as qawaal bachchas, though brothers, drifted apart. Jealousy could well have been the reason. Makkhan Khan got a position in the court of the Maharaja of Gwalior, one of the bigger native states. And in due course his son Naththan Peer Baksh not only succeeded him but also became the guru of Maharaj Daulat Rao Scindia. Nothing is known about Shakkar Khan except that he died young, but his son Bade Mohammad Khan became the court musician of the Maharaja of Rewa, a comparatively smaller state famous for its white tigers.

As far as I can make out, the khayal that Naththan Peer Baksh taught Khuda Baksh of Agra tended to move heavily at a slower tempo and was adorned with huge larazdar taans, which were slightly offbeat. Voice throw was full-chested and the use of gamaks was favoured. Pandit Dilip Chandra Vedi, a disciple of Ustad Faiyaz Khan and Bhaskar Buwa, had heard Khuda Bakhsh's son Ghulam Abbas Khan in person. He was well over a hundred at that time. Bhaskar Buwa had learnt from Fayez Muhammad Khan who was a disciple of Qadir Baksh, son of Naththan Peer Baksh. Thus Dilip Vedi, who died a few years back in his early nineties, was in the best position to authenticate this view, which he did in an interview with me.

Hassu, Haddu and Natthu Khan, the three grandsons of their guru Naththan Peer Baksh, sang this gayaki which both Maharaja Daulat Rao Scindia and his son Jayajirao were fond of. Descriptions are available of taans with unusual names that the Gwalior ustads used to practise. There was the kadak bijlee (lightning and thunder) taan, nangaa talwaar (naked sword) taan and the hathee chingar taan (the one which was capable of bringing elephants out of the stables). Once, Hassu, singing a duo with his brother Haddu Khan in the durbar, took up the terrible hathee chingar taan, with frightening gamaks. In the middle of the long taan, he stopped and spat blood. Naththan Peer Baksh left his seat, came over and wiped his grandson's face with his shawl and said, 'Marnaa hai to beta taan pooree karke maro (Die if you must, son, but finish the taan first')!

It is interesting how these stories travel from generation to generation. Ustad Nissar Hussain Khan, who was attached to the ITC Sangeet Research Academy till his death in 1993 at the age of ninety, was the son-in-law of Ustad Inayat Hussain Khan, the famous singer and composer of the durbar of Rampur. Inayat Hussain had married the daughter of Haddu Khan. Nissar Hussain Khan told me that Haddu Khan, after a hundred sit-ups in the morning, would have his bath in cold water from the well. His breakfast consisted of half a seer (one litre) of milk in a bucket with forty sweet jalebis thrown in. Thereafter he would do his daily riyaz for four hours with gamak taans, which would rattle the windowpanes. Lunch was 'simple'—half a seer of meat korma and rotis. In the evening he would have dinner in the Gwalior palace after a recital. The royal dinner, too, certainly wouldn't have conformed to that prescribed for an invalid: dahi and khichri.

The modern health-conscious reader might note that Haddu Khan was paralysed after a stroke in his early sixties. On the other hand, Krishna Rao Shankar Pandit, who favoured desi ghee, lived till ninety-seven. Alauddin Khan, father and guru of Ali Akbar and Ravi Shankar, respectively, is reported to have completed his century. Ustad Badal Khan, the sarangi-player, lived till the age of a hundred and ten. Ustad Rajab Ali Khan, who lived on rich food and country liquor, died at the age of ninety. So did Alladiya Khan, founder of the Jaipur gharana. Ustad Ahmad Jan Thirakwa was the most famous tabla-player of the last century whose midnight dinner of biryani, korma and kebabs cooked in desi ghee helped him to live to a ripe old age. The doctors, of course, would no doubt tell us that with a more balanced diet, free from cholesterol, and with regular exercise, he would not have died an untimely death at a mere ninety-three. Be that as it may, Muslim ustads I have known—with the sole exception of the diabetic Faiyaz Khan—in old age were all hearty eaters of rich food, kept highly irregular hours and were none the worse for it. Also, most of them would have been able to drink modern-day musicians under the table, Bhimsen Joshi excepted.

The medal, however, goes to Ustad Keramatulla Khan, the famous dhrupad singer whom Ustad Vilayet Hussian Khan of Agra Gharana acknowledges in his book as one of his forty-one gurus. This story has been narrated to me by Aqil Ahmad, another surviving ustad of the same gharana, a disciple of Ustad Tasadduq Hussain Khan. At the time this incident took place Aqil Ahmad was in Bombay learning from Vilayet Hussain Khan. Apparently Latafat bhai, my last guru, a young man then, came up with the idea that a music conference should be arranged by members of the Agra gharana residing at Gwalia Tank in Bombay. After all, people who hardly knew music, and had few connections, were making money by staging shows of dance and music, even arranging minor festivals. All that would be easier to accomplish for Latafat Khan with a houseful of well-known ustads. Accordingly, it was decided to send a message to Ustad Faiyaz Khan at Baroda. Vilayet Hussain Khan was keen on getting his guru Keramatulla Khan, also, who was visiting Baroda at that time.

Till the morning before the inaugural day of the conference, there was no news from Baroda. Those were the days when few people kept telephones, certainly not musicians. Latafat Khan, by nature a nervous person, was in a state of considerable agitation and ran to Bai Kesarbai, the then premier female singer of khayal in the city. She refused categorically to act as a substitute, be it for Ustad Faiyaz Khan or Miyan Tansen. In a dither, they ran to Narayan Rao Vyas, a popular singer of Gwalior gharana khayal and Marathi songs. On returning home they were greatly relieved to find Faiyaz Khan alighting from a carriage. With him was a very old gentleman with a flowing white beard in white kurta-pyjama, slightly dishevelled after his train journey. Latafat Khan thought he looked almost indecently ancient and that it was a miracle he had survived the journey. When Latafat Hussain learnt from Vilayet Khan, his uncle and father-in-law, that Keramatulla Khan was a good five years past his hundredth birthday, he promptly suggested the pride of place at the end of the inaugural session should be given to him the following day, in case he lasted that long.

When the curtain lifted the following evening and a

suitable introduction with respectful eulogies was made by Ustad Vilayet Hussain Khan, the audience saw an ancient person doubled up with age with a flowing white beard dressed in a spotless white pugree and sherwani. There were Vilayet Hussain himself and Latafat's elder brother Khadim Hussain on the tanpuras and Makhkhan Singh on the pakhawaj. No sound came from the singer whose head was suspended above his knees. Then slowly, very slowly, as the head started going up, came the sa as if from a distance, gradually increasing in volume till it became a flowing note without a quiver—something unexpected from a person even thirty years younger. Aqil Ahmad wondered how such a battered old instrument, which legitimately belonged to the attic, could produce such a gorgeous musical sound.

When the alaap, which consisted of all the known alankars, ended after half an hour, Makhkhan Singh's pakhawaj came into play with the dhrupad's sthayee. Three or four minutes passed but the pakhawaj player could not locate the sam. When he did, he could not come back to it after a couple of full cycles. This happened once, twice, three times. Keramatulla Khan, totally blind then, turned vaguely around and said: 'Vilayet Hussain!'

'*Ji*, Ustad.'

'Who is playing the pakhawaj with me?'

'*Ji*, Makhkhan Singh.'

'*Toh khoontaa nahi pahchaantaa?* Even a half-witted calf recognises the bamboo pole to which it is tied.'

Nobody said anything. Ustad started singing again but at the end of the cycle the sam kept on eluding the pakhawaj player. Both Vilayet and Khadim Hussain were masters of dhrupad dhamar and specialised in layakari. When they sang their jugalbandi with a tabla on one side and a pakhawaj on the other, Marathis, who liked the intricacies of rhythmic variations, attended their recitals in hundreds. They were also trying to keep the taal with their hands but not coming to the sam. This went on for a while when Makhkhan Singh stopped playing and with folded hands said, 'Ustad! I am like your *bachcha*, your son, please carry me with you.'

Khansaheb smiled, 'So, Makkhan (meaning butter), your makkhan is already churned, is it? All right, let us proceed. Please pay attention.'

Vilayet Khan later told Aqil Ahmad it was an old trick of casually dropping a beat here and there and changing the mukhda (refrain) slightly and unobtrusively that made the accompanist look like a fool. But the beauty of it was that it was done with such consummate skill that the two ustads on the tanpuras could not easily spot it.

The venerable ustad had been installed in a small hotel nearby and Aqil Ahmad had been given the charge of looking after his meals. Vilayet Khan had, however, cautioned Aqil Ahmad that the ustad ate more than a man of his age and that the kitchen should be somewhat generous in sending the portions. Accordingly, young Aqil had got about thirty chapattis and half a seer of korma and a quarter seer of gajar ka halwa (the popular, rich north Indian dessert of finely grated carrots soaked in thickened milk, cooked in ghee and sugar and seasoned with cinnamon powder and dry fruits), hoping that it would be enough for three persons, which included Vilayet Hussain and himself. When he got to the ustad's room, Vilayet Khan made a sign to Aqil to keep absolutely quiet. As the food was unpacked from the tiffin carrier, the ustad came out of his reverie and said, 'Vilayet Hussain.'

'At your service, Ustad.'

'Is there anyone else here?'

'No, nobody, Ustad.'

'Let us taste the korma. Mmmm... it is good. Where are the chapattis? Pile them up, pile them up! I am hungry. I eat once in twenty-four hours, you know. Give me one *baalisht* of chapattis. You know Vilayet Hussain, my khuraak, my intake, is diminishing with age. Even ten years ago I would take two *baalishts* of rotis.'

One may add that 'baalisht' means the distance between the end of the extended little finger to the other end of the thumb, which could safely be ten inches. Aqil Ahmad says Vilayet Hussain Khan was not a big eater and what was left at the end of the meal was just enough for a child. He also added that this one meal a day of Ustad Keramatulla was a myth since milk and jalebis had to be provided for his breakfast. He lived for many more years. Babban Rao Haldankar recently told me that he had heard Keramatulla Khan in 1942 when the ustad was a hundred and sixteen. Babban Rao was far too young to remember anything except his voice, which was sonorous and tuneful, but on the thinner side. Babban Rao's brother, not as well known a painter as his father, made a sketch of the ustad, which hangs today in the famous Debal Club of Kolhapur.

To go back to young Haddu and Hassu Khan, they were great favourites of the maharaja and their recitals took place virtually every day in the durbar when Bade Mohammad Khan arrived and upset all the arrangements. In addition to heavy gamak and larazdar taans, which have remained to this day a notable feature of this gayaki, his qawaali-based drut khayals and their lilting rhythm appealed to one and all. I have heard a few of these khayals and have learnt one in raga Bahar, 'Aye damanua laye sondhi sugandhi,' which S.N. Ratanjankar had recorded for Hindustan Co. of Calcutta more than sixty years ago. Bade Ghulam Ali Khan told me that he also had heard from his predecessors that Bade Mohammad Khan and his son Bade Mubarak Ali Khan used to sing this composition. It has a typical qawaali-like movement. Maharaja Daulat Singh wanted Haddu and Hassu to add this song to their repertoire and could have easily asked Bade Mohammad Khan to teach them. One can only guess the reasons for not doing it.

Maybe there were objections from Naththan Peer Baksh. What was done instead was rather unethical. Haddu and Hassu were made to sit behind a heavy curtain when Bade Mohammad practised. Apart from his recitals, which the brothers attended, they listened to him in this clandestine manner for well nigh two years. At the end of this period when the brothers felt that they had the hang of Bade Mohammad Khan's style and a fair part of his repertoire, the Maharaja announced a public recital of the two boys at which they were expected to come out in the open and sing Bade Mohammad's gayaki and compositions. It did not strike the Maharaja that there was a moral side to it. Bade Mohammad Khan heard them and on Daulat Rao's request, accepted them as his disciples by performing the formal gandabandhan ceremony, but did not forgive the Maharaja. He went back to Rewa where he was treated with great respect by the ruler. Reappointed on a salary of twelve hundred rupees he was given an elephant and an anklet made of gold for the left foot, a sign of patronage those days, which entitled him to sit beside the Maharaja of Rewa in the durbar as the premier court musician.

At this stage the Gwalior style appears to have taken a distinct shape and shifted more and more to taans. Acharya Brihaspati corroborates this view. Other gharanas that owed their births to Gwalior, like Patiala, Sahaswan and Jaipur, leaned towards adorning their gayakis with different varieties of taans. Only Agra, which stuck to its long tradition of dhrupad and dhamar, never gave up the alaap or the detailed unfolding of the raga in slow movement. Kirana followed later. All the above-mentioned schools of khayal had one thing in common, their loyalty towards traditional compositions and the punctiliousness with which they tried to adhere to the nayaki anga in rendering the bandish.

The term nayaki signifies the exact manner in which a bandish or composition is sung as taught by the guru. Our musical tradition has been strictly an oral one, until the middle of the nineteenth century when the system of notation was started in Bengal by Kshetra Mohan Goswami, Krishna Dhan Bandopadhyaya and Dwijendranath Tagore, eldest brother of Rabindranath, and was later taken up by Vishnu Digambar Paluskar and Vishnu Narayan Bhatkhande. It was therefore necessary that the pupil should faithfully render the composition sticking to every word and every nuance as taught by the guru. The nayaki anga of the bandish gave the singer the liberty to adorn the lines of the composition allowing his own imaginative faculty to come into play. This discipline is gradually disappearing in recent years, especially in eastern India. Political freedom has brought about a growing sense of freedom from convention and a certain lack of discipline in every walk of life. Indian classical music is no exception.

Before the young musician of the new generation calls me a conservative old fool after reading the above paragraph, that is if he is given to reading at all, I must try and defend the virtues of strict talim. First, traditional compositions form an important part of our musical education. It is the bandish that holds the key to the raga. The greater one's repertoire of bandishes of a particular raga, the better is one's knowledge of its anatomy. Further, every raga has its own character, its own personality. Take, for instance, Bhairavi, Raamkali and Kalingadaa, which share more or less the same notes. The first should be sung with plenty of meends and gamaks but no fast taans or unnecessary alankars like murkees and khatkas which disrupt the atmosphere of peace, tranquillity and sanctity of dawn associated with this raga. Talim teaches us to concentrate on the madhyam, the fourth note, the degree of oscillation of the re and dha, the minor second and the minor fifth, and the shrutis or the microtones. In raga Raamkali, the concentration is on the pancham, the constant fifth, and it is not as sombre as Bhairavi. It, therefore, admits of taans. Kalingadaa, which employs exactly the same notes as those in the Bhairavi, is a lighter raga with a flighty character. Its movement is also different and it uses the pet phrase of sa ga re ga. Every raga has its major and subsidiary phrases. Bandishes give you these phrases, without which the anatomy of a raga is never properly perceived. All this clearly cannot be learnt from books, music being a performing art.

The older gharanas, where dhrupad flourished before the advent of the khayal in the form we know today, are Gwalior and Agra. The founder of the Jaipur gharana, Ustad Alladiya

Khan, was originally a noted dhrupad singer. Kirana is traced to Bande Ali Khan who was a famous beenkar and taught dhrupads as well as khayals, although the present Kirana gayaki owes its existence to Abdul Karim and Abdul Waheed Khan who were not known as dhrupadiyas. My ustads as well as my father, Shrikrishna Ratanjankar, Thakur Jaidev Singh, Pahari Sanyal (whose opinions I value more than those of anyone else) were firmly of the view that every student of music must begin with dhrupad. Dhrupad offers many more traditional compositions than khayal and for proper delineation of a raga, initial training in dhrupad is essential.

Further, those who shaped my opinion held the view that dhrupadiyas of the past were masters of meend, gamak and shruti, the three pillars on which our raga sangeet rests. I remember my father telling me more than once that those who had not heard the alaapchari of Allabande Khan, who used to sing with his elder brother Zakiruddin and son Nasiruddin, could not conceive what shruti and swarasthaan meant in Indian music. Pandit Dilip Chandra Vedi used to say that when Nasiruddin Khan sang, his command over sur seemed the last word. When Zakiruddin opened his mouth it seemed his shruti and swarasthaan were even more accurate and the notes acquired a luminous quality. Much as Vediji tried to like the music of Moinuddin and Aminuddin Dagar brothers, he could not think of mentioning their names in the same breath with that of their father Nasiruddin and granduncle Zakiruddin Khan. Among the khayaliyas who had mastered shrutis he would mention his two mentors Bhaskar Rao Bakhle and Faiyaz Khan, both of whom belonged to such gharanas as patronized dhrupad through centuries.

Abdul Karim Khan did not receive proper talim in dhrupad although on occasions he is reported to have sung dhrupad marvellously well and displayed great command over layakari in his early years. In the words of my father, 'Whatever he sang, of course, was music.' I have not heard the great dhrupad singers, though I have been on terms of intimacy with my generation of Dagars. I have heard Faiyaz

Khan and have marvelled at the use of dhaivat, which is neither komal nor shuddh, in his 78 RPM record of *Lalit* not only in slower movement, but even in the fast one, which the instrumentalists call jod. So is the sahakaari dhaivat in his *Desi Todi Dhamaar* and *Khayaal* which are also available in commercial cassettes. Among those I have heard whose command over shrutis was phencmenal was Shrikrishna Ratanjankar.

My own opinion, born out of my experience of listening to ustads and discussions with musicologists spanning over sixty years now, is that sur in Hindustani classical music is like a flowing river. We have consciously tried to build the ghats (landings) like the komal re (minor second) of Bhairav, and a separate one for the komal re of the Marwa and Shree, which is slightly higher. There are komal gandhars (minor third) of Kafi, Nayaki Kanhra, Darbari Kanhra and Miyan Malhar. All are different. The shrutis are not static either. For instance, the komal ga and komal ni of raga Bhimpalasi are higher in the ascendant scale than the same notes while going down. The komal ga of Miyan Malhar is higher than that of Darbari because it is approached from the top with madhyam. Darbari and Nayaki Kanhra's gandhars, though slightly different from each other, are approached from the bottom with the help of rekab. In other words, shrutis are not independent of meends. The moment you freeze a shruti, it becomes a static note. Unlike in European music we do not hop from one note to another. We glide, except in the case of sargams.

Dhrupadiyas used to call khayalias besuraa (out of tune) because of taans, which are a series of staccato notes in vowels. Drut alaap in dhrupad, the equivalent of taans in khayal, is a series of consonants woven together with the help of halaq and gamaks. In the earlier days of khayal gayaki also, there were plenty of halaq and gamaks in taans, which helped to join one note to another. Another variety of taans without danas, called manja, prevailing in Gwalior and adopted by Jaipur gayaki, is a series of notes pronounced with akar but strung together with the help of meends. Both these types have obviously been evolved by khayal singers who were not bereft of the dhrupad tradition.

Khayal gayaki, of course, has been changing, as it must over the years, but my elders were lucky to have missed the invasion of Punjabi harkats and murkees from the bazaars of Lahore and Peshawar, reserved earlier for their brand of thumris and ghazals by petty tawayefs. A few years back, a famous khayaliya with a strong predilection for this variety of cheap ornamentation was talking to Nivruttibuwa Sarnaik, then attached to the ITC Sangeet Research Academy. He said, 'Buwa, as you know, like you I never sing thumris but everywhere at the end of my recitals there are shouts for thumris. Do you think I should start singing thumris as well?' Nivruttibuwa, with the typical mischievous sparkle in his eyes, replied, '*Jo gaate ho, wohi gaate raho. Sirf theka badal dena* (Go on singing exactly the way you do, just change the taal').

As the Gwalior gayaki became taanpradhan, it developed the mannerism of using more and more linear taans and sapaat taans. This is not a desirable feature because unlike Karnatak music Hindustani ragas do not deal with arohi and avarohi, the ascendant and descendant scale and paltas, but are dependent on chalan, or a certain laid-down movement. For instance, Chhayanat is best established when the phrase sa re, re ga, ga ma, ma pa, pa re are used while ascending, and sa dha ni pa re ga ma pa ga ma re sa when coming down. This zigzag movement cannot be replaced by re ga ma pa ni sa, sa dha pa ma ga re sa. Similarly, Bihag has the essential phrase of pa ma ga ma ga without which the raga appears naked. The taan ni sa ga ma pa ni sa re sa ni dha pa ma ga re sa irons out the features of the raga ruthlessly.

My first guru, Rabindra Lal Roy, told me in the course of a conversation in his later years that this was a deliberate attempt to create a contrast. My second guru, Mushtaq Hussain Khan, who sang Gwalior, used to go a step further. Some of his linear taans would ignore grammar: such as in ga ma pa dha ni sa or ni sa re ga in Bihag. His argument was once the raag-bhaav, or the atmosphere of the raga is established, these minor departures do not stand out. On the contrary, they become part of the general atmosphere of the raga. Maybe. I feel about the abundance of such linear and sapaat taans the same way I do when I see on the TV large sprinklings of men and women in Australia, South Africa and even in the sanctum sanctorum of English cricket, at Lords, watching cricket in summer with next to nothing on. They also fit into the general atmosphere nowadays.

The importance that an artiste should assign to a bandish and the manner in which it is to be delivered, sometimes playfully, as Faiyaz Khan used to, enjoying and loving each of the phrases while adorning them with short taans in the manner of qawaals, is almost a lost art. However, I am reminded of an incident from my days in Lucknow. Usually, after the annual examinations, some of the examiners would be invited to sing by Ratanjankar, principal, Marris College of Music, now known as Bhatkhande University. On this occasion it was Pandit Mahadev Prasad who opened the evening's proceedings. He was a pundit all right but he had an unusually raucous voice and his taans sounded like a piece of brick rubbed against a tin roof at great speed. Half an hour of Mahadev Prasad was enough for a normal adult listener but an hour and a quarter for listeners that included Ratanjankar, Mushtaq Hussain Khan and Alauddin Khan must have been the limit. At this point Wadilalji, one of the external examiners with a long association with Bhatkhandeji and his institution, thought it was time to call D.L. Roy to assist Mahadev Prasadji. Now this D.L.Roy had already taken ten years to get to the final year of the graduation course of five years and was a born besuraa who could not sing in tune for more than a minute to save his mother's life. As soon as Roy made his appearance Wadilalji said to him, 'Can't you see Panditji is getting tired? Why don't you give him voice support?'" Which, of course, Roy proceeded to do with the enthusiasm of a dog attacking a bone after being on a vegetarian diet for a month. Panditji picked up his turban and betel case and brought his recital to a close to delighted clapping from the audience.

Ustad Mushtaq Hussain Khan followed. I remember he sang Jhinjhoti and developed the raga with unusual patience. But what I particularly recollect were his taans which covered three octaves and cascaded like a fountain. He was in exceptional form and his dry virtuosity, not always everybody's cup of tea, was greatly appreciated by the ustads and the staff of the Marris College. He also sang for over an hour. Who then would sing after him? There was only one musician senior to Mushtaq Hussain in age and that was Rajabhaiya Poochwale. He had a dull voice like a much-used faceless copper coin, reportedly due to excessive riyaz, but he was a disciple of Krishna Rao Shankar Pandit's father and, therefore, an eminent guru of the authentic Gwalior gayaki. Reluctant though he was, he was persuaded by all the artistes. And how long did he sing? Not more than twenty minutes! He sang 'Barajo na mane' in Basant Bahar, the composition in slow medium tempo, which seemed like the dignified swaying gait of an elephant. This was followed by a tarana in Bahar. No taans, only bahlawa. Believe me, the impact of all the fireworks of my guru Mushtaq Hussain Khansaheb was completely wiped out in minutes.

Jiyajirao Scindia's rule ended in 1886. He, like his father, was a great patron of music and became a gandabandh disciple of Natthu Khan, the youngest brother of Haddu and Hassu. Hassu was gone by that time and Haddu was touring other centres of music. He loved travelling by train. Bombay, by that time, was connected by rail to Calcutta—then capital of India. Haddu Khan came to this city of merchant princes. It is not known where he had his recitals but a description is available in P.N. Chinchore's book in Hindi on Rajabhaiya. It appears that his virtuosity and taans, of which he was so proud, had a totally unexpected effect on his audience. Shortly after his recital began, his listeners started disappearing one by one, and by the time he finished only his host and his courtiers remained in the hall. It took Haddu Khan a couple of days to get over his trauma when he was told that but for Taj Khan and Ali Baksh Khan of Wajid Ali Shah's court in Metiabruz (the present dock area in Calcutta), there was virtually no khayaliya in Calcutta.

Also, the court musicians of the exiled Nawab were not easily accessible to the public. What audiences were accustomed to hear were dhrupads which had a long tradition because Calcutta was the meeting point of the famous Vishnupur and Betia gharanas. Except in tappa, imported by Ram Nidhi Gupta (Nidhubabu), taans, khatkas and murkees were strange to the ears of the music-loving citizens of Calcutta. Haddu Khan, on realizing this, requested his host to arrange another soiree in a different locality. That evening he eschewed all the adornments, which are taboo in dhrupad, and sang his khayal without a single khatka, murkee or taan. The taal was ektaal instead of chautaal, both of which have the same twelve matras or beats. After all, Haddu Khan was a born artiste and it did not take him long to win over the hearts of the Bengalis. One gathers that he also travelled to Krishnanagar and sang before the Maharaja. The Diwan (prime minister) Kartikeya Chandra Roy, the grandfather of my first guru Rabindra Lal, as well as the poet, singer and mystic Dilip Kumar Roy of Pondicherry, formally became Haddu Khan's disciples.

I have some doubts about the veracity of this story. There was a court musician called Hasnu Khan in Krishnanagar and this may be the reason for the confusion.

Haddu Khan had many disciples outside his family members. Most of them were Marathas from the then Bombay Presidency. There were one or two who had settled in Gwalior whose Maharaja was also a Maharashtrian. Haddu Khan was fond of saying he was not in favour of teaching Muslims who were as a rule namak-haraams.[1] Once they started gaining recognition they would disclaim their guru and declare they had learnt from their father and uncles as if they were gharanedar musicians. Haddu Khan taught Hindus, preferably Brahmins, because they were supposed to be brighter than members of other castes. Of these several were responsible for spreading the Gwalior gayaki in Bombay and what is known today as the state of Maharashtra. No one, among these, is more responsible for converting the musicians of western India from Karnatak sangeet of the south to Gwalior of the north than Balkrishnabuwa Ichalkaranjikar and his equally famous disciple Vishnu Digambar.

Professor B.R. Deodhar, in his book *Pillars of Indian Music*, gives us a glimpse of the kind of harrowing life of hardship and poverty that these musicians had to endure to receive talim from their gurus. They worked as domestic servants-cum-cooks, were often denied two square meals a day and begged for their food from neighbours. The gharanedar Muslim ustads did not care to give talim to Hindus, especially if they were poor, as in the case of the great Bhaskarbuwa Bakhle (who deserves a separate chapter). Even Muslims who were poor and had no family connections with musicians had little chance of receiving talim from a reputed ustad. Ustad Alauddin Khan, whose dynasty includes Ali Akbar Khan and Ravi Shankar, desperate for talim from Ustad Wazir Khan, the court musician and guru of the Nawab of Rampur, had to throw himself before the carriage of the nawab before he obtained entry into the sacred premises of the 'Rajguru's' household.

Balkrishna of Ichalkaranji was born in the village of Chandore, not far from Kolhapur, into a family of professional beggars. No stigma was attached to mendicancy in Indian society if one was a Brahmin or a sadhu or a Buddhist monk. On the contrary, it was considered an act of piety to give alms to mendicants. Possessed with an indomitable desire to become a musician, he left home in his early teens, went from one guru to another, travelled hundreds of miles on foot, got involved with a lot of fake sadhus, and became a disciple of Devjibuwa (Ramkrishna Paranjpay) whom he served as domestic servant and cook—only to be thrown out after four years by Buwa's wife who hated the sight of him.

Devjibuwa, who had learnt dhrupad from Chintamani Mishra, also got extensive talim in khayal and tappa from Haddu Khan. Balkrishna had hardly any time left for his riyaz after his domestic chores but learnt compositions on the way to the temple every evening when he accompanied his guru. When he was thrown out on the streets he had neither money nor any clothes to speak of. At one stage he decided to starve himself to death in front of a Kali temple in Monghyr. Ultimately, he found refuge in the house of Vasudev Rao Joshi, another disciple of Haddu Khan. For six years he cooked food for his guru, cleaned the house, taught his guru's junior disciples and in return received talim for four hours every morning from four to eight. In due course his talents received recognition not only from discerning listeners but from Jiyajirao, the Maharaja of Gwalior, who suggested he should take talim from the court musician Ustad Haddu Khan himself. Balkrishna politely refused the offer saying he could not go to any other ustad without his guru's permission.

On the occasion of the wedding of Haddu Khan's daughter with Bande Ali Khan, the famous beenkar of Kirana gharana, the festival of music lasted seven nights. Mohammad Khan, the eldest son of Haddu Khan, sang on the first evening, with Balkrishna and Vishnupanth Chhatre on the tanpuras, to lend him voice support. Haddu Khan announced at the end of the recital that Chhatre was his *shagird* and Balkrishna was his grandson, his *shagird*'s *shagird*. One of the listeners said, 'Yes, both of them are good but is your grandson capable of giving a full-fledged recital on his own?' That evening Balkrishna's solo performance was of such a high order that even the great Haddu Khan embraced him in public and expressed his hope that Balkrishna would be a true torchbearer of his gharana.

What was Balkrishna's gayaki like? Professor G.H. Ranade, disciple of Mirasibuwa, has written that his voice was as sweet as the purest honey and there was no change in quality in the higher and lower octaves. He has gone to the extent of stating that the tonal quality of his voice was superior to that of Abdul Karim Khan and his mentor Rahmat Khan, the younger son of Haddu Khan. Balkrishnabuwa's gayaki was unadulterated Gwalior except that he paid somewhat greater attention to the vistar, or unfolding of the raga, than other members of his gharana. His halaq and gamak taans, covering the best part of three octaves, were famous and there was no trace of falsetto in the application of notes in the higher octave. His breath control and stamina were remarkable. He was known to have sung for four hours in the morning followed by an evening recital extending to three-and-a-half hours. Professor Ranade concludes his assessment of Balkrishnabuwa by saying that he was unquestionably a great singer but even greater was his contribution to music in the length and breadth of Maharashtra. He was the first to open a school of music with the help of influential citizens like Dr R.G. Bhandarkar, N.C. Apte, R.R. Kunde and Justice K.T. Tilang. The credit of bringing out the first journal on music also goes to Balkrishnabuwa Ichalkaranjikar. Among his disciples were big names like Manohar Pandit, Bamanbuwa Chafekar, Nilkanthabuwa (the first guru of Mallikarjun Mansoor), Gundobuwa of Oundh, Mirasibuwa, his own son Annabuwa and, of course, Pandit Vishnu Digambar.

Fortune made up for its earlier lack of attention to Balkrishnabuwa—till a year before his death in 1925 when his favourite son and disciple Annabuwa died. Till then, his fame as the court musician of the Raja of Ichalkaranji and the premier singer of Maharashtra had spread to every corner of western India, although he was comparatively unknown in the north and not known at all in Calcutta or eastern India. His affluence had not changed his earlier attitude of indifference to money matters. Once, Debal Club of Kolhapur had paid him sixty rupees for three recitals. He thought this was more than what the club, of which he was a founder-member, should spend on a single artiste, even one of his standing, and returned half the fee. One does not know whether Balkrishnabuwa was a male chauvinist, for in his school the male students paid five annas to five rupees per

Mallikarjun Mansoor

month depending on their parents' income. The girl students were required to pay thirty rupees, which in those days would have covered the expenses of a small family for a whole month.

Many years ago, in a railway compartment on the way to Bombay from Lucknow, I heard Shrikrishna Ratanjankar and my father discuss the respective merits of the great voices they had heard. They finally agreed to five names: Ustad Zakiruddin Khan, the grand-uncle of the late Dagar brothers, Vishnu Digambar, Faiyaz Khan, Bhatkhandeji and Bade Ghulam Ali Khan. Why they did not include Pandit Omkarnath Thakur in the list still puzzles me. Panditji's melodramatic gayaki might have irked purists, but unquestionably he had a wonderful voice.

As a youth my father had the opportunity to listen to Vishnu Digambar in the house of Bhupen Ghosh of Pathuriaghata. Bhupenbabu, a member of a well-known, rich, aristocratic family of north Calcutta, was a passionate devotee of classical music. Later, in the thirties, he started the All Bengal Music Conference and gave Calcutta a chance of listening to the great musicians of northern and western India. But for him this city could not have played host to Ustad Alladiya Khan, Faiyaz Khan or Abdul Karim.[2] Much before the birth of the All Bengal Music Festival, Vishnu Digambar had come to Calcutta and was staying with Bhupenbabu in his Pathuriaghata Palace. Vishnuji had, by that time, virtually given up singing khayal and had turned to bhajans, religious songs based on ragas without adornments, which had mass appeal in those days when film songs had not yet made inroads into the living rooms of the middle class. Bhupenbabu told my father that Panditji was averse to singing khayal in public but still got up at the crack of dawn to do his riyaz. My father walked three miles at 4 am to get to Pathuriaghata and sat outside Vishnu Digambar's room. His eavesdropping was adequately rewarded by an alaap in Bhairav in a voice that would haunt my father even thirty years later.

Vishnu Digambar was probably the only musician of Maharashtra whose initiation into classical music was not fraught with the kind of hardships his contemporaries had to undergo. Vishnu's father was a kirtan singer who received the patronage of Srimanta Daji, brother of the Raja of Kurundwar. Vishnu was a fair-complexioned, good-looking child with pleasant manners. He grew up with Dajisaheb's son and was so accepted by the family that his sacred thread ceremony was performed along with that of Daji Sahab's son with considerable pomp and splendour. Vishnu was also good at studies and would have found a position in the Kurundwar state service had it not been for an injury to his left eye. That was the turning point in his life and the beginning of his tutelage under Balkrishnabuwa Ichalkaranjikar.

Vishnu's untutored voice was big, somewhat inflexible and harsh. Sheer hard work and dedicated practice for eight to nine hours a day turned him into an accomplished singer in ten years. His voice also acquired timbre and flexibility and remained his main asset in a reasonably long musical career. He had also imbibed ourtly manners through his association with the royal families of Meeraj and Kurundwar, which helped him later in life. He went to Baroda with a recommendation from the Raja of Kurundwar and impressed the Maharani Jamunabai. He could have stayed on at Baroda or could have got a position in any of the native states but he had other ideas.

He was aware of the kind of demeaning experience talented but poor aspiring musicians had to undergo, if at all they got a chance of learning from ustads, who were the jealous keepers of our classical music at the turn of the nineteenth century. Ustads, too, unless they were at the top of their profession, hardly received the right amount of patronage and spent their days teaching their kith and kin and tawayefs. With the advent of English education a new middle class emerged, which aped the masters and was indifferent to its own traditional culture. Learning music, associated as it was with illiterate Muslim musicians and women of ill fame, was unthinkable for children of lawyers, doctors, middle-level bureaucrats, well-to-do entrepreneurs, and fiercely respectable members of the Brahmo Samaj and Arya Samaj in the north, which formed the bulk of the new middle class. But for Vishnu Digambar and Vishnu Narayan Bhatkhande in Maharashtra, and the Tagore families, both of Raja Sourindra Mohan and Prince Dwarakanath in Bengal, classical music would have remained anathema to 'bhadralok' class.

The biggest contribution of Vishnu Digambar is the Gandharva Mahavidyalaya, a school for teaching music to young students, with branches in other states. This concept, which preceded Bhatkhandeji's Marris Music College by twenty-four years, is not the first of its kind. Very few people are aware that the Banga Sangeet Vidyalaya was founded by Raja Sourindra Mohan Tagore in 1871 in Calcutta, where violin, sitar and vocal music lessons were given by a number of well-known musicians. This was followed by the Bengal Academy of Music which received a grant from the government apart from considerable financial support from Raja Sourindra Mohan himself. Oddly enough, the Gandharva Mahavidyalaya was founded by Vishnu Digambar, not in Bombay but in distant Lahore in 19?1, on the advice of a sadhu whom Vishnuji had met in Girnar.

He introduced textbooks containing traditional compositions with notations, much as Bhatkhandeji would do a couple of decades later. For this purpose, Vishnu Digambar learnt the staff notation system from one Mr James, a bandleader in Jodhpur. However, his own system of notations was different and he never could listen to a composition and put it down on paper without help. Here again, the credit for introducing a notation system for the first time goes to Krishna Dhan Bandopadhyaya of Calcutta, in his publication called *Banga Oikya Tan* in 1867, followed by a similar one by his guru, Kshetra Mohan Goswami a year later, though his rough draft was drawn up as far back as 1858. The eldest brother of Rabindranath Tagore, Dwijendra Nath, claimed the credit of being the first to introduce the notation system in our music, but this was not correct. Kshetra Mohan Goswami, the guru of Krishna Dhan and Raja Sourindra Mohan, preceded him.

The second Gandharva Mahavidyalaya was founded seven years later in Bombay in 1908. It rapidly became so popular among the Maratha middle classes that Vishnu Digambar had to take three small buildings on rent adjacent to the present Congress House. In 1913, his friends advised him to buy a plot of land on Sandhurst Road for Rs 48,000 and this place became his headquarters from where a regular journal called *Sangeetamrit Pravaaha* was published. In addition to all this, he arranged five music festivals on a national scale between 1918 and 1922. The first grand conference, for which Bhatkhandeji was responsible, was held at Baroda in 1916. It looks as though Vishnu Digambar had shown the path to V.N. Bhatkhande in more than one direction.

From 1917 onwards, Vishnu Digambar became so involved with the administration and financing of his Gandharva Mahavidyalaya and its branches that his role as a performing musician became less and less important to him. One of the reasons for his recitals becoming scarce was that he fixed his fee at five hundred rupees when his guru Balkrishnabuwa hardly ever charged more than a hundred for outstation performances. Not that Vishnu Digambar was avaricious, but he was firmly of the opinion that a musician's place in society was not lower than that of a physician or a barrister. One is not sure, however, whether even the most successful doctor or barrister in the Twenties could demand the kind of fee Vishnu Digambar asked for. But he did not neglect his riyaz, which he kept up assiduously till he took to saffron and became mainly a singer of bhajans.

The second part of his musical life is an uninteresting one for his chronicler. He was a very good singer but not a great one, who fell among Rambhaktas. Finally, he retired to his ashram in Nasik and spent his days reading *Ramcharitmanas* by Tulsidas and singing bhajans and kirtans. Some of his favourite bhajans were popularized by his son D.V. Paluskar and were available in 78 RPM records. 'Chala Mana Gangaa Jamunaa Teer', 'Thumaka Chalata Ramachandara', Raghupati Raaghava Rajaram', all based on ragas, were much in demand during the Fifties and Sixties.

My father used to say vocalists have two kinds of voices. One resembled string instruments and the other wind instruments. The voices of Ustad Faiyaz Khan, Bade Ghulam Ali Khan and Amir Khan, which had a lot of timbre, belonged to the first. Dattatreya V. Paluskar's piping voice resembled a flute dipped in honey and sounded as if he was born without an Adam's apple. He had very little talim from his father, who died when Dattatreya Paluskar was a child. He received lessons mainly from Vinayak Rao Patwardhan who, along with his contemporary, Narayan Rao Vyas, allowed the classical dignity of the heavy Gwalior style to be contaminated by the lighter Marathi Natya Sangeet, so much so, that one could not imagine that it had anything to do with the Muslim tradition. The difference is not between *attar* and incense, the fragrance of both of which is rich and overpowering. It is the difference between a dish of biryani with the flavours of garlic, onion and saffron, and a dish of bland vegetable curry.

It would be wrong to call the Natya Sangeet Hindu or Marathi gayaki just because Bhaskarbuwa, Anantamanohar Joshi, his son Gajananbuwa, Shrikrishna Ratanjankar and his disciples, members of the Pandit clan like Krishnarao and his sons, and Ulhas Kashalkar, the present-day major exponent of the Gwalior gharana, all belong to Maharashtra, and are of course Hindus. None of them resembles Patwardhan or Narayan Rao Vyas, though their roots are the same. Patwardhan and Narayan Rao further introduced fast sargam into the Gwalior gayaki, where none exists even now. However, those who like this style would unquestionably put D.V. Paluskar on a higher pedestal than his mentor.

It is a pity that D.V. died in his forties. Had he lived longer, his music might have acquired with age the requisite touch of dignity and tranquillity associated with his father's music. Those who have listened only to his 78 RPM records and the two cassettes of half an hour's duration may perhaps not agree with me. But I have listened to him a dozen times since P.N. Chinchore introduced me to a thin young Paluskar in a buttoned-up long coat and Marathi round topee outside the gates of the Marris College hostel one evening in the mid-Forties. Standing there, me leaning on my bike, Chinchore made him sing a number of compositions. I have always found his music sweet and melodious but lacking in poise and depth.

I have mentioned Gajananrao Joshi in the previous paragraph. He had lessons from his father Ananta Manohar Joshi, known as Antubuwa, a disciple of Balkrishnabuwa Ichalkaranjikar. Not satisfied with the talim in Gwalior gayaki, Gajananrao went to Bhurji Khan, the son of Ustad Alladiya Khan, the founder of the Jaipur gharana. He then became a gandabandh disciple of Ustad Vilayet Hussain Khan of Agra. Since he did not have a particularly good voice, he took to the violin and is the only artiste in north India who had separate national programmes on AIR to his credit as a singer as well as a violinist. Balamuralikrishna is the only other musician who has performed this feat in the south.

Remarkably enough, as a vocalist, Gajananrao would seldom mix the Gwalior, Jaipur and Agra styles. When he sang, for instance, *Natbihag* a la Agra, *Puria* in the traditional Gwalior style and *Patbihag* in the Jaipur gayaki at the same mehfil, it seemed as if the artiste had changed clothes in between. His disciple, Ulhas Kashalkar, has also inherited talim in Gwalior and Jaipur styles from his guru. Endowed with a good voice and aesthetic sense, he is on his way to becoming the premier khayal singer of India, a position held by the octogenarian Pandit Bhimsen Joshi for the last twenty-five years.

Gajananrao used to say he could sing the Agra gayaki but not that of Faiyaz Khan. In his drawing room, among many

Ustad Alladiya Khan

photographs of famous musicians, the pride of place went to Aftab-e-Mousiqui, whom he had heard for the first time in Mysore. This is where young Gajananrao Joshi was requested by Ustad Faiyaz Khan to sing Shuddh Kalyan. Gajananrao begged Khansaheb's pardon and said he would, with the ustad's permission, prefer to sing Yaman Kalyan. At the end of the recital, Faiyaz Khan asked him about his talim. When he heard that Gajananrao had learnt only from his father Antubuwa, Faiyaz Khan wondered how there was such a strong influence of Rahmat Khan on Gajananrao's gayaki. The mystery was solved when Gajananbuwa explained that his father used to play tanpura behind Ustad Rahmat Khan for nearly four years.

Not that Rahmat Khan gave lessons to Antubuwa or anybody else for that matter. He was perhaps genuinely unaware of the existence of Antubuwa. Once, when he sang over three days in Ichalkaranji, he enquired from his host on the third day whether he knew the whereabouts of Balkrishnabuwa who, Rahmat Khan said, sang his brother Mohammad Khan's gayaki better than anybody else. The interesting part of the story is that Balkrishnabuwa, the court musician of the Raja of Ichalkaranji, had been playing tanpura and giving Rahmat Khan voice support over those three evenings. Rahmat Khan was Haddu Khan's younger son and was, therefore, the Khalifa of not only Balkrishnabuwa but also that of his gurus Devjibuwa and Vasudevrao Joshi.

Amiyanath Sanyal of Calcutta, a friend of my father, received talim from Ustad Badal Khan, the famous sarangi player, as well as from Shyamlal Khetri, disciple of Bhaiyya Saheb Ganpat Rao of Gwalior, the famous harmonium player and also the guru of the legendary Moijuddin Khan. Amiyanath was fortunate enough to have grown up in Calcutta at a time when the greatest tawayefs had settled in the city. His lineage was upper middle class but he had married into the family of the Maharaja of Natore. He was, therefore, above the inhibitions of the then respectable middle class about frequenting the jalsas of tawayefs, usually arranged by zamindars and rich, non-Bengali, businessmen of Calcutta. He hardly ever missed the recitals of Gauhar Jaan and Malka Jaan of Agra in particular.

Moijuddin Khan has been made immortal to Bengali readers in his book *Smritir Atale* (from the depths of memory). Amiyanath's rendering of the thumri *'Baajuband khul khul jaye'*, according to my father, was second only to Faiyaz Khan's. He played been as well as esraaj (dilruba) with such a fantastic touch that the great Hafiz Ali Khan, father of Amjad Ali, the famous sarod player of today, once said to Amiyanath, 'Paanchubabu (that was his pet name), why don't you lend me your hands for a month or two?' Here is the story of young Moijuddin from Amiyanath's book in the words of Shyamlal Khetri:

'Moijuddin was what we call a shrutidhar. Do talk to him and you will realize he knows no raga, he knows no taal. He has had no training whatsoever. He can sing a composition by listening to it just once. When he sings, he instinctively sings the raga and taal, any taal, correctly. In fact he is not even aware of the notations, the sa re ga ma of music. He sings the way a duckling takes to water just after being hatched. And as you know, no one dares sing after him, such is the impact of his music, especially his thumris. How would you explain it except by the sanskaar of his previous birth?

I have seldom come across a more modest, well-mannered and dignified person as the tawayef Malka Jaan of Agra. Once, she invited Ustad Bhaiyya Sahab Ganpat Rao and some of us to her house to listen to Suggan Bai, her guest. This was Suggan's first visit to Calcutta, though I had the pleasure of hearing her earlier. Her thumris were very good but her dadras were remarkable. It is not easy to sing a dadra. Its movement, unlike in thumri, is lilting and requires special technique. However, on this occasion she hurried through a khayal and tarana, a warming-up prologue to her three dadras. Everybody was full of praise, except Moijuddin.

While Suggan Bai was taking a brief respite and preparing her paan-tambakoo, there were several requests for Moijuddin Khan to sing. Malka, the hostess, no doubt felt uncomfortable but had to accede to public demand with a formal request to Moijuddin. There was no tanpura for men available. So, with the harmonium and the accompaniment of one sarangi, Moijuddin settled down to sing. When he opened his mouth he took my breath away by his unpardonable defiance of etiquette. He started singing the same dadra, *Nadiya nare heraye aayi kanganaa*; the third and the last of Suggan Bai's dadras, with more colour, skill and feeling than Suggan or any of the tawayefs were capable of. Within moments, Suggan's *kanganaa* was lost forever. Suggan Bai, red in the face, left the room with Malka Jaan hurriedly following her.

When we mentioned to Ustad Bhaiyya Sahab that he could have easily prevented Moijuddin, now his disciple, from creating such an indecently awkward scene, he turned round and said, 'When Moijuddin sings, it is not he but the Saiyad of Mousiqui which possesses him. Never, never stop him from singing whatever he wants. Otherwise, he will go mad, like Rahmat Khan.'

One day, in Moimurganj in Kashi, we were settling down to lunch when Rahmat Khan suddenly descended on us without prior intimation. Before we could go through the formalities of welcoming the illustrious son of Haddu Khan, he said to Bhaiyya Sahab, 'I understand there is a young man called Moijuddin who sings very well. I want to listen to him.' Now, Ustad Ganpat Rao was from the royal family of

Gwalior³ and deserved some deference from the son of the Maharaja's premier court musician. The courtly manners of those days, too, did not admit of the abrupt style of Rahmat Khan. Bhaiyya Sahab uttered some formal words of welcome to which he added that it was Moijuddin's singular good fortune to sing before the great ustad but would he, Khansaheb, not like to rest for a while and partake of the frugal meal in that humble abode before a soiree could be arranged— preferably in the afternoon? Rahmat Khansaheb responded with a firm 'No!', and demanded to hear Moijuddin then and there.

So, Moijuddin had to be produced. He was made to sing with a single tanpura and to the accompaniment of me on the harmonium and Bashir on the tabla. Moijuddin started at high noon with a pedestrian composition in raga Malkauns. Of course, with Moijuddin, even an ordinary bandish became extraordinary. Rahmat Khan liked it. 'Shabash beta, now let me hear a thumri,' he said. Moijuddin started his patented 'Baajuband khul khul jaye' in Bhairavi and Ustad Bhaiyya Sahab took the harmonium from me. The wizard that my ustad was, his single-reed harmonium created the illusion sometimes of the flowing stream of notes of a sarangi, sometimes a flute and even the zamzamaa of a string instrument, especially with the laggi. He was at his best when he played with Moijuddin, and vice versa. Even before Moijuddin's thumri could come to a proper end Rahmat Khan's taareef started and went on for what seemed like hours. He actually started weeping and muttering over and over again, 'Hai Allah! Why have you not given me Moijuddin's voice and taaseer. How am I ever going to sing after this? I shall give up singing.'

By the time everyone was sick of Khansaheb's wild lamenting as well as with hunger, Moijuddin, directed by Bhaiyya Sahab, fell at the feet of Rahmat Khan and said, 'Huzoor, what you are saying is positively sacrilegious. My music at best is for the raees and the tawayefs. If you would care to sing after this, you would yourself realise your music is meant for ustads. Compared to your music mine is not worth a pie to your silver rupee.' Wonder of wonders, the mad fellow who would not sing even when requested by rajas and maharajas, immediately burst into a halaq taan, covering two octaves in raga Todi. It was such a perfect taan, such wonderfully accurate notes strung together like pearls in elegant patterns, that Moijuddin spontaneously cried out in wonder. The whole gathering automatically exclaimed loud praises. Rahmat Khan looked intently at Moijuddin and said, 'Do you really think that I sing better than you do?' He paused for a while, got up and left muttering to himself, 'Yes, yes, I sing really well. Moijuddin says so. Praise be to God! Alhamdulillah! I sing really well.' He was gone without having even a glass of water.

According to Pandit Dilip Chandra Vedi, Ustad Rahmat Khan was the best exponent of the Gwalior gayaki he had heard. Rahmat Khan lived with Vishnupanth Chhatre, Haddu Khan's favourite disciple, who was the manager of a circus at which Rahmat Khan was made to sing during the intervals. Whenever he refused, which he did often, Vishnupanth threatened to cut off his daily dose of opium. Outside the circus, Rahmat Khan's recitals were dictated by his whims. Nobody knew when and where he would consent to sing or whether he would walk out in the middle of a recital. But for Vishnupanth, this highly eccentric son of Haddu Khan would have starved. When Vishnupanth Chhatre retired, he took his Khalifa to Kurundwar in Maharashtra.

This is where Abdul Karim Khan first heard him and fell in love with his music. According to Dilip Chandra Vedi, 'Abdul Karim used to imitate Rahmat Khan's voice throw but could not produce a single taan of his. That only Bhaskarbuwa Bakhle succeeded in doing, merely by listening to him on a few occasions.' The late Shaqoor Khan, the well-known sarangi player of Delhi, who was distantly related to Abdul Karim Khan by his first marriage, mentioned to his son Mashkoor Ali that during a recital of raga Miyan ki Malhar,

Abdul Karim, the mesmerizing quality of whose music was a byword, suddenly stopped singing and said to his audience, 'For the last fifteen days I have been trying to sing this asthayee, *'Karim nam tero'*, the way Ustad Rahmat Khan sings it, but I am getting nowhere close to it.'

A couple of years ago Jalsaghar of Calcutta arranged a series of analyzes of different gayakis by me with the help of prominent artistes of respective gharanas who demonstrated the salient features of their styles. On the evening devoted to Kirana Gharana, which featured Firoz Dastur and Pandit Bhimsen Joshi, I played the famous Bhairavi thumri, *'Jamuna ke teer'*, a 78 RPM record of Abdul Karim preceded by the same song sung by Rahmat Khan whose disc must have been cut during one of his lucid moments in the very early Twenties of the last century. Most of the listeners present were hardly familiar with the name of Rahmat Khan but those who were, and quite a few of them well-known musicians, were intrigued to notice the astonishing similarity between the two.

A few other records of Rahmat Khan are also available in the ITC Sangeet Research Academy archives. The Bhupali is wonderful but there is a slight suspicion of a madhyam. In the Yaman the komal nishad makes a fleeting appearance. So does the *rekhab* in Malkauns. All this indicates the state in which Rahmat Khan was during the latter part of his life. But there is no denying the impact of his music on Ananta Manohar Joshi (Antubuwa), Bhaskarbuwa Bakhle, Abdul Karim Khan and even Manji Khan, the son of Ustad Alladiya Khan, who along with his brother 'Bhurji' Khan, used to spend a month in Kurundwar every year as long as Rahmat Khan was alive.

Krishnarao Shankar Pandit died in 1989 at the age of ninety-seven, according to his son Lakshmanrao. Amjad Ali Khan's calculation indicates that he could not have been less than a hundred and five because Panditji once told Amjad Ali that he had heard Nanhe Khan, Amjad's grandfather, also a court musician of Gwalior.

In 1978 Calcutta Music Circle and Amir Khan Kala Kendra jointly held a five-day festival dedicated to Ustad Faiyaz Khan. As the main organizer, I mentioned in my short opening speech, that the ages of Ahmad Jaan Thirakwa (tabla), Ghulam Rasool Khan (harmonium) and Krishnarao Shankar Pandit added together would perhaps be more than the sum total of the ages of the rest of the participants at the conference. The best part of this occasion was that each one of them gave such an account of himself that no one believed that they were nonagenarians. Today, Abdul Rashid Khan, attached to the ITC Sangeet Research Academy at Calcutta, is well above ninety. In a recent recital, on the occasion of Holi, his powerful voice and his ability to climb up at will to the pancham in the upper octave with full-throated ease were the objects of envy of musicians half his age. Who, then, is afraid of cholesterol?

Krishnarao's grandfather Vishnu Pandit was a kirtan singer and was well versed in Sanskrit. He also was attached to the Gwalior durbar. Haddu Khan learnt a number of Sanskrit shlokas from Vishnu Pandit, which he sang in various ragas. In fact, Jaidev's *Geetagovinda* has been a part of the repertoire of successive generations of musicians of the Gwalior gharana. Maharaja Jiyajirao Scindia was not a mere patron but had learnt by heart well above five hundred compositions from Naththan Peer Baksh. Haddu, Hassu and Natthu Khan were given sumptuous quarters at the Imambara and this is where Krishnarao's father Shankar Pandit's ganda was tied by Natthu Khan. Haddu Khan by this time had lost the use of his legs after a stroke. He would teach his sons Mohammad and Rahmat Khan along with Shankar and his brother Eknath Pandit, sitting on his bed.

After the death of Haddu Khan in 1883, followed a year later by that of Natthu Khan, it was Bade Nissar Hussain, the adopted son of Natthu Khan, who became the premier court musician. Unfortunately, Jiyajirao Scindia also very soon left this world, leaving behind his infant son. The administration of the state was handed over to a regency council appointed by the British government. The British administrators, as expected, drastically cut down expenses on music, dance and such other seemingly useless activities, with the result that Bade Nissar Hussain lost his job. Shankar Pandit, who became his disciple after Natthu Khan's death, said to his family, 'Well, it does not matter whether we can afford it or not, Ustad cannot be on the streets. As long as I am alive, he will stay with me.' Which Bade Nissar Hussain Khan did for the next thirty years.

Shankar Pandit left no stone unturned to attend to Khansaheb's comforts. The only thing that could not be allowed in a conservative Marathi household was non-vegetarian food. Every night, a rupee was placed under Khansaheb's pillow for his dose of opium. The sight of silver first thing in the morning got the ustad into the right mood for the rest of the day. All this was not easy for the Pandit *parivar*, which was not particularly well off. Bade Nissar Hussain, however, adapted himself to his new surroundings with magnanimous ease. After taking his early morning bath he would wear a dhoti and mark his forehead with sandal paste like a devout Hindu, which he used to say he had been in his previous birth when his name was Nissar Bhat. He loved reciting and exchanging Sanskrit *shlokas* with the Pandits.

Once, when Shankar Pandit went on a pilgrimage to Puri, Nissar Hussain accompanied him to the sacred temple of Jagannath, dressed as a Hindu. On their way back they went to the Kali temple at Calcutta, the city of merchant princes, where the two of them gave quite a few recitals. The Lieutenant Governor-General of India was invited to one of these where Bade Nissar Hussain Khan sang 'God Save the Queen' in raga Bada Hans Sarang. The Chhota Laat Saheb was so pleased that he gave them two all-India railway passes and a large, handsome pocket watch from West End Co. Years later, Khansaheb used it to crack walnuts and almonds for his breakfast.

It must have been around 1885 or 1886. A good-looking

boy in his teens was seen in tattered clothes in Gwalior begging from door to door. In the evenings, he would be seen at impromptu soirees of musicians. Gwalior at that time was the home of pandits and ustads who came from distant parts of the country. The boy, known as Ramkrishna Vaze (pronounced Vaazay), would go to them with the hope of getting talim in return for domestic chores done willingly by him. Occasionally, someone would give him a meal and advise him to go back to his native village. Bal Guruji, one of the many vocalists, took pity on him and suggested he should approach the Kirloskar Theatre Company visiting Gwalior at that time. With luck he might land a female role since the boy could also sing a bit. In reply Ramkrishna said that at least a hundred aspiring musicians were learning music in Gwalior, out of whom at least twenty or so were lucky enough to get talim from well-known ustads. 'If you live that long, you will find that Ramkrishna will be the one whose fame will prevail.'

After this, whenever Bal Guruji spotted him in a mehfil, he would welcome him thus, 'Oh come, Miyan Tansen junior, go and sit in front. Ustadji is waiting for you to start his recital which he can't without your *ijaazat*,'.Ramkrishna would say, 'Musicians, Bal Guruji, are not born; no one, not you or even Miyan Tansen. It is talim and hard work which make a singer. If I am lucky, the day will come when you and many others will pay good money to hear me.'

I have a tape of a special radio recording of Miyan Malhar that begins with an announcement by Z.A. Bokhari, the then director-general of AIR, who says, 'Our scheduled programme has been cancelled because Pandit Ramkrishnabuwa Vaze has been kind enough to agree to sing without prior notice. He will be accompanied by Ustad Bundu Khan on the sarangi and Ustad Allarakha[4] on the tabla.' Big names indeed. Unfortunately, the recording was done at a time when Buwa Vaze was old and well past his prime. There are quite a few of his 78 RPM records in my collection which, though recorded not much earlier, are better and his taans do not lack variety. I used to hear him broadcasting from AIR Bombay in the late Forties when I noticed his ability to ornament phrases with difficult combinations but I did not like his voice. I was far too young at that time to appreciate that in Hindustani music, a good voice is not essential, though it certainly helps.

One of Vaze's old records, on which he has sung '*Bala bala bala jaiye*' in Bhatiyar was a favourite of Tarapada Chakraborty. Other 78 RPM records contain ragas like Bhairav Bahaar, Jaunpuri, Todi, Khambaj, Vrindavani Sarang, Tilang, Khat, Barwa, Natbihag, Marwa, Miyan Malhar, Tilak Kamod, Kafi, kanhara and Khambhavati. If one listens carefully, one notices that his taans are different in quality and variety from those of his contemporary Gwalior artistes. This is because he got his main talim from Bade Nissar Hussain Khan but never let go the opportunity of frequenting the company of well-known ustads visiting Gwalior. Later, after the death of Bade Nissar Hussain, he learnt from Inayet Hussain, son-in-law of Haddu Khan, Dilawar Khan of Rewa, Sadat Ali Khan of Nepal, Mahmood Ali of Jaipur and Daulat Khan of Raigarh. He especially learnt hori and tappa from Chunne Khan of Benaras.

This is why his music was called '*chaurangee*' by his admirers in Maharashtra. He specialized in singing different bandishes in different taals and had an immense repertoire. According to Nivruttibuwa Sarnaik, he had heard only one artiste besides Abdul Karim Khan who would get lost in his own sur and that was Ramkrishnabuwa Vaze, and that his conquest of mehfils was a byword in Maharashtra. He was known to hold his own in a soiree where the other participants were Miyan Jaan, Shankar Pandit and the great Bhaskar Rao Bakhle. He had equal command over the common major ragas and rare ragas like Panchkalyan, Gaudi, Manjh, Garabageshree, Madhyamavati, Paraj-bahar, Manjari, Tirban, Garakanhara, Khat, Khokar and Vasanti-kedar, Bageshri-kanhara and Dhakka.

Frankly, I had not even heard the names of quite a few

of these till the other day. Finally according to Nivruttibuwa, some of his taans like *mukhbandi* (sung with a closed mouth), *matthi and jabra* were remarkable, though he never favoured speed at the cost of clarity. Pandit V.G. Jog, however, would make fun of Ramkrishnabuwa's *jabra* taans because apparently his tongue would hang out in the process and the jaw would quiver simultaneously and violently, something which would, no doubt, have met with serious disapproval from the purists.

The two main recipients of talim from Shankar Rao, the host and premier disciple of Ustad Nissar Hussain Khan, were son Krishnarao Pandit and Rajabhaiya Poochwale. When I first saw Rajabhaiya in my early teens, I found his appearance amusing. He was fat, had a huge unkempt moustache, walked with a limp, generally with a hand on the shoulder of his son or a disciple, and never without his typical Gwalior topee shaped like a flying saucer. Finally, his surname Poochwale caused much merriment among my friends because it literally means one who has a tail. Much later, I learnt he was from a place called Pooch, near the town of Jhansi, hence the name.

His ancestors were from Satara, some way from Pune in Maharashtra, and they came with the in-laws of the famous Rani of Jhansi, who fought against the British during the Sepoy Mutiny. The Jagir, named Pooch, was awarded to Rajabhaiya's great-grandfather by the Rani. Rajabhaiya was incidentally christened Balkrishna. How and why his name was changed to Rajabhaiya is not known. At the age of two and a half, he was struck by polio and lost the use of his legs. The story goes, and Rajabhaiya used to swear to it, he was taken to Puri by his father when he was barely five, and sitting before the idol of Jagannath, the child cried out, '*Mujhe payer de Bhagwan* (God, give me legs),' and the next day, he started walking.

Rajabhaiya's first guru was Bamanbuwa, a well-known dhrupad singer. He learnt more than four hundred compositions in dhrupad and khayal from Bamanbuwa and son Lalbuwa. By that time his father was gone, two sisters had to be married, which meant the sale of the house in Gwalior, and the necessity for Rajabhaiya to look for work. Thanks to Lalbuwa, Rajabhaiya was given the job of a harmonium player with the local dramatic society called the Amateurs' Club. A year later, the prince Madhavrao Scindia, who was keen on Marathi musicals on stage, became the patron of this club, which was rechristened 'Gwalior Sangeet Natak Mandali'.

It was Lalbuwa who introduced Rajabhaiya to Shankar Pandit before he died in 1907. One day, he was roaming absentmindedly around in Sarraf Bazaar when he went past a gramophone shop where a record was being played. It was a song in raga Dhani, *'Krishna Murari binati kar Hari'*, sung by Shankar Rao Pandit. He found the music so enchanting that he spent eight annas (fifty paise) to hear the record eight times and made up his mind that Shankar Pandit would be his guru. His search led him to Shankarrao's son-in-law, Kashinath Mulay, who duly put in a word and in 1907 Rajabhaiya was accepted as a disciple.

The gandabandhan ceremony, held before invitees, was concluded with formal talim in raga Bilawal. The khayal that was taught on this occasion was with *'Mai ek to katha'* as the mukhda (refrain) which resembles Deshkar in the use of the phrase pa dha pa dha with the sam on dhaivat. Years later, I heard it from Rajabhaiya's son Balasaheb, and also from Ulhas Kashalkar once on request. It is a pity Shuddh Bilawal, a major morning raga, and a thaat according to Bhatkhandeji, is not heard nowadays.

My old college friend Prabhakar Chinchore has written a book on Rajabhaiya Poochwale. Dr Mrs Sumati Mutatkar, several years my senior, also learnt from him after she left Marris College. Both these sources confirm the authenticity of the following story. Within a week of the formal ceremony, Shankar Pandit, possibly due to pressure from the family, stopped teaching Rajabhaiya. Lakshminarayan Garg, in his book, *Hamare Sangeet Ratna*, mentions that Rajabhaiya used to follow Shankar Rao Pandit endlessly, wherever he went, especially to the temple of Bitthal Das every morning, and would sit silently before his guru with folded hands and entreating eyes. One day Shankar Pandit took pity on the young man and said, 'What can I do, Raja? I cannot teach you. I have given my word not to part with our precious *khazana* to outsiders. But do not get disheartened, my boy. I will sing for you every morning and evening at the temple and repeat the sthayee and antara of the composition until you pick them up. I will also show you how the raga should be delineated, and I am sure, if you are attentive enough, you will, by God's grace, become a true representative of our gharana some day. My prayer and blessings are with you.' This kind of clandestine talim was accompanied by assiduous practice by Rajabhaiya with the tanpura in one hand and the bayan in the other for eight to ten hours a day. I think excessive practice or incorrect voice production, or both, robbed his voice of its timbre. In 1916 Bade Nissar Hussain Khan died, followed six months later by Shankar Pandit, and thus ended Rajabhaiya's talim.

Members of the Pandit family, interviewed by me, called the story a pack of lies and referred me to Krishnarao Shankar Pandit's statement in the July 1986 issue of a journal called *Sangeet Kala Vihar* edited by B.R. Deodhar. Krishnarao had said in the interview that if the current story were correctly attributed to Rajabhaiya, then he had not only committed the unpardonable sin of abusing his guru's trust and reputation, but also unnecessarily spread lies about the innocent Pandit parivar. In 1907, he, Krishnarao, was already married and was an established singer. Rajabhaiya came later and in any case was not talented enough to be considered as Krishnarao's potential rival. He further added that Vinayakrao Kotwal, a disciple of Krishnarao's uncle Ganpat Rao Pandit, had managed to steal his guru's collection of bandishes with incomplete notations. These reached Rajabhaiya and found their way into Bhatkhandeji's five volumes of *Kramik Pustak Malika*. In any case, Shankar Pandit, to his son's best knowledge, taught Rajabhaiya for seven years, along with one or two others in a room rented in Maharajganj in Gwalior.

Whatever may be the truth of this much-publicized story, it is clear that there was no love lost between the Pandit clan and Bhatkhandeji's camp, which included Krishnarao's uncle Eknath Pandit and Rajabhaiya Poochwale. In 1915, Vishnu Narayan Bhatkhande came to Gwalior in search of old traditional compositions and was captivated by Shankar Pandit's '*Nakshaa kaam kaa khayal*'. Panditji, however, refused to part with any of the bandishes. The reason was one that confronted Bhatkhande all his life. The khayal compositions of Bade Mohammad Khan, Haddu and Hassu Khan and Bade Nissar Hussain were priceless possessions that were not meant for public consumption in printed notations.

Bhatkhandeji had already received the active patronage of Sir Sayajirao Gaekwad, Maharaja of Gaekwad. Through him he approached Maharaj Madhav Rao Scindia and convinced him of the necessity of spreading Shashtriya sangeet among the masses, or at least the educated middle class. The system of musical education, as developed by Bhatkhande, thus found its way to Gwalior, the home of khayal and tappa hitherto guarded zealously by the ustads, and Rajabhaiya, who became a disciple of Bhatkhandeji, was appointed the first principal of Madhav Music College. Krishnarao Pandit not only refused to cooperate with Bhatkhandeji, he actually established his own school in the same city. The feud between the two Maharashtrians never ended during their lifetime. Krishnarao outlived not only Bhatkhande but also his successor Shrikrishna Ratanjankar.

The President's award was conferred on Rajabhaiya Poochwale. When the news reached Gwalior, Rajabhaiya was in a coma after suffering a massive cerebral attack. The family placed a pugree on his head, applied sandal paste on his forehead and garlands round his neck. Sweets were distributed among the students of the Madhav Music College. Three days later Rajabhaiya died, leaving behind his wife, daughters and son Bala Saheb Poochwale. Bala Saheb is eighty-seven now and still capable of singing his father's gayaki. But even he could not revive the memory of the Shankara, Hameer and Chhayanat that I heard from his father sixty years ago. Rajabhaiya's rendering of '*Aadi Mahadeva*' in Shankara and '*Chameli phoolee champaa*' in Hameer (the sam of this song in Jhoomra taal is on pancham and not on ni dha) with its dignified swaying elephantine gait, and heavy larazdar taans ending invariably with swift sapaats, for me is unforgettable.

Once, Begum Akhtar, the queen of ghazals, was smoking and nibbling at an ice cream cone at the same time in the green room just before her recital. An admirer asked her whether it did not affect her voice. Begum Sahiba smiled and said, '*Gale se thhode hi gaanaa gaayaa jaataa hai?* (Do you think one sings with one's voice?).' She of course had an intoxicating voice while Rajabhaiya's was like an old tyre that had lost its tread years ago, but it was no impediment to the overall effect of his music, the like of which I have not heard from any other exponent of the Gwalior gharana.

Krishnarao had his talim from his father Shankar Pandit as well as Bade Nissar Hussain Khan, his father's guru. He was gifted with acute intelligence and obstinacy in equal measures as a child. If he failed to pick up a bandish after a few attempts he would burst into tears but would not let his father go until he got it by heart. Neela Bhagwat, a disciple of Sharat Chandra Arolkar of the Gwalior gharana, has written a short biography of Krishna Rao Shankar Pandit, which has raised a frown or two from the members of the Pandit parivar. She has mentioned a small incident in Krishnarao's childhood. When he was no more than eight or nine, he got into a fit of uncontrollable rage and threatened to jump into the well if his father did not promise then and there that all the bandishes that Shankarrao had learnt would go to his son and no one else. This incident has some bearing on the controversial story of Shankarrao's dilemma vis-a-vis Rajabhaiya, his disciple. Anyway, it was no wonder such a boy would rapidly develop into a singer of some merit even before he reached adulthood. Krishna Rao's first public recital took place in Mathura when he was barely fourteen, or twenty-one, if we accept Amjad Ali Khan's assessment. At this age he would assist his father or even Bade Nissar Hussain Khan on the tanpura at mehfils.

Bade Nissar Hussain Khan, I have mentioned, was adopted by Natthu Khan, the youngest brother of Haddu and Hassu Khan. Vilayet Hussain Khan in his book mentions that Natthu Khan's style was somewhat different from that of his brothers and his rendering of khayal and tarana was quite distinctive. He specialized in taranas and *trivats*[5] were his trademark. The entire repertoire of Natthu Khan, as well as those of Haddu and Hassu Khan, in due course were inherited by Krishnarao through his father and Dadaguru Bade Nissar Hussain Khan. Unlike Ramkrishnabuwa Vaze, the Pandit parivar did not turn to any other ustad.

When I was in my early teens Krishnarao Pandit was an elderly musician. When I reached middle age, Panditji had qualified to be called ancient, though he remained extremely well preserved throughout. In the earlier stage of my musical development I did not take to Panditji's music. I found his voice gruff, his mannerisms comical and his taans verging on acrobatics. This was due to my early addiction to Kirana because of my friend and mentor Pradyumna Mukherji and subsequent conversion to Agra after hearing Ustad Faiyaz Khan.

My favourites, whom I heard regularly on the radio, were Sureshbabu Mane, Roshanara Begham, Hirabai Barodekar, Gungubai Hangal of Kirana and, of course the records of Abdul Karim Khan. I do not remember any of the Jaipur gharana artistes except Moghubai Kurdikar and Lakshmibai Yadav. Kesarbai never agreed to broadcast at all. I did listen to quite a few Maharashtrian Gwalior artistes but at that age I did not particularly care for them. Even Mushtaq Hussain Khan, who sang Gwalior and could be very erratic at times, was not everybody's cup of tea. It is not unusual for someone in his teens, therefore, to come to the conclusion that members of this gharana were short of aesthetic sense and cared more for taans than sur and gradual unfolding of the raga. As a generalization it holds good even today, Ulhas Kashalkar excepted. Bade Ghulam Ali Khan, whose gayaki is ninety per cent Gwalior, would not have sounded so great if he had Krishnarao Pandit's voice and comparative lack of musicality.

Today, with the departure of the greats, I feel differently about Panditji's music. I heard some of his early 78 RPM records in the house of his son Lakshman Rao Pandit. His Gaud Sarang, Desh, Malkauns, etc. would open the eyes of the members of the Patiala gharana. He sounds so much more in sur than how he sounded when I was young. The change is not in him but in me. And his virtuosity is amazing.

In the Seventies I had the opportunity to listen to him more than once in Delhi and Calcutta. He was nearing eighty. Once, at the monthly sitting of the Calcutta Music Circle, run by Vijay Kichlu, A.T. Kanan and myself, I heard his Bhupali. Like all Gwalior gharana singers he started his madhya-vilambit (slow-medium) khayal in Tilwara, which has the same sixteen beats as teentaal but is slightly more compact. Maharashtrians as a rule have better command over laya than their compatriots in the north or east India. Krishnarao Shankar Pandit was equal to the best of them. Twice he sang the sthayee but the tabla-player, who was not just anybody, missed the sam on both occasions. Panditji gave a benevolent laugh and said, 'Never mind, you play simple ektaal, if that is the fashion nowadays.' The tabla-player, now no more with us, went red in the face and gave simple theka in Tilwara with ostentatious care, even during baant and bol-taan. Gradually, a variety of taans, heavy larazdar ones extending over two-and-a-half octaves, chhoot taans, wonderful phirats and sapaat taans came out of Panditji's armoury. Suddenly, he took a huge taan from pancham in the lower octave which went straight through the middle octave to dhaivat in the taar saptak (higher octave) and came back at double the speed to the dhaivat again in the mandra saptak, each note as clear as a bell.

This was followed up by half a dozen extremely complex

taans covering all the three octaves. Muhammad Sagiruddin, the famous sarangi player, stopped playing and exclaimed, 'Subhaan Allah! Subhaan Allah!' Munawwar Ali Khan, son of Bade Ghulam Ali Khan, sitting next to me, gripped my hand in sheer excitement and cried, 'Kumarbhai, this is the stuff I was brought up on. Wonderful!' Every note was hit right in the middle. Can one say the same about all musicians in their eighties? Possibly only about the late Mallikarjun Mansoor and Nissar Hussain Khan.

Krishnarao Shankar Pandit's nature was typically Brahmanical. He was a simple man proud of his lineage but not vain or arrogant. He came to sing at my conference in Calcutta in 1978. The notorious Calcutta smog had affected his voice though the listeners could hardly make that out. He blamed it all on koraa matkaa, the brand new earthen pitcher he had bought for his train journey. He told me to use a new pitcher only after soaking it for twenty-four hours. He distrusted the refrigerator, of course. The last time I met him was in Delhi, shortly before his death. There was a huge gathering on the lawns of Pupul Jayakar's house. On the occasion of the Festival of India in the USA, a set of records of old masters was brought out by Sheila Dhar. This was going to be presented by the Prime Minister to the oldest musician in the country after the youngest, Rashid Khan, then eighteen or so, had sung for us.

During Rashid's recital, we saw Panditji sitting next to Rajiv Gandhi with his hand patting the Prime Minister's back affectionately. One or two of my friends asked me, 'What do you think Panditji is saying to Rajiv Gandhi?' 'Possibly,' I said, 'he is asking him, "Son, I do not seem to have seen you before. What do you sing? Which gharana? Who has given you your talim?" Rajiv Gandhi's reply would be, "Panditji, whatever talim I have received is entirely from my mother Indiraji, but before she could impart her very own diabolically complex taans to me, she left this world, to my great misfortune."' Within an hour the story came back to me with one or two juicy additions. This, I suppose, is what is known as velocity of circulation in economics.

Srimati Lalith Jaywant Rao recorded well over a hundred traditional bandishes by Sharat Chandra Arolkar for the Ford Foundation Project before I took over from her. Sharat Chandra was past eighty at that time and died shortly thereafter. At that great age he was finding it difficult to stay in tune but gave us a fair glimpse of what the authentic Gwalior gayaki was like. Sharat Sathe, who accompanied him to Calcutta, also recorded a hundred compositions, some of which he sang so well that one of his extended recordings of Yaman Kalyan reminded me of some of the best Gwalior artistes of the past. Sharat Chandra Arolkar's earlier recordings in the archives of the ITC Sangeet Research Academy give me the impression that even in his youth he had inherited little of his guru Krishnarao Pandit's virtuosity but that he displayed a somewhat higher order of musical intelligence and artistic sense. Those who are close to him attribute it to the talim from Eknath Pandit and Krishna Rao Mulay, as well as his own spiritual development.

I was present during his interview by Lalith Rao when he mentioned two salient features of Gwalior gayaki. The first is the importance of bandish, which should be viewed from ashta-dishaa, or eight angles. What the eight angles were have remained unclear to me, but he reiterated what my ustads, for that matter all the ustads of Gwalior, Agra and Jaipur used to insist upon—'*Bandish ko chipak ke gaao.*' In other words, embrace the bandish and build your innings around it, to borrow a phrase from cricket terminology.

The second was the need for developing the ashtaanga, or eight aspects of khayal gayaki. When I asked him, he gave me a list of alankars that the singer should use, e.g., khatka, murak, kampa, andolan, meend, soot, etc. I thought these were the tools of the trade of an artiste, not features of khayal gayaki. However, detailed investigation and analysis of various traditional styles of the major gharanas for the same Ford Foundation Project over ten years have led me to the following features of khayal singing that were at one time common to all gayakis. These are:

1) Bandish nayaki—A composition should be sung exactly as the guru has taught it and as he has inherited it from his ustad.

2) Bandish gayaki—Here one is entitled to depart from the laid-down composition, play with each line in any manner commensurate with the chalan or movement of the raga. Here the artiste's own imaginative faculty comes into play. Balasaheb Poochwale, in a tape that I possess, has first sung 'Kaise sukh soye' in Bihag in three aavartans (cycles) of ektaal in the nayaki anga. He then sings the same madhya-vilambit composition in the gayaki anga in two aavartans and even one aavartan without disturbing a single notation of the original composition.

3) Vistar—The slow unfolding of the raga as distinct from the unfolding and ornamentation of the composition. Vistar can be done in any tempo depending on the artiste's mood. In khayal, however, it was not the custom to make the vistar as long and dilatory as in dhrupad alaap. In fact in Gwalior gayaki the vistar portion was minimal in the beginning and the tempo was slow-medium where the character of the taal was well defined. Gradually, in the course of time, some vistar has crept in, but it is certainly not as detailed and elongated as dhrupad alaap or bol-vistar in Kirana gayaki.

4) Bahlawa—Long meends are a speciality of Gwalior gayaki. Bahlawa is a play of combination of notes and phrases with the help of heavy taans and meends. Bahlawa slowly evolves into taans at a later stage. Plenty of examples can be given from the gayaki of Krishnarao Shankar Pandit's tapes as well as D.V. Paluskar's vilambit khayals. Among artistes of today, Ulhas Kashalkar's recitals give ample examples of this anga. Bahlawa is seldom used in drut khayals. Some of the best Bahlawa I have heard is from Ustad Faiyaz Khan, Mushtaq Hussain Khan, Bade Ghulam Ali Khan and Khadim Hussain Khan—as well as from his disciple Babban Rao Haldankar. All of them owe their styles to a greater or lesser extent to the Gwalior lineage.

5) Bant—It is a rhythmic division of taal with the help

of words. While doing bants the Gwalior style makes it mandatory to use all the words of sthayee or antara in proper sequence, without disturbing their meaning.

6) Bol-taan—Here the words and rhythmic taans are combined together, a speciality of Agra gharana, also to be found in Gwalior. For ready reference, the reader may turn to Ustad Faiyaz Khan's drut khayals of Lalit and Raamkali in 78 RPM records.

7) Layakari—This anga, once an essential part of the khayal gayaki of Gwalior and Agra, is gradually disappearing. To play with taal with the help of words, as in dhamar and ladant tehaees, cross-rhythmic variations and anaghat sams are not favoured in the vocal music of today, though layakari continues to flourish in instrumental music, especially in Maihar Gharana. This may well have to do with unaesthetic overdoing of this anga by some ustads of the Agra and Gwalior gharanas.

8) Taans—Taans are taboo in dhrupad and dhamar, but are favoured by all khayal gharanas. There are different types of taans developed by different gharanas. Gwalior's speciality is heavy larazdar linear or ekharaa taans with or without gamaks covering at least two octaves. They are slightly off-beat. Rhythmic taans are not so common to all Gwalior artistes. One can find examples in records of Rahmat Khan, D.V. Paluskar, Gajananbuwa and Ulhas Kashalkar, among those who belong to the true Gwalior tradition. I am not referring to Ustad Nissar Hussain Khan or Pandit Shrikrishna Ratanjankar because they have combined Agra with Gwalior. Yet another variety of taan introduced by Gwalior and popularized by Jaipur are manja taans without danas where notes are joined together with meends, e.g., sare, sare, rega, rega, gamapa, gamapa, gama. Sapaat taans, as I have mentioned earlier, were originally a trademark of Gwalior, now common in all gayakis.

Layakari can be done with sargams also, as in the Patiala gharana. Gwalior has never favoured sargams as a rule, the exceptions being exponents Narayan Rao Vyas and Vinayak

Rao Patwardhan who indulged in fast sargams that often sounded inartistic if not tedious or comical. Sargams play an important part in the synthetic khayal gayaki emerging in India, especially in the east, thanks to Bade Ghulam Ali Khan and Amir Khan, but this is not a new feature in Hindustani music. Ustad Bairam Khan, the ancestor of the Dagars, who flourished in the Jaipur court in the nineteenth century, was well known for sargam patterns in his alaapchari. So was Ustad Alladiya Khan, the dhrupadiya, before he turned to khayal and founded the Jaipur gharana. Sargams can well be recognized as the ninth anga now.

One word before I conclude the chapter on the Gwalior gharana. There is little doubt that all the known gharanas have evolved out of Gwalior. As such, the angas enumerated above are common to all schools of khayal just as the fundamentals of all religions are more or less the same. Which is why the term 'fundamentalist' continues to irk me. The days of fighting between gharanas and khandaans are a thing of the past. In these days of constant exposure of aspiring musicians and serious students of music to styles of different musicians through festivals and electronic media, a synthetic gayaki is bound to emerge. But if adequate attention is paid to all the nine angas described here, the essential structure of authentic khayal will survive. Style is a matter of shabda-tatwa, sound production, mannerism and the impact of a great personality that gives birth to and perpetuates a particular gayaki. Enthusiastic budding talent is likely to fall in love with a gayaki for superficial reasons. Analysis of the angas and their cultivation are far more important. These alone will lend variety and authenticity to a musician's recital irrespective of the school he belongs to.

4

Patiala and Sahaswan

The year 1942 was when Calcutta was bombed by the Japanese. A few twenty-pounders fell in Hatibagan and Kidderpore docks, causing an unprecedented sensation among middle-class Bengalis, who promptly left home and hearth for Madhupur, Deoghar, Shimultala and such other well-patronized health resorts in the neighbouring state of Bihar. Marwaris left their gaddis behind and left in droves for their ancestral villages in Rajasthan. Panic was widespread. The Red Road was enclosed and served as a runway for a makeshift aerodrome of the Royal Air Force. It was the year of sensation-mongers and of patriotic Bengali youth who saw and welcomed the towering figure of Subhash Chandra Bose behind the Japanese.

For a sixteen-year-old youth who had yet to begin to shave, and who had come during Christmas to Calcutta from Lucknow, the winter of 1942 would best be remembered as the year when he heard Kesarbai, Roshanara Begham and Ustad Bade Ghulam Ali Khan perform. I was already sold on classical music irrespective of the various forms and schools prevalent at that time about which I had little knowledge. I had come in contact with Ustad Mushtaq Hussain Khan of Rampur who came twice a month to Lucknow for his radio recitals and became my guru. I had once heard Ustad Faiyaz Khan, whose music had already cast a spell over me. Shrikrishna Ratanjankar was a friend of my father and the cerebral content of his music was beginning to evoke responses from my embryonic musical intellect.

But 1942 offered me a feast, which was sumptuous and overwhelming. Here was Kesarbai with her deep melodious voice, her shuddha akar and her taans, each of which was as intricate as a Catherine Wheel, Roshanara Begham with her elongated raga vistar, lightning gamak and dooni and chaudooni tans, and finally, the one and only Bade Ghulam Ali Khan whose voice was like a supple body without angles and bones. It was worth going miles by public transport just to hear him. For me, an adolescent fanatically devoted to music, it was a discovery of untold riches, a treasure house of a lifetime. This was my first encounter with Jaipur, Kirana and Patiala gharanas—and all under one roof!

My undeveloped power of analysis could notice the stylistic difference in the presentation of the three great artistes of the three gharanas broadly and instinctively, but not the subtleties and the varying emphases on the different angas of khayal gayaki, which I perceived much later. Oddly enough, Bade Ghulam Ali Khan's music—and I do not mean his voice alone—found an immediate responsive chord, possibly because of my association with Mushtaq Hussain's Gwalior gayaki.

Eyebrows might be raised by some who have not delved deep enough into Gwalior, the parent gharana, and the Patiala gayaki of Bade Ghulam Ali Khan. To me, however, the negligible difference between themir, such as it is, can be attributed to Khansaheb's personality and his individual contribution, especially in taankari. The late Jnan Prakash Ghosh, who had heard Ghulam Ali Khan as much as his near and dear ones had, was totally in agreement with me on this point.

Whenever I made the above observation it would annoy Khansaheb's son Munawwar Ali, who was a dear friend, now no more with us. He once told Malabika Kanan, 'Kumarbhai seems to think Gwalior has given birth to every gayaki. Even an artiste from Kanya Kumari in the deep south would be labelled by him as a product of Gwalior!' The same Munawwar Ali grasped my hand in sheer excitement when both of us

Kesarbai

were listening to Krishnarao Shankar Pandit, and said, 'Kumarbhai, this is the stuff that I and my Baap-Dada were brought up on.' I would pull his leg often and tell him that he need not be ashamed of his ignorance since he was like a frog in the well and had hardly heard anyone except his father, his uncle Barkat Ali Khan and myself.

In fact, even to an untrained ear, Krishnarao Shankar Pandit, the last stalwart of the Gwalior gharana, sounded amazingly like Khansaheb, minus of course his golden voice. Lakshman Rao Pandit, Krishnarao's son who worked for the AIR for some years, once arranged a soiree for his father in Delhi and invited his friends and colleagues, not all of whom were musicians but well initiated into classical music. Quite a few of them later wanted to know whether Ghulam Ali Khan ever had talim from Panditji who must have been in his mid-eighties at that time but in total command over his sur, laya and taankari. I have in my possession a few of Krishnarao Pandit's old 78 RPM records of Gaud Sarang, Yaman Kalyan, Malkauns and others that I played to one of my senior disciples and her husband, who is a well-known music critic. Their response was identical.

Bade Ghulam Ali Khan was endowed with a remarkable sense of artistry and skill but had not inherited the erudition of his ancestors, neither was he bothered about it. His emphasis was on riyaz and riyaz alone. He did not care about the gradual unfolding of the raga, and his repertoire of ragas, in any case, was limited. He would plunge straightaway into the bandish, in slow-medium tempo, and the treatment of the vilambit composition was scrupulous but not extraordinary. This was followed by bahlawa full of wonderful meends and heavy taans. The linear taans that grew out of the bahlawa would cover three octaves and, for sheer clarity and tonality, were unparalleled. His drut khayals were adorned with rhythmic sargams, bol-taans and taans often four times the tempo of the composition. While his linear taans were in the Gwalior mould, his taans and bol-taans, at double the speed of the taal, were not unlike in Agra. And in his chaudooni taans, he had no rival in India or Pakistan.

His gayaki was taan-pradhan or based predominantly on bahlawa and taans which constituted nine-tenths of his presentation. He was impatient with vistar when certain ragas like Todi or Darbari demanded it. He was most at home with taans, sargams and difficult paltas, i.e., fast permutation and combination of notes, born out of years of dedicated practice. In fact, except when he was eating or sleeping, the swarmandal never left his hands. His idea of entertaining a guest was to sing for him. If there was no one, he would sing to himself. In my long association with Ustad Amir Khan I have heard him practising for no more than an hour in the morning and an hour in the evening. Ustad Faiyaz Khan gave up practising at the age of fifty. Not Bade Ghulam Ali Khan, who after the stroke that paralyzed his left side, staged a comeback through fanatic riyaz and willpower.

There is little doubt that Ghulam Ali Khan's style of presentation resembles Gwalior's more closely than any other gharana. Endowed with a sense of beauty, though not of discipline, he scrupulously avoided the Punjabi mannerisms of his compatriots which sound grating to our ears. His voice production was scientific and hearing it meant instant intoxication. Ustad Amir Khan used to say that the moment Ghulam Ali opened his mouth, he got ninety out of hundred from the audience whereas he (Amir Khan) would probably get seventy, or thereabouts. 'One had to use one's brains to compete with him (*Dimag ke sahare se unka muqabala karna parta hai,*') he would say.

It all started with Miyan Kaloo, a sarangi player of Kasur, a village near Lahore. His son Ali Baksh Khan and a friend Fateh Ali Khan used to sing jugalbandi in khayal. For twenty-four years, they practised taankari before they came to the Doab. Ustad Faiyaz Khan, in one of his rare interviews on AIR, Lucknow, mentioned that Ali Baksh and Fateh Ali, known variously as 'Alia-Fattu', 'Jarnail' and 'Kaptan', came to sing in Jaipur. Pandit Vishwambhar Nath was one of the court musicians whose name is mentioned with reverence by Ustad Vilayet Hussain Khan of the Agra gharana as one of his forty-one gurus. He was well versed in dhrupad and the heavier type of khayals. The young musicians Alia-Fattu were naturally keen to ascertain the reaction of the venerable old pandit who heard them in the court. Not being satisfied with the customary words of praise, they wanted to know his true opinion. Pandit Vishwambhar Nath invited them to his house, made them sit on a charpoy and brought out a looking-glass. 'What do you see in the mirror?' he asked Ali Baksh.

'*Ji*, my face.'

'Can you see your face clearly?'

'*Ji, haan.*'

'Now look at your face once again,' said Panditji, shaking the looking-glass.

'How can I see my face when the glass is not steady? Sometimes the ears are missing, sometimes the nose.'

Panditji laughed and said. 'My boy, that is exactly the trouble with you and your music. If you had worked just as hard on your swarasthaan and ragaroop all these years, instead of taankari alone, you would have been great singers. Your violent taankari is clipping the ears and noses of the ragas you sing.'

Apparently they took his advice and became disciples of Ustad Tanras Khan of Delhi, who later became a court musician of Gwalior. They also became formal disciples of the legendary Haddu Khan. Fateh Ali Khan's son Ashiq Ali Khan was a tremendous tanaiyat whose music on the radio caused a lot of amusement among my friends in my early years. Apparently, he paid little heed to the advice given to his father by Pandit Vishwambhar Nath. On top of that, Ashiq Ali's voice was far from melodious and his aggressive taankari often sounded like a violent disagreement between two tomcats.

However, the historical link between Gwalior and Patiala is clear. Ali Baksh Khan went to the Maharaja of Patiala while Fateh Ali Khan drifted to Tonk, a small native state in Rajasthan. The Nawab of Tonk was himself a musician and a composer who used the takhallus, or pen-name, of Ibrahim. Among his well-known compositions, *'Sakhi mana lage na'* in raga Bageshri and *'Sa sundara badana'* in Malkauns deserve special mention. These facts are based on the history of the Kasur gharana, as imparted to me by Munawar Ali Khan, the elder son of Bade Ghulam Ali Khan. However, according to Professor B.R. Deodhar, Ali Baksh went to Tonk and Fateh Ali to Patiala.

While Fateh Ali Khan served the Nawab of Tonk, Ghulam Ali's uncle Kale Khan went to him for talim, which, however, was denied to his brother Ali Baksh (not to be confused with the senior partner of Fateh Ali who bore the same name). It is not clear why Fateh Ali Khan was opposed to the idea of teaching Ali Baksh, father of Bade Ghulam Ali, though he was extremely talented and, according to Shakoor Khan, the well known sarangi player of Delhi, ended up as an excellent player of dilruba. In addition, his singing earned him a position in the court of Jammu and Kashmir. When Fateh Ali taught Kale Khan, Ali Baksh used to listen attentively.

He had a natural gift for imitation, which often caused merriment among other disciples. This reached the ustad's ears and Ali Baksh was asked to give a command performance. A great deal of mirth and laughter followed Ali Baksh's caricature of the court musicians, at the end of which Fateh Ali Khan asked him whether Ali Baksh could give an imitation of Fateh Ali Khan's own style and mannerisms. Quite naturally, Ali Baksh resisted the idea saying, 'Huzoor, you are the badshah of music, how dare I give an imitation of your inimitable way of singing?' When he was persuaded and finally ordered to do so, Fateh Ali Khan was astonished by the verisimilitude in their styles. He said, 'This is amazing! I've never ever taught you—when and how did you learn all this?' With folded hands Ali Baksh said, 'I have been listening while you were giving lessons to Kale; Allah's kindness and your *meherbani* have made it possible for me to absorb a little of what you sing.' Fateh Ali Khan realized that this boy was capable of no mean accomplishment and richly deserved serious talim from him.

Ustad Kale Khan had a powerful round voice, sweet yet manly. Amiya Nath Sanyal, in his book, *Smritir Atale*,[1] has devoted a whole chapter to this eccentric personality, a great singer who harboured a secret vanity about his accomplishment as a player of veena. In general appearance he resembled his nephew Bade Ghulam Ali, which was not likely to sweep the tawayefs off their feet. Nonetheless, according to Amiyababu, Kale Khan fancied that the famous Gauhar Jaan of Calcutta, an outstanding singer and a great beauty, harboured an unrequited passion for him. Amiya Nath, related to the Maharaja of Natore, arranged a soiree in the Natorehouse on Lansdowne Road in Calcutta. Amiyababu was completely captivated, so was the Maharaja. 'His voice,' recalls Sanyal, 'was like a sarangi, without the sharp edges.' It reminded him of Abdul Karim but unlike that of Karim Khan, Kale Khan's voice in the upper octave did not resort to falsetto. It retained its original rich rounded character. As to his style and virtuosity, unimpeded by the heavy meal of puris and rabri which had preceded the recital, the author recalls the intricate harkats (a very short phrase consisting of complicated taans), heavy halaq taans mixed with lightning sapaat ones. Kale Khan's music reminded him of mannered baroque art, and he had not come across anything like it in any khayal, born out of the dhrupad tradition, before or after.

From Amiyababu's description, I feel he should have noticed the stylistic affinity between Kale Khan and Bade Ghulam Ali Khan whom he also heard in his later years. The latter's music had a lot of filigree work reminiscent of the baroque and rococo styles. On second thought, I would not carry the analogy to its extreme point. The baroque style was born out of a protest against classicism. The same could not be said about the music of Kale Khan and Bade Ghulam Ali Khan. The baroque style also did not ignore proportion and perspective, something which Bade Ghulam Ali failed to observe scrupulously in his presentation. I did not find the architectonic quality in his music that I did in Faiyaz Khan's alaap or Amir Khan's vistar. Ghulam Ali Khan's music was like a magnificent display of fireworks of many colours in the sky. Like Shelley's skylark, Ghulam Ali's music was not earthbound.

The reason I have specifically dwelt on Kale Khan is that Bade Ghulam Ali learnt from this uncle of his, from the age of five till twelve or thirteen, which was not enough talim for the son of an ustad those days. Amiyababu is reported to have told his daughter Reba Muhuri that there were many points of dissimilarity in their respective styles. Kale Khan adhered more to tradition and took more time to unfold the raga. He paid somewhat greater attention to detail in the vilambit khayal than his nephew did. I have no clue as to whether he was addicted to sargams, like the generation after him, which includes Ashiq Ali, Ghulam Ali and even Fateh Ali and Amanat Ali, who came even later. That Kale Khan, like his celebrated nephew, was known for his predilection for paltas and fanatic riyaz, is illustrated by the following incident. It has been recounted in the chapter on Bhaskarbuwa Bakhle in B.R. Deodhar's book *Pillars of Hindustani Music.*[2] Balwant Rao Barve, a devoted disciple of Bhaskarbuwa, narrates to Deodhar:

> One evening Buwa Sahab took five or six of us for a stroll with him. We went to a house near Bhindi Bazar. There was a large rectangular courtyard after one entered through the outer door. From where we stood in a group inside, we could hear someone singing in one of the rooms on the ground floor. Buwa Sahab signalled to us to listen quietly and we stood frozen where we were. The singer was doing endless repetitions of the scales, ascending and descending, of Bhoop raga. We must have stood there for about an hour, during which time the musician just did the scales over and over again. After the first half hour, each note of the passage

came out clear and sweet, and towards the end, that single exercise began to appear so fluent, each note seemed round like a perfect pearl—clear, appealing and full of power.

Buwa Sahab took us into the room where the music was being practised. The singer, a Muslim vocalist, stopped singing, greeted Buwa Sahab and asked the reason for this unexpected visit. Buwa said, "These boys are my disciples. They find music practice boring. The grinding of the same taan a thousand times is not known to them. So I have brought them here to show them what even such a skilled musician like you had to do before he made a name for himself. The musician in question was from Punjab, Kale Khan, the uncle of Bade Ghulam Ali Khan Sahab."

Apart from B.R. Deodhar, Dr M.R. Gautam, a noted musician and musicologist and the ex-vice-chancellor of Khairagarh University, thinks Khansaheb's voice production is the most scientific among all the Indian musicians he has heard. Bade Ghulam Ali Khan once told Mr Deodhar that he used to practise standing before the wall of a palatial masjid in Lahore, where his guru Kale Khan first took him. 'The two stood facing the massive wall and Kale Khan asked him to start. Ghulam Ali was able to hear the echo from the wall in front. Then Kale Khan started singing. Every once in a while he would stop and tell Ghulam Ali to listen to the echo. He found that his guru's voice and its echo were both tonally perfect and identical. When Ghulam Ali heard the echo of his voice, he discovered that the latter was lacking in tonality. Thereafter, the masjid became his favourite place for practice.' *(ibid)*

Basically, Khansaheb was a self-made musician. His talim was limited to seven or eight years, i.e., till the age of thirteen.

He once narrated a story to me, which, no doubt, others had
also heard from him. At the age of seventeen he decided to
sing to his father Ali Baksh Khan. His father listened to him
patiently, got up and left without a word. Later in the
evening over his supper, young Ghulam Ali enquired from
his father why he had not said anything. Was it because he
did not like the singing? Would he please correct the errors,
if any? Ali Baksh Khan kept quiet for a few seconds, then
replied with a sigh, 'What can I say? One who does not have
sur has nothing (*Jis ke paas sur nahin, us ke paas kuchh bhi
nahin*)'.

I could not believe my ears. Bade Ghulam Ali Khan did
not have sur? Even at that tender age how could the great
Ghulam Ali deserve such a caustic remark from his father. It
however indicates two things. First, he had no talim from his
father, because soon after this incident Ali Baksh took a
second wife and Ghulam Ali left his father's home with his
mother. Secondly, he was not a born musician. The great
Bade Ghulam Ali Khan owed his stature to riyaz, unimaginable
hard work and, of course, an innate sense of artistry. From all
accounts, Bade Ghulam Ali had no talim from anyone except
a few months of it from Pandit Dilip Chandra Vedi. Vedi
claimed to have taught him a few age-old compositions of the
Gwalior gharana, one of which, *'Sugreeva Raama kripa'* in
Chhayanat was Khansaheb's favourite. According to Professor
Deodhar, Ghulam Ali learnt the song and a few more from
Baba Sinde Khan, the 'mad fakir' from Punjab, who settled
in Bombay for a while and also taught Deodhar. Kirana
ustads claim Bade Ghulam Ali had approached Ustad Abdul
Waheed Khan, the unacknowledged mentor of Ustad Amir
Khan, for talim with a nazrana of twenty-one rupees, but was
refused.

Khansaheb once told me that he used to practise night
after night in the Hindu burning ghat and would return home
in the small hours of the morning. Obviously, he could not
do his full-throated riyaz at night in the congested mohalla
where he lived. In the day he had taken up practising on the

sarangi for a living and selling cups of tea at the railway station. This was the hardest period of his life. Later, he would attach himself to a petty tawayef called Gigbai and play the sarangi with her.

However, his nightly sojourns to the burning ghat continued. He could not carry a tanpura all the way there, hence came about the invention of the 'swarmandal', which is like a mini-harp. It became his lifelong companion. It is this instrument that put the idea of changing the key while singing audav (pentatonic) ragas into his mind. This he used to do with telling effect, switching to Durga, Dhani, Hansadhwani and Malkauns while rendering a raga like Bhupali in his later days. For sheer virtuosity there was no one his equal in the entire subcontinent. After the death of Abdul Karim Khan and Faiyaz Khan, Bade Ghulam Ali was the numero uno in the eyes of all except some traditional purists.

Professor B.R. Deodhar, in his *Sangeet Kala Vihar Patrika* (June 1949 issues in Marathi and Hindi), mentions an incident in Bombay. Professor Deodhar is reported to have told Bade Ghulam Ali, 'Khan Sahab, your recitals leave some of us in a state of unfulfilment. You neglect raga vistar and are anxious to go on to taans. Even then you do not create the impression of following the conventional system. Taans are interspersed with bahlawa, followed by taans again. This might appeal to that section of the audience that looks forward to fireworks, but the cognoscenti cannot help feeling and saying openly that Khan Sahab's recital lacks unity and defies traditional form. We, your admirers, do not like to hear such criticism.'

Bade Ghulam Ali kept quiet for a minute. He did not take umbrage. He merely said, 'All right, I will reply to their criticism in the next mehfil, not in words but through my music.' Two days later, Khan Sahab was to sing for one of the suburban music circles of Bombay. He sang Darbari Kanhra. For the first twenty minutes, he slowly developed the raga with uncharacteristic patience. He then switched over to

bahlawa followed by badhat, sargams and finally an abundance
of heavy taans in keeping with the sentiment of the raga—
no murkee, no khatka, no frivolity—a genuine serious rendering
of Darbari that could satisfy the staunchest of purists. When
Professor Deodhar asked him why he did not sing like that
always, Ghulam Ali simply said, 'Deodhar Sahab, do not
forget I am not singing only to you in a mehfil. My audience
expects sensation. It wants acrobatics. If I sing only like this,
my public would wonder whether I was keeping well. I
cannot disappoint them, can I?'

I had a similar experience with Ustad Bade Ghulam Ali
Khan. The previous evening Khansaheb had sung at Mahajati
Sadan. As it happened, my recital preceded his. When I
finished, I turned around and, to my horror, found Khansaheb
sitting in the wings. Apparently, when he heard I was
singing, he wanted to be carried there. As I bent down to
take his blessings, he said with a mischievous smile, '*Kyun,
Agra gharane ke hote hue bhi itna achcha gate ho?* (Fancy you
managing to sing so well despite your belonging to the Agra
gharana?)' This was not such a joke as one might think it to
be. Khansaheb actually did not care for gayakis other than
Patiala, though he had once mentioned Zohrabai Agrewali in
glowing terms to me. However, I was lucky enough to earn
his approval and affection despite the Agra stigma.

The following morning, which was a Sunday, I dropped
by at his Balu Hakak Lane residence. On such occasions my
friend Munawwar always managed to be absent. Khansaheb
sang a nom tom alaap in Todi for half an hour for me. There
was no one else present. The latter part of the drut alaap
became taans, that is, vowels replaced the consonants in
natural course for him. It was quite remarkable since he was
not in the habit of doing dhrupad alaap a la Agra before his
khayal. Neither did it suit his temperament. Nonetheless, it
was alaap at its best. When I ventured to ask him why he did
not sing like that more often, he asked me with a smile, '*Kya
shikrebaaz ko kabutar bananaa chahte hain aap?* (Do you want
a hunting falcon to turn into a pigeon?)'

Bamanrao Deshmukh, in his book *Indian Musical Traditions*,[3] has squarely blamed Bade Ghulam Ali Khan for flouting tradition. His view is that the taste of the audience is created and influenced by ustads and organizers of music festivals. They will ask for the diet that is fed to them over a period of time. After all, I also cannot but feel Hindustani classical music is raga sangeet. If raga is not established through alaap, and Bade Ghulam Ali Khan wishes to cater to what he assumes to be public demand for excitement and acrobatics, the audience will gradually accept that in preference to serious music in course of time.

What, then, is the future of khayal and its traditional form? Is Test cricket going to be replaced by One-Day cricket? I am inclined to agree wholeheartedly with the views of Professor Deodhar and Bamanrao Deshmukh. Murkees and Punjabi harkats have no place in khayal—just as taans are taboo in dhrupad and dhamar. Secondly, excessive taankari and sargams, even in the hands of ustads, interfere with the ragaroop, which in any case has to be established through alaap or vistar. We Indians—Hindus or Muslims—follow the shastras or the canons dictated by tradition over a period of time. Individual talent, however remarkable, cannot afford to ignore tradition. Within the confines laid down by tradition, ustads like Abdul Karim Khan and Faiyaz Khan have brought about certain changes that have been accepted by all. Kumar Gandharva and Pandit Jasraj have wilfully stepped beyond the boundaries. Not poor Bade Ghulam Ali Khan who has not been guilty of anything of that sort. He had been the willing victim of his own virtuosity that tended to flout the musical discipline expected from a great ustad.

Let me cite an analogy in cricket. Those of my generation might remember Mushtaq Ali Khan, the Indian opening batsman. He had exceptional talent and footwork. He also had sound talim from Sir Jack Hobbs, Herbert Sutcliff and the great C.K. Naidu. Mushtaq Ali's defence was so sound that he could not be bowled out if he made up his mind to eschew strokeplay. He actually scored thirty-odd runs in three-and-a-half hours as captain of the Muslims against the Hindus to save a match. But his love for strokeplay was such that he would not be satisfied with less than a couple of boundaries against the new ball in the very first over of a Test match. He would hit a fast good length ball from outside the off stump to midwicket or even square leg. When set, he would toy with the bowling, however good, with his unorthodox strokeplay. Keith Miller of Australia, unquestionably the greatest all-rounder after Sir Gary Sobers, has called Mushtaq Ali the Errol Flynn, the gay buccaneer, of cricket. Both Dennis Compton, another great cricketer, and Keith Miller, who played against and with Sir Don Bradman, actually said that they had never seen the equal of such devastating batting as that of Mushtaq Ali in their lives.

Needless to say, the results were not always rewarding. The question that arises is, why did Mushtaq play like that? The simple answer is, because of a certain temperament and the desire to play to the gallery. Like Bade Ghulam Ali, he, too, was a victim of his own skill and virtuosity. Those who are lucky enough to amass wealth easily can be wild spendthrifts. This applies to Ghulam Ali Khan's music. He was the slave of his own exceptional skill and talent, not their master.

Apart from riyaz, the secret of Ghulam Ali Khan's virtuosity was total relaxation of muscles while singing. In cricket parlance, I had never come across a more relaxed stance. That and his total control over his voice, even when afflicted by cold, helped him to do wonders. His range covered a full three octaves without a hint of falsetto. Jnan Prakash Ghosh mentioned two incidents from the early days of his acquaintance with Khansaheb, who stayed with Jnanbabu in his ancestral house in Dixon Lane. As usual, Khansaheb was singing and Jnanbabu was on the tabla. There were not many people except for a few of Jnanbabu's disciples and members of his family. In slow-medium ektaal, Khansaheb was doing bahlawa till the eleventh matra was reached. Jnanbabu's dha dha dhin coincided with a lightning sapaat taan from the singer, covering two octaves and ending in the sam. On another occasion, while being shaved with an old-fashioned razor by a barber, Khansaheb felt like taking taans. The barber promptly stopped but was asked to go on shaving. It was a bizarre sight. Khansaheb's mouth was closed, there was not a single quiver in his double chin, but his taans were roaming in three octaves.

Music was Ghulam Ali's life. Everything he saw, heard or uttered was in musical terms. Looking at a fish flitting from one corner of its aquarium to another, he would say, 'Dekho dekho, see how it darts around with its quivering fins and tail—just like desi Todi—pa dha, ma pa, ga ma, re ga, sa re, ni sa.' Lying on his deathbed in Hyderabad in the middle of the night, the last thing he said to Munawwar Ali, his son, was, 'If you take the drone of the table fan as the shadja, the tonic, that street dog's bark would give you the rekhab and gandhar of Todi.'

Professor Deodhar recollects, 'One day, Khan Sahab had a radio broadcast at 1 pm. As I was working for the Bombay radio station at that time, I, too, had to be in attendance. After he had finished, Khan Sahab said, "Wait for a while. I have sent for a taxi. We will go together." It was mid-July and rain was coming down in torrents. Besides, I was hungry. But I did not have the heart to say "No" to Khan Sahab. The taxi came along and we got in. Water in any form would make Khan Sahab very happy. The rains, in particular, were pure bliss for him. Some of the rain water seeped into the taxi and began to drench us but Ghulam Ali Khan was in high spirits. He said, "Come, Deodhar Sahab, let us go to the sea shore. The sea will be something worth seeing right now." I protested, "Let me go straight home . For one, I am famished, and my clothes are beginning to get wet, too."

'However, by way of compromise I agreed to let the taxi driver take us via Marine Drive. We arrived there and Khan Sahab asked the taxi driver to stop his vehicle at a spot where there was a concrete projection. The waves of the turbulent sea at this point were thirty to forty feet high. Khan

Sahab said, "The time and the place are just right for doing riyaz. Listen." And he began to sing. Whenever a particular massive wave broke and water spouted up, Khan Sahab's taans rose in synchronization and descended when the water cascaded down. The sea water rose in a single massive column but split at the top and fell in broken slivers. So did Khan Sahab's taans, in raga Miyan Malhar. Sometimes, if his ascending notes failed to keep pace with the surging water, he was angry with himself and would try again. This went on for three quarters of an hour. I got so immersed in the whole proceeding that hunger and thirst were forgotten. Finally, Khan Sahab's son, who happened to be with us, said to his father, "Let us go now. It is three-thirty and we are both hungry."[4]

It was this single-minded obsession with music and refusal to yield to any other distraction in life that distinguished the musicians of the past from the ones today. For Ghulam Ali Khansaheb nothing else besides music existed—except possibly biryani and korma cooked in pure ghee, a large tin of which accompanied him on his tour. Certainly the best biryani I have ever tasted outside the kitchen of the Nawab of Rampur was at Khansaheb's house.

Bernard Shaw once said that an artiste had to be ruthless about his art, for which no sacrifice should be too great. He must not make any compromises. Music is a jealous mistress. She does not permit worship of Mammon, politics or even public relations—as appears to be the norm nowadays. Ghulam Ali Khan made no more compromises with his music than he did about desi ghee, both of which occupied the top of the table of his value system. Once, as a guest at Santosh Banerjee's house at Ekdalia Road, Ballygunge, he ran out of his store of desi ghee. Alternatives were provided by his host but Khansaheb was adamant. Either he got his ghee from Ludhiana or all his scheduled recitals in Calcutta were to be cancelled and immediate arrangements made for his journey back. Ultimately, a man had to be sent all the way to Punjab to bring Khansaheb's ghee. I used to stay opposite Banerjee's house those days and shared his family's anxiety over the whole affair. After Khansaheb had his stroke, he told me once with tears in his eyes, 'What good is this Ghulam Ali who cannot sing, and has to live on bland food cooked in *groundnut oil?*' He mouthed the words 'groundnut oil' with the kind of horror and contempt the pucca saheb of my youth would refer to one who cheated at cards.

Sheila Dhar of Delhi, an old friend, possessed a talent for mimicry and eye for detail that made her a superb entertainer. She was persuaded by me and some of her other close friends to put experiences with musicians she had met into print. This she did a few years before her death and the result was irrefutable evidence that she was a perceptive, thoughtful, Indian writer of some of the funniest writings in English.[5] I used to tape-record her sometimes during our regular sessions at the India International Centre in Delhi, and the recordings remind me that she was an even better raconteur in Hindi interspersed with smatterings of English. Her first encounter with Bade Ghulam Ali Khan makes hilarious reading but the tape sounds better.

Sheila, in her childhood, had shown distinct talents, and her father, who was a patron of the arts and a founder member of the Bharatiya Kala Kendra, New Delhi, was keen to expose his sixteen-year-old daughter to the customs and manners of the music world of the Forties. During one of the annual festivals, she was given the job of welcoming and looking after the sensational young discovery from Punjab, Bade Ghulam Ali Khan of Lahore. It was decided to put him up at the residence of Nirmala Joshi of Sangeet Natak Akademi. She was a Pahadi Brahmin and Khansaheb a fierce carnivore. It was, therefore, a classic case of not fitting in.

Sheila had not even seen a photograph of Ghulam Ali, though she had heard some of his fabulous recordings. 'The power and magnitude of his voice,' wrote Sheila Dhar, 'had conjured up an image of him that I had been nursing in my heart for quite some time. However, what alighted from the car in Nirmala Joshi's porch had no resemblance whatsoever to the handsome singing star of my imagination. The real counterpart was huge, dark, unsmiling and ungainly. His thin black moustache curved downwards at each end of a rather mean mouth, just stopping short of the jawline. His small beady black eyes, which moved constantly, made him look ferocious. Nor did there seem to be any connection between his speaking voice and his singing voice. The exchange in Punjabi between him and the two disciples who had come with him was loud and rough. I was not familiar with the natural accents of the language, so even the pleasantries they exchanged sounded like angry outbursts.

'I brought out the words of welcome I had rehearsed over and over again... I managed to convey that hot water for his bath, and his dinner, were both ready and that if he wished we could proceed to the pandal, where the music was in progress, as soon as he liked...

'After a while his huge body, clad in a pale blue kurta of embroidered silk appeared in the dining room where we were waiting. The old-fashioned cook, dressed in a clean white dhoti, brought us four gleaming silver thalis one by one. Each had seven small silver bowls containing an assortment of thin sauces of different hues—yoghurt white, spinach green, lentil yellow, potato brown, squash beige, beetroot red and so on. The maestro scowled at the unfamiliar food and lowered the large and rather shapeless thumb of his right hand into each bowl in turn, hoping against hope that it would encounter a piece of meat on a bone. When the thumb met no resistance and sank clean to the bottom of each bowl right through the thin gravies, the horrible truth dawned on him. He was trapped in a puritanical vegetarian household and there were no prospects of getting meat...

'I was the person in charge, so the maestro turned to me, pushing the thali roughly away, "Such music as mine and this food (*Yeh gana aur yeh khana!*" the tape says), he thundered in a shocked tone. "I am going to cook my own dinner. I will make a list of what I need. It is impossible for me to sing without proper nourishment. Even when we sit down to practise at home, a big pot of good food is always at hand and we dig into it regularly to keep up our strength. Somebody told me that every note that I sing has the aroma of kebabs. Do you think I can sing the way I do if I have to feed on grasses swimming in different fluids of various kinds?"'

The taped version ends here with the maestro in our imagination driving off in a horse-drawn tonga into the sunset in search of a dinner in Jama Masjid mohalla that could aspire to the minimum gastronomic standards of the Patiala gharana. But there is more to it in the book:

'I was sure my father would think I had made some horrible mistake when we did not arrive even six hours after we were expected. The disciples had set off with a long shopping list that featured six broiler chickens (for the three of them), a kilo of khoya, or solidified whole milk, a kilo of almonds, a tin of clarified butter (ghee), fifteen different spices and a huge stack of tandoori rotis. A charcoal fire was lit and a portable stove set up in the open courtyard because no meat of any kind was allowed in the family kitchen. Full-scale cooking operations started around nine with great enthusiasm and expertise and a delicious one-dish meal was triumphantly produced within two hours. The maestro heaped vast quantities on a china plate since the thalis were not available for this kind of depraved eating. Nor was there any space inside the house, so the dinner took place outdoors and was all the more enjoyable for that. Three or four hearty belches announced the end of this phase of the proceedings and we finally set off for the site of the concert.'

For a man of this kind of food habits, a trip to Madras must have been quite an ordeal. In December 1951, Bade Ghulam Ali Khan gave a recital at the Madras Academy and caused a sensation with his voice, taans and sargams. G.N. Balasubramanyam, an MA in English literature, the leading vocalist in Karnatak music and president of the academy fell at his feet and said, 'You are the greatest!' The devout orthodox Brahmins of Mylapuram were shocked at this adulation of a Muslim, and decided to virtually blackball Ghulam Ali. G.N.B. told them, 'There is no caste system among musicians. He may not be a Hindu but I bowed to Devi Saraswati, the goddess of learning and the arts, who resides in his throat.' G.N.B. invited Khansaheb to stay in his house. His wife told him in no uncertain terms that if fish or meat entered the house, she would promptly hang herself. Ultimately, a separate house was hired and Khansaheb, who loved to do his own cooking, was equally relieved. He stayed for a couple of months in Madras and conquered the south.

Khansaheb was a God-fearing, kind-hearted, generous person. He was also a spendthrift and, according to Ustad Amir Khan, was capable of gambling away a month's earnings in one Diwali night. For a man who looked like a Punjabi village butcher, of uncontrolled eating and drinking habits, he had a mind of perceptive poetic quality. Professor Deodhar recalls, 'I believe the year was 1945. Khan Sahab and I were seated on the sands of Chaupatty beach of Bombay. The sun was about to set and its last rays fanned out and bathed the west in red. The picturesque scene above was reflected in the calm waters of the Arabian Sea. As he sat transfixed by the scene before us, Khan Sahab turned to me and said, "Deodhar Sahab, this is the precise hour to sing Marwa. I am amazed by the ingenuity of our ancestors! Consider their perceptive artistry in employing that particular re and dha. The hour of sunset is a fascinating time. Lovers, who have been separated, begin to wonder how they are going to spend the night in loneliness. The same thing happens to those who do not have a roof over their heads. The day passes by itself—but the night? They are worried about finding a shelter. In all the notes of Hindustani music the most important resting place is shadja (sa). But in Marwa the very note sa virtually vanishes and whenever we use it briefly we feel a sense of relief. I feel that the chief aim of raga Marwa is to portray this anxiety and uncertainty.' (*ibid*)

Some, like Ratanjankar, say that Bade Ghulam Ali Khan was a greater thumri than khayal singer. Thumri in Punjabi anga offers little peace to the serious listener. There is hardly any scope for 'thahran', or dwelling at length on the notes. Further, this anga favours the chromatic arrangement of successive major and minor notes, which goes against the very essence of Indian classical music and can be traced to the traditions of traders from West Asia. Munawwar Ali used to say Punjab never had thumri, it was imported from Purab (East). That Bade Ghulam Ali Khan could sing both varieties at will, and better than his contemporaries, would be evident from his records. I am inclined to say the same about his ghazals, which not many have had the privilege of hearing.

I once persuaded Ustad Amir Khan to sing thumri in my house over a drink and, of course, not before an audience. He sang it exquisitely, changing the *murchhanas*. When I asked him why he refused to sing thumris in public, he simply said, 'Well, I can't sing better than Ghulam Ali, can I?'

Ustad Haddu Khan had two sons-in-law. The elder, Bande Ali Khan, was a famous player of been and a dhrupad singer. At the same time there is evidence that he taught khayal to young Bhaskarrao Bakhle. The other son-in-law was Inayet Hussain Khan. Members of the Kirana gharana claim that Bande Ali Khan, their own ustad, was the real son-in-law. Inayet Hussian was married to a goldsmith's daughter adopted by Haddu Khan. Sahaswan ustads vehemently object to what they consider a sheer canard and claim that Kirana on the other hand is descended from Mirasis[6] and therefore belong to a much lower echelon of the society of musicians.

A Muslim IAS officer of UP once confided in me that he always refused tea and refreshment in the house of his minister who was a member of the scheduled caste, a 'chamaar'. Another friend, the second son of the Nawab of Chhatari, nearly went crazy looking for a suitable Rajput Muslim boy for his daughter. Apparently, the Rajput Hindus who embraced Islam in the days of the Mughals claimed

Ustad Bande Ali Khan

aristocratic lineage. They were true 'upper-caste' Muslims. So much for Islam that preaches brotherhood and equality among Mussalmaans, leaving the devout Hindus to their absurd caste system.

The state of Rampur in the UP of the British days was known for its Shia nawabs, descended from Afghan warriors in the employment of the Mughal emperors, who became famous patrons of music. Some of the great names of music are associated with the Rampur durbar. It was during the reign of Nawab Kalbe Ali Khan that they started gathering in the Nawab's court (1860 onwards). In the late Nineties of that century, the Nawab's son Hamid Ali Khan not only kept up the tradition but became a disciple of Ustad Wazir Khan, a descendant of Miyan Tansen's on the daughter's side. Wazir Khan's wife also belonged to the same Seniya dynasty and as such, this elite family was considered to be superior in caste to the rest of the musicians in the country.

Wazir Khan became the guru of the two most eminent sarod payers, Alauddin Khan and Hafiz Ali Khan, and can therefore claim to be the fountainhead of instrumental music in northern India. The other important gharana, that of Ustad Imdad Khan, the grandfather of Vilayet Khan, also owes its allegiance to the Seniyas, though in a somewhat indirect way because of Imdad Khan's association with Sajjad Mohammed, the blind surbahar player of Raja Sourindra Mohan Tagore's court. Sajjad Mohammed was the son of a disciple of Umrao Khan, the grandfather of the same Wazir Khan, the Rajguru of Rampur.

The khayal singers who adorned the court of Rampur were Kale Nazir Khan, Bahadur Hussain Khan, Haidar Khan, Inayet Hussain Khan and Mushtaq Hussain Khan. Most of them were from the hamlet of Sahaswan in the neighbouring Badayun district. Hence came the name Sahaswan-Rampur gharana—though all the stalwarts mentioned here sang Gwalior.

Inayet Hussain Khan, possibly the biggest name in the Sahaswan-Rampur gharana, had his talim from Ustad Bahadur

Ustad Alauddin Khan, Pandit Ravi Shankar and Ustad Ali Akbar Khan

Khan, even though his father Mehboob Baksh was also a singer of the nawab's durbar and his maternal grandfather Fahebuddaula Khan was a well-known singer from Lucknow. Ustad Bahadur Khan was a player of been and sursingar as well as a dhrupad singer. But he is remembered as a prolific composer of madhyalaya taranas in khayal which were sung by Mushtaq Hussain Khan and Nissar Hussain Khan with great gusto.

Nissar Hussain, who married Inayet Hussain Khan's youngest daughter, gave me an interesting and unusual insight into Bahadur Hussain Khan's method of training. After a young student practises the sa re ga ma for a year or two he is given paltas in two sampurna[7] ragas like Yaman in the evening and Bhairav in the morning. Instead, Inayet Hussain was given paltas in a 'sankeerna' raga like Gaud Sarang, the main phrase of which is ga re ma ga dha pa re sa. Sankeerna literally means narrow, i.e., it allows restricted movement, not as free as sampurna ragas where one can sing the scale up and down with all possible permutations for practice during one's training period. I have questioned at least fifty musicians of different gharanas and they all started with Yaman or Bhairav. Most of them confirmed that Gaud Sarang, the afternoon raga, would be considered extremely complicated and a very unusual choice for an absolute beginner.

There is a locality called Peele Talab in the city of Rampur where relations of Ustad Hafiz Ali Khan used to reside. Some of them, friends of Mehboob Baksh's family, had unmarried daughters and were naturally interested in young Inayet Hussain. When asked, Bahadur Hussain Khan's usual reply was, 'The boy is going through the early stages of training. He should be able to sing a bit after a couple of years.' The fathers of the prospective brides agreed with Inayet's ustad but nonetheless were curious about the young lad's progress. There was Shabban Khan, one of these visitors from Peele Talab, who was keen on having Mehboob Baksh's son as his disciple and was not happy over the choice of Bahadur Hussain as the young lad's ustad. It was his insistence that ultimately prompted Bahadur Hussain Khan to invite them to dinner the following week.

Meanwhile, Bahadur Hussain called Inayet Hussain and said, 'Come, memorize these two bandishes in Bihag and I shall show you the movement of this raga and the way it should be unfolded.' Bihag, which has the same notes as Gaud Sarang, even the two madhyams, but has a totally different movement, skipping re and dha in the ascendant scale, was the raga that the ustad chose and altered some of the paltas to suit Bihag. The performance of Inayet Hussain, a week later, surprised Khansaheb's guests and they were all praise for the boy and his ustad. Nissar Hussain Khan also believed in the motto: '*Ek sur sadho to sab sur sadhe* (Practise one raga and master all),' which may not find acceptance with all ustads.

While Inayet Hussain Khan inherited a large stock of bandishes and taranas in medium tempo from his ustad, he himself turned out to be one of the most brilliant composers of all times. Thanks to Girija Shanker Chakravarty who went to Rampur for talim from Inayet Hussain Khan, Bengalis are familiar with some of them, such as '*Jhanana jhanana*' in Chhayanat, '*Papi dadurwa*' in Gaud Malhar, '*Tarapata raina dina*' in Maru Bihag and '*Dekhi aisi piyari*' in raga Hameer. He also came to Calcutta in the early 1920s and charmed the cognoscenti.

He was not so successful in the Senate Hall where he faced a large crowd of university students. Rabindranath Tagore was present. As soon as Inayet Khan finished his recital of the first raga, there were cries for 'Robibabu', which gradually built up into a crescendo. Tagore went to the stage and rebuked the students with his impromptu song, '*Tumi kemon kore gaan karo he gunee, ami abak hoye shuni* (Oh you wizard, I listen with wonder to the magic you put into your music)'. Lots of people who recount this incident confuse Inayet Hussain with Inayet Khan, the illustrious sitar player and father of the famous Vilayet Khan. However, I have heard this story from my father, who happened to be one of the crowd that day.

While Inayet Hussain belonged to an era when more or less everybody sang Gwalior, his final talim was from the legendary Haddu Khan. For quite some time the two sons of Haddu Khan, Rahamat and Chhote Mohammad Khan, were looking for a suitable boy for their sister. They heard Inayet Hussain Khan, liked his music and his looks, and reported to their father. An invitation to dinner was duly extended. The following evening, Inayet Hussain presented himself to the great man who also liked what he saw and requested the young man to sing. Inayet Hussain, whose manners were above reproach, said with repeated salaams, 'Khan Sahab, you are the greatest, and this naacheez, good-for-nothing toddler, in the world of music does not dare open his mouth in your august presence.' Haddu Khan was modesty incarnate. He said, 'You are quite right, my boy, there is not a single offspring of a swine among the musicians who would dare sing before me, but I am giving you my *ijaazat*. Go ahead, I would like to hear you.'

Inayet Hussain's penchant was for heavy larazdar taans covering three octaves. He delivered with unusual skill and finesse the brilliant taranas of Bahadur Hussain Khan. This pleased the great man and a formal proposal of marriage followed. Inayet Hussain had two children by this marriage. The daughter, in the words of Ustad Nissar Hussain Khan, had the golden locks and complexion of a European lady and Inayet Hussain doted on her. Unfortunately, both the son and the daughter died. But from the story related to me by Nissar Hussain Khansaheb, one can clearly see how the authentic Gwalior gayaki, together with the compositions of the 'qawaal bachchas', crept into the Sahaswan-Rampur gharana.

At the Grand Conference of 1924-'25, organized by Pandit Vishnu Narayan Bhatkhande in the baradari at Kaisarbagh, Lucknow, the second prize went to Ustad Mushtaq Hussain Khan. Bhatkhandeji is reported to have declared at that time that a fourth of all famous khayal compositions could be found in the ustad's repertoire. Amiyanath Sanyal, after hearing his famous larazdar taans covering three octaves, prayed for Mushtaq Hussain's good health and long life in his book. Shrikrishna Ratanjankar's gayaki would indicate the extent of the influence of Mushtaq Hussain's taans. These can also not be heard any longer, nor are there any records of Ratanjankar's music of his younger days. Such tapes of the ustad, as we can find in the archives or at the Sangeet Natak Akademi, Delhi, and the AIR, were recorded when the ustad was in his eighties, and was teaching at the Bharatiya Kala Kendra in Delhi after the merger of the old native states. Even these give us a fair idea of his gayaki though obviously not of his virtuosity.

Mushtaq Hussain's father was a qawaali singer known as Langra Kalhan. He belonged to a family of qawaals which had settled in the village of Sahaswan, in the Badayun district of UP, two hundred and fifty years ago. Till the other day, Jaffar Hussain, a nephew of Ustad Mushtaq Hussain Khan, sang superb qawaali, the like of which I have not heard on either side of the border. Pandit Ravi Shankar was all praise for him at a soiree specially arranged for him by Naina Devi in her house in Delhi a few years back. Jaffar Hussain on this occasion was being assisted by a young grandson of Nissar Hussain Khan who, like other members of this Sahaswan family received talim in khayal before opting for qawaali.

Mushtaq Hussain's preliminary talim from his father began at the age of ten, and thereafter from his maternal uncle Puttan Khan and his famous cousin Mehboob Khan (Daras Piya) of the Agra gharana. At the age of fourteen he was taken on as a disciple by the grandfather of Nissar Hussain Khan, Ustad Haidar Khan of the Rampur durbar. Mushtaq Hussain's first wife was Haidar Khan's daughter. His third wife was the daughter of his fifth guru Ustad Inayet Hussain Khan. By that time Mushtaq Hussain was thirty-five and his talim was more or less complete. His last guru was Ustad Wazir Khan, without whose blessings it was impossible for Mushtaq Hussain or anyone else to find employment in the Rampur durbar.

Ustad Wazir Khan, as mentioned earlier, played been and sang dhrupad. No one knows whether Mushtaq Hussain Khan had any formal talim from the famous ustad of the Seniya gharana. I had never heard him sing dhrupad at any time. His temperament was that of a khayaliya, and his repertoire of khayals ranged from Daras Piya's bandishes to Inayet Khan's brilliant compositions, not to mention the taranas of Bahadur Hussain Khan. Unfortunately, out of his four wives and twenty-one children, none of the sons is alive to carry on the tradition. Ghulam Sadiq, who married Mushtaq Hussain's youngest daughter, and is attached to the music department of Delhi University, could offer barely ten per cent of the huge Sahaswan khazana for the Ford Foundation project when I recorded him a few years back. Other disciples of Khansaheb include Sulochana Brihaspati, Sumati Mutatkar (now in her middle eighties), Shanno Khurana, who is my age, and Naina Devi, who is no more with us.

It is highly unlikely that the gayaki of Mushtaq Hussain Khan and the bulk of his repertoire will survive. Ishtiaq Hussain, the eldest son of Mushtaq Hussain Khan, had inherited both the gayaki and the repertoire, but spent most of his life assisting his father in mehfils. After Khansaheb's death at the age of ninety, Ishtiaq Hussain gained recognition briefly when he came over to the ITC Sangeet Research Academy, Calcutta, where his services were hardly put to proper use. Nor was he given a chance to appear at the ITC music conferences.

Mrs Sushila Mishra, a well-known disciple of Pandit Ratanjankar, wrote in the *Illustrated Weekly of India* some time in 1952 that Ustad Mushtaq Hussain Khan was 'easily the best exponent of Gwalior gayaki today'. Both Krishnarao Shankar Pandit and Rajabhaiya Poochwale were alive then. Sharat Chandra Arolkar was an able member of that gharana as were Anant Manohar Joshi and Mirasibuwa; not to talk of popular artistes who belonged to Gwalior like Vinayak Rao Patwardhan, Narayan Rao Vyas and D.V. Paluskar, all of whom were very much in the limelight.

Pandit Omkarnath Thakur was in the forefront of this group. As such, Mrs Mishra's claim could well have been a contentious one. Moreover, Mushtaq Hussain Khan's disciples had already named their gharana as Sahaswan-Rampur and not Gwalior. However, if Mrs Mishra's point was that what Khansaheb actually sang was indeed uncontaminated Gwalior, some of us might be inclined to agree with her. Like the older Gwalior artistes, he also eschewed detailed unfolding of the raga. He preferred what is known as *aochar*, i.e., a general outline of the raga, with its main phrases lasting about ten minutes or so, before taking up the bandish of the vilambit khayal in the nayaki anga—which would be a scrupulous replica of what his gurus had taught him.

He was fond of bahlawa and heavy larazdar taans in shuddh akar, covering three octaves in the true Gwalior tradition. He did not overindulge in the baant and bol-taans, which found favour with a number of Gwalior and especially Agra ustads. I mention Agra because Khansaheb had his early talim from his celebrated maternal uncles of the Atrauli branch of the Agra gharana, but the influence was barely noticeable except in the better-known compositions of Daras Piya which he loved singing. The taans, both without danas and the ones that had the staccato effect, were pure Gwalior. His sargams were ordinary and made occasional appearance in his drut khayals. He preferred to sing his vilambit khayals in medium slow teentaal instead of the tilwara (which also has the same sixteen beats) much favoured by the Gwalior gharana.

I have never heard Mushtaq Hussain Khan sing to other taals liked by the Gwalior gharana, such as jhumra, ada chartal and tilwara. In vilambit khayals his taans were linear, slightly off-beat and replete with sapaats in the descendant scale. He reserved the faster taans for his taranas, both in madhya laya and in drut, which are to be found in Nissar Hussain Khan's gayaki. Like his predecessors, Mushtaq Hussain Khansaheb never sang thumris, which he associated with tawayefs.

Once, at the end of his recital at the Aligarh University, there was a clamour for thumris. Khansaheb's solemn reply, in stentorian tones that amused the students, was, '*Main koi rundee nahin hoon* (I am not a prostitute)'. All in all, the conclusion one arrives at is that he followed in the footsteps of his fathers–in–law rather than his maternal uncles'. Both Haidar Khan and Inayet Hussain Khan sang Gwalior. In fact, at that time there was hardly any other gayaki except Gwalior that put on slightly different faces in Agra, Patiala and Rampur. Even within the Gwalior gharana, the style of some of the Maharashtrians, which was influenced by Natya Sangeet, was quite different from, say, Krishnarao Shankar Pandit's or Inayet Hussain Khan's gayaki. That is bound to happen since, apart from regional influences, music, after all, is a vehicle of the expressions of the musician's personality. One notable exception in Mushtaq Hussain Khan's gayaki, which he did not imbibe from Gwalior, was the tappa anga and the tap-khayal which were exported by Ghulam Nabi (Shori Miyan), brother–in–law of the qawaal bachchas of Lucknow.

As mentioned earlier, Mushtaq Hussain Khan favoured teentaal even in vilambit khayal. I heard him sing Daras Piya's famous composition, '*Piharwa ko birmaye*', in raga Jog with its two nishads in medium-slow teentaal, which my third ustad, Ata Hussain Khan, son of Daras Piya, sang in ektaal and in a slightly different manner. One of the reasons could be that Ahmad Jan Thirakwa, the famous tabla-player and Khansaheb's fellow court musician of Rampur, who accompanied him, called teentaal the king of all taals.

Ahmad Jan Thirakwa was also an enthusiastic singer. On one occasion, Ustad Faiyaz Khan was made to try his hand at the tabla when Thirakwa sang. This, of course, was in the privacy of Khansaheb's room in the Empire Hotel in Lucknow, after three-fourths of a bottle of John Haig had been consumed. Once, in an informal get-together in Naina Devi's house in Delhi, Thirakwa took the tabla and started singing '*Pee ki boli na bolo*', a thumri in Piloo, and made all of us sing a bol or two in turns. The participants that evening, apart from the hostess, were Amir Khan, Vilayet Khan, Amjad Ali Khan, Debu Chowdhuri, Hafeez Ahmad Khan, Yunus Hussain Khan and Shanta Prasad.

Ahmad Jan Thirakwa had an exceptional musical brain and had heard a lot of good music in his childhood and youth. This was thanks to his brother–in–law, Kale Nazir Khan, who reportedly had learnt dhrupad from Bahram Khan, the ancestor of the Dagars. Bhatkhandeji owed a lot of compositions to Kale Nazir Khan as did Thakur Nawab Ali of Lucknow, who published a collection called *Marfoon Naghmaat*. Thirakwa's childhood and much of his youth were spent in the company of Aman Ali Khan and Mubarak Ali Khan of Bhindibazar. This is the same Aman Ali whose influence on Amir Khan was noticeable in his rendering of '*Lagi lagan*' in raga Hansadhwani.

Aman Ali's disciples included Anjanibai Malpekar, T.D. Janorikar, Ramesh Nadkarni and Shivkumar Shukla, all of whom developed the distinctive style of their guru and called it the Bhindibazar gharana, noted for its striking arrangement of sargams after the Karnatak fashion and some beautiful khayal compositions. The daily get-together of Aman Ali, Mubarak Ali and very often Thirakwa, when in Bombay, was scheduled at the *kotha* of Munnibai, a disciple of Abdul Waheed Khan, a revered ustad of the Kirana gharana (Munnibai is not to be confused with Amir Khan's second wife, who bore the same name). Waheed Khan and Mubarak Ali were *doodhbadal bhai* who exchanged cups of milk as children and thus became brothers. Later in life, the milk was replaced by stronger drinks, in larger quantities—at Munnibai's expense.

One day, Abdul Waheed Khan told his friends, 'I got a wonderful tarana in Sohini from my uncle years ago, I have been racking my brain for the last two days but for the life of me I cannot remember the antara. It goes like this...' He sang the sthayee which drew immediate exclamations of praise from Mubarak Ali and Aman Ali. Mubarak Ali said,

'It is wonderful, and I think I can compose an antara which will match the sthayee, but I will need at least a couple of days. I will miss our evening sessions but it is a challenge I will be glad to accept.'

So he sang the sthayee three or four times with Abdul Waheed and went home humming. Two days later, he turned up at the usual hour of the evening and Waheed Khan said, 'Come in, Mubarak, come in. Have you brought me the present you promised?' Mubarak Ali nodded his head and gestured to Ahmad Jan Thirakwa to take the tabla. Then he asked Abdul Waheed to sing the sthayee. As soon as the sthayee was over, Mubarak Ali started the antara. It was a *trivat* with such beautifully intricate patterns that it was not easy to follow it. Everybody asked for an encore, a request headed by Ahmad Jan who promptly sang more than half of it and said, 'I remember it up to this point. It matches the sthayee beautifully. Just sing it once more, Mubarak, please!' Mubarak helped himself to a large drink, turned his back to Ahmad Jan and said, 'Absolutely not. He has already stolen half of it just by listening to me once. If I sing it again the bastard will digest the rest and will claim it as his (*Adha to ekbar sun ke hi uda liya, dobara gaunga to sala poora hazam kar jayega)*'.

Ahmad Jan Thirakwa was unquestionably the most famous tabla player of his generation. Years ago, Dr M.R. Gautam, who started his career as a producer in AIR, witnessed a scene at the Delhi radio station. After a solo recital, Ahmad Jan was escorted by him to the duty officer to receive his cheque. 'Where is the pad for the thumb impression?' asked the great man. There was an expression of utter surprise on the face of the duty officer, followed by a smirk, which incensed Thirakwa. 'Why are you smiling?' he asked in a voice which kept on rising. 'Is it because I cannot sign my name? Is it because I am not as literate as you are? What is so funny about asking for the pad for the *angutha chhaap* (thumb impression)? How far have you studied, young man? Why don't you answer instead of grinning like an idiot? Why don't you answer me?' The successive queries were each accompanied by the thump of a huge walking stick on the floor. The young duty officer, who was distinctly nervous by this time, mumbled a few words indicating that he was a graduate of the Delhi University. 'Is that so? And how many graduates are there in this country?' demanded Khansaheb, pointing his walking stick at the middle of the young officer's chest. 'What did you say? You don't know? Maybe a hundred thousand, did you say? Well, remember, there is only one Ahmad Jan Thirakwa in the whole of Hindustan.'

The third important figure in the Sahaswan–Rampur gharana is Ustad Nissar Hussain Khan who spent the last fifteen years of his life in the Sangeet Research Academy, Calcutta. I got plenty of opportunities to talk to him. He told me that his early talim, for that matter, almost his entire talim, was from his grandfather Ustad Haidar Khan. Fida Hussain Khan, Nissar Hussain's father, was born with a voice which was harsh and unmusical. Sheer hard work and dedicated practice made it eminently acceptable and he managed to get into the court of the Maharaja of Baroda. He was neither an outstanding singer nor an erudite one like Mushtaq Hussain Khan, whom he imitated. I heard his broadcast more than once over the Lucknow radio and to me, in my teens, he sounded like a clone of my ustad.

Nissar Hussain's talim from his grandfather Haidar Khan was limited to a few years. After the death of Kalbe Ali Khan, the Nawab of Rampur, Haidar Khan went to Nepal. By the time he returned to Nawab Hamid Ali Khan's court, Nissar Hussain had received a state scholarship to go to Baroda for enrolment in the Sir Sayaji Rao Music College. The teachers were Ustad Ata Hussain Khan of the Agra gharana, Jamaluddin Khan Beenkar who also was a competent singer, and Nissar Hussain's father Fida Hussain Khan. Senior musicians of the Agra gharana claim that Nissar Hussain Khan, during his prolonged stay at Baroda, was greatly influenced by Ustad Faiyaz Khan, the premier court musician of Maharaja Sir Sayaji Rao Gaekwad. This certainly was understandable. They further claim that he learnt from Ata Hussain Khan.

In the 'Charcha' series in the Ramakrishna Institute of Culture in 2002, I presented an analysis of the gayaki of Sahaswan gharana followed by recitals of Afzal Hussain Khan and Rashid Khan. I played an excerpt from one of the earlier tape-recordings of Nissar Hussain Khan's raga Pancham side by side with Ata Hussain Khan's Darbari Kanhra. The musicians present admitted that the resemblance in their taans and bol-taans was uncanny. Even in the 78 RPM records of Nissar Husain Khan, the impact of Agra gayaki is noticeable. Also the songs he sang, e.g., *'Ba he kala hot'* and *'Paiyan parungi'* in Jayjaiwanti, *'Tu aori aori'* in Gobardhani Todi, *'Acche peer mori'* in Vrindavani Sarang, *'Piharwa maika deho bataye'* and Ata Hussain Khan's composition *'Hat na karo mohe chhand'* in Khem Kalyan are those which I have learnt from my Agra gharana ustads. When I questioned Nissar Hussain Khan about it, he replied, 'Ata Hussain was like an elder brother to me. There was not a day when we did not spend at least a couple of hours together, singing or chatting about music. Naturally, I got a thing or two from him.' In a recorded interview in the Sangeet Research Academy, he has repeated what he had said to me earlier: *'Phir hamne do-chaar cheezen lee unse* (So I took a thing or two from him).'

Two musicians succeeded in achieving a happy blend of Gwalior and Agra, Shrikrishna Ratanjankar being the other. In the course of time, however, the influence of Agra got diluted and that of Nissar Hussain Khan's father or, to be precise, certain features of the style of Mushtaq Hussain Khan, became more and more prominent. Nissar Hussain Khan claimed that he had picked up features he liked from ustads that he had heard in his youth and prepared a *'guldastaa'*, his own bouquet of flowers. My own impression is that like Bade Ghulam Ali Khan, his emphasis throughout was on riyaz and not on raagdari. Quite a few of his recordings in the Sangeet Research Academy indicate that his virtuosity was often at the expense of the shastriya delineation of the raga. His linear taans, covering two-and-a-half octaves, remind one of Mushtaq Hussain, but Nissar Hussain's sargams, paltas and combination of notes, and rendering of taranas, seem to be his very own.

The last recital of his that I heard, when he was eighty-seven, of the raga Puriya Dhanashree, and the freedom with which he moved around in his taans and sargams would have been the envy of an ustad half his age. His style was faithfully imitated by his son Sarfaraz Hussain, now no more with us, and son-in-law Hafeez Ahmad Khan, currently the seniormost member of the Sahaswan dynasty. Hafeez Ahmad, gifted with artistic sense and a voice which has depth but drifts into falsetto in the upper octave, is not heard any more, which is a pity because there is no one left to remind us of Nissar Hussain Khan's gayaki.

Rashid Khan, unquestionably the most talented of all the members of this gharana, has, of late, drifted away from his ustad, Nissar Hussain Khan's style. His sur, 'swar-prayog', or application of notes, and the pianissimo-fortissimo effect that he creates with his voice-throw are just as extraordinary as his taans. One wishes sometimes, though, that he would slowly increase the tempo of his taans instead of hurling the jet-propelled ones right from the word go, and also concentrate more on patterns than on speed. He favours the Kirana type of vistar in the vilambit portion. There is nothing wrong with a young man searching for a style, but one wishes all the same, he would not forsake the bahlawa bant and bol-taans of his ustad's gayaki.

What Nissar Hussain Khan sang was considerably different from the original Gwalior gayaki of Sahaswan. What Rashid Khan sings today bears no resemblance to the music of Mushtaq Hussain Khan. Is it appropriate then to label Sahaswan a gharana? I think it would be more in the fitness of things to call it a 'khandaan' (family) which has produced quite a few outstanding vocalists. No doubt the dynamism of a gharana depends on fresh contributions from successive generations but the process should not attempt to depart from the mainstream, nor should there be any major structural alterations in the gayaki. Quite a few musicologists are of the opinion that at least three generations should follow the same shailee, or artisitic style, to qualify as gharana members.

When I first listened to Ustad Mushtaq Hussain Khan, he was in his late sixties. I never had the chance of hearing him in his prime, but met many who had. When I went to him he had lost his 'mizaj'—an untranslatable word which loosely combines mood and temperament. He would not spend more than ten to fifteen minutes on the slow exposition of the raga, even such major ragas as Todi, Yaman and Darbari. The main ingredients of his music were bahlawa and taans. The reason for this was the nature of Nawab Raza Ali Khan. Raza Ali's father Hamid Ali Khan was a great connoisseur and a reasonably competent singer of dhrupad and dhamar. During his reign the young Mushtaq Hussain's music was more stable than it became in later years. Prince Raza Ali Khan became the disciple of the ustad and gave him a 'nazrana' of three thousand rupees which in today's currency would easily be three or four lakh. The ustad did not take the money. Instead he spent it on a 'chadar' woven with silver threads for the grave of the Peer Sahab of Bareilly. Ustad Mushtaq Hussain of course was held in great esteem by Raza Ali after he succeeded his father to the throne but he was a whimsical and impatient man incapable of listening with concentration to even the best of music for any length of time.

Raza Ali Khan's eldest son-in-law, Syed Nurul Hasan, joined Lucknow University as a lecturer in history when I was an undergraduate. In later life he gained recognition as a scholar, diplomat and finally as the governor of West Bengal. Famous for his enormous girth and love of good food, which he would not eschew despite high blood sugar counts reminiscent of Don Bradman's scores, he had been a slim, handsome young man in my college days.

Back from Germany after my second bypass surgery, I was

invited to lunch at the Raj Bhavan in Calcutta, where I had to witness the 'Laat Sahab' devouring his favourite kebabs and pulao while I was served boiled food. Nawab Raza Ali's youngest son-in-law, Sudarshan Mehta, was a senior executive in Shaw Wallace in Calcutta. Thanks to both of them I have had the pleasure of sampling some of the choicest dishes from the kitchen of the nawab. The last time I met the nawab was at Sudarshan and his wife Naheed's residence in Calcutta. Ustad Dabeer Khan, the grandson of Nawab Hamid Ali's guru, Wazir Khan, of the Seniya gharana, played the been. Omar Khan of Lucknow also played his 'besura' sarod for a while. Nawabsaheb listened to Dabeer Khan's alaap in Behag for fifteen minutes, then demanded to hear Kamod. Right in the middle of his recital he called upon Ishaq Hussain, son of Ustad Mushtaq Hussain and shagird of Raza Ali Khan, to sing some of Nawabsaheb's compositions. No wonder the nawab's patronage gradually led to Ustad Mushtaq Hussain losing a great deal of his aesthetic sense and mizaj and turn more and more to his earlier penchant for taans.

I doubt if Miyan Tansen himself could have survived under such conditions for long. On top of all this, Nawab Raza Ali Khan loved making disciples out of eminent musicians. Ustad Amir Khan managed to escape that distinction, by an early morning train from Rampur with the help of Begum Akhtar. Raza Ali Khan played the castinets on the strength of which he tied the black thread round the wrist of Ahmad Jan Thirakwa.

One gathers that the nawab fell so deeply in love with Akhtaribai Faizabadi that he carried her off to his palace and held her in luxurious imprisonment for many years. To quote Sheila Dhar once again, 'She was showered with gifts and allowed to wear the priceless heirlooms of the state including a 'satlada', a seven-stringed pearl necklace. The nawab was rumoured to have said openly in the palace that the only thing brighter than the seven diamond pendants of the famous necklace was Akhtaribai's smile. However, his fixation soon made her claustrophobic and she began to resent her gilded cage. Partly as revenge and partly as a game to test her power, she ordered coins to be struck in her name and had them embossed with her profile. She thought it was time to bring matters to a head and this seemed a stylish way of doing just that. When the nawab's intense devotion began to turn into displeasure with what she steadfastly regarded as nothing more than a lark, her mood changed to one of anger. She expressed it by decamping with the necklace, no doubt to teach him a lesson. The nawab's men were despatched in hot pursuit but could not find her anywhere because she immediately stopped singing publicly and went underground. When she emerged years later, it was as Begum Akhtar, the respectable wife of a barrister from an eminent family of Lucknow. The protection of such a husband made all the difference. The wild and now outdated allegations of the princely state now seemed absurd.'

Mushtaq Hussain Khan was a deeply religious man. When he died, virtually in the arms of his disciple and well-known singer Naina Devi at her residence, his last words were, 'Oh Lord! Your divine grace touched me and made me a singer. Please forgive my sins, *khataa muaaf karnaa*.' He was a simple soul and took great pride in his lineage. Whenever he sang any of Bahadur Hussain's taranas or his guru and father-in-law Inayet Hussain Khan's compositions, he would say, 'He was a *sher*, a lion, the king of the jungle, I am a pariah dog. *Hum to kutte hain, kutte!*' His full-throated taans could cover three octaves or nearly three, because he would touch the *ati taar sa* in falsetto. He would inform his audience that he received the knack from his father-in-law as part of the dowry. He was jealous of Ustad Faiyaz Khan and sometime said unflattering things about a khayaliya of the Agra gharana, the son-in-law of Mamu Daraspiya, singing dadras and thumris in public and doing dhrupad alaap before singing his khayal. All this obviously, in his opinion were not in the true tradition of khandaani khayaliya.

Prabhakar Chinchore, my friend of college days, sat for his Sangeet Nipun examination a year before he left university.

On the day of the practical examination, outsiders were allowed. The examiners were Ustad Alauddin Khan, Rajabhaiya Poochwale, Mushtaq Hussain Khan, Badilalji and, of course, Shrikrishna Ratanjankar. Though Chinchore did not answer one or two questions too well, his performance on the whole was satisfactory. I remember he sang Shyam Kalyan, Megh and Patbihag. When principal Ratanjankar turned to Mushtaq Hussain Khan for his opinion, the ustad asked how many marks he was entitled to give the examinee. On being told he had to allot marks out of a hundred, he said, *'Sau to de hi dijiyega, aur das pandra meri taraf se inam bhi* (By all means give him the hundred, also add ten or fifteen as baksheesh from me). For a boy his age he has accomplished a great deal.'

5

Agra Gharana and
Ustad Faiyaz Khan

The history of creativity in Hindustani music cannot but take serious cognizance of the two greats, Ustad Abdul Karim Khan and Ustad Faiyaz Khan, both of whom flourished at the beginning of the twentieth century, for they changed the form of khayal without departing from tradition. To people of our generation they were and still remain the two musicians of the century.

Comments on Ustad Faiyaz Khan's music, that is from those who had heard him in person, remind one of the parable in the *Jataka* about the blind men and the elephant. The one who felt the trunk thought what he touched was a python, another touched a leg and thought it to be a solid pillar. Yet another touched the tail which he thought was a moving rope. None of them could visualize the whole animal.

Ustad Hafiz Ali Khan, the great sarod player and the father of Ustad Amjad Ali Khan, told me once, 'Hai, hai. What an artiste! Be it at khayal or thumri, no one in Hindustan could equal Faiyaz Khan in bol banana.' Mintoobabu, a well-known sitar player in our youth, called him the master of rhythm and layakari. Ustad Vilayet Khan, who in a recent interview acknowledged his debt to the three major influences in his life, viz. his father Ustad Inayet Khan, Ustad Abdul Karim Khan and Ustad Faiyaz Khan, talked of Faiyaz's drut khayals and his sapaat halaq taans from the

Ustad Faiyaz Khan

Taar-Saptak-Gandhar. Pandit Ravi Shankar talked of the maestro's gift of expression, as did Ustad Amir Khan, who used the term 'majestic'. Professor D.P. Mukherjee, who had his early initiation into dhrupad under Radhika Goswami and khayal under Pandit Bhatkhande, used to mention Khansaheb's raagdari and the architectonic quality of his alaap. One could see, in the mind's eye, the sandstone castle building up in the air, tier upon tier, to a massive skyscraping structure like that of the Buland Darwaza.

Pandit V.G. Jog, who in his youth accompanied Faiyaz Khansaheb more than once on what the ustad used to call a fiddle, talked of the intoxicating spell of his music which lasted several days after the recital. Only Bhishma Dev Chatterjee, the famous khayal singer of Bengal who subsequently took some talim from Ustad Faiyaz Khan in Baroda, and Thakur Jaidev Singh, the well-known philosopher-musicologist of Benaras, talked of the totality of Khansaheb's music, calling him a 'complete musician'.

The present-day listeners of classical Hindustani music, of course, have not had a chance of hearing Ustad Faiyaz Khan. At best, they have heard his 78 RPM records which belong to the pre-electronic age when the recording equipments were not only primitive but the microphone actually had to be placed at least two feet away to prevent his powerful voice from leading to distortions. Alternatively, they have heard the AIR wire recordings of Khansaheb, sung at the fag end of his life, when tuberculosis had affected both his lungs and he was actually coughing blood between his halaq-taans.

The late Sunil Bose of AIR was in charge of the Baroda station in 1949 and 1950. But for him and his desire to provide Khansaheb's family the wherewithal for his treatment, even this music, such as it is, would have been lost to posterity. While they are still precious to people of the new generation, in these recordings Khansaheb is barely a shadow of himself.

The genealogy compiled by Ustad Vilayet Hussain Khan of the Agra gharana, and his worthy son Yunus Hussain Khan who is also no more with us, clearly indicates that this gharana chronologically claims to be the oldest, even older than Tansen's Gwalior. Jaywant Rao, in his book on Ustad Khadim Hussain Khan, talks of *nauhar vani* going back to Nayak Gopal of Devagiri, who was brought by Amir Khusrau to Delhi during Alauddin Khilji's reign. The first Muslim name belonging to the Agra gharana appears to be that of Haji Sujan Khan, a contemporary of Miyan Tansen. The emperor Akbar bestowed the title of 'Deepak Jyot' on him, presumably because he was a master of the Deepak raga which, if Bollywood and New Theatres are to be believed, Miyan Tansen sang to light fires all round him.

Shrikrishna Ratanjankar composed two songs in this raga on the basis of some evidence from the scriptures, and it resembled Bihag and Jhinjhoti in parts, and did not sound as if it could set a house on fire. What we do know, however, is that Haji Sujan Khan composed a dhrupad, 'Pratham Man Allah', in raga Jog. The khayalias neglected this raga till Ustad Mehboob Khan (Daras Piya), the father-in-law of Ustad Faiyaz Khan, composed the first well-known khayal, 'Peeharwa ko birmaye'—with two nishads and not one komal nishad, as it is sung nowadays.

Haji Sujan Khan got the village of Gondpur as a gift from the emperor Akbar. Here his descendants lived till 1857 when the Mutiny moved them to Agra. The dynasty boasted of two other big names, Miyan Sarasrang, during the time of Aurangzeb, when music was taboo, and Miyan Shyam Rang, during the time of Mohammed Shah Rangile. The song 'Aye Badra Kare Kare' in Birju Ka Malhar is credited to him though it is difficult to believe that khayal existed in the Agra gharana at that time.

In fact, khayal gayaki in Agra is credited to Khuda Baksh, the son of Miyan Shyam Rang or Qayyum Khan. Khuda Baksh, along with three other brothers, had rigorous training in dhrupad, dhamar and alaapchari. But Khuda Baksh, while not lacking in virtuosity, was widely ridiculed because of a voice that was so harsh and unmusical that it earned him the nickname of 'Ghagge'. Unable to put up with the taunts and derision of his family members, he left for Gwalior and decided to become a disciple of Naththan Peer Baksh whose father and uncle were Makhkhan Khan and Shakkar Khan. (The famous qawaal bachchas had imported khayal from Lucknow in the late eighteenth century.)

Here, Khuda Baksh learnt the art of voice production as well as khayals and tap-khayals from his ustad for fourteen years. When he returned to Agra, his music was scarcely recognizable and his voice had become so tuneful and sonorous that he would bring tears to the eyes of listeners. In fact, he would not be allowed to sing at weddings and festivals as tears were considered inauspicious.

As Khuda Baksh's fame spread, he was invited to join the court of Jaipur's Maharaja Sawai Ram Singh, who had already collected luminaries like Pandit Bishwambhar Nath, Rajjab Ali Veenkar, Imrat Sen, a descendant of Miyan Tansen, Sadruddin Khan Dilliwale, and the great Bahram Khan, ancestor of the Dagars.

This is where Khuda Baksh and Bahram Khan became great friends. They exchanged caps and became brothers. People said that Bahram Khan was *numero uno* in Hindustan because of his profound knowledge and raagdari but as far as artistry and 'taseer' went, Khuda Baksh was ahead of him. In fact, the Gwalior brand of khayal lacked vistar which was not foreign to Khuda Baksh who was steeped in the tradition of dhrupad and dhamar. In addition, he borrowed bol-bant and layakari from dhamar and incorporated them into his khayal. These features were further developed with great artistry by Ustad Faiyaz Khan, as we shall presently see.

Ustad Alladiya Khan, the founder of the Jaipur gharana, was born two years before the revolt of 1857 and he died shortly before the Independence of India. In his long life he had met and heard everybody who was anybody in the world of Hindustani music. This is what he has to say about Bahram Khan.[1]

'Among the Muslims Bahram Khan was a pandit. He

went to Benaras in order to learn Sanskrit, lived there for twelve years and acquired the Sanskrit knowledge of music. In those days Sanskrit was not taught to anyone except Brahmins. Therefore, Bahram Khan dressed and behaved like a Hindu. He applied sandalwood paste on his forehead and performed rituals like *sandhyavandan*. But he was so honest that he did all these things only for the sake of appearance, but never went into a temple breaking religious rules.

He served his guru well and acquired knowledge of Sanskrit by pleasing him. There were a number of books in Sanskrit, and his specific intention in learning Sanskrit was to be able to read them. He behaved in such a way that neither his guru nor anybody else suspected him for twelve years. He studied *Sangeet Ratnakar, Sangeet Kalpadrum* and other ancient works on music with great attention. At last, while returning home he revealed his secret to his guru, fell at his feet and asked for his forgiveness. He truthfully told his guru his intention. His guru was pleased and bade him farewell with blessings.

Bahram Khan was well disposed and affectionate towards all singers, old and young. He wished that the knowledge of music and the secrets that he had acquired with great difficulty could be made known to everybody.[2] He taught music to weavers' children although weavers were perceived as a non-musical community. Many of them began singing extremely well and composed sargams in difficult ragas with facility. Bahram Khan would allow them to sing in important concerts. His intention was to show that while these persons from non-musical families could sing *as* well, we musicians neglected the art.

Bahram Khan sang dhrupad and dhamar extremely well and knew many compositions. He would compose excellent sargams in every raga. This talent continues in his family of Dagars. Before him, some four hundred years earlier, all the singers from Dagar, Khandar, Nauhar and Gobarhar *bani* (traditions) had good knowledge of sargams. But they did not pass it on to anybody except their children and disciples. Bahram Khan popularised it among people of all communities.[3]

In the old days all the singers from the four traditions maintained cordial relations with one another. Bahram Khan belonged to the Dhadhi community. He requested Haidar Bakshi (grandson of Nityamat Khan) and Alam Sen to teach alaap, dhrupad and dhamar to his grandsons Zakiruddin and Allabande. Although Bahram Khan was apart from all the four traditions, the traditional singers acceded to his request and taught his grandsons. Bahram Khan died at the age of hundred.[4]

Bahram Khan and Khuda Baksh pulled each other's legs relentlessly in public. Bahram Khan's constant refrain was *'Ama Yaar Ghagge,* why don't you take a few lessons in raagdari from me? Everyone can see you still don't know how to sing.' Once, while Khuda Baksh was singing, he brought tears to the eyes of his listeners, which included Bahram Khan. At the end of the recital, Khuda Baksh said, *'Hame to gana nahin ata,* I don't know how to sing, why then the handkerchief, Bahrambhai?' Bahram Khan replied, *'Isi afsos ke mare toh ro rahen hain* (that is precisely why I'm crying)! All these years of riyaz and hard work have come to nothing. What a great pity!'

In 1916, the first Grand Music Conference was held at Baroda under the patronage of Maharaja Sayaji Rao Gaekwad through the efforts of Pandit Vishnu Narayan Bhatkhande. Ustad Aminuddin Dagar's grandfather Ustad Allabande Khan, and his elder brother Ustad Zakiruddin Khan, who was an even greater alaapiya were singing dhrupad. In the middle of the recital, Ustad Allabande addressed the audience and said, 'Alaapchari in Hindustan is sadly coming to an end and hardly exists outside the Dagar clan.' The following day, when young Faiyaz Khan's turn came, he did an alaap in Darbari which lasted over an hour, before be came to his dhamar and khayal. Ustad Allabande Khan embraced Faiyaz Khan and said, 'When I referred to my clan, I did not exclude you, Faiyaz Hussain, you are very much one of us, *tum toh hamare hi ho.'* This has reference to the topee-badal bhais, Bahram Khan and Ghagge Khuda Baksh.

Both lived to a great age. Khuda Baksh died in his nineties while Bahram Khan comfortably scored his century. Khuda Baksh, towards the end, hardly sang, because his memory was failing him. He would forget the names of ragas but remember the compositions or vice versa. One has heard the story from Faiyaz Khan about a singer from Punjab who appeared one fine morning in Khuda Baksh's residence in Jaipur and requested him to sing raga Jait. Poor Khuda Baksh racked his brains but could not remember a single composition nor the raga. Disappointed, the singer from Punjab picked up Khuda Baksh's tanpura and said, 'Shame on you. I can sing to you compositions in Jait, Jaitshree, Jaltkalyan, any number of them. Fancy you calling yourself a great ustad and you do not know even Jait. I am taking your tanpura with me.' Apparently that was the custom in those days. If an ustad lost in a musical duel he had to forfeit his tanpura to the winner.

Khuda Baksh's two sons Ghulam Abbas and Kallan Khan were returning from the bazaar and met the stranger on the doorstep, carrying the tanpura. They were amazed and asked their father, 'This man says you could not sing Jait. How can that be when you have taught us dhrupad, dhamar as well as khayal compositions in that raga?' Having said this, they tuned the tanpura and sang the sthayee of a dhrupad in Jait. Khuda Baksh immediately said, 'Oh, is that the raga this gentleman wanted to hear?' He proceeded thereafter to sing one composition after another until it was well past two o'clock and a message came from the kitchen that it was already late for lunch. The singer from Punjab apologized profusely, saying, 'I had heard from my guru that you were a great artiste but I did not realize till now that you were an equally great ustad, a great pundit.'

Khuda Baksh trained his two sons, Ghulam Abbas Khan and Kallan Khan, as well as his nephew Sher Khan. The last named passed his art on to his son, the celebrated Naththan Khan, guru of the equally famous Bhaskharbuwa and Babli Bai. Just as Balkrishnabuwa Ichalkaranjikar promoted the Gwalior gayaki in Maharashtra, Sher Khan and Naththan

Khan kept the flag of the Agra gharana flying in Bombay with Gwalia tank as their headquarters. Their descendants include quite a few renowned ustads like Vilayet Hussain Khan, Khadim Hussain Khan, Anwar Hussain Khan and Latafat Hussain Khan. Ustad Alladiya Khan, the founder of the Jaipur/Atrauli gharana, lived with them when they were in Babulnath in Bombay.

Apart from the matrimonial connections that bound Atrauli and Agra together for many generations, there was the outstanding example of Munshi Ghulam Hussain who had trained many of the Atrauli ustads. Jaywant Rao, in his biography of Ustad Khadim Hussain Khan, entitled *Sajan Piya,* about the musician who had trained Jaywant's wife Lalit Rao, mentions an interesting incident. When Ustad Alladiya Khan came to live with the Agrawallas in Bombay, Khadim Hussain was a mere child. One day he was so overwhelmed by Ustad Alladiya Khan's compositions and taankari that he said, 'Dadaji, please give me a little of your *'ilm'*, your vast repertoire. It would indeed be a great favour to me.' Ustad Alladiya Khan, to the great surprise of young Khadim Hussain, stood up, placed his hands on both his ears as a mark of respect to his ustads, closed his eyes and started muttering to himself. Khadim Hussain fell at his feet and said 'Dadaji, please forgive me if I have talked out of turn and asked for something which does not belong to me.' Alladiya Khan promptly placed his hand on Khadim's head and said 'No, no, my child! Of course it is your legitimate right, *tera to huq hai mujh se mang ne ka,* it is your granduncle Munshi Ghulam Hussain, a favourite disciple of Ghagge Khuda Baksh, who first placed the tanpura on my shoulder; Agra and Atrauli are one and the same, *woh dono to ek hi hain.'*

To the usad of bygone days, *'iman',* honesty and loyalty to the guru, and khandaan formed the cornerstone on which the entire gharana system rested for generations. Ustad Vilayet Hussain Khan of the Agra gharana in his book *Sangeet Sansmaran* mentions that he had forty-one gurus! He would include among them even those from whom he had received only two or three compositions. As a result he had a vast repertoire, possibly larger than that of any of the virtuosos like Ustad Tasadduq Hussain Khan, Khadim Hussain Khan or my guru Ata Hussain Khan. The last, son of the famous Daras Piya, inherited countless bandishes from his father and became the devoted disciple of his brother-in-law Faiyaz Khan with whom he spent the major portion of his life at Baroda.

Any reference to Ustad Vilayet Hussain Khan of Agra and Ustad Alladiya Khan of Atrauli/Jaipur gharana would not be complete without what the famous Kesarbai Kerkar had to say about him, quoted by Babban Haldankar in his Marathi book *Zulu Pahnare Dou Tambure* on both these gharanas. He is eminently fit to write on a subject like this, having received extensive talim in Jaipur style from Moghubai Kurdikar (mother of Kishori Amonkar) as well as Ustad Khadim Hussain Khan of Agra. It is not common knowledge that both Moghubai and Kishori took talim from the ustads of the Agra gharana, the former from Ustad Vilayet Hussain Khan and the latter from Anwar Hussain Khan.

On the occasion of the funeral of Ustad Vilayet Hussain Khan in 1963, Kesarbai recalled the close relationship between Vilayet Hussain's father, the great Naththan Khan and her own guru Ustad Alladiya Khan, and said, 'Just as they were like brothers, so were Vilayet Hussain and I. What a great pandit he was, a veritable ocean of learning! The more I listened to him, the more I wondered about the inability of present-day disciples of the Agra gharana to benefit from their close association with this great ustad. I myself have not only got a lot out of him but have incorporated some of the angas of Ustad Faiyaz Khan's music into my khayal and thumri.' Frankly, I would not have believed this had I not recently heard a private recording of Kesarbai's thumri *'Babul mora'* in Bhairavi.

Naththan Khan, unquestionably an outstanding singer of his time, known for his special treatment of vilambit asthayee, would have perhaps been an even greater singer but for his

predilection for the bottle. When he was invited to sing
before the Maharaja of Mysore, one of the bigger native
states, it was considered an honour by the Agra clan in
Bombay. The Maharaja, whose Yuvaraj was a man of enormous
girth, was a great patron of Karnatak as well as Hindustani
music. The son was also an accomplished pianist who carried
a cottage piano on his jungle safaris. On his arrival from
Bombay, Naththan Khan was received by the Maharaja's
emissary at the railway station, put up in the state guest
house and was told that the Maharaja, who had heard much
about Naththan Khan, would like to hear him the very same
evening. When Khansaheb was escorted to the palace, he
was in such an advanced state of inebriation that he could
scarcely sit down for his recital.

The following morning he could not remember what had
happened beyond the fact that he had started on the raga
Kamod and the courtiers had laughed at him. Very soon, the
same man who had received him came with a purse of two
thousand rupees and suggested that Naththan Khan not take
the trouble of staying on in Mysore and, if he pleased, leave
by the night train. Naththan Khan kept quiet for a minute
and said, 'Please convey my salaams to his highness and tell
him that I am indebted to him for his overwhelming kindness
and generosity, but I am unable to accept this gift as I could
not perform yesterday due to high fever. I shall, if it pleases
the Maharaja, be honoured to sing before him in a day or
two.' As every member of the Agra gharana knows, Naththan
Khan's subsequent recital impressed the Maharaja so much
that he stayed on as the premier court musician of Mysore.

Ustad Alladiya Khan, who used to call Naththan Khan
'Bhaisahab'(brother) recounted a similar incident:

'Naththan Khan came to visit me at Kolhapur. I
informed Maharaja Sahab that a very famous singer
had come from Mysore and that he sang very well
indeed. The Maharaja invited Bhaisahab to sing that
very day. Bhaisahab was in the habit of drinking.

Before going for the concert he went out and drank
and when we reached Maharaja Sahab's palace, he
drank a great deal there too. By the time he sat down
to sing, the alcohol had had its effect. He wanted to
sing one thing, but something else would emerge. On
that day Bhaisahab just could not sing. The Maharaja
asked me if it was the same guest I had praised so
much. I said "Maharaja, you were in a hurry—he has
arrived only today and is tired and unwell after the
long journey. Let him rest for a day or two and then
listen to him. The Maharaja fixed his recital after
two days. Before leaving for the concert Bhaisahab
got ready and appeared to be leaving the house. I
knew his intention and said, "Bhaisahab, today I will
not let you go out. If you go, then the doors of my
house will be closed to you forever." Bhaisahab
stayed back and we proceeded to the palace. The
Maharaja's arrival was announced. Bhaisahab came
up to me and said that he needed a drink badly or
else he would not be able to sing at all. I called for
a drink and gave it to him and warned all the
servants not to serve him any more. The concert
began. Bhaisahab sang extremely well. Maharajasahab
was very pleased. Naththan Khan was indeed a very
skilled singer.'[5]

Obviously, Alladiya's close friendship with Naththan Khan
did not extend to sharing drinks. Alladiya Khan, who traced
his lineage to the Shandilya Gotra Brahmins, was a devout
Muslim and a teetotaller. Naththan Khan, apart from his
affection for Alladiya Khan, held him in great esteem as a
musician. He would often tell young musicians, 'Before you
utter the name of Alladiya Khan, make it a point to wash
your mouth with rose water first.'

Talking of iman and loyalty to one's guru, and khandaan,
I am reminded of an incident in the late Fifties. My second
guru, Mushtaq Hussain Khan of the Rampur/Sahaswan

gharana, came to Calcutta to stay with my third ustad, Ata
Hussain Khan of the Agra gharana, in the outhouse of the
palace of the Raja of Mahishadal. There was only one cot in
Ata Hussain Khan's room. There was a double bed in the
next room occupied by his daughter and son-in-law. Mushtaq
Hussain Khan, though an elder cousin, refused to occupy the
cot because Ata Hussain Khan's father Mehboob Khan
(Daras Piya) had taught young Mushtaq Hussain in his
childhood. He insisted on sleeping on the floor, his sole
reason being Ata Hussain was after all his 'khalifah', and son
of his 'mamu' and ustad. Ultimately, an extra cot had to be
brought from the adjoining palace to save his iman.

To go back to Faiyaz Khan and his ancestry. I had
mentioned the two sons of Khuda Baksh, Ghulam Abbas
Khan and Kallan Khan. The latter succeeded his father in
the Jaipur court and tutored a number of disciples who went
on to make a name for themselves, the most famous of them
being Zohrabai Agrewali, who also learnt from Sher Khan
and Mehboob Khan. Two others were Firdausi Bai, and
Bibbobai Jaipurwali. Ghulam Abbas Khan did not leave
Agra. The elder of his two daughters, Abbasi Begum, was
married to Safdar Hussain of Sikandra Rangeela gharana and
the younger, Kadri Begum, to Kale Khan (Saras Piya) of
Mathura. Kale Khan had several well-known compositions to
his credit like 'Chatur Sughar Bayian' (Kedara) and 'Manmohan
Brij Ke Rasiya' in Paraj. His son, Ghulam Rasool Khan,
accompanied Faiyaz Khan on the harmonium all his life.
Faiyaz Khan had a special soft corner for Ghulam Rasool—
not because he was a great harmonium-player but because he
was a matriculate and could, therefore, speak English with
'an accent like that of a sahab'.

Safdar Hussain Khan died a few months before Faiyaz
Khan was born. Abbasi Begum returned to her father who
took full charge of his favourite grandchild's musical education.
Faiyaz Khan belonged on his father's side to the Rangeela
gharana, named after Ramzan Khan Rangeele, an eminent
ustad whose beautiful compositions incorporated the Nayaki

Kanhra, Nat Bihag and Chhaya Bihag. Faiyaz Khan also got a lot from his uncle Fida Hussain Khan, but his talim came more or less exclusively from his mother's side, from Ghulam Abbas Khan and his brother Kallan Khan. In later years young Faiyaz was also influenced by Ustad Naththan Khan and even more so by his son Abdullah Khan who was a bit of a hero in Faiyaz Khan's eyes.

Latafat Khan recounted to me a recital of Lachari Todi by Faiyaz Khan in the Santa Cruz Music Circle sometime in the Forties. He would dwell on the Shudh Gandhar with great dexterity, and with a dazzling harkat, would go back to rekhab via the Komal Gandhar. Every time he did that he would draw spontaneous applause. Suddenly, Khansaheb stopped and said aloud as if to himself, '*Hai*, how wonderfully Bhai Abdullah Khan sang this Lachari Todi. I am not even a small particle of Ustad Abdullah Khan, *mai to unka ek zarra bhi nahin boon.*'

Ghulam Abbas and Faiyaz remained very close to each other even after Faiyaz Khan's mother married again. Ghulam Abbas died at the ripe old age of a hundred and nine. Even in his fifties, Faiyaz Khan would close the door when he ordered his hookah, as a mark of respect to his mentor, as was the custom those days.

Ghulam Abbas, on his part, was an extremely nervous listener and would seldom attend Faiyaz Khan's recitals. He would prefer to stay at home and wait for his disciples to come back and report to him. '*Kaisa hua gana?* How did it go?' he would ask Khadim Hussain or Ata Hussain, 'I hope Faiyaz did not make any mistakes. What did he sing?' This, mind you, was at the height of Faiyaz Khan's glory in the Thirties. When reassured that Faiyaz Khan had captivated the audience as usual and was not allowed to conclude his recital till the early hours of the morning, Ghulam Abbas Khan would repeatedly praise Allah that the boy was shaping up well after all.

Ghulam Abbas Khan was a fitness fiend and remained addicted to free-hand exercise even when he crossed his century. One day he called young Dilip Chandra Vedi and asked him what he was learning from Faiyaz Hussain.

'*Ji, newar ki jhankar* in Chhayanat', replied the young disciple.

'*Kai saans me asthayee bharte ho?* How many breaths do you take to sing the composition?'

A strange question, thought Dilip Vedi. He had never given it any thought.

'*Leo suno,*' continued Ghulam Abbas. He then proceeded to sing the long vilambit asthayees in two breaths, claiming that he had not needed even the second one in his youth!

Latafat Khan told me once that Ghulam Abbas Khan ate twelve almonds with his breakfast after his customary hundred push-ups. As he had lost all his teeth, the almonds had to be reduced to a paste. Once, not finding any almonds in the house, Faiyaz Khan's wife ground a few peanuts instead. The old man took one helping and spat it out promptly. 'I have dealt in *sachcha* sur all my life,' he said,. 'I know the difference between almonds and peanuts.'

This should not be interpreted as bragging. According to Ustad Vilayet Hussain Khan, he had heard only two '*sureela gavaiyas*' (musicians known for their extreme tuneful quality). One was Abdul Karim Khan and the other one was Ghulam Abbas Khan. 'His Bageshri was so compelling that we could not hold back our tears,' says Vilayet Hussain Khan in his book.[6] This is exactly what Bala Saheb Poochwale, the octogenerian stalwart of the Gwalior gharana, told me about Faiyaz Khan's Bageshri, a few years back.

No wonder young Faiyaz Hussain's training under his grandfather was a rigorous one. Musical exercises were punctuated by regular push-ups and wrestling. Faiyaz started at the tender age of five and till he was twelve was not permitted to sing any songs, only the twelve notes and their usual combinations, or paltas. Khansaheb once told us that as a child he was very fond of the raga Iman and since singing ragas was prohibited at that age, he had climbed a tree in the backyard to sing '*Eri ali piya bin*'. Ghulam Abbas Khan asked the servant to bring the boy to him and Faiyaz was given a royal thrashing, first for disregarding his orders, secondly for singing a raga and thirdly, horror of horrors, for singing a khayal with taans and embellishments! In later years Ustad Faiyaz Khan himself would insist on teaching the children in his family (he had none of his own) only dhrupad in the beginning. Khayal was taboo until the voice settled down after adolescence. And taans, of course, were unthinkable, although I think the ustad did make an exception in the case of Sharafat Hussain whose taans were prolific even when he was barely in his teens.

I have mentioned earlier when I first heard Ustad Faiyaz Khan. It was at a private soiree in Calcutta. I was barely eight. Khansaheb was preceded by Ustad Hafeez Ali Khan on the sarod. What remains in my memory more than anything else is the tabla sangat of Bhishma Dev Chatterjee who was a well-known khayal singer of Bengal. He made all of us laugh, especially the children, by repeatedly massaging his left arm with the right hand during the jhala while the fingers kept on drumming the bayan at jet-propelled speed. Faiyaz Khan followed with alaap and '*Phulawan ki Gendanwa*' in Jaunpuri. It must have been difficult for an uninitiated child to sit and listen to orthodox classical music for three hours, but I recollect no sense of boredom. On the other hand, I have faint memories of the exquisite pain which his pukars from the Taar-Saptak-Gandhar evoked in me.

Years later, an evening at the Empire Hotel in Lucknow readily comes to mind. Firoz Dastur, a distinguished singer of the Kirana gharana, once described to me the enthralling effect of Ustad Faiyaz Khan's alaap in Bihag, which made his hair stand on end. '*Hamare rongte khare ho gaye the,*' he said. The memory of Khansaheb's Megh Malhar, sung in honour of a Rana of Nepal, thrills me even now, more than half a century later. His voice seemed to grow in depth and dimension as it descended in the mandra saptak. As Khansaheb reached the bottom of the lower octave, I felt as if I had been carried on the crest of a wave to deep, deep waters. I also recall the barhat in the middle octave step by step, jumping one note and descending with a massive meend to the tonic, when Khansaheb's disciples would finish on their tanpuras with a chorus of re ni sa re.

Then began the drut jod ang in his dhrupad alaap with its mosaic of rhythmic patterns, showers of larhi and thok and the roar of the ocean in his gamaks. I felt like I was being swept away by a tornado. When it died down eventually, I left with the feeling that anything after this sublime experience would be an anticlimax. Outside, there was the scent of rain. A half moon briefly peeped out of the cloud on top of the Kaisarbagh Baradari and 'the air was all in spice'.

Close proximity to nature at its most glorious, and great art, have an ennobling effect on one. It is the provenance of the higher self. Memories of such moments are many. Reading *The Brothers Karamazov* and *War and Peace* in my teens, listening to David Olstrakh play Beethoven's violin concerto, trekking on the mountain path to Pindari glacier in the Himalayas, watching elephants swimming at misty dusk in the Tipong gorge near the Burma border, a bright moonlight safari on a bitterly cold night in the Kanha forest with the shadows of towering trees all around us, watching the smouldering volcano from a coconut grove on the island of Bali or sitting on the Waikiki beach watching an exquisite sunset, each of these is an experience that is inexpressibly more enriching than hedonistic pleasures on a purely physical level. 'Great art does not merely startle or attract applause,' points out Rabindranath Tagore in a letter to my father.[7] 'It is not merely something which brings tears to the eyes or overwhelms one in an excess of emotion. Its job is to take one to the high point of imagination and creativity, where all is beauty. That creativity is like the creation of Nature, it encapsulates the strength of truth.' That evening's Megh Malhar belonged to this realm, an experience which probed the depth of one's being and brought one closer to the gods.

D.P. Mukherjee, somewhere in his journals, mentions Ustad Faiyaz Khan as a 'master of atmosphere'. Ustad Ahmad

Jan Thirkuwa, the legendary tabla player, also used to talk of this '*mahawl*' or atmosphere. He said there had been other great musicians in the past but no one ever exercised a greater hold on the audience. He could make his listeners laugh with joy. Total strangers would embrace one another in Khansaheb's mehfil. He could also bring tears to their eyes.

Aqil Ahmad Khan, one of the few surviving ustads of this gharana, which is increasingly resembling a graveyard, mentions a mehfil in Sundaribai Hall in Bombay at which the great Alladiya Khan was present. Aqil Ahmad was barely in his teens at that time. All he remembers is Ustad Faiyaz Khan's bol banao in Lalit. Every time he played on the phrase '*Balma moso raho na jaye,*' it was in subtly different ways. 'Gliding down to madhyam from the shadaj in taar saptak, it would bring tears to the eyes of the audience around him. When the recital ended, Ustad Alladiya Khan wiped his eyes, clasped Faiyaz Khan to his bosom and said, 'Faiyaz Hussain, you are truly Faiyaz, *Waqai tu Faiyaz hai, kya gana gaya tune aaj.*'

One wonders what helped him in creating this kind of atmosphere. In the ultimate analysis what great musicians like Abdul Karim and Faiyaz Khan possessed was an indefinable quality, a charisma which does not lend itself to analysis. In the absence of any other definition it is known among musicians as '*Khuda ki den*' or the light from above. Nonetheless, it is worthwhile examining in some depth the various facets of Ustad Faiyaz Khan's music.

First, his voice, the quality and *taaseer* of which cannot be ascertained from the primitive recordings available today. Its timbre, pitch, volume and coloration of tone were entirely different from those of any musician dead or alive. It did not have the rubber-like flexibility which Abdul Karim Khan, Amir Khan or Bade Ghulam Ali Khan's voices possessed. But in one word, it could be summed up as majestic. It was part of the regal personality which dwarfed those who gathered round him, even in the court of Maharaja Sir Sayaji Rao of Baroda which Khansaheb adorned for decades.

Next, his ragadari. Usually, artistes of his kind are not pundits. Khansaheb's music was an amazing blend of artistry, knowledge and taste. He had great command over uncommon and difficult ragas, but he never chose them in mehfils because he knew what his audience wanted. Also, major ragas which have stood the test of time have a greater impact on listeners than the 'achhop' (uncommon) ragas. Ustad Faiyaz Khan had taught the Raja of Mahishadal, the late Deba Prasad Garg Bahadur, some of these, viz. Tankashree, Ramgauri, Kapargauri, Gayatri, Pradeepki, Pancham etc., but always added that these were like 'hathi ke dant, dikhane ke waste, chabane ke nahin. Pet to bharta hai wohi Iman, Bihag, Jaijaiwanti, Darbari se (like elephant's tusks, not for chewing food but for show. One has to fill one's belly with common and major ragas like Iman, Bihag, Jayjaiwanti and Darbari').

In Faiyaz Khan's youth, Pandit Vishnu Narayan Bhatkhande had arranged for an invitation to him from the Maharani of Kashmir. There, for ten days he sang eighteen different kinds of Kalyan. Out of these, eight were in Iman Kalyan and were different from one another in subtle respects, with supporting bandishes of dhrupad, dhamar and khayal. Alaapchari also changed with the bandish, as was the rule those days.

Yet another great point with him was his ability to bring out the character of the raga while allowing associated ragas to appear and disappear, what is known as avirbhav and tirobhav. Barwa has to come close to Deshi, Kafi and Sindhura, yet must retain its own identity. While singing Chhayanat he would flirt for a while with Kedara and Kamod but never to disadvantage. In Jhinjholi he would give us a glimpse of Tilak Kamod, but only a glimpse, not a close-up. He was really a master of raagdari. As Pandit Shrikrishna Ratanjankar once said, 'Hum toh rag ke ghulam hain. Khan Sahab jab gaate the raag unka ghulam ban jata tha (We singers are slaves of the raga but when Khan Sahab sang, the raga would become his servant, he the master.' No wonder Pandit Bhatkhande handed over to him his favourite pupil 'Baburao' (Shrikrishna Ratanjankar) after his Kashmir trip.

The third notable feature was his accuracy of shrutis. Komal Gandhars are different from one another in Todi, Nayaki Kanhra, Darbari or Miyan Malhar, and this was common knowledge among the ustads of yesteryear. That Faiyaz Khan with his dhrupad tradition behind him would be able to execute them is not remarkable. But he would illustrate the point further by using a static gandhar in Darbari instead of the traditional oscillating one. He would take the liberty of andolit nishad and gandhar in Bageshri to establish that they are complementary notes.

Faiyaz Khan has sung a remarkable Lalit alaap and khayal in one of the early 78 RPM records which is complete in all respects. In a total duration of five minutes, the character of the raga and its salient features have been established in a masterly fashion and produce the same effect as a live concert—except for his voice, which the record could not possibly capture. Usually, khayal singers use the komal dha in Lalit which is hazardous, as with the madhyam as shadaj, the top half can meander into Todi. That is why dhrupad singers used the sahakaari dhaivat which is somewhere between the shudh dhaivat and the komal one. In alaap, this shruti ascends a bit with the meend and changes position slightly when used as a descendant note. That Faiyaz Khan does it with consummate ease in alaap is spectacular enough, but to be able to do it in drut jod and in taans is breathtaking. Khansaheb's *Desi Dhamar* (HMV 78 RPM) also has a sahakaari dhaivat which is deliberately used as a direct static note.

The mention of desi Todi reminds me of a story which is traced to Krishna Rao Mazumdar of Indore, an amateur but a highly competent musician and a disciple of Ustad Rajab Ali Khan of Dewas. Actually, I heard it from Dr M.R. Gautam when he was at AIR, Indore, and before he donned the mantle of a highly respected scholar and musicologist.

Ustad Faiyaz Khan was singing Desi Todi in the Indore durbar. The Maharaja heard him with closed eyes for an hour and a half and got up at the end of the recital. It was announced that the next recital of Khansaheb was scheduled for the following morning.

Next morning, Rajab Ali Khan began the day with Todi. His taankari was a byword those days and on this occasion he excelled himself. Ustad Faiyaz Khan, though junior in age, was the guest artiste and was therefore scheduled to sing after Rajab Ali Khan. When his turn came, he looked to the Maharaja for his command. 'Desi,' said the king and closed his eyes. Once again Faiyaz Khan sang desi, alaap, dhrupad, dhamar and khayal. Once again, the Maharaja departed soon as the recital was over.

The third day began again with Rajab Ali. Once again Faiyaz Khan looked to the Maharaja for his 'farmaish'. Once again came the terse command: 'Desi!' Ustad Faiyaz Khan later told his brother-in-law Ata Hussain Khan that it was easily the most awkward moment of his life. What kind of a test was this? Was this a conspiracy to belittle him in the presence of Rajab Ali, the court musician of the nearby state of Dewas, or just royal whim? Once again he sang the alaap, this time in a different vein, with different bandishes. When he finished he folded his hands and asked if the 'Sarkar' desired any thing further! The Maharaja got up and said, 'No, there can be no music after this.' Having said this he took off the pearl nacklace which adorned the royal neck and presented it to Faiyaz Khan. He also announced an inam of eleven thousand rupees to Faiyaz Khan and two thousand five hundred to Rajab Ali, the court musician.

Rajab Ali Khan was a great connoisseur of itar, the costly indigenous perfume which the raees and musicians of the past fancied. When he came out of the durbar he decided to hire a tonga and return to Dewas via an itar shop. What he chose was a very expensive one. The shopkeeper gave him a dubious look and said it would cost a hundred and fifty rupees.

'Is that so? And how many of these tiny bottles have you got?'

There were ten of them and the price was fifteen hundred.

'Excellent,' said Ustad Rajab Ali Khan producing the

brand new currency notes. 'Now pour the whole bloody lot into my shoes.'

For a while the incident at the Indore durbar soured his relationship with Faiyaz Khan who, after all, was a good friend. But Rajab Ali always said. '*Haan, reet ka gana to wohi hai, jo Faiyaz Khan gata hai* (what Faiyaz sings is the real, authentic traditional music'). So Krishna Rao Mazumdar confided in me when I visited him in 1973.

Latafat Khan, who lived in Bombay and was a distant nephew and disciple of Faiyaz Khan, rushed to Baroda when the ustad's death was announced on the radio. Recorded music followed the announcement on November 5, 1950. On the train to Baroda, Latafat Khan met Rajab Ali Khan. '*Hai hai*,' said Rajab Ali. 'What a musician, what a *gawaia!* You will not hear the like of him in a hundred years. *Sharab unko le gayi.* Alcohol killed him. What a great loss!' Having said that he brought out his bottle of country liquor and finished it in an hour. This of course was canard, for Faiyaz Khan died of diabetes and TB, and in old age he scarcely drank much of his favourite Scotch.

When Faiyaz Khan came to the Baroda durbar he was young and promising but quite a few years away from the superstar that he was to become. It was on Bhatkhandeji's recommendation that the Maharani of Baroda, daughter of Travancore, employed him. Ghulam Rasool Khan, his favourite cousin who moved in with him, told me that it was the young Faiyaz Khan's ambition to be engaged in a 'riyasat', or a native state as it was known in the British days. Baroda exceeded his expectations. It was one of the biggest states and Sir Sayaji Rao Gaekwad was an extremely progressive ruler. He founded the first arts and music schools in northern India and had the unique privilege of appointing two legendary ustads, Abdul Karim Khan and Faiyaz Khan, as his court musicians at different points of time. Both were paid from Rs 150 to Rs 200 a month. The latter claimed a tonga allowance of Rs 16 per month. In a few years, Faiyaz Khan's pay rose to Rs 300, which in the Twenties was affluence.

Ustad Latafat Khan

Sir Sayaji Rao was a patron of the arts but had little taste for or knowledge of classical music in his early days. Faiyaz Khan had to sing every Monday evening behind an exquisitely carved marble screen in the durbar, irrespective of the presence of an audience. Ghulam Rasool Khan reminisced in my presence, 'It was a bizarre experience. There would be no one in the hall most of the time, except the tabla player and me on the harmonium. What was worse was that parties would occasionally be thrown to honoured guests who would include the political agent or British civilians. God knows what they made of Khan Sahab's kind of music! Once, Ustad Faiyaz Khan made a petition to the Maharaja saying artistes sometimes need an audience. They do not get much satisfaction out of singing in the wilderness. Promptly came the order from his royal patron that all the Class IV staff who finished their duty in the afternoon would hereafter sit and listen to his music every Monday.'

Later, Sir Sayaji Rao became quite an admirer and would listen to Faiyaz Khan more than once a week. When the Baroda radio station was installed, Khansaheb's programme did not have a time limit. The station director would often receive calls from the palace. The Maharaja was listening with his family. Closing time would depend on the sweet will of Khansaheb and his patron. The prince, Pratap Singh, was addicted, like all other native princes, to race horses, cricket and frequent sojourns to Europe. The grandson Fateh Singh Rao Gaekwad became the gandabandh pupil of Faiyaz Khan. I had only heard of him as the cricketer and the president of the Board of Control, until I was invited to participate in a festival in memory of the late Aftab-e-mausiqi Ustad Faiyaz Khan years later. While inaugurating the festival, which was held in the same durbar hall, he welcomed all of us and said, 'Faiyaz Khan had not only adorned the Baroda court as the greatest vocalist of his time but was also my guru. After his demise, I have stopped listening to any other musician.' This was a diplomatic statement which was, no doubt, an excellent excuse for his subsequent absence from the festival. Ghulam

Rasool Khan's presence was of considerable encouragement to the gharana artistes, two of whom were Latafat and Sharafat Hussain. Ghulam Rasool Khan showed me the marble screen behind which Faiyaz Khan used to regale minions with his severely classical art.

Faiyaz Khan was steeped in the classical tradition. Therefore, his presentation was, initially, strictly traditional. In course of time, however, he gradually changed the form of khayal as well as that of his thumri. As such, I would not call him a romantic but a neoclassicist. I am not referring to the romanticism in his expressions. I am, of course, using the term romantic in the sense it has been used to connote the movement in literature, art and sculpture implying a protest against classicism which led to revolutionary changes in the form. Faiyaz Khan effected several significant changes without departing from the classical tradition. First, he felt the absence of slow and systematic exposition of raga in the Gwalior khayal, and took resort to the dhrupad alaapchari. This he followed with dhamar and then a drut khayal. Later he often dispensed with the dhamar but went straight to vilambit khayal which was sung in the Gwalior fashion in madhya vilambit tempo (medium slow, in ektaal, jhumra or tilwara). It did not contain vistar but bahlawa, bol-bant, bol-taans and heavy larazdar taans. This was again followed by a drut khayal.

First, the alaapchari. This was strictly a dhrupad alaap with all the alankars which are associated with it. It did not contain the murkees or khatkas associated with khayal. Later on, he occasionally introduced one or two 'gale ka kam' if he was going to sing a khayal after the alaap. His alaap, though it proceeded step by step in the manner of dhrupad, did not have 'meerkhand' or 'khandameru' known in the shastras i.e. mechanical or mathematical combinations of notes. On the other hand, the alaap highlighted the main phrases of the raga without which the 'raag-bhaav', or the anatomical characteristics of the raga, cannot be brought out. This was his speciality.

Pandit Ravi Shankar also remarks that the raga, in his hands, quickly came to life. But though a dhrupadia by tradition, he had glamorised the dhrupad alaap, especially the jod ang—the faster part—just as the been alaap was glamourised and taken to a different level by Pandit Ravi Shankar, Ustad Ali Akbar and Ustad Vilayet Khan. Pandit Ravi Shankar, in his book *Raag Anurag* in Bengali, remembers Faiyaz Khan with a trace of nostalgia, especially for his non tom alaap and the jod ang, which was neither like the been nor like the rabab alap but something which was very much his own. Panditji had not heard the like from anyone before or since. Examples of this are to be found in the AIR archives and in capsule form in his 78 RPM records of Lalit, Raamkali and Darbari. The jod portion of his alaap culminated in gamak jod at fantastic speed. The clarity of the notes and their weight have to be heard to be believed, though the Rajmata of Mahishadal, mother of the late Deba Prasad Garg, is reported to have told Faiyaz Khan that his gamaks represented only four annas (twenty-five per cent) of that of his nana (maternal grandfather) Ghulam Abbas Khan!

When Faiyaz Khan skipped the dhamar and came straight to khayal after his alaap, there was no repetition of the alaap portion in his vilambit khayal. What attracted immediate attention was the bandish bharna, or the manner, in which the composition was sung. First came the nayaki anga, the nibaddha, or the way it had been passed on by the guru. Then came the gayaki anga or the manner in which he sang the phrases of the composition differently, with expression, almost in the manner of a thumri singer. The same technique was used in the bol banana in drut khayal which he obviously borrowed from qawaali. It was followed by embellishments in the shape of short bol-taans and taans which made his arrival at the 'sam', always a bit of an event.

The tehais, which are still prevalent in instrumental music but are now rare in vocal music, heightened the effect. The climax was reached when he came to the taans in 'barabar laya' i.e. at twice the speed of the composition.

These involved halaqs and gamaks, the weight or gravity of which was never sacrificed for the sake of speed—the fetish of classical singers today. He would occasionally take very fast tappa taans in his khayal. One gathers he borrowed this from the gayaki of Ustad Tanras Khan of Delhi, but made it his own.

The bol-bant and layakari prevalent in Gwalior gayaki constitute a special feature of the Agra style. This was especially true of the bol-taans, thanks to their Dhamar tradition, though, of course, taans are taboo in Dhamar. There is an innate sense of rhythm in every person. Khansaheb fully exploited that in his rendering of dhrupad, dhamar and khayal. 'Nritya, vadya aur geet, yeh teen milé to sangeet (Dance, instrument and song, all here together make up music).' All these elements were there in Ustad Faiyaz Khan's music.

Vamanrao Deshpande, in his book *Indian Musical Traditions*, has branded the Agra gharana as extremely taal-oriented and lacking in musicality. He has been careful to exempt Faiyaz Khan whose 'swara', impact, has been recognized by Mr Deshpande. However, according to him Faiyaz Khan did not belong to the Agra gharana but to the rangila named after Ramzan Khan Rangeele, an ancestor of Faiyaz Khan from his father's side. To discuss Agra gayaki without Faiyaz Khan is not unlike staging *Hamlet* without the good prince. It is common knowledge among musicians that Faiyaz Khan's entire talim came from his maternal grandfather Ghulam Abbas Khan, whose 'sureelapan' was a byword in his time. I have already written about his father, Ghagge Khuda Baksh's, extraordinary voice and sureelapan.

Naththan Khan's music attracted high praise from all musicians, particularly Alladiya Khansaheb. Elsewhere, I have mentioned the impact of Abdulla Khan's music on Faiyaz Khan. In the post-Faiyaz Khan era, Sharafat Hussain had a golden voice. He had received excellent talim from his uncle Ata Hussain Khan and father-in-law Vilayet Hussain Khan. His fault lay in that he was over-elaborate and repetitive in his vistar but he never sacrificed sur for taal. It is also a fact that no music conference was complete without Sharafat whose untimely departure was a great misfortune for his gharana. It is true a lot of ustads from the Agra khandaan ruined their voices by trying to imitate Faiyaz Khan's voice, but there were quite a few who did not. Among the disciples who did not, I quote Srikrishna Babbanrao Haldankar from his book[8]:

> 'The Faiyaz Khan stream was perpetuated by musicians like Sohan Singh, Kumar Mukherji, Swami Vallabhdas, Ramarao Nayak and Pandit Ratanjankar and his disciples. The Vilayet Hussain stream was perpetuated by Ramakant Ramnathkar, Saraswatibai Narvekar, Jagannathbuwa Purohit, Ram Marathe and Pandit V.R. Athawala. Pandit Kanebuwa of this stream is no more with us. An altogether different stream was represented by Khadim Hussain Khan.'

Despite being a non-professional for the better part of his life, Babbanrao himself, in my opinion, was an outstanding product of this stream as his gayaki was far more authentic and difficult than that of most ustads of the Agra gharana. His bahlawa, or permutation of notes at medium-slow tempo, with the help of long meends and heavy taans in the Bidar anga, reminded me of what I have heard of Puttan Khan of Atrauli. He was the first guru and uncle of Mushtaq Hussain Khan who, according to Aqil Ahmad, could sing bahlawa for a quarter of an hour. This he did in various combinations with the help of four or five notes, all of them organically interrelated, without repeating himself. Puttan Khan's bahlawa, as distinct from vistar, in a major raga like Todi or Iman could last half an hour without boring the listener.

Other successful disciples of Khadim Hussain and Anwar Hussain Khan were Govindrao Agni, Mohan Chikkarmane, Anjanibai Lolekar, Jyotsna Bhole and Saraswatibai Faterpekar. Potentially the best of all female artistes was Krishna Udiyavarkar who was in college with me and who, for some reason, took saffron and gave up music. Her talent disproved the myth that the Agra gharana gayaki does not suit women. Starting from Zohrabai in the first quarter of the twentieth century, who was considered the greatest in her time, down to Lalit Rao and Lalita Ubhayakar, many took to the Agra style and made a name for themselves. None of them was accused of sacrificing 'tunefulness' for the sake of layakari. However, a few ustads of this gharana, with their harsh voices and offensive mannerisms, and known also for their penchant for unending duels with the tabla players, may have been responsible for the view taken by Vamanrao Deshpande, who started life in the Gwalior gharana, became a disciple of Sureshbabu Mane, son of the great Abdul Karim Khan, and ended up with Jaipur. That being the case, the association of two big names of the Jaipur gharana with Agra should have diluted his prejudice against the Agra gharana. Moghubai Kurdikar learnt from Vilayet Hussain Khan of the Agra gharana, besides, of course, from her original guru Alladiya Khan Sahab. Her daughter Kishori Amonkar also became a gandabandh shagird of Anwar Hussain, younger brother of Khadim Hussain Khan.

Dr Ashok Ranade, noted musicologist and erstwhile professor at the University of Bombay, is of the opinion that it took a bit of courage in Faiyaz Khan's time to sing on a key as low as C or B sharp when there was no microphone. But his open-chested, full-throated voice, with its rich timbre and remarkable volume, was such that even when he dropped his voice and introduced delicate nuances, even the person sitting at the back of the hall could hear him distinctly. He had trained his voice in the manner of the great stage actors like the late Sisir Bhaduri of Bengal, whose monologue in whispers could be heard clearly in the last row.

This is what is known as the fortissimo pianissimo effect in opera music, erroneously called 'modulation' in our country. This was particularly noticeable in Khansaheb's thumri, along with his dramatic alankaar, the Kaku-prayog and pukars (which often brought tears to the eyes of listeners). If our classical music is a branch of the *Natya Shastra*, it has to have an element of drama, not melodrama, as we found in the music of Pandit Omkarnath, Kumar Gandharv and, of late, in the singing of Pandit Jasraj. The dramatic element in Khansaheb's music was heightened by the refrain sung in unison by his shagirds on the tanpuras. He had all the angas in his gayaki and the knack of presenting them in his own inimitable manner. Above all, he had his finger on the pulse of the audience. According to Dr Ranade, 'there was no chink in his armour'.[9]

Ustad Faiyaz Khan got the top prize for khayal, a gold medal, in the 1925 Grand Music Conference arranged by Pandit Bhatkhande. The first prize for dhrupad went to Ustad Zakiruddin Khan and Allabande Khan and the second to the latter's son Nasiruddin Khan. There was no prize for thumri. In fact, none of the participating vocalists, like Mushtaq Hussain Khan, Chandan Chaubey and Ali Baksh Khan (father of Bade Ghulam Ali), sang thumri. No one in the Agra gharana before Faiyaz Khan would dream of singing thumris, dadras and ghazals which were associated with tawayefs.

Dilip Kumar Roy, of Pondichery fame, had spent a fortune touring the whole of India with the sole objective of listening to ustads and tawayefs before he became a sadhu. In his Bengali book *Bhramyamaner Din-panjika*, he mentioned that he was disappointed with the dhrupad singers for their never-ending alaapchari with gamaks, the excessive taanbazi of Mushtaq Hussain Khan and even Faiyaz Khan's khayal in Multani (the reason for which would become clear in the succeeding pages). But for Faiyaz Khan's thumri, he had nothing but the highest praise:

'It was as if Faiyaz Khan had on that day demonstrated conclusively to me 'the precise difference between true music and the counterfeit. Of all the singers participating in this festival [in Lucknow] the greatest unquestionably were Faiyaz Khan and Chandan Chaubey, the famous dhamar singer of Mathura. It is

Dilip Kumar Roy

difficult to say who was greater. While the tonal quality of Chandan Chaubey's voice was undoubtedly sweeter, Faiyaz Khan was probably the more complete singer and a greater artiste . . . his music seemed to come from his life blood. I had already been fascinated by his thumri at Baroda, but in Lucknow he seemed to surpass himself. An artiste, by his own inner quality, can suddenly conjure up a vision of great beauty to the amazement of the beholder or the listener. It is not an effect which can be achieved by mere hard work. If a certain extra, a divine inspiration does not illumine from within, no amount of practice or effort can produce the exquisite cascade of sensation that Abdul Karim or Faiyaz Khan can. There is no truth in the absurd saying that genius is the capacity of taking infinite pains: Allabande Khan could never aspire to the genius of Faiyaz Khan just as Ramdas Paramanik, my barber, could never write poetry like Rabindranath Tagore. The visions and sounds which Faiyaz gave us in that morning session of Bhairavi belong to this category. His rendering of thumri proved what an extremely superior genre this can be. It was no ordinary rendering of thumri. He brought to it a unique gravity that was peculiarly his own. He synthesized in his thumri the gamak of the dhrupad, the sparkling rhythmic halak taans from khayal, the grainy quality of tappa and rippling meends of the thumri. The total effect was indescribably enthralling. When Nasiruddin Khan sang his alaap and dhrupad earlier, it had seemed to me that nothing could ever destroy the mind-blowing vision of his Mayapuri magic palace. The magic of Faiyaz Khan's thumri almost erased the deeply ingrained memory of Nasiruddin Khan's alaap. This was no mean achievement.'

My father, D.P. Mukherjee, had joined the university as a young lecturer a few years prior to this event. Thanks to his passion for music and his closeness to Pandit Bhatkhande, I was able to obtain his comments on his boyhood friend Dilip Kumar Roy's version, whom he compared to a horse with blinkers. In his opinion:

'Dilip did not have the musical sense to appreciate Allabande and Zakiruddin Khan. Those who have not heard the trio, Allabande, Zakiruddin and Nasiruddin, do not know what heights dhrupad alaapchari can attain. I have never heard such use of meends and shrutis. With the help of the physics department of the university, we hung a series of clay pitchers from the ceiling of the old white baradari hall of the Nawabs of Oudh to help the acoustics. There was no microphone of course. Mushtaq Hussain, though he overdid his taans, sang well. Faiyaz Khan, in the previous evening's session, did not sing his khayal very well, largely because he was violently sick before his recital through imbibing large doses of whisky in the bathroom. Bhatkhandeji had warned me against this and specifically asked me to keep an eye on Faiyaz. How the devil was I expected to know that he had a bottle hidden in the toilet! We were all frightfully disappointed, indeed shocked that he had made such an ass of himself. Faiyaz Khan was also deeply embarrassed. He was young then, no more than in his early forties, which made him a toddler in that august company of venerable ustads. He went with folded hands to the organizers, Thakur Nawab Ali, Bhatkhandeji and others, and asked for a half-hour's session in the morning. And would you believe it, the half-hour ran to two! The crowd would not let him go. Nine gold medals were awarded by the public which largely consisted of Rajas and Nawabs of UP, and they knew their music. I also remember Aldous Huxley, who came with the Nawab of Chhatari. You will find this mentioned in his *Jesting Pilate*.

Faiyaz Khan told his brother-in-law Ata Hussain that the audience had got tired of dhrupad, dhamar and khayal. What the festival needed was a touch of the lighter stuff. For Lucknow, he chose '*Babul mora naihar chuto jai*', the famous Bhairavi thumri of Wajid Ali Shah, the last Nawab of Oudh who was banished by the British to Metiabruz in Calcutta. The venue was the same baradari of the Nawab whose legendary pursuit of music, poetry and beautiful women still lingered in the memory of the older generation. Khansaheb, who was in the habit of introducing couplets from famous Urdu poets into his thumris and dadras, chose the last Mughal Emperor Bahadur Shah Zafar's '*Daro diwar par hasratse nazar karte hain, khush raho ahle watan hum to safar karte hain*'. Such was the impact of the music that Ata Hussain Khan behind the tanpura could scarcely hold back his tears. 'Bhaisahab looked back to admonish me for not giving him support and found me in tears,' Ata Hussain Khan told me. '*Hai, woh sab kya din the* (Those were the days of great music.)'

I remember two programmes compered by S.K. Chaubey on Lucknow radio. The first one ran to a full one hour in which Ustad Faiyaz Khan took on the role of Miyan Tansen singing dhrupad in Darbari Kanhra and Miyan ki Malhar before the Emperor Akbar (played by Chaubey). The second consisted of thumris and dadras where Faiyaz Khan adopted the role of the famous Ustad Moijuddin Khan.

Those who heard him—and they included Thakur Jaidev Singh, Amiya Nath Sanyal and my father—swore that it was not possible for anyone to sing in a mehfil after Moijuddin. The great Rahmat Khan, son of the legendary Haddu Khan of Gwalior, wept profusely after hearing Moijuddin in Benaras, and wanted to give up singing. It was the same Rahmat Khan whom Abdul Karim Khan imitated and whose taans Bhaskarbuwa copied! Faiyaz Khan used to say that no one in the Agra gharana had ever sung thumri, dadras and ghazals before him. One gathers from Ustad Alladiya Khan's memories that Mehboob Khan (Daras Piya), father-in-law of Faiyaz Khan, composed thumris besides khayal. He never sang thumris in public but taught Zohrabai Agrewali. The khandaani ustads would have died of shame if any of their progeny had been heard singing what they considered the prerogative of the courtesans and tawayefs. But Bhaiyya Saheb Ganpat Rao of the royal family of Gwalior, and his brilliant disciple Moijuddin Khan, gave this genre a new respectability. Faiyaz Khan admitted that it was Moijuddin and his disciple Malkajan, with whom young Faiyaz had a romantic involvement, who inspired him to sing thumris. From Moijuddin's old 78 RPM records recently reissued in cassettes by HMV, one can, however, detect precious little resemblance to Faiyaz Khan's *'Bajubandh khul khul jaye'* (Bhairavi), *'Bande nanda kumaram'* (Kafi) or his *'Mere jubna pe ayi bahar'* (Dadra), all available with HMV in 78 RPM.

Talking of thumri, Ustad Faiyaz Khan's most memorable triumph before the grand conference at Lucknow was at Mysore, one of the richest states in British India. The Maharaja himself, an accomplished piano-player and composer of several kritis in Karnatak music, was also a great patron of Hindustani music. Ustad Naththan Khan, grandnephew of Ghagge Khuda Baksh, adorned the Maharaja's court. When Faiyaz Khan gave his memorable performance in the Mysore court he was in his early thirties. To quote from Dipali Nag's book on Ustad Faiyaz Khan[10]:

'The court was rich with the presence of Shishodia Mohia Bhagvat of Karnatak. Hafiz Khan of Kirana gharana and Bashir Khan, who excelled at taans. The Maharaja of Mysore wanted some excitement and arranged for a duel between his court musician Hafiz Khan and Faiyaz Khan. What he envisaged was more of an intellectual confrontation between the two ustads. Waze, the household officer, announced that a gold medal studded with precious stones would be given to the winner. The eminence of these musicians and the possibility of a brilliant encounter drew people from far and wide. Musicians like Naththan Khan and his sons Abdullah Khan and Vilayet Hussain Khan were already there. Ghulam Abbas, then 92, advised Faiyaz to tune his tanpura half a note higher and requested Hafiz to tune his half a note lower. The air of expectancy was everywhere.

Finally, it began. The competition of dhrupad and khayal between the two musicians held everybody in raptures, and it was difficult to decide who had more claims to the coveted prize from the king. One, two, three, four, five, six days went by. It was on the seventh day that the king wanted to listen to thumri. Unfortunately, like most senior gharana ustads those days, Hafiz Khan did not indulge in thumri and Faiyaz Khan did. Being the only contestant, he sang with great confidence and created a world of infinite beauty with his music. The Maharaja was visibly overwhelmed and made his decision. Faiyaz Khan won the medal, four shawls, two big thaals and several thousand rupees.'

Years later, Ustad Faiyaz Khan, the undisputed number one in Hindustan after Abdul Karim Khan's death, was given the title of 'Aftab-e-Mausiqi', the 'Sun among Musicians', by the very same court of Mysore in 1938.

It is also mentioned in Dipali Nag's book that Sri Sayaji Rao Gaekwad, Maharaja of Baroda, through exceedingly pleased and proud of the title bestowed by Mysore on the Baroda court musician, could not but feel that it would have been in the fitness of things for him to have the privilege of honouring Faiyaz Khan with titles and riches instead of allowing the Maharaja of Mysore to have an edge over him. After a couple of months he issued an order which entitled the great ustad to sit next to the Maharaja in the durbar, resplendent in jewellery and medals. On his next birthday, Gaekwad presented Khansaheb with a purse of 11,000 rupees and conferred on him the title of 'Sangeet Ratna' (Jewel of Song). It is of some interest that there was the usual increment of twenty-five rupees in his pay scale which coincided with this solemn occasion.

Faiyaz Khan had become a legend in his lifetime. His music, his dignified carriage, regal manners, unstinted praise for other musicians and generosity—the last almost to a fault—made him fit to consort with the aristocrats of his day. The late Deba Prasad Garg, the Raja of Mahishadal, who was one of Khansaheb's favourite disciples, once mentioned to me that if there was even a remote possibility of controversy, Khansaheb would quickly bypass it with *'Kya kahna!'*, his favourite expression. In fact, he had told Garg that opinions among musicians invariably differed and often differed violently. One should never take sides on the basis of preferences, because one's own taste and judgment are not sacrosanct. Imagine such advice from the mouth of a professional musician whose custom those days, no different now, was to praise one to one's face with plenty of *'Masha Allahs'* and *'Subhan Allahs'* and say *'taoba taoba'* behind one's back!

There are anecdotes galore about Faiyaz Khan's generous nature. In 1944, a few of my college friends in Lucknow got together and formed a circle which was inaugurated by a performance by Ustad Faiyaz Khan followed by Bismillah Khan and Shrikrishna Ratanjankar. Sharafat Hussain, who was a lad of twelve or thirteen then, sang Kedara wearing a cap embroidered with zari on a freshly-shaven head. That day Khansaheb's alaap in Iman scarcely touched the teevra madhyam, followed by a matching asthayee, *'Gori surat mana bhai re,'* which I have not heard from any other member of the gharana since. I also remember a superb halaq taan from the taar saptak in Darbari, which drew instant applause that evoked a smile from him and a caution that this taan was from Vrindabani Sarang, *'Isko kabhi mat lena'!*

The following morning, I visited him in the Empire Hotel with great trepidation and only sixty-nine rupees against the hundred and one we had offered and which itself was a trifle compared to Khansaheb's usual fees in those days. I need not have worried. The ustad heard my tale of woe, took the money, added thirty one rupees from his purse and gave it back to me, muttering to himself that Allah would promptly despatch him to Jahannam (Hades) if he robbed the pocket-money of children.

Unnao railway station is on the Lucknow-Kanpur line. The stationmaster had a dream. He wanted to host a soiree of Khansaheb's music. On the occasion of his son's sacred-thread ceremony he approached Thakur Jaidev Singh who at that time was teaching in the D.A.V. College in Kanpur. Thakursaheb assured him that Khansaheb could be persuaded to come to sing in Unnao for a fee of eight hundred rupees, which would include his railway fare from Baroda. When Khansaheb arrived in the morning to stay with his host, he took Thakursaheb aside and whispered to him that the gentleman concerned did not appear to be particularly affluent and what did Thakursaheb imagine his earnings would be? 'Oh, I don't think they would be more than a hundred and fifty a month at the most'. 'Good Lord!' exclaimed Khansaheb. 'That means the poor man is going to spend more than six months' pay on me!' Having said that he quietly went out for a stroll to the bazaar.

Thakursaheb remembers that the mehfil in the evening was one of the best and Faiyaz Khan treated the host with the same courtesy which he would extend to a feudal lord, repeatedly asking for his 'farmaish'. The following morning he accepted his return ticket and nothing else. Then he called the child whose sacred-thread ceremony was to be performed and presented him with a gold ring in a velvet case. Thakursaheb was ninety when he recounted this incident with tears in his eyes. At that great age he found it difficult, I suppose, not to allow his emotions overcome him.

Latafat Hussain Khan recollected a trip to Himmatnagar with the ustad on the occasion of the Raja's birthday. It was the custom of the subjects to leave their 'nazrana' on a huge silver plate in front of the ruler who gave them his annual 'darshan'. Before Khansaheb gave his recital, the Raja made it a point to display the huge plate to his durbar. The contents, according to Latafat Khan, ran easily to 20,000 rupees, which was presented to Faiyaz Khan after his recital. Khansaheb bowed low and accepted the gift with appropriate words of gratitude. He then made an unusual request. He asked that the entire domestic staff be assembled before him. The Raja of Himmatnagar, though he found the request strange, promptly asked the hundred-and-fifty-odd servants to gather before him, whereupon Ustad Faiyaz Khan handed over the entire plate to the headman for distribution with the announcement that that was a gift from their Raja on the auspicious occasion of his birthday.

This, however, is not the end of the story. When dinner was served, Khansaheb and his retinue were completely taken aback to find the Raja waiting on the guests at the table in the livery of the major domo. He smiled and informed his guests, 'Let me have the honour of waiting on Khansaheb. He is not only the greatest musician of Hindustan. He is truly the Badshah, the Emperor, I am a mere Raja of a small riyasat.'

In money matters Faiyaz Khan was not merely generous, he was also careless. Mohan Kapoor, the nephew of the late Damodardas Khanna who was the chief organizer of the All India Music Conferences in Calcutta, was then living in Bombay. He was a frequent visitor to Jaddan Bai's house and would arrange special soirees of Khansaheb's music at her place almost every month. He also wanted Faiyaz Khan to sing compositions which featured the name 'Mohan'. A number of bandishes was composed by Khansaheb like '*Nadan ankhiya lagi mohanso*' in Jayjaiwanti and '*Nainso dekhi ek jhalak mohanso*' in Sughrai, which were later recorded by the Hindustan Recording Company. After the first of these compositions was presented by Faiyaz Khan in a private recital hosted by Mohan Kapoor, he gave him an envelope, which Khansaheb tucked in the pocket of his silk sherwani and forgot all about. When the washerman returned the envelope, he opened it and found a single currency note. He called Ghulam Rasool and said, 'Have a look at this. I have never seen the like of such a note before. How much money is this?' Ghulam Rasool was astonished to find that it was a thousand-rupee currency note which Khansaheb had absentmindedly consigned with the dirty clothes for the weekly washing! Khansaheb kept quiet for a minute and said 'How would I know, Ghulam Rasool, that the envelope which Mohan Kapoor gave me had a thousand rupees when he had already paid my fees for the recital? At my age, I am not expected to remember these details. Anyway, imagine a raees paying a thousand rupees for a bandish! If my late father-in-law Daras Piya were alive he would be minting money today, wouldn't he?'

Anecdotes about Faiyaz Khan would be incomplete without the mention of Ustad Jagatguru Mullick of Calcutta who incidentally was the guru of Khansaheb's two other cronies, Ustad Hafiz Ali Khan and Ustad Inayet Khan. To the present generation they need to be reintroduced as the fathers of Ustad Amjad Ali Khan and Ustad Vilayet Khan. The incidental reason behind Jagatguru's exalted position was that he owned a liquor shop in Dharmatala, Calcutta. He also was fond of taking taans and sargams covering five octaves which were such a constant source of entertainment to his disciples that they could not help calling on their guru at his shop whenever they felt like a drink.

Their horse-driven carriage would be parked outside and the three shagirds would troop in with Faiyaz Khan leading the procession and a servant bringing up the rear with an empty basket. Faiyaz Khan, after he bent and touched the guru's knees, would explain his difficulty in reproducing the particularly difficult taan which Guruji had taught him three days earlier. Sheltered behind Faiyaz Khan's broad back,

Hafiz Ali Khan would promptly start filling the basket with an assortment of their favourite tipples. I have heard a tape of Jagatguru and am of the opinion that the great homeopath musician Bhawnra Piya of Agra just about pips him to the post. For sustained entertainment he is marginally superior to Jagatguru. The followers of the Buddhist scriptures who firmly believe that life is a long tale of sorrow and misery (*Sarvam Dukkham*) should have free access to these private tapes, currently in the archives of the ITC Sangeet Research Acdemy in Calcutta.

Faiyaz Khan had a quiet sense of humour. A friend of ours, Farhat Sayeed Khan, the second son of the Nawab of Chhatar, never sang but decided to become the gandabandh disciple of Ustad Faiyaz Khan after hearing him once. The family virtually owned half of Aligarh, and Rahat Manzil, where the recital took place, was an imposing palace. The recital was memorable and at its conclusion, one of the distinguished listeners started to praise Khansaheb, ending up by calling him the Miyan Tansen of the twentieth century. Precisely at that time, a small mouse went running past and disappeared through the door. With a pleasant smile the ustad thanked the gentleman profusely for his eulogies, '*Arre main kis kabil hoon!* I am only a singer of moderate stature. When Miyan Tansen, his guru Swami Haridas or Baiju Bawra sang, herds of deer would come and listen to their divine music. My music makes even a tiny mouse run away.'

Rabindranath Tagore, who grew up under the influence of Jadu Bhatta, the legendary dhrupad singer of Bengal, preferred dhrupad to other forms of music, especially khayal. That Ustad Faiyaz Khan had sung for him at his ancestral palace at Jorasanko in north Calcutta is known to very few. To me it is an event comparable to the meeting of Beethoven with Goethe. My father and Deba Prasad Garg were present. Tagore sat through the recital with closed eyes as if in a trance. Khansaheb sang atop, dhrupad and khayal in Raamkali, followed by thumri in Bhairavi for the greatest '*shayer*' (poet) of Hindustan.' Tagore paid him a nazrana of twenty-one gold

mohurs and said, 'Look at this man! It took him only a
moment to knock off fifty years from my age.'

Let me end the anecdotes about Ustad Faiyaz Khan with
the one from the reminiscences of Syed Muztaba Ali, the
famous writer and a 'pir murshid' (spiritual guide) of the world
of Bengali *adda*, whose background included student days in
Santiniketan, a year at the Al-Hazar university of Cairo, a
few years as a teacher in Kabul, a doctorate in comparative
religions from the university of Bonn and quite a few years in
Baroda college when Faiyaz Khan was there. The story is to
be found in his book *Panchatantra* in Bengali:

> 'I have no idea what Chaudhuri had said to his guru
> Khansaheb. One day, he turned up, large as life, at
> my doorstep. I was stunned. How would I receive
> him? Where would I ask him to sit? I could not for
> the life of me decide. Not even a visit from Maharaja
> Sayaji Rao himself would have found me feeling at
> once so proud and so helpless.
>
> 'And the ustad! You won't believe this—he took
> both my hands in his and repeatedly pressed them to
> his bosom, he seemed even more nonplussed than I
> was. In truly courtly style he bowed to me. Apparently,
> somebody had told him, to my eternal mortification,
> that I came from a lineage of great teachers and that
> I had acquired my knowledge at Al-Hazar, Cairo, the
> great seat of learning in the Muslim world—so much
> so that the Maharaja had himself brought me from
> there to Baroda.
>
> 'Why am I telling you all this? It is to explain to
> you how simple and innocent the great Faiyaz Khan
> was, the Shahenshah, the king of kings, of the world
> of music. Much later, I realized that just as he stood
> at the summit of the world of music, he genuinely
> believed that if Sayaji Rao thought highly of me, I
> must similarly be at the top in my field. If he had
> found favour with royalty for his knowledge and

great artistry, the same logic, in his mind, would no doubt apply to me.

'We met frequently after this at music soirees. There were also intimate personal meetings. I often tried to explain to him, 'Look, Ustad! Many kings will come and go, many Shams-ul-ulemas and supreme intellectuals. For that matter, even the Diwan (Chief Minister) of Baroda with his seemingly endless pomp will depart and be duly replaced, but who knows when the likes of you will come again? I shall in my own lifetime see other kings and other diwans but no one like you.

'He was an incredibly handsome man even in middle age. The face, the complexion, the moustache, all together made me feel he was the 'Nandakumar' of his own song, except that Nandakumar (Sri Krishna) had a dark skin while he was very fair. "When may I come and sing?" he asked. "*Tauba, tauba*," I softly swore, "why should you take the trouble, Khansaheb? I shall go to you some evening, with your permission." At his own insistence, however, he came frequently. He would arrive at seven in the evening and stay often till five the following morning. On many occasions he gave me a glimpse of 'bahisht', (heaven) which none else has been able to do since his death. Knowing that I loved his rendering of *Nandakumar*, he sang it for an hour and a half for a humble, insignificant listener like me.

'But how much more can I write? I can only say that he reigns supreme in a large chunk of my happiest memories.

'Let me conclude with one last anecdote. I had once organized a soiree at my house at the request of a Bengali lady residing in Baroda. Ustad was in great form that day. The temperature had been as high as 114°F that afternoon in Baroda. It was unbearably hot even at night and the monsoon was still two months away. Ustad sang for three hours and then looked to the lady for requests. After much persuasion the shy young lady said "Megh Malhar" in a thin, hesitating voice. The ustad responded immediately.

'It was as if he poured all his years of training, his creativity, his heritage, the skills of his forefathers and his entire genius into the magic of that rendering. I sat entranced, absorbing the music through my ears, my eyes, through every pore of the skin and every fibre of my being. And just then, outside, there were raindrops! There was pandemonium in the mehfil— some rushed to congratulate the ustad, some gazed at him transfixed in awe as if they were witnessing a miracle, one or two of his admirers cavorted on the farsh (carpet) like bumpkins—I can't describe the event. Justice can be done to it by someone who has the same precious gift and inspiring power with the pen.

'The ustad did not respond with the deep salaams with which he normally received applause or praise. After a salaam or two he sat quietly with his palm against his cheek, not uttering a word and in deep thought. I was puzzled.

'Even after this he sang through the night to daybreak. After the last Bhairavi, when the guests had left, he bade me farewell. I suggested he take a bit of rest after such an exhausting performance. A long silence ensued while the ustad looked at me with a peculiar expression on his face, the meaning of which I could not fathom. In a voice filled with humility and pathos he finally said to me, "Tell me, Syed Sahab, why do people embarrass me in this fashion? Can I possibly bring the rains down with my Megh Malhar?"

'I answered without hesitating, "That Allah alone can answer. What I do know, he was with you last night."'

Ustad Faiyaz Khan died on November 5, 1950. About fifteen years later, I had occasion to visit Baroda again. In Independent India, the Maharaja was now an ordinary citizen like you and me, though with remnants of a few privileges and wealth, which you and I cannot aspire to. I finished my business in course of the day and was due to leave for Bombay the following morning. In the evening, I had an urge to place flowers and light a candle on Ustad Faiyaz Khan's grave. Baroda was now part of the state of Gujarat. Like the French, the Gujaratis refuse to speak or comprehend any language but their own. I had quite a problem buying candles. The smaller shopkeepers had no idea what I was looking for. Thanks to a kindly fellow-shopper I learnt that a candle was not a '*mombatti*' but a '*membatti*', perhaps on account of its white colour.

I would not have found the grave that day, had it not been for Ustad Ghulam Rasool Khan. If people had not heard of Faiyaz Khan, it was hardly likely that they would know about his final resting place. Ghulam Rasool Khan solved my problem by asking a young lad to accompany me. The car traversed many a small lane and a byway in the city before it stopped outside a garage. Inside, two boys, ill-clad in grease-stained shorts were going hammer and tongs on the skeleton of an old car. All around were scattered the tools of their trade and used tyres. We crossed over the obstacles and through the rear door of the garage reached a small open space. Several goats grazed there amidst a number of unmarked graves. In one corner there was a grave with a marble canopy. Beneath lay in eternal sleep Aftab-a-Mausiqi Ustad Faiyaz Khan, the last emperor of the golden age of Hindustani music.

6

Jaipur Gharana and Ustad Alladiya Khan

Ustad Alladiya Khan lived from the middle of the nineteenth century to the middle of the twentieth. Even in that star-studded era, when ustads emerged in the dozens in every region, Alladiya Khan could safely be called a genius. He came from a distinguished family of dhrupad singers. Yet he not only sang khayal but within the confines of tradition, he created a new school, a new Khayal gharana, which has now run to three generations and has produced eminent singers like Manji Khan, Kesarbai, Moghubai, Mallikarjun Mansoor, Nivruttibuwa Sarnaik, Kishori Amonkar, Gajanan Rao Joshi and his disciple Ulhas Kashalkar. Alladiya Khan, a great musician and a system-builder, was fortunate enough to have seen his gharana flourish and gain increasing popularity in his lifetime.

Son of a versatile dhrupad singer, Ahmed Khan, the court musician of Uniyara, a small state near Jaipur in Rajasthan, Alladiya was originally named Ghulam Ahmed Khan. Unlike the sons of the ustads of his time, Alladiya went to school and learnt Arabic and Persian. Side by side, lessons in music were given to him by his father, and grandfather Juggan Khan. Ahmed Khan died at the age of eighty, leaving behind his teenage son to provide for a family of twelve. If young Alladiya were to pursue his studies he would at best be a teacher in a madarsa, earning ten to fifteen rupees a month. It was better, everybody thought, that he should learn his ancestral business. Jahangir Khan, the uncle, took charge of the boy. In the next ten or twelve years, training was imparted to Alladiya in great earnestness.

Jahangir Khan left Uniyara and entered the service of Nawab Kallan Khan, brother of Nawab Kalbe Khan of Rampur, who took up permanent residence in Jaipur. 'My training,' says Khansaheb in his memoirs, 'went on even when my uncle was employed in singing for the nawab. As soon as he returned home from the court, he sat down to teach us. In this way, I continued to memorise compositions for three years... He made us practise separately. I used to sing all night. My uncle would stay up and I would practise in front of him. My memory was good and I managed to learn dhrupads, dhamars and asthayees[1] of ten or fifteen ragas in a single day. In this way, I learnt 10,000 or 12,000 compositions from Jahangir Khan Sahab, and by Allah's grace I remember them to this day.'

Should the reader think this is an exaggeration, I quote what Alladiya Khan had to say about his father, Ahmed Khan, who, according to him, knew 25,000 compositions in dhrupad and dhamar:

'I sang at the court of Maharaja Ram Singhji of Jaipur. All the musicians of Jaipur were very fond of me and were happy with my singing. When I went to pay my tributes to Bahram Khan Sahab (who was ninety or ninety-five years old and had become blind with age) said to people present, "I have never heard a singer like his father. He knew innumerable compositions." He used to touch his ears as a mark of respect whenever he heard my father's name. He was a great friend of my father and often visited Taunk when my father was alive.

'Once they were conversing about music in the afternoon. Bahram Khan expressed his wish to hear a few dhrupads in Shuddha sarang, a raga sung in the afternoon. It was about three then. My father sang dhrupads in Shuddha sarang and continued till six. It was getting so late that Bahram Khan said, "Let us stop now. It is time for namaz. Your memory is truly astounding". They used to discuss music together for long hours. Once, they were arguing about the raga Barari Todi. In the end, Bahram Khan had to accept the interpretation of our gharana and learnt our dhrupad *'Birhan baawari begi sudh liyo pyaare'.'*

Incidentally, Raja Deba Prasad Garg of Mahishadal had learnt the same dhrupad from Muzaffar Khan who belonged to a different gharana. Also, he claimed he had heard Alladiya Khan sing the same composition in khayal.

Bahram Khan, the great-great-grandfather of the late Moinuddin and Aminuddin Dagar, was a famous dhrupadiya; but when he proposed to teach young Alladiya, Ahmed Khan did not consent because Bahram Khan was from the Dhadhi community. It is intriguing indeed that Alladiya Khan, coming from a famous khandaan of dhrupad singers and acutely conscious of it, should turn to khayal and eventually receive widespread recognition as the founder of a new khayal gayaki. Govind Rao Tembe, a well-known harmonium-player, playwright, actor and disciple of Alladiya Khan, has written a biography of his guru in Marathi wherein he traces the switchover to khayal to an incident in Amleta, a small state in Rajasthan. The Raja of Amleta, a connoisseur of dhrupads, was very keen on Alladiya Khan's singing and would invite him often to his court. Once he made Alladiya sing for a whole week, morning and evening. This apparently damaged Khansaheb's voice. It took him months to recover from it and even when he did the 'taaseer', the bloom, was gone forever. This is probably the time when he discarded the gamaks of Khandarbani dhrupad and decided to change over to khayal permanently. Again, this does not often qualify as an adequate explanation for the transformation. Alladiya Khan's memoirs, however, indicate that he not only learnt asthayees[2] from his uncle but also continued to impress aficionados all over the country with his khayal in his youth. Here, for instance, are a couple of memorable occasions in his own words:

'One day, Nazir Khan was singing in the Jodhpur court. Mirach Khan was accompanying him on the sarangi. He gave excellent accompaniment to Nazir Khan. Mirach was from Delhi and he had laboured so hard sitting in front of the dargah of Hazrat Nizamuddin Auliya that his right hand was permanently curved as if he was holding the bow, the fingers of his left hand were stiff and bent and his bottom was hard like the heel of the foot from so much exercise and sitting... Through the grace of Hazrat he became so skilled that no sarangi player in the country could ever play khayal like him on the sarangi. Especially difficult ragas like Kamod Nat—I have never heard anyone play them like Mirach did. When Nazir Khan finished singing, the Maharaja ordered me to start. I began and gradually came to *'firat'* [a variety of fast taans] after developing the raga and a few brief bol-taans which use the words of the composition].

'Mirach was accompanying me very well. After a while, I rendered such a forceful and intricate fikra that Mirach was left staring. He tried to reproduce it but started putting his instrument down. I said, "What are you doing? Please continue, you are playing very well." But he would not agree and replied, "I will just play the sur. I cannot keep up with you." Putting the instrument down he addressed the Maharaja, "Your Majesty, Alladiya's music is so difficult that I cannot accompany him properly. The phrase that he just executed was so heavy and forceful that when I tried to play it, it seemed my wrist and fingers would break. He took the bow in his hand and, looking at Nazir Khan, exclaimed, "I could swallow up such singers and shove the bow into their throats."'

And again:

'I went to Calcutta where I stayed for a year or more. At a function Aliya-Fattu (Ali Baksh and Fateh Ali Khan of Patiala gharana) were singing and so was I. They started the recital and after every taan they would say, *"Janaab,* these are not taans but cannon-balls." That was in fact true. They were really very skilled and rendered taans in a very forceful manner. A very old gentleman known as Mirza Sahab was present. He was a hundred, maybe even more. He had been a student of Mir Ali Soz who was very famous for his 'Soz' and 'Mirsiya' compositions in every raga. Aliya and Fattu sang and then my turn came. As soon as I started, Mirza Sahab stood up and gestured to me to stop. It seemed as if the ground was slipping from under my feet and I thought I had made some horrible mistake. But Mirza looked at Aliya and Fattu and indicating me said, "Children, truly you should have been gunners. But the real music has started only now." Hearing this I was relieved and sang with great enthusiasm.'

Ustad Alladiya Khan does not spare even his friend, Naththan Khan of Agra, whom he addressed as Bhaisahab:

'In Allahabad Bhai Naththan Khan and I sang together with great energy. There was a great deal of cutting across each other's taans. Nazir Khan and Azam Khanji were very pleased with my singing and they held me close and prayed for my health and long life. Naththan Khan on that day wanted especially to surpass me but with the blessings of my elders I sang better and more complicated taans than he did and my singing was full of verve and great skill.'

All these events described by Khansaheb took place much before Amleta. While it does not indicate excessive modesty on his part, it is clear that he had made his name more as a singer of khayal than of dhrupad and dhamar.

But what was his style like? We have three clues. First, the ustad whose khayal gayaki exercised the greatest influence on young Alladiya Khan, Bade Mubarak Ali Khan. Second is a detailed examination of the gayaki of his disciples. The third will be the direct evidence of those who heard him and have tried to describe it in their books or to us. It is extremely unfortunate that no gramophone record of his exists although he died as late as 1946. Neither can I remember him singing on the radio although quite a few of his disciples did.

The one singer whom Alladiya Khan put on a pedestal above everyone else was Mubarak Ali Khan, the illegitimate son of Bade Muhammad Khan of Rewa, whose style was imitated by Haddu and Hassu Khan. Alladiya Khan had the opportunity of learning from Mubarak Ali Khan but refused to do so because, in his own words, 'I was afraid of compromising the reputation of my family tradition.... Singers of my family never learnt from people whose musical lineage was uncertain... He loved me very much and kept insisting that I learn from him. I, however, did not do so. Today I realize what a great mistake I made at that time and feel sorry for it.'

Elsewhere he says:

'I have not heard a singer like Mubarak Ali Khan Sahab in my whole life. Tanras Khan, Haddu Khan and he were in reality the three gods of music. It is not possible to imagine the way they used to sing. Mubarak Ali Khan Sahab's firat was extremely skilful and intricate... His taans would unroll as if they were threads of silk woven together. He would create such an intricate web out of them that listeners would be awestruck and wonder how he would get out of it.

But it was child's play for him. He would get out of
it as if he was separating each strand from another.
His taans were difficult to comprehend. If he sang a
fikra in the five-beat rhythmic pattern, thousands of
fikras would emerge from it. The wonder of it was
that each one would have its own distinct beauty but
the rhythmic pattern would be the same. His taans
were calculated with the precise perfection of an
arrow. Suppose it was a taan of two rhythmic cycles,
the listener would be counting the beats, and when
the two cycles were about to end and the third about
to begin, he would surprise everybody by reaching
the sam with such precision that people could neither
nod nor indicate the sam. His hikka taans would soar
up like a whirlwind and explode, showering flowers
of different kinds. When he began to sing taans, he
would rub his palms together and fikras would reel
off, one more beautiful than the other. And, in the
name of Allah, the fikras were so heart-wrenching! It
is impossible that such a singer be born again.'

We will presently examine the close similarity of the taans
described here with those of Kesarbai. She was the only one
who worked harder than anyone else on Alladiya Khansaheb's
talim for years.

The only time I heard Ustad Alladiya Khan was in 1942,
when he was eighty-seven and I was a lad of fifteen with
indistinct comprehension of what the great man had to offer.
He sang Nayaki Kanhra, so I was told, and much later, I
heard the same composition, 'Mero piya rasiya', from other
members of the Jaipur gharana. What I remember after sixty
years were the shuddh akar and resounding gamaks in his
taans. Years later I heard similar gamak taans from Mallikarjun
Mansoor's recital of raga Bhausakh at the Calcutta Music
Circle's conference in the early Seventies. Such gamak taans
of Khansaheb may have had their origin in the following
story narrated by him:

'One day, I had gone to Mubarak Ali Khan Sahab's house. It was evening and he was sitting on a cot in the courtyard. Bahram Khan, Ghagge Khuda Baksh, Mohammad Ali Khan and Khairat Ali Khan were sitting around him. Bahram Khan was fond of making mischief and he was making fun of everyone... Finally he came to Mubarak Ali, saying, "What kind of music do you khayaliyas sing! *'Ooi meri ye lagi, ooi meri wo lagi!* (That's my this, and that's my that!)' Mubarak Ali got angry and took up such a forceful gamak taan that the legs of the cot broke and it crashed. All of them were caught in the ropes of the charpoy. We ran up to them and extracted each one. All of them were ashen-faced. Mubarak Ali said, "If anyone tried to sing a forceful gamak taan like this he would be spitting blood. Such is the way we khayaliyas sing." Indeed it was a taan of that kind.'

Before we come to Alladiya Khan's disciples, most of whom I have heard, I cannot resist quoting yet another incident from Alladiya Khan's memoirs when his 'three gods of music' sang together:

'Once, Haidar Bakshji had invited Haddu Khan over. I too was present on the occasion. Haddu Khan started singing. Then he executed a good fikra, and seeing that it had been successful, he recited a riddle: "*Chaar ghade ras ke bhare, chor take le na sake* (four pots of honey and the thief couldn't take any)." Tanras Khan and Mubarak Ali were present. They stood up angrily and demanded an explanation. Haddu Khan replied, "*Mujhe jo kahna tha wo maine kah diya, ab himmat ho to saath baith ke gaao* (I have said what I wanted to, come and sing with me if you have the guts)." So Tanras Khan and Mubarak Ali started singing with Haddu Khan. They continued to sing the same composition, and when the taans started, it seemed like a cockfight. When Tanras

Khan was singing it seemed that nobody could possibly sing better but when Mubarak Ali started one had the vision of a new and strange world. His singing was difficult, with complex and incomparable taans. This went on for an hour. It was a shower of taans, one better than the other and all the singers were firm in their respective places. Seeing that no one was retreating, Haidar Baksh stood up and said with folded hands, "For Allah's sake, please stop now. Come and have your dinner." Everybody was happy and sat down to eat. They joked with one another and talked about other things. The great thing about singers, those days, was that they did not let bad feelings linger for long. Quarrels ended as soon as they began.'

Later in his memoirs Alladiya Khan mentions that some purists criticized Haddu and Hassu Khan as 'rang bhariye' singers, those who sacrifice purity for the sake of adding colour. Their virtuosity and artistry were often at the cost of raagdari. Tanras Khan was meticulous about raga depiction and truly magnificent. Mubarak Ali Khansaheb, according to Alladiya Khan, was incomparable. He had not heard such music before or since and it must be remembered that Alladiya Khan belonged to the golden age of Hindustani classical music. One thing is clear, however, Mubarak Ali Khan's style was taan pradhan. So was Alladiya Khan's. Despite being a dhrupadiya he cared little for slow unfolding of a raga, the alaap or vistar. His stock of khayals was from the Manarang and Agra gharanas, possibly due to his close association with the Bombay branch of the Agra gharana when he stayed with Naththan Khan's family in Babulnath. He also composed a large number of bandishes and often changed dhrupad compositions into khayals.

We will try and analyze this Jaipur style in greater detail in this chapter. For the moment we are concerned with Alladiya Khan's gayaki and how it evolved over the years.

One can safely assume that until Alladiya Khan came under the spell of Mubarak Ali Khan, his khayal singing was based on the Gwalior style, in fact the only style prevalent in those days. This is reflected in his use of heavy gamaks on one hand and the taans which avoid the staccato effect on the other. The notes sa re, sa re, re ga, re ga, sa re ga, re ga, re ga ma, ga ma, etc., are conjoined with the help of meend. Dhrupadiyas disapprove of taans because they go against the very essence of our music which admits only gliding and not hopping from one note to another. In the faster portion of the dhrupad-alaap, the vowels in the taans are replaced by consonants like ri re na na, etc., joined with the help of halaqs and gamaks. Alladiya Khan's gamak taans, which I had the privilege of hearing six decades ago, were indeed like cannon balls in the true tradition of Haddu Khan, Mubarak Ali Khan and Ghulam Abbas Khan of Agra who excelled in similar heavy gamak taans which, from various accounts, sounded like artillery engagements.

Swami Dharmavrat, a biographer of Alladiya Khan, remembers the reverberating sound of his taans, which never lost their musicality. Govind Rao Tembe, in his book in Marathi titled *Alladiya Khan Yanchi Charitra*, mentions that the ustad used to excel in gamak bol-taans at twice or sometimes four times the laya of the composition; something that one has always associated with the Agra gayaki, which also has been nurtured by the dhrupad-dhamar tradition. It must also be reiterated that Alladiya Khan was closely related to the Atrauli branch of the Agra gharana. His first guru was Munshi Ghulam Hussain, a disciple of Ghagge Khuda Baksh, the founder of Agra khayal gayaki. Alladiya Khan was also very close to Naththan Khan of Agra and often sang together with him. Both of them were accustomed to sthayee bharna in vilambit laya in the dhrupad style, which calls for tremendous '*dum-saans*' or breath control. This, in fact, is an outstanding feature of Jaipur gayaki even today.

Shrikrishna Babban Rao Haldankar, in his book[3], adds a few more features of Khansaheb's gayaki:

1) 'The swar-vistar of his music, or the progression of notes, could be compared to the movement of a snake. When a snake moves forward it touches the ground with every part of its body. Govind Rao Tembe writes in Khan Sahab's biography that his music progressed with a similar continuous movement in which a note merged into the following note.
2) 'Rare and combined ragas (jod ragas) were Khan Sahab's forte. His taans revealed an ingenious and skilful combination of the notes of both the ragas.
3) 'Khan Sahab would swoop down on the 'mukhda' (refrain) in an uncanny manner. One could compare this to the sudden attack of an eagle on its prey in a downward plunge.

'The last point bears striking similarity to Alladiya Khan's own description of Mubarak Ali Khan's taans and his spectacular and totally unexpected manner of arriving at the sam.'

I first heard Kesarbai, unquestionably Alladiya Khan's premier disciple, in 1942. The same year I also heard Roshanara Begum and Bade Ghulam Ali Khan. The previous evening Roshanara had made a tremendous impression on the Calcutta audience with her extremely tuneful and systematic vistar of Malkauns and taans which never lost their clarity despite their fantastic speed. To me and my friend Putuda, at that impressionable age, the ease with which she shot up to the tonic in the 'atitar saptak' (top of the higher octave) without falsetto was no less miraculous than her 'chaudooni' gamak taans at four times the normal speed. She was already the numero uno in our eyes among the top female musicians until we heard Kesarbai on the last evening.

As the curtain went up we beheld a middle-aged lady of imposing appearance in white silk accompanied by a single tanpura and Majid Khan on the sarangi. The pitch was lower than usual, possibly G sharp, and her first enunciation of the sa, the tonic, revealed a quality of voice somewhat heavier

than most female musicians'. As she progressed with her raga
Lalita Gauri, the luminous quality of every note she struck
with her open-chested shuddh akar was such a departure from
anything we had heard before that we clasped each other's
hands in sheer joy. Neither my friend nor I was acquainted
with Lalita Gauri, and thought it was Poorvi, but that did not
interfere with our enthusiastic appreciation. What struck us
immediately was the quality of her execution. It seemed every
phrase, every meend in the bahlawa, every taan had been
rehearsed a hundred times. Her approach was almost European,
with meticulous attention to detail and flawless well-rehearsed
execution.

Then came the intricate taans of Alladiya Khan's gayaki,
which would not allow a single pause for breath until the sam
was reached. The teentaal was slow, almost as slow as the
tabla accompaniment provided for a Maseetkhani Gat on the
sitar, which is indeed very slow as far as teentaal goes for
vocal music. Kesarbai would start as soon as a quarter of the
sixteen beats was over, often even earlier, and finish her taan
in one breath exactly at the point where the mukhda began.
Very often one would get the impression that she would not
be able to finish the taan as it started ascending, when there
was hardly any time left for the arrival of the mukhda. With
surprising speed she would swoop down on the mukhda in a
manner which was perfectly in keeping with the intricate
original pattern of the taan. Never did the listener feel that
the last movement was contrived or done in haste.

Babban Rao Haldankar mentions that at one concert
Kesarbai was taking a taan in a composition which was set to
'dheema' (very slow) jhaptaal. Suddenly, at a point, she
realized that she would not reach the sam with precision. She
continued her taan over the next 'aavartan' (cycle) in the
same breath without breaking the tempo, and built the
pattern so ingeniously that she hit the next sam with perfect
precision. On this occasion I marvelled at the Catherine-
wheel effect of her taans, the perfect blend of sur and laya,
the occasional syncopatic emphasis on a note which

momentarily destroyed the jewel-encrusted ornamental pattern of the taan and built yet another new one, and more than anything else, the effect of continuity in her music largely because of her amazing breath control. The previous evening I had been bowled over by Bade Ghulam Ali Khan's mastery over his taans, both linear and palta-based patterns, and felt he could do anything he wished with his voice. When I heard Kesarbai's Jaipur gayaki, I realized there must be a bigger brain, a system-builder behind this unique style. Kesarbai's credit lay in its faultless execution.

I am putting on paper exactly what I felt at that tender age when every recital of a stalwart, and there were many those days, seemed wondrous and incomparably beautiful. I realized as I do now that comparisons are invidious. To say that so and so ustad was better than another is as silly as stating that a gazelle is better than a greyhound or a lion superior to a Royal Bengal tiger. One can, at best, compare the angas of the respective styles of musicians or express one's regret over certain essential angas of the khayal gayaki omitted or not developed adequately by a particular school.

It is common knowledge that the Jaipur gharana, like the Patiala and Sahaswan, or the original culprit Gwalior, ignored the slow unfolding of the raga which Kishori Amonkar has incorporated into her gayaki. All credit to her, despite her occasional erratic and even ungrammatical treatment of major ragas. Jod ragas are her forte. When I heard her in Jagdish Goenka's house more than thirty years ago, I exclaimed to a friend, 'Where has she been all my life?' Gradually, her eccentricity and overt exhibition of emotion got the better of the highly disciplined gayaki of her mother and guru Moghubai Kurdikar. Her drut teentaal khayals, sung in addha, are what a friend calls 'pure Juhu beach stuff'. Divested of her Bollywood syndrome and with greater attention to her original Shastriya training, she would continue to be the first lady of our Hindustani music today.

I realize now, of course, that Kesarbai's gayaki, though sophisticated and dignified, had severe limitations. Her 78

RPM records of Gauri, Kafi Kanhra, Bihagada, Nand, Durga, Maru Bihag, Lalita Gauri and Tilak Kamod are absolute gems which aspiring female students of khayal must hear repeatedly. But her recitals seemed like elongated versions of these records and ran the risk of sounding monotonous to a fastidious ear after a while. Her limitations, of course, are the limitations of the Jaipur gayaki. Without bol-vistar, bol-banao, bol-bant and with a somewhat limited imagination, her treatment of raga, like that of other members of her gharana, could not last more than half an hour without repetition.

But it was impossible not to admire her as long as she sang. Her imposing personality, her 'swar-lagav' (application of swara), the purity of her notes, the fantastic riyaz that had gone into her music, the overall impeccable taste—all combined to produce the impact that her recital had on the cognoscenti as well as the lay listeners. Her well-rehearsed taans were like ladders to the sky from which her swooping dive to the mukhda and her arrival at the sam was always an event. Rahmat Qureshi, brother-in-law of Majid Khan, the sarangi-player, and the lifelong accompanist of Kesarbai, once played with me in Delhi. He gave me a memorable description of Kesarbai's style. '*Jab bhi lambi taan lekar wo wapas aati thi, muhkda bhi dulhan ban kar aa jata tha* (As soon as her long taan came to an end, the mukhda would come along like a newly-wedded bride).'

A fantastic amount of hard work had gone into her gayaki. Professor B.R. Deodhar, who has written more than one book on music and has produced quite a few disciples, the most eminent of whom was Kumar Gandharv, used to edit a journal called *Sangeet Kala Vihar* in Hindi and Marathi. In an interview Kesarbai had been surprisingly frank about her origin, upbringing and early initiation into classical music. She was proud of her looks and complexion and hinted that eminent ustads were keen on imparting free lessons to her in her youth. Of the names she mentioned, the prominent ones were Bhaskarbuwa Bakhle, sitarist Barkatulla

Khan and Ramkrishnabuwa Vaze. This was when she sang Natya Sangeet and bhajans and managed to receive the patronage of a rich businessman, Seth Vitthaldas, who set her up in a flat in Shivaji Park in Bombay.

It was Sethji who approached Alladiya Khan with the request that he teach Kesarbai. Ustad was not so interested in teaching women at that stage. This was despite the fact that he had given talim to Tanibai who was, according to some, the best of his female disciples, when he was the court musician of Sahu Maharaj of Kolhapur. Ultimately, of course, Alladiya Khan relented when a large fee was promised, but he made Kesarbai take an oath that she would have to follow his instructions to the letter even if they were not pleasant. Five hundred and one rupees were paid to the ustad (more than a hundred times the value in today's currency) on the occasion of the gandabandhan ceremony. The time-table laid down by Khansaheb was a rigorous one—practice from 4 am till 8, breakfast with her guru, talim from 9 to 1 o'clock in the afternoon, rest for a few hours, again talim and practice in the evening until a late dinner after which the ustad had to be dropped off at his residence by Sethji's chauffeur.

This went on for nearly a year and only two ragas were taught—Todi and Multani. An abacus was presented to her by her ustad and every taan had to be practised five hundred times. Any mistake in the execution of the taan would mean starting all over again. Ten months later, Khansaheb suggested a soiree where she would have to sing before half a dozen knowledgeable musicians. If she passed the examination with credit, her postgraduate talim would begin thereafter. Bai herself used to say that by that time her breath-control was such that she could take a taan covering a whole cycle in vilambit teentaal in a single breath. Her command over laya was also such that she was confident that the best of tabaliyas in Hindustan would not be able to shake her even if he were to deny theka and play lehera for a whole aavartan.

This inhuman labour went on for year after year, which is why she was legitimately proud of her music and later in life would charge the highest fee for a recital, possibly the same the conference organizers would offer Ustad Faiyaz Khan or Pandit Omkarnath Thakur. While she was deferential towards the great ustads of Agra, from Naththan Khan to Faiyaz and Vilayet Khan, she genuinely believed her khayal singing was the best in the country and that there would never be anyone, male or female, to equal her in her own gharana or—for that matter—in any other. Most listeners tended to agree with her which made her not only proud but arrogant as well.

Sheila Dhar in her book[4] remembers her when Sheila was in her teens and Kesarbai was often her father's honoured guest in Delhi. Although she got all the adulation she needed, 'she still felt insecure and was often ungracious, and even nasty, without any visible provocation, to people who deserved better'. On one occasion, when Kesarbai was billed to sing in the Bharatiya Kala Kendra conference, writes Sheila Dhar, 'she swept regally into the green room in her diaphanous white chiffon sari, her head literally in the air. She saw Rasoolanbai, the consummate thumri singer from Benaras, sitting meekly on a rug on the floor, waiting to go on stage as soon as her tabla-player finished tuning up. It was well known that in order to hear herself better in concert, Rasoolanbai had cultivated the habit of covering her left ear-hole with the little finger of her left hand. This had become an idiosyncrasy that her many admirers loved. As a technical aid to perfect pitch she found it so invaluable that she used it in every recital. All concert-goers associated the gesture with her, and so did Kesarbai, as I was soon to discover.

As soon as Rasoolanbai sighted the great Kesarbai, who was an awesome presence for all musicians, she courteously stood up and folded her hands in greeting. She not only respected the singer, but also considered the khayal form she represented somewhat superior to the genre of the thumri and dadra that she herself specialized in. Besides, she was by nature a soft-spoken, cultured and humble person with practically no ego. Far from appeasing Kesarbai, Rasoolan's deference provoked her to bare her claws.

'Rasoolan, what on earth are you doing here? I am told it is a serious music conference. Can it be that you have come here to sing?' she asked haughtily, trying to disguise the dig as good-humoured banter.

'Baiji, when you have graced this city with your presence, it would be nothing but impertinence for me to claim that I have also come here to sing.'

'*Kyun nahi, kyun nahi, kya chhungliyan thak gayeen teri?* (Why not? Why not? Unless, of course, your little finger has got too tired of working and needs a little rest?)'

I asked Sheila Dhar how old she was when this happened.

'I was in my eighth class in school.'

'Do you remember anything more about her?'

'Yes, I remember how she would appear every morning at the breakfast table after spending an unconscionably long time over her bath and toilet, always in a white sari, pearls in the morning and diamonds at night. She would apply kajal on her head.'

'Kajal! On her head? What do you mean?'

'Yes, kajal. She had become rather thin on top by then and she applied kajal on a big bald patch. Under the chandelier it would shine like a freshly tarred road under a full moon. I also remember she was rude to Ratanjankar in D.V. Paluskar's presence and called him a grammarian, not a musician.'

'That's a shame. In his youth he was a very fine artiste and his knowledge was profound. As it happens, I once questioned him about Kesarbai's Kafi Kanhra and Kukubh Bilawal. The two main features of any Kanhra are ni pa and ga ma re sa. At least one should be there in her rendering of Kafi Kanhra. Ratanjankar agreed with me and said that the taans she took in Kafi Kanhra were mostly those of Kafi and Bageshri. Her Kukubh Bilawal also does not agree with our famous sadra, '*Shambhu patha shesh*'. Nivruttibuwa told me what Kesarbai sang was not Kukubh but Sawani Bilawal. Some call it Sukhiya Bilawal. Since Nivruttibuwa also learnt from Ustad Alladiya Khan, it just adds to the confusion.'

'Well, I don't know about that. Maybe her knowledge of ragas was not very deep but she was a grand singer.'

Which she certainly was, though Mallikarjun Mansoor used to call her music *'baithaya hua gana'*, or crammed music. But as far as her execution goes she certainly was second to none and she was quite conscious of it.

When the national programme was introduced by AIR, the inauguration was done by Faiyaz Khan. Those days the programme ran for one-and-a-half hours, beginning at 9.30 in the evening. The honour of doing the second national programme went to Kesarbai who earlier refused to sing on radio on the ground that she could not stand the idea of her music being played on street-corners and paan-bidi ki dukaan (betel shops). On this occasion, however, she did perform. When Gangubai Hangal's turn came, the great Kesarbai promptly wrote to AIR saying it should never play her tape again. Gangubai of Kirana gharana was no mean singer—but obviously not fit to be included in such elite company.

The following story I got from Nivruttibuwa Sarnaik. Seth Vitthaldas was a regular operator on the Bombay Stock Exchange and had made his pile. Alladiya Khan used to give a portion of his savings to Sethji and got a fair return. Any loss sustained by Khansaheb was borne by Vitthaldas. This way Alladiya Khan's capital, such as it was, increased slowly but steadily until he insisted on being initiated into the mysteries of speculation. After a few solo flights, which did not turn out to be particularly profitable, Khansaheb received a hot tip from Vitthaldas who said that he himself was investing ten lakh. Alladiya Khan chipped in with twenty thousand, his entire savings. The inevitable happened. Seth, having lost a fortune, departed from this world via a massive coronary attack, leaving behind a huge family and his mistress. Khansaheb was shown the door by his favourite Baisaheba.

In 1971, A.S. Raman of *Sunday Standard* interviewed Kesarbai. The answers to the three questions he put to her flabbergasted me. First, she stated she had received talim in Kolhapur and Bombay from her ustad without a break from

1920 till his death in 1946. This, according to Mallikarjun
Mansoor and Nivruttibuwa, is highly questionable; to say the
least. To the second question she said she always gave voice
support on the tanpura to Alladiya Khan till his death in
1946 and never accepted a solo engagement. This, of course,
is a silly and blatant piece of untruth and an unwarranted
one. The third question was whether Ustad Alladiya Khan
had taught anyone else. The answer was, 'None. Plenty of
musicians claim that they are disciples of Khan Sahab.' As an
afterthought, she added, 'Well, none who could be called a
serious musician.'

This is yet another amazing statement. Even if she
excluded Alladiya Khan's sons, Manji Khan and Bhurji
Khan, and brother Haidar Khan from her list, what about
Bhaskarbuwa, Govind Rao Shaligram, Govind Rao Tembe,
Nivruttibuwa and his uncle Shankar Rao Sarnaik, Tanibai,
Moghubai Kurdikar and a few also-rans like Gulu Jasdanwala
and Sushilarani Patel, wife of the editor of *Filmindia*? Obviously,
at her age—she was eighty-two then—her memory must have
been playing wild tricks, or else they were not serious
musicians in her eyes. A grand singer Kesarbai was, but a very
complex person indeed!

Those were difficult days for Alladiya Khan. Accustomed
as he was to affluent surroundings and Seth Vitthaldas's
kindness, he had to fall back on help from his sons. The
eldest, Badeji, who had serious problems with his voice, had
forsaken talim and taken up farming in Uniwara. Manji
Khan, the second son, was a bit of a spendthrift, liked his
drink and was one of the few musicians in India who kept a
car. He was a family man with the usual number of dependents
and hangers-on as was the custom in middle-class households
those days. The third son, Bhurji Khan, and Alladiya Khan's
brother, Haidar Khan, depended entirely on tuitions to a few
students who were attached to this gayaki in spite of its
complexity. After twenty-five years in the court of Sahu
Maharaj of Kolhapur, the only steady patron Khansaheb had
found was Seth Vitthaldas, and now he, too, was gone.

Nivruttibuwa Sarnaik

Alladiya Khan's musical engagements at this age were also getting scarce. Fortunately, it was at this juncture that Shankar Rao Sarnaik of Kolhapur, uncle of Nivrutti, chose to become Alladiya Khan's disciple. Shankar Rao was a rich man and had his own dramatic troupe in Bombay. Khansaheb, with the intention of making the most of this windfall, demanded 2,500 rupees as gurudakshina for the gandabandhan. Invitations were sent out to prominent members of the world of music and in the presence of a hundred guests the huge plates of sweets and the thread were placed before the ustad, along with a bundle of notes. Khansaheb kept on counting them—one, two, three, four thousand—and still there was more than a half of the bundle left. At Khansaheb's surprised look, Shankar Rao said, 'I understand Ustad is in need of money. Whatever I have been able to raise is nothing compared to the honour Ustad has done to me by accepting me as his disciple.' The bundle contained ten thousand rupees. This was not an inconsiderable sum those days when Raza Ali Khan, Nawab of Rampur, paid three thousand rupees to Ustad Mushtaq Hussain Khan for his gandabandhan.

Alladiya Khan attached himself to Shankar Rao's dramatic troupe but there was hardly any work for the ustad. After an enthusiastic beginning, Shankar Rao scarcely found time for talim. All this, no doubt, hurt Khansaheb's vanity. Here he was, the great Ustad Alladiya Khan, the very mention of whose name made hundreds of musicians touch their ears as a sign of respect, willing to teach a disciple who could not find time to sit with his ustad. Khansaheb's conscience finally made him collar the young nephew Nivrutti and say, 'I am *'ehsaanmand'* (indebted) to your family but if your uncle refuses to take lessons, you jolly well sit with me every day and, Inshallah, I will make a musician out of you.' Nivrutti Sarnaik had just entered his teens, had a flair for tabla and little inclination for studies. Thus started his talim, which went on for a number of years until Khansaheb's death, when Nivruttibuwa went to Rajjab Ali Khan.

Khansaheb's style had evolved over a number of years

and his disciples appear to represent the various stages of this evolution. It is also possible that the talim that Khansaheb gave his female disciples took into consideration their limitations. For instance, Mallikarjun Mansoor, who learnt from Manji Khan, the son, sang in a style slightly different from that of Kesarbai. He used gamaks, not as much as Govindbuwa Shaligram who did, copying Alladiya Khan blindly, but his style was masculine. He lacked Kesarbai's breath control and as such, his taans used to be punctuated by sudden intakes of breath (which are noticeable in his records).

Haidar Khan learnt from his brother Alladiya Khan and was never a successful performer, but it was through him that Lakshmibai Yadav received what one might call second-hand training by Alladiya Khan. Her style was different from the presentation of Moghubai or Kesarbai. Lakshmibai concentrated much more on vistar than any of her '*gurubahens*' (sisterhood of disciples under the same guru). Nivruttibuwa's tans, too, were altogether different from those of Govindbuwa, Anantbuwa Limaye or Mallikarjun Mansoor. He would proceed with his taans with a cluster of five notes, switching over to four midstream and then suddenly to three or six, but ending invariably in true Jaipur style with clockwork precision at the point where the mukhda waited for him. His taans had more '*aad-kuaad*', cross-rhythmic patterns, than those of his fellow disciples, possibly because of the subsequent influence of Rajab Ali Khan. At the same time they resemble the taans of Azmat Hussain Khan, brother-in-law of Vilayet Hussain Khan of Agra, and disciple of Alladiya Khan.

Azmat Hussain, like Nivruttibuwa, lacked the shuddh akar, an essential trademark of the Jaipur gharana, and indulged in bol-bant and layakari. He had family connections with three separate gharanas, the Khurja, Agra and Atrauli-Jaipur, and was proud of his lineage, his khandaan, so much so that he would insist on singing after other ustads. He did this with Bade Ghulam Ali. Bade Ghulam yielded to Azmat Hussain's seniority and pedigree and sang a beautiful Multani at a soiree where Alladiya Khan was present. Azmat Hussain followed him with a rare raga, Shri Tonk, with a fireworks display of intricate taans. Everybody praised him, including Bade Ghulam Ali. His only comment was, 'So, what's new? It is an acknowledged fact that I sing better than anyone here—except my ustad.'

He tried to do the same thing with Ustad Amir Khan at an informal soiree in the Suin Walan Lane in Old Delhi. Amir Khan categorically refused to let Azmat Hussain sing after him and instead threw him a challenge by saying, '*Agar himmat ho to sath baith ke gao* (If you have the guts, sing *with* me and let all present here judge who the superior artiste is)'. Latafat Khan, who was married to Azmat Hussain's niece and lived in the same house in Bombay, acted as the mediator and managed to prevent an awkward and indecent brawl. Azmat Hussain picked up his sola hat and briefcase, which he sported ever since he got the job of a producer in AIR, and left in a huff. He did not speak to Latafat Khan for a year after this incident.

Nivruttibuwa, like Azmat Hussain, also sang drut khayals, something that Mallikarjun did occasionally. Kesarbai sang faster khayals rarely. Moghubai Kurdikar sang drut khayals and taranas and had quite a few compositions to her credit. She also indulged in tasteful bol-bant and layakari, no doubt, because of her association with Ustad Vilayet Hussain Khan of the Agra gharana. So did Gajanan Rao Joshi, who had talim from the same ustad. Some of Gajananbuwa's drut compositions, that one hears from Ulhas Kashalkar, are not without merit. But Ustad Alladiya Khan, from all accounts, hardly ever sang drut khayals. Shrikrishna Ratanjankar confirmed it once during my conversation with him. He also told me that none of his disciples had been able to reproduce Khansaheb's taan patterns which were far more complex and were like a spider's web woven with silken thread. He demonstrated a few of them and I regret not having noted down the sargams at that time.

Gulu Jasdanwala, another disciple of Alladiya Khan, in

an interview broadcast on Bombay radio in 1967 on the twenty-first death anniversary of his ustad, said more or less the same thing. According to him, Khansaheb once sang Yaman Kalyan assisted by his son Manji Khan and brother Haidar Khan. Neither of them had a clue to the taan patterns of the ustad, which were beautiful but unimaginably complex and difficult to follow.

It was a clear November morning in Delhi, the best time of the year, when it is neither hot nor too cold. The sky was a cobalt blue, the grass was a dewy green and the potted chrysanthemums were blooming. I had finished my tea, read the newspaper and was feeling appropriately lazy on a Sunday morning. The last thing I felt like doing was to shave, get dressed and drive fourteen kilometers to the *Times of India* office where Mallikarjun Mansoor was scheduled to sing on the spacious lawn. But Buwa had sent word to me the previous evening and it was not everyday that one got a chance to hear him.

Thanks to the telecasting time of the popular serial *Mahabharat* on TV, the roads had little traffic, and the distance, which in Calcutta might have taken an hour, was covered in less than twenty minutes. When I entered through the gate, the sight that greeted me was like a colossal kitty party of affluent housewives. Punjabi menfolk normally steer clear of such occasions though they are aware of their tremendous snob value. For the ladies, on the other hand, to be invited to the ITC Music Conference or to one such as this is both a status symbol and a splendid opportunity to display their saris and jewellery.

Gangubai Hangal had just finished her recital when I arrived and Mallikarjunbuwa was halfway through his 'Vidyadhar gunijana' in Khat raga. Faced by hordes of dumb females decked out in splendour, the poor Lingayat Brahmin, brought up on vegetarian diet and pure Shastriya music, was feeling a bit lost. It was the kind of atmosphere which would have suited Mehdi Hasan, Chhote Ghulam Ali or Jagjit Singh, big names in the world of ghazal. Buwa's enthusiastic greeting, the moment he saw me, sounded like that of a lone explorer meeting his long-lost gun-bearer in the jungles of Congo. After I manouevred myself acrobatically to the front, through numerous females seated on the carpet, and settled down to serious listening, Buwa finished his rendering of Khat with a dozen taans and looked questioningly at me. I asked for Gaud Sarang, my favourite midday raga.

At a gathering such as this one, I had expected, at best, a stock recital. What happened in the first minute or two was totally unexpected. I thought I had become totally blasé after listening to great music over fifty years. But the very first phrase of re ga re ma ga in Gaud Sarang, the sur, the 'swayambhu gandhar' (in which the four strings of the tanpura throw up the third note) arising from the two well-tuned tanpuras, the purity of the notes uttered by Mallikarjunbuwa with shuddh akar and the manner in which he did his swar-prayog made me shiver all over in sheer ecstasy. The upsurge of emotion I felt was unlike any experience I had had in recent years of listening to Indian music.

I remember a recital of Manjh Khamaj by the one and only Ali Akbar Khan twenty years ago and a brief pukar of Bhimsen Joshi, when he hit the gandhar in the taar saptak in Maru Bihag, which brought about an identical feeling. I thought the days of the greats, who could reduce a listener like me to a zombie, were dead and gone. But the totally unexpected impact of the simple main phrase of Gaud Sarang, without any ornamentation, made me ponder what real music was made of. I still ponder—when I listen to young vocalists on the trapeze nowadays.

All this however does not mean that Mallikarjun was above giving stock recitals. In fact, eight times out of ten, his public recitals of a particular raga sounded the same. This is a criticism which is levelled against most artistes of the Jaipur gharana. But I have had the advantage of listening to a relaxed Mallikarjunbuwa in private on many occasions, when he would allow his imagination full play. I remember one such occasion in the late Sixties when, in my house, he was singing the song *'Jhan jhan payel baje'* in Nat Bihag. It was a song made famous by Ustad Faiyaz Khan. This is a drut composition in teentaal of sixteen beats, and the refrain covers five of them. He started taking taans of eight matras, gradually extending to nine, ten and eleven beats. It went on for eight minutes by my watch—and there was no repetition. The only listeners were Vijay Kichlu, Brij Bhushan Kabra, my favourite guitar-player of classical music, and myself. That was a most un-Jaipur-like act which would have been the delight of Bade Ghulam Ali, Faiyaz Khan or even Bhimsen Joshi. It would not, however, have pleased those of Alladiya Khan's disciples who favoured taans covering the same teentaal but only in the vilambit laya. The other outstanding exception was Nivruttibuwa Sarnaik, who might have managed to perform this feat himself, if so challenged.

The credit for introducing Mallikarjun Mansoor to Calcutta audiences goes to the Calcutta Music Circle organized by A. Kanan, Vijay Kichlu, Farhat Sayeed Khan and myself. Farhat Sayeed Khan was the son of the erstwhile Nawab of Chhatari, who was a gandabandh disciple of Faiyaz Khan but never sang even in his bath. In his first appearance, Buwa sang Nand which is a comparatively recent contribution of the Agra gharana but popularized by Jaipur. (Several musicians belonging to different gharanas sing this raga under the name of Anandi or Anandi Kalyan. It is difficult for me to approve of this practice. It is like borrowing someone's car and changing the number plate.)

The vilambit khayal *'Dhoondhu ware sain'*, composed by Mehboob Khan Daras Piya) is the only one in currency even now. There was no drut composition in existence until Vilayet Hussain Khan's *'Aj hoon na aaye'* was taken up by Agra artistes of later generations. Jaipur, however, was content, as usual, with the vilambit composition. It has been a great favourite of all the artistes of this school, from Kesarbai to Kishori Amonkar. Buwa's Basant Kedar on that occasion was a beautiful blend of two major ragas and assumed a new identity. He concluded his recital with what most thought was Nayaki Kanhra but which later was identified as Bhausakh, with resounding heavy gamak taans the like of which I never heard from him before or since. When reminded of it Buwa would laugh and say, 'Woh budhaape ki cheez nahin (Such taans do not go with old age)'. What struck all of us was the incorporation of some south Indian idioms into his gayaki, which made it particularly endearing.

Mallikarjun was born in the village of Mansoor in 1910 and died of cancer in September 1992. Out of his eighty-two years, seventy-seven were spent on music and very little else. The business of earning a livelihood and raising a family was incidental. Music was his life and except for the last fortnight before his death, when he could hardly utter a word, he would not have dreamt of spending a single day without singing or teaching music. His father was a small-time farmer who was fond of Marathi drama and Natya Sangeet.

Dharwad, where Mallikarjun lived and died, was a small town not far from the border of the present state of Karnataka. It was full of people who were bilingual and favoured both Hindustani and Karnatak systems of music. Mallikarjun's initiation was at the age of six, into Karnatak music, by Swami Aiyappa who was a violin-player. Mallikarjun's elder brother was keen on north Indian music and left home barely in his teens for a job with a Marathi drama troupe which took in young boys with good voices for female roles. Soon after, Mallikarjun, who showed unmistakable promise as a child, joined his brother. The manager of the dramatic society, Panduvabuwa, was an accomplished singer by provincial standards and took the boys in hand. Marathi Natya Sangeet is strictly based on the classical and requires talim, which Panduva had received from Nilkanthbuwa, a disciple of Balkrishnabuwa Ichalkaranjikar.

When the troupe camped at Bagalkot, Nilkanthbuwa was invited to see their play and was particularly impressed by the singing of the ten-year-old Mallikarjun; so much so that he made up his mind to adopt the boy, having no child of his own. For the next six years, Mallikarjun received serious talim in Gwalior gayaki, as well as genuine affection, from Nilkanthbuwa and his wife. Meanwhile, his elder brother had teamed up with Gauhar Karnataki, an actress of rare accomplishment, and started his own company.

Gauhar Karnataki was known for her beauty and charisma. The great Bal Gandharva, the doyen of the Marathi stage, married her and made her his partner. All that Basavraj Mansoor needed for his troupe was his younger brother's voice. For the next seven or eight years, that is till Gauhar Karnataki joined Bal Gandharva's troupe, they were a happy family in want of neither money nor popularity.

The Gramophone Company of India, to whom music-lovers of our generation would remain ever grateful, used to employ talent-spotters. Their objective was the same as that of the present Marwari management of the same company (which regrettably has changed its name to Sa re ga ma) and that was, to make money. Unlike present times when film music, aadhunik Bengali and Tagore songs, ghazals—both 'geetnuma' (sung without appropriate embellishments) and in imitation of the Pakistani stars—have been receiving priority over Shastriya Hindustani music, His Master's Voice looked for up-and-coming classical artistes in the Twenties of the last century. They appear to have displayed great foresight in picking up two budding artistes—Gangubai Hangal and Mallikarjun Mansoor—when they were virtually toddlers in the world of classical music. Mallikarjun was barely twenty-three when his first record came out. This 78 RPM record has two drut khayals, 'Kanganawa mora' (Adana) and 'Saiyan mora re' (Gaud Malhar). The stylistic similarity with Narayan Rao Vyas, no doubt because of the influence of Natya Sangeet, is evident. Though the voice is supple and tuneful and the taans show clarity, the music is bland and gives scarce indication of Buwa's style of later years. HMV brought out thirty such records within two years, most of which were Natya Sangeet, one thumri which shows embarrassing affinity with the Marathi bhajan and a couple of khayals.

According to Dilip Vedi and Govind Rao Tembe, two

outstanding disciples of Ustad Alladiya Khan were Tanibai and Manji Khan. Tanibai died young and did not pose a serious threat to Kesarbai. Manji Khan (Badruddin was his original name) was a powerful singer who thoroughly disapproved of his father's habit of keeping the company of tawayefs. Manji Khan's ambition was to become an *'afsar'* (officer) in British administration. He would punctuate his conversations in Urdu or Marathi with a few English words that he had picked up, preferred European clothes and loved cricket in the company of a few Englishmen in Kolhapur where his father was a court musician of Sahu Maharaj. (His elder brother Nasiruddin, who never followed his ancestral profession, was a highly accomplished cricketer, according to Ustad Alladiya Khan.) The Maharaja in due course appointed Manji Khan as a range officer in the forest department of his state on the condition that he not give up his music. Once, Khansaheb was giving talim to Kesarbai, who sang her taan touching the gandhar in the higher octave. Manji Khan, who was combing his hair after his bath, standing in front of the mirror on the hatstand, took the same taan with more intricate patterns and came to sam after touching the sa in atitar saptak. Ustad came out and slapped Manji's face, saying, 'Don't you know it is infra dig for an ustad's son to compete with a tawayef?' 'How would I,' retorted Manji, 'since you spend most of your time with them?'

In 1921, after the death of Sahu Maharaj of Kolhapur, the state went to the court of wards. Alladiya Khan settled down in Bombay and spent most of his days with Kesarbai, teaching her, dining with her and Seth Vitthaldas, and talking stocks and shares with the latter. Kesarbai, a highly possessive woman, used to throw tantrums every time Khansaheb took on a new pupil like Moghubai Kurdikar or Lilabai Sirgaonkar. On one such occasion, she decided to learn music from Manji Khan instead, and took an attaché case full of currency notes worth ten thousand rupees to him. Manji Khan had expensive habits. He liked his drink, went to a good tailor and maintained a car. His answer to Kesarbai was a firm no. When requested by Mallikarjun to give the matter serious thought, he merely said, '*Aap kya chahte hain main bhi apne* art *ko gandi nali main utar doon* (Do you want me also to throw my art into this filthy drain?)'

Mallikarjun Mansoor came to Bombay in 1934 in search of a guru. The Gwalior gayaki practised in Maharashtra under a veneer of Natya Sangeet, he felt, had reached saturation point. He was toying with the idea of taking talim from Krishnarao Shankar Pandit, in search of the authentic Gwalior style, when he met a singer called Fadnis Krishna who became famous for his role of Sant Tukaram on the stage. In private life he was a jeweller and his shop was a meeting-place for actors and musicians. One day, Manji Khan dropped in while Mallikarjun was there and on his request went to the gramophone shop next-door to hear the young singer's record. Manji Khan agreed to take Mallikarjun on as his disciple.

The talim lasted only three-and-a-half years but it was pretty intensive, involving not less than six or seven hours of learning a day. After six months, Mallikarjun had the privilege of accompanying his ustad to every mehfil, and giving him voice support. He once recalled that in the course of two months, Manji Khan did not repeat a single raga. Apart from talim, Buwa aped his ustad's mannerisms and his way of life.

The prestigious Debal club, in Alladiya Chowk in Kolhapur, sports framed photographs of all the famous musicians who had sung there. During my maiden visit to the club with V.G. Jog, I was intrigued to find a picture of the conservative Lingayet in a jacket and tie which, no doubt, formed a part of the talim. To Buwa Alladiya Khan was God and Manji Khan was the son of God—Jesus Christ himself. He did not consider it worth his while to listen to any other musician, or even talk about one, as long as Alladiya Khan was alive—and precious few afterwards.

Much as Buwa and many other Bombayites praised Ustad Manji Khan, the latter's one and only visit to Lucknow in 1936 was not much of a success. The musical climate of Lucknow, soaked in Nawabi culture, did not admit of music without emotional content. Taankari, however intricate and difficult, belonged to the domain of acrobats. Manji Khan was so disappointed with the lukewarm response of the patrons and audience that he refused to accept even the railway fare from the organizers of the conference. The conference was part of a large exhibition. I was only nine years old and have no recollection of anything except the huge tents on the banks of the Gomti river, and the bright colours of Nicholas Roerich's paintings.

What was Manji Khan's style like and what did Alladiya Khan think of his favourite son's music? There are only one or two brief references in his memoirs to the talented boys, Manji and Bhurji, when they were learning from him and his brother Haidar Khan. Nothing at all about Manji Khan when he was an established artiste:

'One day, in Bapu Sahab's [one of the important men in Sahu Maharaj's court] mansion, Haidar Khan, Nasiruddin (Badeji)] and Manji were accompanying us. Both the brothers were singing a little along with us. I began singing the composition *'Mero piya rasiya'* in Nayaki Kanhra. The children had heard this composition in Tanibai's house, and they must have practised it at home. While singing they got engrossed in it. Both of them began singing freely. Haidar and I stopped and told them to continue. Both sang very well. Bapu Sahab Maharaj said, "Khan Sahab, you keep telling us that you still teach them only dhrupad and dhamar. How is it that they are singing the asthayee of khayal so well?" I said, "I myself am intrigued. I have not started teaching them asthayees yet, but sometimes I take them to Tanibai's house. It seems they have been practising what they have been listening to..." The children felt encouraged by that day's performance and by our praise. I was very happy and hugged them both and blessed them.'[5]

Manji Khan's style, apparently, was not a carbon copy of that of his father. That was partly because of his own musical personality and partly because of the influence of Rahmat Khan. After Vishnupanth Chhatre wound up his circus and settled down in Kurundwad with his khalifa, Alladiya Khan used to send his children to him every year for a month. Mallikarjun did not think one could get a fair idea of his late ustad's gayaki without listening to him. Unfortunately, like his father, Manji Khan never cut a disc, though his disciple already had thirty records to his credit when he got his ganda tied by Manji.

Behind the hectic and intensive talim that Manji Khan gave to Mansoor was probably a premonition of his sudden and untimely death. He died in an accident one evening when Mallikarjun was singing in the Santa Cruz Circle. The news was not conveyed to him until his recital was over. By the time he rushed to the hospital, Manji Khan was gone. Alladiya Khan, with tears in his eyes, said, 'Three hundred years of my khandaan's music has gone today with Manji.'

Buwa was once again in a quandary. Alladiya Khan said, 'You would do better to go to Bhurji. I am no longer fit mentally or physically to give you talim.' Bhurji Khan was a good teacher but not a performing artiste. He had quite a few disciples, which included Gajanan Rao Joshi and Menkabai Shirodkar, mother of the well-known thumri singer Shobha Gurtu. It is reported that a Mr Jayakar, a well-known lawyer, used to bear the expenses of Menkabai Shirodkar's talim and the British Governor of the Bombay Presidency was more fond of her than her music. The only person whom Khansaheb was still teaching assiduously was Moghubai, mother of Kishori Amonkar. It was Mallikarjun's duty to accompany the old man to her house thrice a week.

I have heard a record of Mallikarjunbuwa of those days. On one side, he sang Yamani Bilawal, and on the other, Bihagada without komal nishad. When this disc was out, Mallikarjun was naturally keen, not without trepidation, on Khansaheb hearing it. He approached Bhurji Khan who

Kishori Amonkar

made a couple of attempts to play it, but every time he did so, Khansaheb would lose his temper and ask him to stop it. One day, Bhurji Khan asked him, 'Abbajaan, don't you want to listen to Mallikarjun's record? He is singing really well and he is the brightest shagird of our gharana!' 'No, no!' shouted Alladiya Khan, 'I don't want to hear it. *Manji bahut yaad aataa hai.* (It reminds me of Manji).'

Till Buwa reached the age of sixty, not many had heard him outside Maharashtra. Luck and the departure of D.V. Paluskar, Bade Ghulam Ali Khan, Amir Khan, Kumar Gandharv, Sharafat Hussain and others brought him to the forefront. Otherwise, an uncompromising purist like him could not have been a favourite of ignorant organizers of music festivals of north India. In his closing years he had honours heaped upon him. He had, of course, received the Sangeet Natak Akademi award and Padma Bhushan earlier, but the Padma Vibhushan, the second highest honour in the country which was bestowed on him shortly before his death at well past eighty, came to us as a pleasant surprise.

In his personal life he was a pious man of simple and frugal habits. He preferred bidis to cigarettes and unending cups of tea before and after his recitals. That his son Rajshekhar managed on his own to rise in the academic world to the post of reader in English literature in Karnataka University, despite sustained hours of talim from his father, was never mentioned, though normally this would have been a matter of pride for a father who was barely literate. In spite of the considerable difference in our ages, he treated me as his friend and tolerated my singing. Thanks to Manji Khan's training, he liked sharing a drink or two with me and every time he would say, '*Yeh pahli martaba main pee rahaa hoon* (This is the first time I am having a drink in my life).' This would be accompanied by a bellyful of laughter which, like his music, came straight from the heart and was highly infectious.

Sheila Dhar, who was steeped in the Kirana tradition, once told me that she had heard musicians of all gharanas occasionally going out of tune or failing to hit a note right in the bull's eye, but never a Jaipurwalla. This statement is largely true, not necessarily applicable to the ustads, but the run-of-the mill follower of other gayakis. Assiduous practice and the clear voice production in shuddh akar by Jaipuriyas may well be the reason. Though insistence on the akar is common to all gharanas during the training period, stylistic deviations account for lack of fidelity to this fundamental norm when the musicians mature. Not so in Jaipur. Except when words of the composition are used in bol-vistar and bahlawa, the Jaipur gayaki favours the akar throughout.

In Jaipur gayaki, since this is also born out of Gwalior, bahlawa receives preference over vistar. The detailed dhrupadi alaap, which is the basis of bol-vistar in Kirana and Agra, is absent in Gwalior, Patiala and Jaipur. Unlike Patiala, which shows a lack of discipline and structural weakness, Jaipur gayaki is faithful to the bandish, or composition, in its limited vistar and bahlawa. Its structure is firmly based on classical norms and since the Jaipur singer's innings is built around the bandish, which is sung with absolute precision, raga anga is given full attention. Although Alladiya Khan was a dhrupadiya, deep heavy glides, which are prominent in Agra and Gwalior, are absent in the gayaki created by him.

Alladiya Khan, according to Govind Rao Tembe, indulged freely in gamak taans as well as bol-taans—but these are notably absent in the gayaki of the female singers of this school. These facets might have been omitted by Khansaheb while teaching Tanibai, Kesarbai, Moghubai and one or two others whose voices would not have suited this anga. I do not recollect Nivruttibuwa using bol-taans nor Anandbuwa Limaye, a disciple of Govindbuwa Shaligram. The last named disciple imitated Alladiya Khan's gamak taans but not his bol-taans. I have heard Mallikarjun Mansoor take bol-taans, but not on a regular basis.

The outstanding feature of Jaipur gayaki, which makes it sound different from other schools, is the feeling of continuity in the sur because of the amazing breath control displayed by almost all the musicians—with the notable exception of Mallikarjun Mansoor. Shrikrishna Haldankar, who had his talim from Moghubai before he transferred his loyalty to Agra, says, 'When a Jaipur gharana artiste takes a sam and begins his rendition in a new aavartan, he takes care that he does not pause in his alaap or break his alaap before he sings the mukhda again to reach the sam. The old records of Kesarbai or Moghubai will amply prove this point...This kind of presentation also requires a continuous thought pattern or process, or the building up of a macro composition. Thus a massively structured improvisation (*deergha rachana*) facilitated by astounding breath control could be said to be the intrinsic feature of this gharana. The impact of this kind of presentation on the audience is such that the listener reacts to the music with awe.'[6] There is no doubt this gayaki cannot be imbibed without proper talim and thus remains to my mind the one gayaki which is different and more difficult than any other for this singular reason. One can imitate the ustads of Agra, Patiala, Gwalior and Kirana—and not only superficially—but Jaipur gayaki cannot be presented in its entirety without proper initiation and of course years of practice and breath control.

There is no gayaki in which the two streams, laya and sur, mingle so perfectly into a meandering river. The movement is continuous, like a huge snake or a view of flowing water from high up in the mountains. This deprives the singer of the pleasure of approaching a note, loving it and viewing it from different directions as in dhrupad alaap as with Agra, or with the bol-vistar of Kirana. Also, when I say laya, I mean laya, not taal. Being a dhrupadiya, Alladiya Khan's emphasis in this gayaki was on beats equally spaced in such a manner that they become mere matras. Thus in Jaipur gayaki, the laya of teentaal, jhaptaal or rupak is the same. The characters of the taals are totally lost.

The manner of treating the ragas is also the same. Just as this gayaki pays no attention to the character of the taal, it does not take into account the varying personalities of the ragas. It will treat the lighter ragas, like Maru Bihag, Tilak Kamod and Nand, with the same sentiment and with the same dignified gravity as the heavier Kanhras or Malhars. Jaipur totally avoids bol-banao, murkees, harkats and khatkas, which can give a light touch to ragas like Kalingada, Kafi, Gara, Khamaj, Tilang and Tilak Kamod. Such ragas are themselves usually avoided. Agra gayaki which, like Alladiya Khan's, had its roots in the dhrupad tradition, borrowed alaap from dhrupad and bol-bant and layakari from dhamar. Curiously enough, Jaipur gayaki sans these angas, and with its emphasis on taans, does not appear to be a logical inheritance from an ustad who comes from a long line of distinguished dhrupad singers.

Says Haldankar:

'This does not mean that Alladiya Khan Sahab could not dwell on vilambit and vistar capably. In one of his mehfils, some *'buzurgs'* (elderly persons) from north India were present who insisted on vilambit and vistar. Khan Sahab was able to adeptly delineate these, winning applause from the older ones. I also had an opportunity to experience such vistar from my guru Moghubai in one of her mehfils. Yet it is not known how far this competence was achieved by other disciples. As stated earlier, Kesarbai Kerkar was found to have delineated vilambit and vistar at length in her last phase, especially after 1960, and taken recourse to taans only for name's sake.'[7]

Layakari is more or less totally absent in this style except to a limited extent in Nivruttibuwa's presentation. Again, according to Haldankar:

'Surashri Kesarbai took to occasional layakari in the later phase of her career. Her cassette *Bageshri Bahar* bears testimony to this... It would have been more impressive had the pronunciation been graceful. Also, her layakari followed in the footsteps of Agra gayaki...

The layakari, which is distinctly different and graceful, is to be experienced with my guru Moghubai Kurdikar and her worthy daughter Kishori Amonkar, ace singer of this era. Their layakari is not simple and straightforward but an unpredictable combination of tisra and chatusra jaati.'[8]

Haldankar traces this to the training imparted to Moghubai by the legendary Khepruji Parvatkar from Goa and goes to the extent of claiming that she is the only lady artiste who would not have hesitated to face a challenge from the best of tabla-players in the country.

It would follow from this analysis that without quite a few vital facets of the khayal gayaki, such as the raga vistar, which is the best and essential part of our music, bol-bant, layakari and adequate attention to the character of the raga and taal, the Jaipur gayaki is bound to sound monotonous to a fastidious listener who has had a taste of other styles demonstrated by ustads like Abdul Karim Khan, Faiyaz Khan and Bade Ghulam Ali Khan representing their respective distinguished gharanas. The strange part of it is that it does not. While Kesarbai, Moghubai and Mallikarjun sang, it sounded wonderful despite the limitations of their presentations, largely because of the harmonious blend of sur and laya, the like of which cannot be found in any other gayaki. And the taans are such that a young aspirant may well feel that this gayaki is totally beyond him. However, the effect does not last once the music stops. This is not the kind of music that you carry home with you.

7

Kirana Gharana

AIR's Calcutta office and studios were situated in those days in a ramshackle old building at 1, Garstin Place in Dalhousie Square. On one occasion there, Bade Ghulam Ali Khan was about to give his recital in about fifteen minutes. The tanpuras and the swarmandal had been tuned. Khansaheb was not one of those ustads whose voice needed warming up. He was patiently waiting for the red light to come on when Biman Ghosh, the programme executive, appeared with a tall dark gentleman in white dhoti-kurta. As soon as Khansaheb heard the name, Pankaj Kumar Mallick, he laid his swarmandal aside, gathered his huge, unwieldy body and stood up with some difficulty. He took the hand the gentleman extended him in both his hands and said to Biman Ghosh, *'Inse haath milana kafi nahin hai, gale lagana chahiye* (Shaking hands with this gentleman is not enough, he deserves to be embraced). I have yet to come across someone whose songs are as popular with the paan-bidiwallahs of Calcutta as with the aristocratic ladies of Lahore.' He hummed the first line of the famous film song *'Piya milan ko jana'* and made loud appreciative noises. 'All credit,' he said, 'to this gentleman and Raibabu. *Wah, wah! Subhan Allah!'*

In my younger days film songs had not acquired the upstart and bizarre characteristics of most such songs today. Thanks to Raichand Boral, the music director of New Theatres of Calcutta, and Anil Biswas of Bombay, film songs were often based on ragas. Sung by K.L. Saigal, Kananbala and Pankaj Kumar Mallick, they were great hits. Raibabu was an accomplished tabla-player himself and Anil Biswas sang old Bengali songs and kirtans, as well as dadra and ghazals wonderfully. Records of classical music could not be expected to be as popular as film songs, but two 78 RPM records brought out by Odeon of Abdul Karim's thumris *'Piya bin nahi avat chain'* in Jhinjhoti, and *'Jamuna ke teer'* in Bhairavi, were extraordinarily popular among the Bengalis. When Abdul Karim Khan came to sing at the All Bengal Music Conference in Calcutta, there was a scramble for tickets.

My father recounts in his journal *Monay Elo*[1]:

'I heard Abdul Karim when he was at the peak of his powers. It was a few days after the death of Deshbandhu C.R. Das. What an extraordinary gathering that was—Rabindranath Tagore, Mahatma Gandhi, Atul Prasad Sen and Sharat Chandra Chatterjee, the novelist, all were there in Dilip Kumar Roy's house... In between one raga and another, Gandhiji got up to collect subscriptions for his Congress party. Abdul Karim sang Anand Bhairavi and a few other ragas suitably edited for a mixed audience, but thanks to Gandhiji, his *"mizaj"* , mood, was lost. I do not think Gandhiji cared for classical music—or for that matter any music other than bhajans, his favourite simple devotional songs. Once, he attended the famous beenkar Murad Ali's recital in Ambalal Sarabhai's house in Ahmedabad. "How did you like it?" asked the host. "Amazing," replied Gandhiji, "but not as sweet as the music of my spinning wheel". Tagore's appreciation was *"saccha"*, true. He would close his eyes and be lost to the world. Atul Prasad got so carried away on occasions that he had to be controlled. And Sharat Chandra? When Dilip had gone to invite him to listen to Abdul Karim Khan, he merely asked, "Does he know when to stop?"'

Ustad Abdul Karim Khan

I have described in my first chapter my impression as a child of the great man who mesmerized his audience. Acharya Girija Shankar Chakrabarty was reduced to a zombie until the lighted cigarette burnt his fingers and brought him back to life. Ustad Badal Khan, at the end of the recital, told his disciple Bhishma Dev Chatterjee, '*Abdul Karim ki swar siddhi ho chuki. Woh jo swar lagata hai wohi saccha swar hai. Saaz ke sath na mile to saaz ki galti, magar ab woh sur mein phans gaya. Yaad rakhna, beta, woh Barodewale ka khayal saccha hai* (Abdul Karim has achieved the ultimate perfection in his application of notes. If the accompanist's instrument does not agree with it, it is the fault of the instrument and the man behind it. But, remember, son, Abdul Karim has got lost in sur unlike the Barodawallah [Faiyaz Khan], whose khayal is authentic).'[2] Two of Bhishma Dev's students, Suresh Chakrabarty and Bimal Chatterjee, were present and were in charge of dispatching the nonagenarian Badal Khansaheb home in a rickshaw.

Thanks to HMV, who have brought out a series of revived 78 RPM records in cassettes called *The Chairman's Choice*, which consist of renderings by old maestros such as Kale Khan, Moijuddin, Piyara Sahab, Faiyaz Khan, Gauhar Jaan, Jankibai and remarkably enough, Abdul Karim in his youth. Like most musicians, he also traversed the beaten path of taiyari and super-fast taans, which would be the envy of the followers of the Patiala gharana even today. There is no inkling of the Abdul Karim of later days, who would get immersed in sur and melody. The only thing common between these early records and the thirty-four 78 RPM records brought out by Odeon was that the pitch was higher than even the D Sharp or E favoured by Marathi Natya Sangeet singers.

There is an intimate connection between Abdul Karim's change in attitude towards music and his spiritual awakening, which may be traced to Tajuddin Baba, the holy man of Nagpur, and Sai Baba of Shirdi. Abdul Karim's meeting with the saint Tajuddin is described in detail by Kapileshwaribuwa

in his Marathi book, as well as by Jayantilal Zariwalla[3]. Abdul
Karim sang before Sai Baba, who blessed him after hearing
his bhajan in Marathi, '*Ho chi dan dega deva, tujha visar na
hvava* (This only do I ask thee, Lord! That thou remain in my
heart forever)'. Baba turned to his devotees and said, 'How
wistfully does this Muslim boy sing your bhajan; how gently
he pleads for the *daan* (gift)—unlike the way you sing, as if
you are bullying God to answer to your prayers.' He asked
Abdul Karim to move in with his family to the heart of
Shirdi jungle where Sai Baba resided. When the time came
for Abdul Karim's departure, Sai Baba gave him a silver rupee
and said, 'Keep this with you always. Do not spend it. Do not
go to Poona, go to Berar, it will do you a lot of good.'

It was in Nagpur that Abdul Karim came in contact with
Tajuddin Baba. To quote from Jayantilal Zariwala's book:

'At Nagpur Khan Sahab stayed with Raja
Lakshmanrao Bhonsle. On coming to know of the
presence of Tajuddin Baba in his compound, Khan
Sahab grew eager to meet him, but he could not see
the saint for three days. He was restless and so
Lakshmanrao suggested, "In the early hours of dawn
Baba goes out for a walk. Follow him then, if you
can."

'Accordingly, Khan Sahab followed Tajuddin
Baba the next morning. They might not have gone
more than a mile when Baba suddenly turned and
shouted, "Go back, why do you follow me, you who
madden the world? Do you want to madden me too?
Begone!" But Khan Sahab was not to be dissuaded
and kept on following Baba. After about three or
four miles, at what seemed to be a particularly dirty
spot, Baba stopped and said, "Why are you after me?
Do you want to sing to me? All right, sit down and
sing a song in praise of Allah."

'Seizing the chance Khan Sahab started singing
the famous *Doha* of Kabir, "*In tan dhan ki kaun*

badaai/ Dekhat naina mittee milaayi" in raga Jogiya. As he took the antara, "*Apne khaatir mahal banaayaa / Aap hi jangal jaa kar soyaa*"[4], the climax was reached and Tajuddin Baba opened his eyes and said, "Thou hast spoken the truth. All this visual creation will one day come to naught. Dust we are and to dust we return. Oh! The wonder of it all! And now, thou must go."

'"I have come to get your blessings Baba. Please bless me," said Abdul Karim.

'"Thou art already blessed. Therefore thou singest so sweet! Goest thou now and we shall hear thee again." So saying, Tajuddin Baba vanished, Khan Sahab wondering how and where he had gone. And the marvel of it was that though he had sat with Baba on one of the dirtiest spots in the jungle, his clothes remained spotlessly clean.

'Thereafter, Tajuddin Baba used to hear Khan Sahab off and on, during the latter's stay in Nagpur for a month. His favourite song, which he never tired of hearing, was, "*Hari ke bhed na paayo Rama! Kudrat teri rang-birangee, Tu kudrat ka wali* (None has yet penetrated the mysteries of Thy working, Oh Lord Rama! All nature is Thy tool and workshop and Thou the master technician at work)." After hearing the words "*Kudrat teri rang-birangee*" he would clap his hands and dance exclaiming, "It is all kudrat (the sport of Allah) and what kudrat (magic endowed by God) there is in your voice too." Highly pleased with Abdul Karim Khan's art, Tajuddin Baba acclaimed him "Gavaiyon ka Sardaar (Chief of Musicians)". This did not mean none could sing like Karim or even better than him. It only showed the extent of Baba's pleasure. But some of the musicians present took Baba's words literally. And when an angry Shende Khan from Punjab challenged the title exclaiming, "What! Abdul Karim Gavaiyon ka

Sardar?" Baba shouted, "Dispute it not or thou shalt rue it for the rest of thy life."[5]

All this lay in the distant future. Like the sons of all ustads, Abdul Karim and his younger brother Abdul Haque did rigorous riyaz for eight hours a day. That Abdul Karim had a touch of genius was evident from the way he was shaping under the tutelage of Nanhe Khan, a cousin of his father, but his talents owed little to heredity. Karim's father Kale Khan was a mediocre singer, and his mother, herself an accomplished laathi player, was the daughter of a famous wrestler, Masid Khan of Hussainpur. She did not come from a family of musicians and cared little for the musical tradition of the Kirana gharana. Even Nanhe Khan, who had retired from the service of the Nizam of Hyderabad, was hardly an artiste of any extraordinary stature. In twelve months Abdul Karim absorbed more than half of his ustad's repertoire. One evening, while teaching a difficult khayal, *'Dard ki safai Allah, Allah ho Akbar'* in raga Poorvi, Nanhe Khan got up to fill his hookah and told his wife, 'Do you know, I doubt whether I shall have anything left to teach this Karim after six months.' No one knew how, side-by-side, the child prodigy had learnt the tabla, nakkara and sitar. One has come across an old gramophone record of Abdul Karim Khan's Darbari Kanhra and Piloo on the veena. There is evidence that he taught Prince Fateh Singh how to play the jal tarang when Karim Khan was in the court of the Maharaja of Baroda.

The first public concert of Abdul Karim was a fortuitous one. At the age of eleven he accompanied his father to a concert at Meerut to hear some well-known musicians play. As it happened, one or two senior musicians enquired whether the two brothers, Karim and Latif, had been initiated into their ancestral profession. This was followed by a request from the organizers to start the proceedings with a duo from the brothers. They tuned their tanpuras to pancham and nishad, very typical of Kirana artistes to this day, and gave such an excellent rendering of Multani with elaborate vistar followed by the drut khayal 'Kangan mudariya mori' with taans and gamaks that there was an encore from the audience as well as from the artistes present. Without a sarangi accompaniment, their khayal in Poorvi, which followed, was of such excellence that Hyder Baksh, the famous sarangi-player from Mysore and the son-in-law of Abdul Karim's guru Nanhe Khan, patted the boys on their heads and kissed them. He gave them a sovereign each and said, 'Eat ghee and almonds and keep up your practice.' He turned to Kale Khan and said, 'You must bring these lads to Mysore for the Dussera celebrations and I will present them to the Maharaja.'

Six years later, Abdul Karim was exposed to Karnatak music for the first time in the court of Maharaja Chamraj Wadiyar of Mysore. Shabboo Khan, a few years older than Karim and nephew of the famous Tanras Khan of Delhi and Gwalior, also participated in the Dussera festival. Maharaja Chamraj Wadiyar was a great patron of Karnatak as well as Hindustani music. His court musicians included the elderly Peer Khan Daroga, an eminent dhrupad singer, Naththan Khan of the Agra gharana, Hyder Baksh and his disciple Gulaabbai. Both the young musicians from the north, Shabboo Khan and Abdul Karim, earned fulsome praise for their khayals and were rewarded with expensive shawls and gold wristlets. The Karnatak musicians were much taken in by the high, melodious voice of Abdul Karim just as he found the preponderance of sargams in Karnatak music highly intriguing. No doubt his simple but beautiful sargams, which we find in his later 78-RPM records, owed their origin to this momentous occasion. The only other Hindustani musician one can readily think of who was influenced by Karnatak sargams— and virtually started a new style of singing—was Ustad Aman Ali Khan of Bhindibazar, Bombay.

Abdul Karim returned to Kirana via Jaipur and found that his wedding had been arranged. The young bride was Gafuran, a cousin of Ustad Abdul Waheed Khan. Abdul Karim was not keen on marriage but was hardly in a position to defy the decision of the family and his ustad, Nanhe Khan.

The outcome of this marriage was an unfortunate one for Gafuran, who led the life of a spinster. Even when she heard that Abdul Karim, who virtually disappeared soon after the wedding, had married again, she refused to remarry in spite of pressure from the family. Like a Hindu wife, she declared there was no place for another man in her life. Abdul Karim never returned to Kirana and the whole affair soured his relationship with Hyder Baksh and Abdul Waheed Khan.

Soon after the wedding, Abdul Karim and his brother Lateef set out for Kathiawar. They stopped at Bhavnagar, Wadhawan and Junagarh and gave recitals. The Nawab of Junagarh was not particularly keen on classical music though he spent a fortune on tawayefs—and famously, on dogs. His son is reputed to have spent a couple of lakhs on the wedding of his favourite mastiff bitch, to which rajas of neighbouring states were invited. It is a pity that he could not take his entire kennel with him to Pakistan at the time of the Partition of India nor the lifesize oil paintings of his pets resplendent in gold chains and collars which still hang in his dilapidated palace in Junagarh. His father, the elderly Nawab, was an insomniac, whom Abdul Karim and Lateef are reported to have lulled to sleep with their melodious vistar of Darbari Kanhra. They were asked to stay on for a year.

Abdul Karim's younger brother Abdul Haq joined him at Junagarh and Lateef went back to Kirana. On their way back Karim and Haq broke journey at Baroda, one of the bigger native states with a progressive ruler like Sayajirao Gaekwad, known for widespread reforms and welfare programmes for his subjects. He also had the habit of doing his rounds at night incognito, like Haroon-al-Rashid of the *Arabian Nights*, with his faithful ADC Taju Miyan. On one such occasion he heard the two brothers practising at night in the house of their hostess, the elderly Allarakkhibai. Enquiries revealed that they were not residents of Baroda and that they belonged to the distant Kirana village of UP, to which they intended to return soon. A month later the Maharaja heard them again during his rounds, and their melodious voices appealed even to his untrained ear. He asked Taju Miyan to get them to sing to Maharani Jamunabai, who came from Travancore in the south and was a connoisseur of both Karnatak and Hindustani music.

Their first duo recital at the palace was a great success. Their khayal was followed by bhajans and Gujarati folk music in Pahadi Mand, which they had picked up in Junagarh. Their extreme youth, courtly manners and melodious voices made such an impression on the Maharani that they were offered positions in the music school. Abdul Karim was appointed with a starting pay of Rs 150 while Abdul Haq got Rs 80, apart from a cash award of Rs 500 each and two expensive shawls. The allowance for a horse-drawn carriage, which Faiyaz Khan received a few years later, was not given at that time. Abdul Karim thanked Maharaja Sayajirao profusely for his generosity and said that their requirements were simple and their salaries were more than enough for hired quarters, dal-roti and flying kites in the daytime.

Soon after this, Aliya-Fattu (as Ali Baksh and Fateh Ali Khan were together called) arrived with a letter from the Maharaja of Patiala. The virtuosity and taankari of Aliya-Fattu was a byword in the world of music and they were the gandabandh disciples of great ustads like Haddu, Hassu and Tanras Khan. The command performance was arranged with due pomp and splendour before His Highness and his entire court. No one, not even Maula Baksh nor Fayez Mohammad Khan, could summon sufficient courage to participate in the same mehfil. The two ustads from Patiala started their recital with the raga Basant in vilambit followed by the song 'Tori gail gaili aindi aindi' in fast ektaal with such dazzling taans and paltas and at such speed, that the musicians present in the audience were dumbfounded. Sir Sayajirao was young, then, and although he was far from being the connoisseur that he became in later days, was piqued by the realization that there was no ustad in his court who could give a fitting rejoinder to these two virtuosos from the court of the Maharaja of Patiala.

When he turned to request Maula Baksh, who was the principal of the Baroda music school, to play, the latter got up and with folded hands whispered into the Maharaja's ears that Ali Baksh and Fateh Ali, apart from being great ustads, were '*mehmaan*', honoured guests, and it would be improper for him or Fayez Mohammad Khan to sing after their recital. This made Sir Sayajirao even more indignant. He burst out loud enough for his entire court to hear, 'I fail to understand the protocol of the ustads. I spend lakhs of rupees on music and musicians every year, only to find now that there is no one here who can save the face of Baroda. You talk about form and etiquette, I call it incompetence. What about the *chhote* musicians, the two young brothers?'

He turned to Abdul Karim and asked, 'Do you have the courage to sing after this?' With folded hands Abdul Karim stood up and said, 'At your service, Maharaj, Huzoor's command will give us the courage.' Then the brothers sat down and tuned the tanpura in nishad and pancham and took everyone's breath away by starting on the same raga, Basant. Their treble and tuneful voices and elaborate vistar wiped away the impact of the fireworks of the older, great ustads in a matter of minutes. To sing the same raga after Aliya-Fattu was a huge breach of etiquette, to say the least. Karim and Abdul Haq further shocked the audience by taking up the same song, '*Tori gail gaili*', in drut ektaal with superb nonchalance and proceeded to outrival Aliya-Fattu by trotting out a series of amazing taans and paltas. Ali Baksh muttered to his partner, 'Let these bastards come to Patiala once, they will be skinned alive!' Maula Baksh, who did not like the senior duo because of an earlier difference on the system of teaching music through notations in the school, now perceived the way the wind was blowing and loudly praised Karim and Haq. Maharaj Sayajirao was overjoyed but the happiest person was young Tarabai, the niece of the Maharani, listening from behind the dainty blinds of fine bamboo strips, which separated the ladies' enclosure from the rest of the durbar. She will return to this story.

Thus began the second chapter of Abdul Karim's tenure in Baroda. The Maharani loved to hear bhajans, which the brothers sang regularly to her. The Maharaja was, of course, very pleased with the way in which the boys conducted themselves with modesty and graceful manners. Their triumphant recital and praise from all and sundry could have easily turned the heads of two such young boys. He was also astonished to discover that they could ride and hunt, activities associated with the well-born and the aristocracy. Apparently they had acquired these virtues while staying at Junagarh.

Meanwhile, Lord Elgin, the Viceroy of India, paid a visit to Baroda, which was easily the biggest event in the reign of Sir Sayajirao Gaekwad, because Lord Elgin, on behalf of the King Emperor of the British Empire, ruled over three hundred and thirty million Indians. (In fact, much later, Edward VIII is reported to have remarked, 'I did not realize what it was to be King Emperor until I visited India and met the Viceroy.') The grand reception was followed by an evening concert when conductor Fredliss and his band played the ragas Yaman and Poorvi. The famous Kathak dancers Kalka and Bindadin from Lucknow performed before the Viceroy. The finale of the evening was a recital by the Karim brothers, who had composed a song specially for the occasion in raga Rasikranjani, obviously an acquisition from the south during Abdul Karim's visit to the court of Mysore. Lord Elgin wanted the words of the song to be translated. Taju Miyan's, the ADC of the Maharaja's effort to render them into English pleased his Lordship immensely: 'O you king of kings, the giver, the protector of the cow and the Brahmins, the arbiter of our destiny, we sing and pray for your welfare.' The young musicians were given certificates with the viceregal signature and two gold rings.

I quote the following from Jayantilal Zariwalla's book because it has a bearing on what I wrote in an earlier chapter on ustads of the Agra gharana:

'After the birthday celebrations of Prince Fateh Singh Gaekwad, two reputed musicians of the Agra

Abdul Karim Khan and Tarabai

gharana arrived at the house of Fayez Mohammad
Khan. They were Ghulam Abbas and Naththan
Khan. In honour of the guests Fayez Mohammad
arranged a dinner recital wherein he invited all the
well-known artistes including the Karim brothers...
At this recital, after Bhaskar Rao Bakhle, Dand
Khan, Alauddin and Abdul Haq had sung, a subject
cropped up when in reply to a request for thumri,
Karim said, "The dhuns and thumris are considered
below the dignity of ustads by my colleagues and it
would offend their sensibility if I sang them here"...
Abbas Tayebji said, "Look at our Rajasahab. See
how many reforms he has introduced for the
advancement of knowledge. He is taking to new and
better ways, and you remain rotting and hugging the
old rubbish. This is not the way to the cultural
renaissance... What is this nonsense that dhuns and
thumris cannot be sung at a concert and that no
other raga cannot be sung after Bhairavi?"... The
rebuke had the desired effect and Abdul Karim sang
a thumri (*"Lagi mori bindiya chamakan"*) and Ghulam
Abbas and Naththan Khan sang another (*"Na
maanungi, na maanung"*).'

This incident is important for two reasons. Earlier, in the
chapter on Faiyaz Khan and the Agra gharana, I had stated
that thumris and ghazals were the sole prerogative of tawayefs
and sarangi players. Ustads of established gharanas would not
touch them in public with the wrong end of the tanpura. The
Agra gharana was one such gharana, which stuck to dhrupad
and dhamars through the centuries until Ghagge Khuda
Baksh imported the khayal from Gwalior in the early
nineteenth century. I further mentioned that Ustad Faiyaz
Khan, inspired by Moujuddin and Bhaiyya Saheb Ganpatrao,
was the first ustad of this gharana, who started singing
thumris in concerts. His father-in-law, the great Daras Piya,
composed thumris and taught Zohrabai but would not have

dreamt of singing those in mehfils. Here, however, is the strange example of two revered ustads, Ghulam Abbas Khan, the maternal grandfather of Faiyaz Khan, and his famous cousin Naththan Khan, singing '*Na maanungi*' in public, a song which virtually became Faiyaz Khan's signature tune in his later days. One assumes the above incident was a rare exception to the general convention until both Faiyaz Khan and Abdul Karim Khan, the two great musicians of the last century, made it a point to end their recitals with thumris and dadras and took this genre to new heights.

Thus the two brothers prospered under the patronage of the Maharaja, happy with their recitals, flying kites and occasional hunting expeditions, until the Maharaja, on the advice of Fredliss, decided to introduce a proper curriculum in the music academy with books containing famous compositions with notations. Abdul Karim was asked to prepare the course under Maula Baksh's supervision. Karim, of course, did not have the foggiest idea of notation. When Fredliss tried to explain it to him, he rightly pointed out that Hindustani music does not deal with static notes. Without meend, gamak, shruti and kan swaras, one can at best put down the bare skeleton of a sthayee and antara in print. Maula Baksh, while appreciating the validity of Karim Khan's argument, insisted on carrying out the royal wishes. Notations, he said, had come to stay, because without them the disciple was entirely dependent on the whims of his ustad and in the process many authentic compositions were getting lost for ever. As Abdul Karim could barely sign his name in Urdu, it was decided that Tarabai, who had been learning from him, would assist him.

The inevitable happened. The respect and admiration that Tarabai had for her guru, deepened to love. Sardar Marutirao Mane, her father, was a man of a highly suspicious nature and given to bouts of heavy drinking and wife-beating. When the wife died the daughter had to bear the brunt. Regular beatings, punctuated by long hours in locked rooms, crossed bearable limits and she decided to leave home. On her insistence, Abdul Karim, his brother and Tahera Begum, as she came to be called, caught an early morning train to Bombay.

Such an act, which involved a member of the royal family, would have called for rare courage even from an accomplished scoundrel. For poor Abdul Karim this was a feat of unprecedented daring. To remain in British India might have been hazardous if Marutirao Mane sought the help of the police. The alternative, arranging a simple double murder to vindicate his family honour, was not outside the scope of privileges enjoyed by a member of the royal household. One does not know on whose advice Abdul Karim sought refuge in Kolhapur, Satara or Miraj, because that was the safest thing to do. His wanderings ceased at Miraj, where he fell violently ill—of suspected bubonic plague. In another supernatural experience, a fakir appeared on Abdul Karim's doorstep next morning, and blessed him and Tarabai with the words, 'Do not worry, take him to the dargah of Khwaja Shamna Meer and let him sing and pray. He will be all right.' Karim was completely cured and this was reason for his prolonged stay in Miraj.

This was when he heard Rahmat Khan for the first time. Rahmat Khan had a profound influence on Abdul Karim's music.[6] On his way from Miraj to Sangli, Abdul Karim stopped at the Dattatreya temple, where the priest gave him prasad and informed him that Ustad Rahmat Khan was scheduled to sing in Kurundwar. He was also told that Khansaheb, an opium addict, was highly unpredictable. He might suddenly get up and leave in the middle of a recital or may go on singing even if the Maharaja felt like bringing the mehfil to a close. Abdul Karim was lucky. Rahmat Khan was in excellent mood and sang a Bhupali which bowled Karim Khan over. Rahmat Khan's uncle Natthu Khan had musical connections with Kirana. When Abdul Karim was introduced to Rahmat Khan, he asked him whether he knew any of Natthu Khan's famous taranas. Abdul Karim sang one in Malkauns. Before he could finish, Rahmat Khan started the slow khayal *'Peer na jaani'* in the same raga. The *sa* in the upper octave, every time it was hit with the *mukhda*, made Abdul Karim shiver all over in sheer ecstasy. Karim accompanied Rahmat Khan for the best part of an hour and told his disciples, including his chronicler Kapileshwaribuwa, that it was an unforgettable experience.

Abdul Karim Khan never returned to Baroda. Even when Pandit Bhatkhande organized the first of his Grand Conferences in 1916 in Baroda, Karim Khan expressed his unwillingness to participate, though Marutirao Mane was gone by that time. Sir Sayajirao was, of course, a man of different quality. When he met Abdul Karim in Mysore during a Dussera festival, he addressed him affectionately and enquired about his family. Abdul Karim asked for the Maharaja's forgiveness, saying, 'Your Royal Highness, it is my destiny which took me away from your magnanimous patronage. I do, however, attach Barodekar[7] to the names of our children. I now have five children. The eldest is Abdul Rahman. My daughter, Champutai, is younger by three years. The third child, Gulab, is also a daughter, followed by Abdul Hamid. The youngest is Sakin Chhotutai. We shall always remember your affection and kindness as long as we live, and we pray for your long life and happiness.'

Of the five children, only Champutai, when she grew up into an eminent singer, would write Barodekar after the name Hirabai. Abdul Rahman became famous as Sureshbabu Mane.[8] I heard him in my youth. He lacked his father's imagination and creativity but his voice and *swar-prayog*, heard on the radio, could have easily been mistaken for those of his father. Gulab, known as Kamlatai, flourished for a while on the Marathi stage and Saraswati Rane, the youngest daughter (Chhotutai), was known for her soulful rendering of Marathi *bhaav-geets*. She is, at the time of writing, still alive.

Abdul Hamid was the most talented of the siblings. At the age of four he could sing the notations of any *taan* of a familiar raga. Once, during a public display of his extraordinary talent, which preceded his father's recital, Pandit Vishnu

Digambar Paluskar climbed on to the stage and sang several taans. The child Abdul Hamid promptly reduced these to sargams with the utmost ease. Interestingly enough, he is the only offspring of the great ustad who did not stick to music. The one who received fame and recognition in every part of the country was Hirabai. Her talim from her father was uninterrupted until Tarabai left Karim Khan and settled in Bombay with her five children. Hirabai then turned to Abdul Waheed Khan who was distantly related to her and better known as the mentor of Ustad Amir Khan.

That was the time when the children were made to adopt Hindu names and the surname of their grandfather Mane. Hirabai's first major recital, in the conference organized by Pandit Vishnu Digambar in 1923, was an instant success. Her voice alone would have made her famous. It was so melodious that she was called 'Kirana ki Koyelia'.[9] Some of the discs of the Gramophone Co. that I was brought upon in my childhood, with the picture of the terrier listening to His Master's Voice, included her Miyan Malhar, Shankara, Adana and Yaman, which did not belie the title given to her.

The mention of Abdul Hamid, whose pet name was 'Papa', reminds me of an article written by Vasant Govind Poddar on Abdul Karim's life. It appeared some years ago in the Bengali journal *Desh*. I gathered from the article that Abdul Hamid was made to change his name to Krishna Rao Mane. He was very young when his parents separated. As such, he never received any talim from his father or his eldest brother Sureshbabu. His extraordinary talent, which had flowered in his infancy, was wasted. He graduated from the Bombay University and for a while managed Hirabai Barodekar's theatre company. At the time of the interview by Vasant Govind Poddar he was fifty-eight.

Vasant Govind asked him, 'Have you kept up your early habit of notations?'

'Not really, but any taan registers in my ears in sargams. That is the easiest thing to do, in my opinion.'

'He plays the violin well, you know. Had he received

talim from his father, his whole life, no doubt, would have changed,' said Nirmala, his wife, with a deep sigh.

'Did you ever meet your father after you left Poona?' asked Vasant Govind.

'Yes, yes! Do tell him about that incident,' Nirmala said with some excitement. "It is almost like a sequence in a Hindi movie.'

'I met him once in 1936. I was travelling from Bombay to Poona. I got a reserved seat next to my father's. He did not recognize me, of course. I also did not tell him that I was Papa, his youngest son. He talked to me nicely and ordered tea. We parted at the Poona Railway Station.'

'This was forty-four years ago,' said Nirmala. 'I cannot help feeling he should have introduced himself. Of course, my husband is one of the shyest and most self-effacing persons in the whole of Maharashtra.'

Among the direct disciples of Ustad Abdul Karim Khan— and they number over twenty-five—the better-known are son Sureshbabu Mane, Rambhau Kundgolkar alias Sawai Gandharva, Ganpatbuwa Bahre, daughter Hirabai, niece Roshanara Begum, Balkrishnabuwa Kapileshwari (Khansaheb's biographer and nominated khalifa, or heir), Shankarrao Kapileshwari, Nivruttibuwa's uncle Shankarrao Sarnaik and Pyare Khan, brother of Azambai of Kolhapur. Except for Roshanara Begum and Pyare Khan all others were Hindus. Khansaheb's biographer and those who were close to him testify that he did not have a communal bone in his body. His spiritual urge took him to temples just as he sang at every important shrine of Muslim saints. He encouraged his Hindu disciples while on tour to visit holy places like Varanasi in the north to Rameshwaram in the south and he bore all the expenses. He would normally end his recitals in Maharashtra with Abhangs—devotional songs in Marathi. He sang '*Hari Om Tatsat*' in raga Malkauns before Lokmanya Tilak, and bhajan and Ram-dhuns to Mahatma Gandhi, who was reported to have said, 'I wish I could take Abdul Karim to every city in India and make him sing his bhajans to Hindus and

Muslims—but where do I find the time, busy as we are in fighting the British, who have created this divide between the two communities?'

Shankarrao Kapileshwari was the disciple who accompanied Khansaheb on the harmonium. Abdul Karim did not approve of the bastardized instrument—with its fixed tempered scale devoid of meends and shrutis—and had a special harmonium made 'wherein the notes were not tempered but concordant. The shadja, or the tonic, of Khansaheb was taken as the shadja of the harmonium and the other notes were constructed in accordance with their positions in the Kalyan and Bhairavi scales. This harmonium could be used for Khansaheb alone. Further, these untempered notes were skilfully joined by delicate touches of the fingers of Shankarrao.'[10] Those unaware of the true nature of the new harmonium often wondered how Shankarrao could produce such marvellous sounds as though he were playing a stringed instrument, often with flowing notes, like a sarangi.

Before this special harmonium was constructed, Khansaheb preferred the sarangi. When a good sarangi-player was unavailable, he would do without any accompaniment. His disciples fought shy of giving him voice support because the best of them generally felt they were out of tune in comparison with Khansaheb. Abdul Karim often sang with one or two tanpuras and nothing else. Nivruttibuwa, nephew of Shankarrao Sarnaik, mentioned to me that on one occasion he tuned four tanpuras. 'No one,' he said, 'could tune a tanpura as perfectly as Khan Sahab. There he was, with four of his disciples behind him, with four huge Miraj tanpuras producing a drone like a swarm of a hundred bees. Suddenly, in the midst of his alaap, he turned around and put his finger on one string which was a shade out of tune. To locate that one out of sixteen separate strings at some distance from Khan Sahab's back goes to show the kind of sensitive ear he had. That is what made him the master of sur that he was.'

On April 2, 1930, Khansaheb invited the musicians of Bombay to a formal dinner where he nominated

Kapileshwaribuwa as his khalifa, investing him with the right
to carry on the Kirana tradition. It would appear, therefore,
that Kapileshwari was closest to him among his disciples and
was perhaps considered by him to be the best and the
brightest. Actually, it was Rambhau Kundgolkar, known to us
as Sawai Gandharva, who has succeeded in carrying on the
Abdul Karim stream of the Kirana tradition effectively. His
disciples include Gangubai Hangal, Firoz Dastur and Bhimsen
Joshi—to name only the famous ones.

When I heard Sawai Gandharva, his voice had started
giving him trouble. V.G. Jog, a lifelong friend who
accompanied me on long musical tours in the Seventies and
early Eighties, was a wonderful companion, full of good
humour and a fund of anecdotes.[11] Very few people know
that Jog, the premier violinist of north India, started life as
a harmonium-player and that his guru Ganpatrao Purohit
accompanied Sawai Gandharva regularly in his concerts.
Sawai Gandharva would start warming up at home three to
four hours before his recital, thereafter continue for another
half an hour in the green room and occasionally, follow that
up on the stage itself. His pupil Firoz Dastur told me, 'A
recital of Rambhauji would be fixed, say, at Laxmibai Hall at
six in the evening. We would sit on Chowpatty beach with
our cups of tea and chaat. Our man would be posted at
Laxmibai. Around seven he would come on his bike, furiously
ringing the bell and shouting, '*Lag gaya, sur lag gaya* (Found
his voice, he has found his voice).' We would rush there to
find people pouring into a half-empty hall, which within
minutes would be packed to capacity. Once Rambhauji
started singing there would be no stopping him. He would
sing for four or five hours at a stretch. The more he sang, the
better would his voice sound. Such sur! Behrebuwa was also
a great artiste but my guru had a better and bigger repertoire.'

According to Ustad Amir Khan, the most faithful, though
not necessarily the most brilliant, representative of the Abdul
Karim stream of Kirana gharana was Firoz Dastur, who learnt
from Sawai Gandharva. In my opinion the pride of place

should go to Sureshbabu Mane, the eldest son and disciple of
Ustad Abdul Karim Khan. That makes him Sawai Gandharva's
khalifa. They worked together in Hirabai Barodekar's theatre
company. Sureshbabu was known for his roles of Ashwin
Sheth in the play *Sanshaya-kallol* and Arjun in *Saubhadra*. He
also worked for a couple of music companies, like Prabhat
and Saraswati Cinetone, as music director, as well as in a few
major roles in such movies as *Satch Hai* and *Devyani*. A top-
class vocalist and an actor of moderate talent, Sureshbabu
was also an accomplished player of the tabla and harmonium.
Govindrao Tembe, a disciple of Ustad Alladiya Khan and
Bhaskarbuwa, was the most famous harmonium-player of his
time in Maharashtra. His duo acts with Sureshbabu were a
regular feature. Among Sureshbabu's disciples were quite a
few big names like the author and chartered accountant
Vamanrao Deshpande, Madhu Kanetkar, Manik Varma,
Menka Shirodkar, Prabha Atre and, of course, Hirabai herself—
before she went to Abdul Waheed Khan. According to
Vamanrao, Bhimsen Joshi also learnt from Sureshbabu for a
while.

I never heard Sureshbabu in person. In my teens the
Bombay radio station would reserve a solid hour in the late
evening for famous musicians, usually vocalists. I remember
some of the names and the kind of impression they created
on young aspirants like my friends and me. There were
Ramkrishnabuwa and Bahrebuwa of Gwalior Gharana, Pandit
Omkarnath Thakur, who had a magnificent voice but
developed a unique melodramatic style which was not without
its comic appeal, Hirabai, Roshanara and Sureshbabu of
Kirana, Moghubai and Lakshmibai Jadav of the Jaipur gharana,
Anjanibai Lolekar, Saraswatibai Faterpekar, Vilayet Hussain
and Khadim Hussain Khan of the Agra gharana and many
lesser artistes who were given half-hour slots twice a day.
Ustad Faiyaz Khan would come over from Baroda once a
month to sing on Bombay radio. I owe a great deal to AIR,
especially the high standard of the Bombay radio station, for
my musical education and my catholic outlook towards all
gharanas, since I heard the best of them in my youth.

When I first heard Sureshbabu Mane, I thought he was a carbon copy of Abdul Karim. His voice-throw and mannerisms were as close to those of his father as to be positively uncanny. Gradually, I realized the son lacked the father's imagination and supreme aesthetic sense. Nevertheless, his class was unquestionable and his ability to bestow a certain incandescence on each and every note did remind a sensitive listener of his father. It is a great pity no adequate proof of this exists except a couple of 78 RPM records. One can, however, quote Vamanrao Deshpande on this subject, since he was very close to Sureshbabu for nearly ten years before he shifted his loyalty to Moghubai and Jaipur:

'In August 1928 I had to leave Bombay for reasons of health and take up a job in Poona. In the two preceding years I had become acquainted with the Gwalior tradition even to the extent of being able to sing jhumras and tilwadas. I thought I must pursue my musical training in Poona. Several evenings were spent in looking for an appropriate guru, but no one pleased me. One evening I went to Sureshbabu's house. The following dialogue took place:

'"I am a student of music. I have picked up some music and I want to study further."

'"Let me hear, at any rate, what you have learnt."

'I sang a khayal for Sureshbabu. He himself provided the basic tabla accompaniment. After I had finished, Sureshbabu said, "If you want to learn from me you will have to wipe out everything you have learnt so far. Then alone I can teach you."

'His remark gave me a rude shock. I had taken to vocal music since my childhood. Later, for a couple of years I had taken systematic tuitions as well—and this gentleman was now telling me to unlearn whatever I had learnt. In other words, I had been struggling in vain all these years! "But before I decide to do that, please let me hear you. Then only I can make up my mind," I said.

'He must have thought this was impertinence. But he did not seem to mind and sang for me for a little while. It was indeed a revelation! I found his music so utterly enchanting that I was instantly enslaved. It was not just music but pure hypnotism.'

Sureshbabu's fee was five rupees which he took in advance and promptly spent on two tickets for a movie and three-and-a-half rupees worth of agarbatti.[12] In the next two years he rarely took any money from Vamanrao and that, too, only when he was in distress and his disciple stuffed the notes into his pocket. Writes Vamanrao Deshpande about his teacher:

'The important point about Baburao's [Sureshbabu's] teaching was how rather than what... Purity of notes was not something completely unknown to me but when I started Sureshbabu's tuition I immediately sensed how imperfect my perception of tonal accuracy had been... He invariably began by asking me to produce the first note sa. But my sa did not sound like his. Every few seconds he would say "Too low" or "Too high" and this went on all the time. In between he would demonstrate how the note should sound. He refused to move up to re until the sa was to his satisfaction... Once in a while I could produce the note that he wanted. On those occasions not only did his face glow with satisfaction but I myself felt so thrilled with the sheer beauty of that one note that I felt the entire magic of music was contained in that tonic... From sa we proceeded painfully to re and ga and the rest of the octave in precisely the same manner... With a correctly pronounced note the tanpura in one's hand sounded intensely melodious whereas the sound created by a false note drowned the drone of the tanpura. Baburao taught me how to apply this unerring test to myself.'[13]

I have quoted Vamanrao at length to establish two points: first, the fanatical emphasis on sur, which is the most important feature of the Kirana gayaki. The second is the kind of training the children of Abdul Karim Khan and his niece Roshanara Begum had received from the great man, which is reflected in Sureshbabu's fastidious precision about fundamentals. Other disciples and their successors have all been highly tuneful but none, with the possible exception of Bhimsen Joshi, could be compared to Sureshbabu, Hirabai and Roshanara Begum. Abdul Karim Khan, of course, stands apart. Bhimsen's voice cannot be called sweet and mellifluous but he hits the notes right in the middle, with un-Kirana like power, reminiscent somewhat of Ustad Faiyaz Khan of the Agra gharana.

The quest for tonal purity, however, did not make Sureshbabu Mane a great khayal singer. His bol alaap or vistar indicated that he had taken a leaf out of Abdul Waheed Khan's book, though it was Hirabai who formally became Khansaheb's disciple. Vamanrao attributes Sureshbabu's failure to lack of riyaz and an undisciplined lifestyle. According to Govindrao Tembe, Sureshbabu's rendering of khayal was initially reminiscent of Abdul Karim Khan but he did not indulge in the long-drawn tonal improvisations of Khansaheb. Also, his fast taans were not always distinct, even though Vamanrao disputes that. Unlike Sawai Gandharva, he was not fond of bol-taans and rhythmic play of words, nor of layakari, though Sureshbabu was an accomplished tabla player. Vamanrao Deshpande, however, maintains that Sureshbabu, in his time, was the king of thumri:

> 'Intricate tonal play of thumri, the minute movement from note to note, subtle suggestions of hardly vocalized notes, microtones and other subtleties and nuances used to come from his voice with such exquisite delicacy that one felt no one on earth could rival him in thumri singing.'[14]

Until 1944, when the Maharashtrans had their first taste of Bade Ghulam Ali's thumri, apparently it was Sureshbabu who held sway in Bombay and Poona. But no indication has been given by Vamanrao of the brand of thumri that he sang. Certainly, Abdul Karim Khan's famous thumris, as we hear them in 78 RPM records, are totally different from the Purab ang-based authentic thumris of Benaras or the Punjab ang of Bade Ghulam Ali Khan. In fact, the dividing line between Abdul Karim's khayal and thumri was certainly a thin one. There is no indication whether Sureshbabu followed his father's brand of thumri or developed a style of his own. One would not be inclined to call any of Sureshbabu's disciples an outstanding thumri singer; and that includes Manik Varma, Prabha Atre and even Hirabai Barodekar who, with Roshanara Begum, were top of the list of female singers of Kirana gharana for well-nigh forty years.

One would be inclined to think that a vocalist of his quality, an accomplished tabla and harmonium-player, who had acted on the stage and in a film or two, would be reasonably affluent. But Vamanrao says Sureshbabu spent the best part of his life with seven children in utter penury. He never sang successfully in a concert. His was, strictly speaking, chamber music; in fact mini-chamber music, which hardly fetched him any money. He lived on tuitions which, at the rate of five or ten rupees a month, could not have helped him to rise above the poverty line even in the 1930s. The one and only white jacket he wore to concerts had turned yellow and his dhoti required so many stitches that he had a needle and thread stuck inside his cap, ready for use.

V.G. Jog, who had accompanied Hirabai and Sureshbabu to East Africa, had a slightly different story to tell. Except the hours when the ship's bar was officially closed, Sureshbabu, clad in a white long coat and trousers purchased by his sister for the occasion, was a permanent part of the scenery, lost to the rest of the world. He hardly sang during the tour despite repeated requests from his hosts and sponsors. On the last morning at Dar-es-Salam, he changed his mind. He sang after

Hirabai's recital. V.G. Jog swears Sureshbabu's komal rishabh Asavari was the best he had heard.

On his return, in a desperate bid to progress from rags to riches, he developed a strange addiction to alchemy on borrowed capital. He turned a corner of his room into a factory where he assembled copper and tin plates, a bellow and chemicals. The madness lasted a year or two—until one evening when he went to sleep and just never woke up.

Among Abdul Karim Khan's close relatives, those who benefitted from his talim were his cousin Abdul Haq and his daughter Roshanara Begum, whose mother was a lesser-known tawayef called Chandabai. In the post-Zohrabai period, the two great female singers of khayal were Roshanara and Kesarbai. Stylistically, they were dramatically different. Roshanara followed the Kirana method of elongated swar vistar at roughly twice the speed of Abdul Waheed, but Hirabai proceeded in a leisurely manner from one note to the next, like peeling the outer layers of an onion. Kesarbai preferred bahlawa to vistar, as is the custom in the Jaipur gharana. Her taans were longer, more intricate and offered bejewelled patterns, each different from the other, rendered in shuddh akar. Roshanara's taans were shorter, just like those of Abdul Karim Khan, but much faster. Her fast taans, some of them with gamaks, were like flashes of lightning. I have never approved of gamak taans taken by women. Roshanara, to my mind, was the outstanding exception to be made. For sheer taiyari, as the word is understood nowadays, she had no equal.

The Partition of India saw Roshanara Begum, who reportedly owed a lot of money in income tax, drifting to Pakistan. She married a police inspector, who did not approve of her singing in public. She continued to sing on the radio and some of these recitals of her later days have come out in pirated cassettes in India. In 1978, more than forty years after she became a Pakistani citizen, Roshanara came to Delhi with Malika Pukhraj, remembered as the ghazal queen of pre-Partition days. Naina Devi arranged a recital on her lawn and everybody who was anybody in the world of music was present. She did not announce the raga but it was Puriya Kalyan with a komal nishad. She started her recital with a brief remark about the poverty of classical music in Pakistan and added that she hardly practised any more, leave alone gave public recitals. Her music, however, showed no signs of age or lack of riyaz. Her extremely melodious vistar lulled us into a feeling of relaxed contentment when, after reaching the tonic of the upper octave, she suddenly took a descending gamak taan, so swift and so perfect that it might have been a ray of light. It was utterly unexpected and so breathtaking that there was a spontaneous chorus of applause from the ustads sitting in the front row. The taans which followed indicated a concealed power behind the feline silkiness of her style. There was not the slightest sign of effort on her face. She was fat and dark and even her most ardent admirers would not have found her appearance alluring. But when she sang, the expression of serenity, the inner feeling of peaceful union with the swaras on her face would convey itself to the audience. The sudden intrusion of a violent yet effortless gamak taan, followed invariably by a smile, would transform her for a fleeting moment into a very lovely person.

Gangubai Hangal also took halaq and gamak taans but Roshanara Begum's taans seemed even more in tune. Gangubai's voice had a masculine touch and her style could not be called feminine either. Her development of raga followed the Kirana tradition but lacks the lyricism of her predecessors. I heard her for the first time in 1943, in Lucknow, in the house of Professor Nirmal Siddhant. His wife, Chitralekha Siddhant, my Jhunumashi, had a lovely voice, extraordinarily powerful for a woman. She could have made quite a name for herself as a singer of Tagore's songs had she lived in Bengal. The Bengalis in Lucknow called her the Nightingale from Santiniketan. But she was crazy about Hindustani classical music and would often tell me, 'Barring your father, I doubt anyone in Lucknow has heard more ustads and tawayefs than myself.'

It was in her spacious drawing room that I heard Gangubai, along with my father and maybe half a dozen others. She sang Lalit with an elaborate vistar and several well-structured and powerful taans. She eschewed all taans in the Bilaskhani Todi that followed with the remark, '*Is raag ki bhaavna mein taan ki jagah nahin hai* (taans do not agree with the personality of this raga).' The remark seemed quite extraordinary at that time. I was barely sixteen then. I realized the wisdom of that statement much later in life. Bhairav is another raga, in my opinion, that does not admit of unnecessary alankars or taans. For that, one should turn to Raamkali, a cousin of Bhairav, with more or less the same notes. Each raga has its own character and a truly sensitive artiste can feel that.

One should be thankful to Providence that in this age of musical poverty, Bhimsen Joshi is still alive and seems to sing better than ever within the limitations forced on him by age and illness. With a fractured tailbone, which never healed properly, and a brain tumour behind him, this octogenarian sits at public recitals, dangling his legs from a chair, and hits the notes in their epicentre with a power that can turn singers half his age sick with envy. That his taans, which he could take at electric speed till the other day, have become a lot slower makes no difference to his drut khayals. He would be the first to deny that he has a sweet voice, but he has attained swar-siddhi.

I heard him first in the Jhankar Music Circle at the residence of Jnan Prakash Ghosh in Dixon Lane in the Fifties. Pahadi Sanyal, the elderly star of Bengali films, was sitting next to me. He was originally from Lucknow and did his Sangeet Visharad from Marris College under Pandit Bhatkhande himself. He learnt dhrupad from the great Nasiruddin Khan, the father of Moinuddin and Aminuddin Dagar, khayal from Baba Nasir Khan, thumri from Benazir Bai and tabla from Acchan Maharaj, the father of the equally famous dancer Birju Maharaj.

All this erudition, however, did not help him to become a performing artiste except as an actor who sang film songs on screen. But as a listener, with his timely daad[15] in polished Urdu, he stood out among Bengalis who were not acquainted with the musical climate and culture of the north. On this occasion, after Bhimsen Joshi finished his recital, Pahadi Sanyal asked for the name of the last raga sung by him. Bhimsen came over and touched Pahadi Sanyal's feet and said, '*Isko Chhaya kahke seekha hamney* (I learnt it as Chhaya).' The confusion in our minds was due to Bhimsen dwelling on the nishad in the ascending scale, which neither Pahadikaka nor myself had ever heard in Chhaya or Chhayanat. Fifty years ago, Bhimsen was a young musician who had already made a mark in Calcutta while Pahadi Sanyal was a well-known aging film star. That Bhimsen touched Pahadi Sanyal's feet was not particularly unexpected but noticing the embarrassment on Pahadi Sanyal's face he said, 'I don't think you have spotted me, Sahab, I am the same Bhimsen who came to you for training when you lived on Raja Basant Roy Road.'

'Good lord!' said Pahadikaka after the usual pleasantries were over and Bhimsen left us. 'I can't believe it is the same boy. He came to me all the way from Poona to learn music. He had a voice like a buffalo calf with a cold. I told him he had no future as a singer but I might be able to find him a petty job in the New Theatres Studio. He lived in my house for a while. I would pay him a tenner or two for running errands and then he suddenly disappeared one day. Good heavens! Astafullah! How can this man be the same Bhimsen?'

In his wanderings, Bhimsen went to Lucknow, Gwalior and finally to Rampur to learn from Ustad Mushtaq Hussain Khan, the then court musician and guru of Nawab Raza Ali. The penniless boy from distant Maharashtra got precious little out of the venerable ustad although Joshi stayed with him for nearly a year. He ran errands for his teacher as well, shopping even for meat, taboo in Marathi Brahmin households. In Lucknow one would find him sitting in a teashop run by D.C. Dutt, otherwise a sought-after singer of geet and ghazals, who drew the highest fee of seventy-five rupees for his radio recitals in those days. On his recommendation, Bhimsen became a regular artiste at Lucknow radio station, singing bhajans for fifteen rupees. All this did Bhimsen Joshi a world of good. He heard all the great ustads of the north and absorbed a lot, traces of which are noticeable in his gayaki.

When we hear records of Abdul Karim Khan and Sawai Gandharva followed by any of Bhimsen Joshi, we realize how dynamic the Kirana gharana is. As Vamanrao Deshpande rightly observes, each generation imported new ideas and yet the basic characteristics of the gharana remained inviolate. Abdul Karim Khan concentrated on sur, and his kan swaras while approaching a note were amazingly beautiful. He liked simple ekhara taans and spontaneous sargams, which were not complicated but wonderfully well-structured. There is no hint of paltas, which have become the rage after Bade Ghulam Ali and Amir Khan. There are gamak taans, which follow the rhythm in Abdul Karim Khan's record of *Shuddha Kalyan.* There is some indication in his record of Darbari Kanhra that he did not altogether ignore rhythm, although one gathers from those who had heard him in person that he did not particularly care for bol-bant.

Sawai Gandharva's presentation was certainly more organized and laya-baddha, or rhythm-bound. His taans also indicate a departure from Karim Khan's penchant for the ekhara taans of Gwalior. Bhimsen Joshi's entire khayal, even the vilambit portion, is rhythm-based. Which is why he prefers ektaal and vilambit teentaal to the elongated jhumra or even the extremely slow ektaal that Karim Khan preferred when accompanied by Shamsuddin.

Like Amir Khan, Abdul Karim, in his vistar, did not wish to be disturbed by the conventional demands of the accompanists for saath-sangat. Bhimsen Joshi, on the other hand, seems to have imbibed the Jaipur gharana's approach of singing regular rhythmic beats. (In an interview with him for the 'Charcha' series arranged by Jalsaghar at the Ramkrishna Institute of Culture in Calcutta, I played the records of Rahmat Khan, Abdul Karim, Sawai Gandharva,

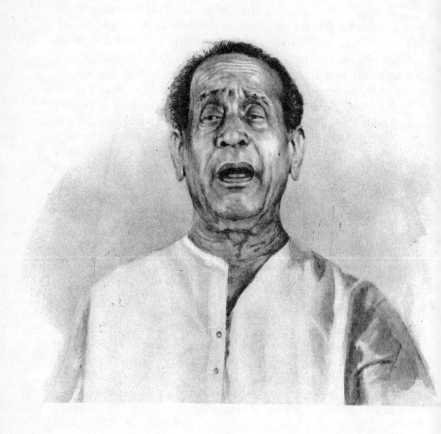

Bhimsen Joshi

Hirabai Barodekar and Sureshbabu Mane, together with my comments and analyzes. In the course of the interview, he did acknowledge the influence of more than one singer from the past and they included Amir Khan on the one hand and Kesarbai on the other, representing the two extremes of the spectrum.) As a result of the influence of Jaipur gayaki, Bhimsen's slow exposition of the raga is knit in a compact and coherent design and never becomes unwieldy or ponderous.

I also have a recorded tape of his Maru Bihag sung a decade ago in the house of the late Mohan Surraiya, where Latafat Khan, Ravi Kichlu and I were present. No doubt our presence encouraged him to indulge in bol-taans and layakari in the true Agra fashion, which he did better than anybody else. Ulhas Kashalkar tells me that Bhimsen once demonstrated to him the bahlawa of the Gwalior gayaki. This was a natural thing to do, after his one-year stint in Rampur with Ustad Mushtaq Hussain Khan. All this, however, has not turned his music into patchwork, which would have been inevitable with a lesser artiste. He has absorbed the features of more than one gayaki and made each his own, while owing steadfast allegiance to Kirana. Chetan Karnavi, in his book *Listening to Hindustani Music,* writes:

> 'As Joshi once told me with a twinkle in his eye, he had processed all these borrowed commodities in his Kirana factory—he has added to this borrowed stuff a certain emotional aura and meditative touch.'

Like that of his famous predecessors, his music is introspective, even meditative. Very often, friends and admirers sitting in front of him would make loud appreciative noises, but it would be obvious from his glazed eyes that they did not register as external stimulus. His dazzling fast taans were triggered by short volleys in the style of Agra, and he preferred rhythmic weaving around three or four notes, culminating in a crescendo in the upper octave where falsetto comes into play. He crashes down to the tonic, invariably with a sapaat, like Amir Khan's. His use of pukars, which calls for hitting the notes in the taar saptak in a full-throated lower register, has tremendous dramatic impact, somewhat reminiscent of Faiyaz Khan's. Bhimsen Joshi's music has drama—never the melodrama of Pandit Omkarnath Thakur and Jasraj.

Some hard-nosed critics fail to discover the cerebral content in his music. Fortunately, I am not one of those who perceive any dichotomy between aesthetic and intellectual appeal. Yet another group of critics finds his limited repertoire of ragas boring. In the days of Abdul Karim and Faiyaz Khan, listeners wanted to hear the elongated version of the ragas which, rendered in 78 RPM records, had contributed to the popularity of the singers. In the days of LPs, cassettes and CDs, it is not unreasonable to expect a bigger repertoire from artistes.

I remember an evening in the Sixties, when I persuaded Bhimsen Joshi to sing Bihag, Kedara and Shankara, not uncommon ragas by any means, but which I had never heard sung by him. On the tanpuras were Ravi Kichlu and I. The audience consisted of my wife and Buddhi, my cocker spaniel. There was no tabla-player. Suddenly, Amjad Ali dropped in wearing a tee-shirt and jeans. He was still in his teens when he had made his presence felt in Calcutta with his distinct sarod baaj. His handsome face, open smile and perfect manners had made him a darling of the crowds. Those days, he would put up at the Broadway Hotel on Ganesh Chandra Avenue, not too far from my flat in Esplanade Mansions. He happily agreed to be the tabla accompanist that evening. But as the AIR station was only a few minutes' walk away, a phone call brought over Jnan Prakash Ghosh, along with V.G. Jog, and Amjad Ali was replaced. I remember with some disappointment that Bhimsen Joshi's handling of those ragas, which fell outside his repertoire those days, was not marked with his usual fluency and ease, nor did they fit into his usual graceful Kirana gayaki.

However, there is more to Bhimsen Joshi's music than

the usual critical response. He may not be a pundit or an
ustad with a bagful of ragas and bandishes, but his open voice
and ability to hit the notes right in the middle with the kind
of abandon not uncommon among the ustads of pre-
microphone days, have tremendous impact. So does the
pianissimo-fortissimo effect of his voice-throw—wrongly called
modulation by Indians. Above all, he has the supreme ability
to get lost in his own music with no thought of pleasing the
audience. I cannot say the same about anyone since the
death of the great Abdul Karim, except Ustad Amir Khan,
who took the Kirana tradition to unexplored heights.

Ustad Abdul Karim Khan was criticised in his time for
the unorganized structure of his recital. At that time he got
lost in sur, just as Tajuddin Baba had predicted, and as long
as he sang his audience sat mesmerized. There was no need
for anything else. The attitude of the followers of Abdul
Karim and Kirana gharana can be summed up by one of their
popular aphorisms: *'Taal gaya to baal gaya, sur gaya to sar gaya*
(If one misses the taal, it is like losing a hair, going out of
tune is as bad as losing one's head)'. Agra gharana ustads, no
doubt, would find themselves in violent disagreement with
Kirana on this issue, nor would this saying apply to Bhimsen
Joshi's music.

According to the cognoscenti of Abdul Karim's generation
such as Thakur Jaidev Singh, the philosopher musicologist, or
my father, who was habitually committed to analysis, any
attempt to dissect Karim Khan's style and music would be as
foolish as trying to measure the merit of a vintage claret by
sending the bottle to a chemical analyst. Nonetheless,
musicologists at home and abroad have attempted to do so on
the basis of the scanty material available to us. I have never
been able to unearth any long-playing recordings of his
though there are avid collectors who have in their possession
such records of Faiyaz Khan and Kesarbai dating back to the
pre-War era. We have to fall back on thirty-four 78 RPM
records of his together with a few which must have been
recorded when he was young. These records, some of which

run to no more than a minute, have found their place in the *Chairman's Choice* series of HMV.

They clearly establish that he was not above the enthusiastic pursuit of taiyari and fast taans common to all young musicians, then and now. None of Abdul Karim Khan's records, therefore, gives us a clear idea of his vistar or bol-alaap which were his forte. Yet those records which are still in circulation convey even to the common listener the magic of his all-pervading sur. To be judged only on the basis of dated gramophone records of the pre-electronic era could be a tremendous handicap for a musician. Yet like the great Russian violinist Jasche Heifetz, whom we also heard only on 78 RPM records, Abdul Karim ranks in our minds as one of the all-time greats. The other day we had an Abdul Karim evening at the ITC Sangeet Research Academy where I played records of my choice to the students and a few outsiders. Some of them, who were hearing the records for the first time, were in tears.

Of the musicians who were born in the second half of the nineteenth century and departed in the first half of the twentieth, two names, those of Faiyaz Khan and Abdul Karim Khan, were on the lips of all music-lovers. Yet no greater contrast could be offered than by these two. Faiyaz Khan's pitch was C, later B Sharp in his old age. Abdul Karim Khan chose F. The timbre of Faiyaz Khan's voice belonged to the string instrument variety with plenty of jawari. Abdul Karim Khan's high-pitched piping voice resembled a wind instrument, which is why the primitive microphone could record the high frequency of his notes. It failed to do so in Faiyaz Khan's case and led to distortions, which is why he was made to sit two feet away from the microphone for his early recordings by the Hindustan Co. Ltd.

Faiyaz Khan liked to dwell on the notes in mandra saptak, or the lower octave, and hardly went beyond madhyam in the taar saptak. Only once, in an AIR recording of Kamod, did I hear him hitting the pancham. Abdul Karim loved the higher octave where the notes hit by him seemed to be pierced by a needle. When he came to the lower octave he preferred to use 'awe' or 'haw' instead of the shuddh akar. It also sounded slightly artificial because his voice lacked depth. It was naturally sweet, melodious and pliant, adjectives which have scarcely been used to describe Faiyaz Khan's voice. Faiyaz Khan's music was called 'majestic' by Amir Khan, while Abdul Karim's was famous for its lyrical quality. Faiyaz Khan did the nom-tom alaap of the dhrupads before he came to his khayal bandish. Abdul Karim did his bol-alaap or bol-vistar in khayal, which was a novelty those days. Each in his own way was a master of sur and shruti with adequate use of kan swaras. Shruti could be best explained to the non-Indian as semitones or microtones, but they are not fixed like notes. They can also be oscillating, like the komal gandhar of Darbari Kanhra or that of Miyan Malhar.

A kan swara is a note particle or a subtle shade of the next or the previous note, which brings out the emotive quality of the raga by hinting at what is to come. For instance when either of the afore-mentioned ustads started with the sa in Darbari, there was just a shade of komal ni, not discernible except to the trained sensitive ear, which contributed to the atmosphere of the raga. Faiyaz Khan liked building his innings round the composition. Karim Khan was so lost in sur that he would not pay adequate attention to the nayaki anga[16] and sometimes forgot to sing the antara. Faiyaz Khan was a purist and would not break any laws. Abdul Karim Khan would break all laws save his own law. Faiyaz Khan liked bol-banana which he had borrowed from qawaali, and bol-bant which has obviously been borrowed by the Gwalior and Agra gharanas, and khayal from dhrupad and dhamar. Neither of these found favour with Abdul Karim Khan though there is evidence that he could sing dhrupad and was capable of layakari. Faiyaz Khan's taans had plenty of halak and gamak, which Abdul Karim Khan was not incapable of producing as is evident in his record of Shuddh Kalyan, but he preferred simple taans like the ekhara linear and sapat taans of Gwalior. The baraabar laya taans of the Agra gharana, which are woven round three or four successive notes in a rhythmic pattern, were scarcely taken by Abdul Karim or other members of the Kirana gharana—with the notable exception of Bhimsen Joshi. Faiyaz Khan rarely did the sargam except, occasionally, in the jod portion of his alaap. Abdul Karim Khan, on the other hand, was famous for his beautifully composed sargams as one found in his records of Bilawal, Dev Gandhar or his thumri 'Piya bin nahin avat chain'.

Dr Ashok Ranade has observed in his book that Karim Khan had borrowed this pattern of sargam from Karnatak music[17], as I suppose, did Aman Ali Khan of Bhindibazar gharana. Both Faiyaz and Abdul Karim sang thumris, which before their time was the sole property of tawayefs. The dividing line between Abdul Karim's khayal and thumri is a very thin one.[18] Faiyaz Khan, in contrast, built his unusual style of thumri on the Benaras bol-banao variety.

In spite of the dramatic differences between the gayakis of the two great musicians, it is possible for the unprejudiced genuine lover of music to equally admire both Faiyaz and Abdul Karim Khan. I have had the unusual fortune of having heard both of them, though at the age of nine I was too young to appreciate Karim Khan. I grew up with tremendous admiration—which I retain in my old age—for both these ustads. Bengalis are emotionally volatile and icon-loving people. When they put someone on a pedestal there is room for just one. Musicians and music-lovers, especially in our part of the world, are ruled more by prejudices than taste acquired through serious listening to all gharana artistes with an open mind. I am happy to be an exception. The reason is simple. Anyone with an iota of musical intelligence, and who has heard the greats of each and every gharana, as I have, cannot afford any prejudice.

Gwalior, the parent khayal gharana, had hardly any raag-vistar, neither did Agra. Thanks, however, to Agra's tradition of dhrupad and dhamar, Faiyaz Khan started the habit of doing a dhrupad alaap before he came to his madhya vilambit

khayal. In the preface of a book called *Raag Nirnaya*, written
by my first guru Dr D.L. Roy, I find that both Faiyaz Khan
and Rajab Ali Khan regretted the fact that Abdul Karim had
introduced bol-alaap or vistar into his khayal. '*Yeh kya kar
raha hai Abdul Karim* (What is this Abdul Karim doing?) Bol-
alaap in khayal? If he has to do an alaap, let him do a
dhrupad alaap followed by khayal,' said Rajab Ali who
belonged to the same Kirana tradition as Abdul Karim but
never did any vistar in khayal. After a few minutes of
bahlawa, he would switch over to taans, for which he was
famous.

Where then did Karim Khan inherit the bol-alaap from?
According to Noor Hassan Khan, son of Abdul Karim Khan's
cousin Majid Khan, all this is the gift of Bande Ali Khan,
founder of the present Kirana gayaki. He was a dhrupad
singer and a famous been-player. That he taught khayal to
Bhaskar Rao Bakhle is also known, which is not surprising
since he was the son-in-law of the great Ustad Haddu Khan
of Gwalior. But there is no proof that Abdul Karim Khan
ever heard him, leave alone got any lessons from him. Bande
Ali Khan spent his advanced years with Chunnabai in a
room attached to the Dargah of Khwaja Saiyad Hasibuddin
Qatal-e-Zarzari Chishti in the jungle in Shanbarwad (Pune).

Vishnupanth Chhatre, the circus manager disciple of
Haddu Khan, who looked after the eccentric Rahmat Khan,
his khalifa, in his old age, visited Bande Ali Khan. Khansaheb,
by then, hardly ever played the been in mehfils. He had
dedicated his music to the saint and played only in the
dargah for his own pleasure. He resented the intrusion of
visitors and reacted violently to Vishnupanth Chhatre's visit.
'Whoever has heard of a trainer of lions and tigers singing
dhrupad and khayal? If you are really a disciple of my father-
in-law, sit down and sing one of his creations,' he shouted.
Chhatre was very apologetic and begged Khansaheb's pardon
for disturbing him. He said it was his lifelong desire to hear
Khansaheb's been and he had come with high hopes to his
khalifa, which Bande Ali was by virtue of his marriage to the

daughter of his guru. Bande Ali Khan picked up the been and threw it to the ground. It landed on the floor with a cacophonous crash whereupon Khansaheb stood up and said, 'Now that you have heard the sound of my been, I suggest you get out of here and not come again.' Chhatre did not give up easily and during one of his subsequent visits with Krishnam Bhatt, a disciple of the Patiala gharana, he heard Chunnabai as well as Bande Ali Khan. He touched Chunnabai's feet and called her the incarnation of goddess Saraswati, which might have softened the eccentric Khansaheb somewhat.

When the young Abdul Karim, during his wanderings with brother Abdul Haq, visited the dargah and paid his respects to Peerzada, descendent of the saint Chishti, he introduced himself as a distant relative of Bande Ali Khan. It did not go down well with the Peerzada who also resented being disturbed by many such intruders who claimed to have belonged to Bande Ali Khan's clan. Abdul Karim noticed it and said, 'I have never heard the great man. His erudition and aesthetics have gone with him to his grave. We have come to pay homage to his memory and light candles on the tombstone. I sincerely believe that with unshakeable faith in Allah, one can rise in any walk of life through one's own efforts.' The reply pleased Peerzada, who blessed the brothers.

The mention of this incident, recorded by Kapileshwaribuwa, is to reiterate my own assumption that the credit for grafting the dhrupad alaap on khayal, by calling it bol-alaap or bol-vistar, goes to Abdul Karim and not Bande Ali Khan. In any case Abdul Karim had never heard nor did he borrow the Meerkhandi alaap from Haidar Baksh, the guru of Abdul Waheed Khan. Abandoning Gafuran, Haidar Baksh's niece, soon after marriage, had soured Abdul Karim's relationship with him anyway. Despite the reservations of Rajab Ali and Faiyaz Khan, the world of music had accepted Abdul Karim's innovation with gratitude. I have called him the father of the romantic movement in Hindustani music, just as I have called Faiyaz Khan neoclassical, not merely because of the lyrical quality of Karim Khan's music but in the sense it has been used in literature, sculpture and allied arts. He challenged the traditional form of Gwalior khayal and changed it—with wide repercussions on other gharanas. Kishori Amonkar's acceptance of bol-vistar, in spite of her rigorous Jaipur training, is an outstanding example. Even latter-day Gwalior musicians, from Patwardhan and D.V. Paluskar to Ulhas Kashalkar, did not turn their backs on bol-vistar, though it was not as elaborate as that of Kirana. Sharafat Hussain of Agra, unlike his predecessors, did vistar in khayal which could run to an hour or more, often to the point of boredom.

In a letter to Rabindranath Tagore[19], my father wrote:

'A good alaapiya would not allow his presentation to be structurally weak. The ways of an established gharana are sound. If any ustad can build new paths through sheer genius, I would welcome him with open arms. Outside Allabande Khan and the Agra gharana, such talent at the moment is extraordinarily rare. However, I rate Abdul Karim highly. You know, perhaps, that in the eyes of old ustads he is not considered a purist gharanedar musician like, say, Faiyaz Khan. He often forgets to sing antaras, uses shuddh notes in Bhairavi and occasionally a shuddh madhyam in Hindol, but he sings according to his own *mizaj* and what *mazaa* there is in that *mizaj*!'[20]

When asked about Khansaheb my father said, 'Abdul Karim would often take liberties with ragas and not always consciously. But whatever he sang was music, words which I am reluctant to use about any musician I have heard.'

The list of Abdul Karim's disciples would be incomplete without Tipu Miyan, the singing dog. It has been mentioned by Kapileshwaribuwa in his book, though there is no mention of the year or the date, as was the meticulous custom of Khansaheb's biographer. Basant Kumar Poddar, who had interviewed Hirabai, was told that she had heard about this incident but it probably happened before Karim Khan's children were born. Basant Kumar feels this must have been before 1908, when Khansaheb was in Bagalkot, because that is where he bought the dog from gypsies for twenty rupees.

He was christened Tipu. The very first non-vegetarian meal served to him was politely refused and he drank only water. In the evening the rice, roti and daal set before him were consumed promptly and without fuss. Karim Khan told his Maratha disciples, 'He must have been a Brahmin in his previous birth. I have never heard of a dog that prefers daal and rice to meat and bones.' Even more strange was Tipu's behaviour when Khansaheb sat down to tune his tanpura. He would pull at his chain violently and bark loudly. The moment he was released, he would follow his new master and sit down quietly to listen to the music for the next several hours with the manners of a true connoisseur. Occasionally, he would make a strange humming sound—unlike anything that anybody had ever heard from a dog.

Four months after this incident, Tipu Miyan was billed for a recital in a music hall in the town of Satara, to be followed by Abdul Karim Khan's recital. The king of Satara, a descendant of the legendary Chhatrapati Shivaji, was a great admirer of Khansaheb. It was but natural that he would lose no time in getting in touch with the ustad and making it abundantly clear that the whole thing was in very poor taste. Whoever heard of a singing dog! Even if he could produce sounds remotely resembling the human voice, the legitimate place for him was a circus and not a music hall where he would share the stage with the great ustad. After a great deal of persuasion the monarch of Satara agreed to attend the show, although he chose the privacy of the adjacent green room to his royal box.

Needless to say, the hall was packed to capacity. Most had come to hear Abdul Karim Khan while some fun-loving people had bought tickets for the bizarre experience of hearing a singing dog. When the curtain went up they saw Khansaheb with two of his disciples on the tanpura. After giving a brief introduction about Tipu's antecedents and his training, he turned around and called Tipu, who was patiently waiting in the wings. Tipu, with a string of pearls round his neck, came and took his seat next to Khansaheb. 'Be careful, Tipu Miyan. You have to sing well before this distinguished audience. *Izzat ka sawal hai* (It is a question of our prestige),' said Abdul Karim. Tipu nodded his head with grave courtesy. Khansaheb's sa was matched by Tipu Miyan's tonic note, very much in tune, followed by re. Slowly, he sang with his master all the notes going up to the sa in the upper octave, and stayed there without a quaver. It brought the house down. With joined hands Khansaheb acknowledged the wild cheers from the audience and the curtain came down.

Grotesque and unbelievable as this may sound, it has been recorded by Abdul Karim's biographer and confirmed by Basant Govind Poddar that the show was followed by two such others, one in Pune and the other in Bombay. The latter was attended by Sarojini Naidu, Annie Besant and B.J. Horniman.

Equally unbelievable is the following story I am quoting from Zariwala's book[21], which is really an abbreviated version of Kapileshwari's biography in Marathi. Khansaheb was a deeply religious person and sought every opportunity to visit holy men, dargahs of departed saints and Hindu temples. He also used to say artistes were above the narrow dictates of religion and caste. His music, he always maintained, was a prayer to God. 'Babu Sahab, from the moment I sit down to sing I pray for the 'kripa' (mercy) of the Almighty,' Abdul Karim told Dilip Kumar Roy. The latter writes in his book[22], 'There is little doubt that he did receive His kripa.' From all accounts his later music was not cerebral, like Abdul Waheed Khan's, nor was it the durbari music of Faiyaz Khan. It was meditative and took the form of a prayer in which he was fully immersed, oblivious of his audience.

Khansaheb had heard of the sacred site and miracles attributed to Dada Qalandar Hazrat, but he had had no opportunity to visit it. So on a Madras tour, he and his party went to Mysore and ascended the hill on which the shrine was situated. They repeated the visit daily for seven days and Khansaheb paid devotion morning and evening throughout the week. On the seventh day they saw a tiger coming out of a cave. The tiger circumambulated the place, sat for a while and disappeared. Thereupon the local priests declared, 'Thy services have been accepted, ask whatever thou wilst.' Khansaheb merely chose to ask that he 'die in sound health; that I may not be a burden to others and myself'. He was quit of all illness thereafter (since 1929) and he departed the world when his time came as instantaneously as he entered.[23]

Abdul Karim Khan was absolutely shattered when Tarabai left with the children. It was the absence of his sons and daughters that he felt more keenly than Tarabai leaving him. An attempt was made by Karim's mother to unite him with Gafuran, his first wife, with no success. Bannubai, one of his disciples, looked after him and according to some, Khansaheb married her when he was well past sixty. They left for Bombay and reestablished the Saraswati Vidyalaya in the city. Although Abdul Karim had lost the zest for life, the best music he produced belonged to this period. What people of the earlier generation remembered and did not have enough words of praise for was what he sang in Calcutta, Bombay and Madras in the Thirties. His listeners were unanimous in recalling the mesmerizing quality of his music.

In 1938, when Khansaheb was approximately sixty-six years of age, he accepted the invitation of the Gayan Samaj of Madras. On an earlier occasion Dilip Kumar Roy had invited him to Pondicherry to meet revolutionary-turned-philosopher Shri Aurobindo, when Karim Khan was visiting Madras. He could not make it. This time he took the slow night train to Pondicherry. On the way he felt unwell. Anyone else would have asked for a doctor. Abdul Karim got down at a small station called Singaperumal Koil. He asked his disciples to tune the tanpuras, sat down with his face towards Mecca and offered a bouquet of sur. In moments of happiness the ustad was in the habit of humming his favourite

Darbari Kanhra. His last brief recital was also in the same raga, on the desolate railway platform of a small wayside station at the dead of night.

Ustad Faiyaz Khan was standing on the balcony of his two-storeyed house in Baroda, when he saw his cousin Ghulam Rasool Khan running up the lane. 'Bhai Sahab,' shouted Ghulam Rasool, 'have you heard? Abdul Karim Khan has passed away. We have just got the news from Bombay.' Faiyaz Khan slapped his leg and cried aloud, '*Hai Allah!* Sur in Hindustan has died with him today.'

The other stream of Kirana gharana has thrown up two great ustads, Amir Khan and his mentor Abdul Waheed Khan. Coincidentally, I was at the end of a recital in Indore, the place where Amir Khan was born and grew up, when the news of his death in a car accident in Calcutta stunned me. It was unbelievable that the last of the giants, whom I had known intimately over the years, would be taken away from us with such shocking suddenness.

As I write this, it is with a heavy heart that I recall the memories of my sixty years of intimate association with another great ustad, Vilayet Khan, who died last year in Mumbai.[24] The sitar and Vilayet were made for each other, just as the shehnai was for Bismillah and the sarod for Ali Akbar. I remember, in the days of my misspent youth, the games of snooker we played when he would beat me hands down matching me drink for drink, the long drives after dinner when we swapped bandishes, evenings in my flat when he would start singing with me on the tanpura and finish well past midnight. On one occasion, Jnan Prakash Ghosh dropped in without notice. Vilayet Khan was singing beautifully. At the end of it, Jnanbabu said, 'Do you know? This is the quintessence of the best of all gharanas I have heard in my life.' Farhat Sayeed Khan, who was also present, said, 'Why not? *Dil aur dimagh to wohi hai jisne unko ahem sitariya banaya* (It is the same combination of head and heart which has made him the great sitar player that he is).'

Vilayet Khan always said, as has been quoted by his

biographer, that there were three major influences on his music, that of Faiyaz Khan, Abdul Karim Khan and of course Vilayet's father Inayet Khan, who died when Vilayet was only nine years old. Vilayet never mentioned Ustad Amir Khan, who had married his elder sister and divorced her later to live with a tawayef called Munnibai, though Amir Khan's influence on Vilayet's baaj is obvious to those who have heard both of them carefully. It is only after Amir Khan's death that Vilayet acknowledged him and that, too, only among close friends.

All this, however, does not explain the astonishing command he developed over his instrument, unmatched by any other sitar-player before or since. It was amazing that a bowless string instrument could reproduce the vocalism of the Kirana gharana, especially the elaborate vistar radically different from the classical dhrupadi alaap of the beenkar of yesteryear that has been glamorized by Pandit Ravi Shankar. His halaq, gamak, meend-bahul and sapaat taans reminded us of Ustad Faiyaz Khan and the '*chhoot*' taans, which jumped with startling suddenness from one note to the other, of Amir Khan. The untimely departures of both Amir Khan and Vilayet Khan have two things in common. Both were tragic in their shocking suddenness, although in Vilayet's case a very short notice was given. The other is: no newspaper gave any prominence to the news of the deaths of two of the greatest ustads of our generation. Vilayet was relegated to the bottom of an inside page, thanks to the impending election and the prowess of our cricketers in Pakistan.

I first met Vilayet Khan when he was seventeen. So was I. He had come to Lucknow to stay with his father's disciple, D.T. Joshi, who, until he was stricken by arthritis, did wonderful alaap in the gayaki ang on the sitar. He also sang well and composed a number of bandishes in khayal and thumri which are distinctly out of the ordinary. It was on Ustad Inayet Khan's insistence that Joshiji became a gandabandh shagird of Ustad Faiyaz Khan because instrumentalists of his generation believed that lessons in vocal music were just as important as technical proficiency in the instrument of his choice.

In Joshiji's later days, musicians and journalists often asked him whether Vilayet had ever learnt from him. His invariable reply was that he was the ghulam, the servant, of this gharana and Vilayet was his khalifa. When Inayet Khan died, Vilayet was a child. Joshiji himself was a college student and could hardly do anything for the family. All he did was to return the amaanat deposited by the ustad to his son. D.T. Joshi was a purist and would not have enthusiastically approved of the liberties that Vilayet sometimes took with major ragas despite his repertoire of traditional compositions. That was something which would have been unthinkable with Pandit Ravi Shankar or Nikhil Banerjee. I like to think that the liberty did not degenerate into licentiousness. Like Abdul Karim, Vilayet Khan's recital would be unorganized sometimes, but it was nonetheless scintillating while it lasted. He was the last of the romantics of this age.

Later in life, Joshiji drifted from Lucknow to Delhi, Santiniketan, and finally to Burdwan, where he was attached to the university. In 1975, on the occasion of Joshiji's sixtieth birthday, Vilayet Khan, with his brother Imrat Khan and family, went to Burdwan with a few other artistes such as Radhika Mohan Moitra and Ustad Mushtaq Ali Khan. They played through the night. In a souvenir published by D.T. Joshi's students, Ustad Mushtaq Ali Khan writes in Bengali:

'I first met Joshiji in 1929 in Calcutta. He was then a college student, learning sitar from Ustad Inayet Khan. He was a disciple, in the true sense of the word, of the late ustad. Joshiji, who was equally well-versed in Urdu, in which he wrote poems, and Bengali (his mother, a Bengali, was a doctor in Lucknow) had grown up in an atmosphere of music. Even his manservant Ramdeen had developed an ear for classical music. There were few ustads of repute who did not accept Joshiji's hospitality in Lucknow. His close association with musicians of different gharanas, who bestowed their affection on this bright young sitar-player, contributed to his repertoire as well as his catholic outlook.

'As far as I remember, it was in 1936 when I had to go to Lucknow. I put up in a desi hotel in Aminabad. Joshiji came over next morning along with his disciple Sunil Bose. He wanted me to stay with him and would not take no for an answer. We were sitting in the lounge, chatting, when I ran out of cigarettes. I went to my room to get a packet and found my belongings had disappeared. It seemed to have been the handiwork of Sunilbabu. I asked for the bill and found that that, too, had been settled.

'I played Darbari Kanhra in Joshiji's house in 1942. When dinner was served, Joshiji asked his servant Ramdeen how he liked my Darbari. "Good," said Ramdeen, "but his Darbari gandhar is not remotely like that of Faiyaz Khan".

'Ustad Bundu Khan, the great sarangi-player, had also come from Delhi and was staying with Joshiji. I was reading the morning paper when he came into the living room. He asked me what was of particular interest in the paper. I said I was reading a statement given by Mohammad Ali Jinnah. "Who is he?" asked Khan Sahab.

'"Qaaede-Aazam," I said, referring to the title bestowed on the leader by his people. "Haven't you heard of him?"

'"Yes, yes," said Bundu Khan, "I know all that, but to which gharana does he belong? Is he a dhrupadiya or is he a khayal singer?"

'That was the climate in Joshiji's house.

A day or two after this, D.T. Joshi did what was virtually impossible and has no parallel in the history of our music. He arranged a recital of various Saakhs

on AIR by Ustad Faiyaz Khan, Mushtaq Hussain
Khan, Sadiq Ali Khan, the great beenkar from
Rampur, and Bundu Khan. The four Saakhs recorded
by Joshiji were Saakh, Lachcha Saakh, Devsaakh and
Bhavsaakh. God knows what happened to that
precious material! I know of no one who had dedicated
his life to the cause of classical music as has Dhruva
Tara Joshi.'

On return from my tour of Madhya Pradesh in March 1974,
I formed a music circle called Amir Khan Kala Kendra and
arranged a music conference on a shoe-string budget dedicated
to the memory of the ustad. Khansaheb had few disciples.
Those who were within reach took part in the festival
without any fees. They included Amarnath and Singh Bandhu
from Delhi, Shrikant Bakre and Purabi Mukherjee from
Calcutta. Shankar Majumdar of Patna was yet another disciple
of Ustad Amir Khan who never grew up into a performing
artiste. So also Purabi's husband Pradyumna Mukherjee, my
Putuda, who was close to Khansaheb and was one of the
lucky few—like his niece Kankana Banerjee—who received
sustained talim from Amir Khan. Putuda, whose talent was
unquestionable, mixed alcohol with music. Gradually, the
alcohol prevailed and the Kirana gharana lost a genuine
artiste.

I first heard Amir Khan on the night of Lakshmi Puja in
Calcutta in 1946. Two artistes preceded him. Chinmay
Lahiri, who is remembered as the guru of Shipra Bose and
Parveen Sultana, was groomed by Shrikrishna Ratanjankar
and D.T. Joshi. He had a thin voice with practically no
timbre but his training and application were of the highest
order. He sang khayal in Jog and Adana, which one would
call 'reet ka gaana' i.e., well-structured and impressive in its
traditional treatment, followed by brilliant taans and sargams.
Those who heard him in his later days, when he was given
to experiment and forgot his lineage, would not have
recognized the Chinmay Lahiri of the Forties. Tarapada

Chakraborty, whose trump cards were his voice and mizaj, followed with a rather tame Malkauns. It was somewhat disappointing for his admirers, which included myself. Even the Jaijaiwanti of the last artiste, Ustad Amir Khan, did not go down particularly well. He switched over to raga Abhogi, which is really a Karnatak raga in the pentatonic scale, reluctantly adopted by the ustads in the north because of Abdul Karim Khan's record, *Charan dhara aaye.*

Amir Khan's rendering and voice-throw that evening bore an uncanny resemblance to Abdul Karim's. I did not care for the raga and am inclined to agree with Nikhil Banerjee, the famous sitar-player, who once remarked that he positively disliked Abhogi until he heard Amir Khan, who gave the raga a new dimension. At the age of nineteen I was musically too immature to notice the subtle distinction between Abdul Karim's stream and that of Abdul Waheed Khan with the latter's over-emphasis on Meerkhand, but I did notice that Amir Khan's taans were completely different to those of other Kirana artistes whom I had heard religiously on the radio in the Forties.

I left Calcutta for Kanpur two years later. Kanpur was a soulless city of mills and slums, known those days as the Manchester of India. But unlike Manchester, it offered no music. I came back towards the end of 1950. It could not have been before the early Fifties when I heard Amir Khan for the second time. It was in a music circle called Jhankar run by Jnan Prakash Ghosh in his ancestral house in Dixon Lane. By then I could recognize the remarkable stylistic affinity between Amir Khan's vistar and that of Abdul Waheed Khan.

But the taans were another matter. Taans of practically all gharanas, Agra, Jaipur or Patiala, are based on patterns arising out of a logical sequence connected with phrases of the raga. In the case of Patiala they are largely based on paltas and are, therefore, predictable. The remarkable feature of Amir Khan's taans and sargam was its sheer unpredictability. It was like the crazy-china floor of an old bungalow. No one, not even the most astute listener or accompanist, could guess what came next. This is because of the chhoots, which in our ancient musical texts are known as *'ullamphan'* and *'avalamphan'*. Literally translated, the terms mean violent jumps from one note to another with large spaces in between, both in the ascending and descending scale.

It is extremely difficult to maintain the ragaroop with such taans. Only an ustad of Amir Khan's calibre could attempt to do so with such resounding success. Further, to continue to hit the notes in the middle, when they are so far apart at a fast pace, is a breathtaking feat. To arrange such combinations, which are not only difficult but aesthetically pleasing would be beyond the scope of lesser mortals. We have experienced that in this part of the country where Amir Khan has a large following among gifted musicians. 'Others abide our question, thou art free', was my reaction then. It still is.

I heard a fair amount of Ustad Abdul Waheed Khan in my teens. After Lionel Fielden, the Bukhari brothers ruled AIR for a number of years before Independence. Some preferred to call AIR the 'BBC' of India, the 'Bukhari Brothers' Corporation'. One of them, Z.A. Bukhari, was very proud of his sartorial elegance and his taste for good food and drinks. His yes-men used to say he was the best-dressed man after Sir Anthony Eden. His airs included a distaste for light music and Tagore songs and a fondness for classical music in a vague aristocratic way.

For some inscrutable reason he was an admirer of Abdul Waheed Khan, who was considered a musician's musician. To an uninitiated listener he could be boring, with the soporific quality of his elaborate Meerkhandi vistar. Anyway, it was because of Mr Bukhari's patronage that Abdul Waheed got chain programmes, which I heard regularly. I also had the opportunity to listen to him in person when he came to Lucknow to give lessons to Akhtaribai Faizabadi, known later as Begum Akhtar.

The half-hour slot on radio was too short for Abdul

Waheed Khan, who would normally devote two to three hours to a major raga at mehfils. He is reputed to have sung a raga like Multani for three-and-a-half hours at a durbar in Indore. He was somewhat hard of hearing and would, therefore, sing with his eyes closed and the right ear glued to the tanpura. Even the Maharaja, who was a connoisseur, must have thought enough was enough and sent a man with the inaam on a silver plate, an indication that his highness needed some well-earned rest from the unending Multani. Ustad Abdul Waheed Khan, deeply immersed in his Meerkhandi combinations and with his eyes closed, was naturally unaware of the intrusion. He later realized his serious breach of manners—but only after concluding his recital.

With the hope that there would be another occasion on which he would be able to repair the damage, he stayed on in Indore for three years in the house of Shahmir Khan, the father of Amir Khan. Shahmir Khan from all accounts was a sarangi-player of less than moderate competence but was otherwise a prominent figure in the Maharaja's court, being in charge of the hospitality meted out to guest artistes. Yet another important court musician was the famous dhrupad singer and alaapiya, Ustad Nasiruddin Khan, the father of Moinuddin and Aminuddin Dagar. It is reasonable to assume that Amir Khan's predilection for elaborate vistar and detailed unfolding of ragas owed their origin to the influence of those two ustads.

I feel at this point that an explanation of the term 'Meerkhandi vistar' is due to readers, especially in the context of the degenerating influence of this technique on the budding musicians in Bengal. I can do no better than quote from an article written by me in the 'Arts and Ideas' supplement of The Telegraph, Calcutta, which appeared on September 19, 1994. It was entitled 'Meerkhand: The Latest Viral Fever':

'At the ITC music festival in Calcutta I heard Sultan Khan's solo sarangi recital. I had heard him earlier as

my accompanist twice in Bombay and once in
Calcutta and was struck by the tuneful tonal quality
of his instrument. This has not diminished over the
years. On the other hand, his virtuosity has increased
to the point of chaotic lawlessness. To a listener
uninitiated to the recent trend of wild permutations
in the name of 'Meerkhand', it might have been
enormously interesting in the beginning. As far as I
was concerned, after nearly an hour of Bhupali,
which seemed longer, the curiosity and interest
degenerated into puzzlement and finally plain
boredom. The recital was a series of disjointed
combinations, most of them extremely difficult, but
not more than half a dozen times did I come across
a familiar phrase of Bhupali, not even the basic *pakar*
of dha sa re pa ga. It was truly an amazing
performance.'

'Meerkhand' is a much-loved term among Bengalis because of
their inherent love for Kirana, and Ustad Amir Khan in
particular, whose influence on budding musicians is no less
than that of the paltas of Bade Ghulam Ali Khan. I refer, of
course, to the young talents, whose real guru is the tape-
recorder. Pandit Dilip Chandra Vedi, whose fame was based
as much on his intricate taans as his belligerent habits in
mehfils, had the good fortune to receive talim from three
great musicians—the legendary Bhaskarbuwa, Aftab-e-Mausiqi
Ustad Faiyaz Khan and Haidar Khan, the brother of Ustad
Alladiya Khan, who founded the Jaipur gharana. His
misfortune, as he was fond of saying, was that he had lived
too long, and, therefore, could not altogether avoid listening
to the synthetic gayaki of modern musicians. About the
prevalent style, he had a singular remark to make, 'At last,
singing has become much easier for the average musician
than for those of us who had to go through rigorous talim in
our youth. All that one has to do now is to open
Bhatkhandeji's books, take the notations of any raga, proceed

with swar-vistar, as distinct from raag-vistar with the help of meerkhand. One does not have to sing the entire sthayee. And antara, of course, has gone out of fashion.

This is followed by sargams and paltas consisting of yet more permutations and combinations, which then are faithfully converted into taans. The question of 'ragaroop', or delineation of the raag with the help of key phrases is a habit of the past, which the modern musician has outgrown. He is constantly haunted by the fear of doing something, which is simple and uncomplicated. The more difficult the combinations of the notes, whether they relate at all to the anatomy of the raag or not, the happier is our modern musician. Actually he has come closer to Karnatak music today than anytime in the past. This is the first distinct sign of national integration through classical music. Film music, of course, had shown the way much earlier.

A correspondent, who appears to belong to a second generation of 'Sunni shagirds', (i.e., those who are inclined to imitate the famous ustads' style with the help of recorded music) has written a long letter to me in which, among other things, he has actually defended the Meerkhand technique with the remark that its base is intellectual. I would be prepared to call it mechanical or arithmetical. Surely ABCD, BCAD, CDAB, CABD etc. are not music. And what does one do if one follows the Meerkhand system with ragas like Gaud Sarang, Chhayanat, Kamod, Anandi, Khat and a host of others whose paths are crooked and anatomical picture complicated?

Yet another friend has pointed out that he learns reliably from the Dagars that they are the originators and avid followers of Meerkhand or 'khanda-meru' as depicted in the Shastras. In that event, the Dagar genealogy and their 'Dagar-vaani' may well date back to the thirteenth century when Sharnga Dev, in his *Sangeet Ratnakar*, took the then 'Kafi' scale of seven notes and listed 5,040 combinations to give us a glimpse of what he thought was the entire universe of our music, something which, as Pandit Ravi Shankar once remarked about the Meerkhand habit, the personal computer can do in seconds nowadays for the benefit of the present generation of musicians without talim.

Further, this was taken up by dhrupad singers and in later days by some khayaliyas as an exercise to train their voices, but never, heaven help us, in their public recitals. And that applies to the Dagars as well, the most important witness to which was Padmanabh Shastri, elder brother of the famous danseuse Rukmini Devi Arundale. Padmanabh Shastri, retired principal of the Holkar College, Indore, was the oldest disciple of Ustad Nasiruddin Khan (Dagar) at the age of ninety-seven in 1997, when Dr M.R. Gautam passed on this story to me. Ustad Nasiruddin Khan had mastered combinations of six ragas and would practise them regularly. He would go on rattling out sare-gare, sare-saga, resa-gare, saga-resa etc. at great speed in the raga Bhairav. Shastri would say, 'Ustad, Yaman Kalyan.' Nasiruddin would promptly switch over to Yaman. Shastri would suddenly shout 'Jaunpuri' and the Meerkhand would change then and there from pancham onward to combinations in Jaunpuri from Yaman without a second's breath. Khansaheb told Padmanabh Shastri that this assiduous practice was necessary to train one's voice for the drut alaap portion (which the instrumentalists call jod) with or without gamaks but was never to be used in recitals in any manner. Paltas born out of Meerkhand, used intelligently, can help khayaliyas in certain sampurna ragas and '*audav*' (pentatonic) ragas like Malkauns, Bhupali, Dhani, Durga etc. Even in sampurna ragas one has to be careful. Ni sa ga re with a pause on re in Yaman brings in the important *pakar* of Khem Kalyan. Ma (teevra) ga re sa re, with emphasis on rishabh, is straight out of Maru Bihag, the note being common to both ragas.

The sarangi-players, too, were immensely fond of meerkhand and paltas but treated them purely as homework and certainly not for social display. A notable departure is attributed to Ustad Hyder Baksh, who was the disciple of the great beenkar Ustad Bande Ali Khan. Hyder Baksh migrated from Mysore durbar to Kolhapur, where he accompanied Ustad Alladiya Khan. He may have been a good sarangi-player but his place in Hindustani music is secure mainly as the guru of two famous ustads: Rajab Ali Khan, the master of taans and Abdul Waheed Khan, the father of Meerkhand vistar in khayal and the unacknowledged mentor of Amir Khan.

Lest I be misunderstood for the umpteenth time, neither Waheed Khan nor Amir Khan in his Meerkhand vistar ignored the topography of the raga. Their talim and their instinct prevented any carelessness. It was an unintelligent imitation of their style that led to well-known pitfalls. Many a leading artiste on the radio would provide adequate evidence of this raging viral 'Meerkhand' fever in my part of the country.

Another point of clarification: alaapchari in dhrupad, akin Amir Khan's style of vistar, is different from what his Sunni shagirds are doing today. What the traditionalists did was to proceed from one note to another with the help of subsidiary notes, bearing in mind the importance of vaadi and samvaadi swaras, as well as what is known as ragaanga. This process must not be confused with mechanical permutations and combinations, which may lead to equal emphasis on all notes. A naïve interpretation of the term 'dhrupadi alaapchari' would imply that Ustad Faiyaz Khan or even Ustad Abdul Karim Khan (who used the same method in khayal though more elaborately) had practised Meerkhand in public recitals!

My real quarrel is with musicians who use the Meerkhand blindly, without emphasizing the key phrases which portray the anatomy of the raga. The least of the unfortunate results of such an approach is monotony, the worst being distortion of the raga itself. To give two more examples, Malkauns, without madhyam as the vaadi swara, would become the lesser-known raga Kosi, in mandra saptak with its dhaivat-gandhar samvaad. Meerkhand in Bhupali will obliterate its distinction from Deshkar. Even a child, when he draws a picture of an elephant, knows that its tail is not as long as its trunk, that all the parts of the creature are not of the same size.

Enough of my prejudices, which may or may not strike a responsive chord in anyone below sixty. Let us return to Ustad Amir Khan in the early 1950s, when I heard him for the second time. He sang a raga like Malkauns for nearly two hours, followed by Adana, vilambit and drut. I must confess that though I enjoyed the recital in parts, I was a bit weary at the end of it. It was more of an intellectual exercise than relaxed entertainment. I could not help following the notations in the vistar portion automatically, as was my habit, and the marathon exercise left me a bit ragged and limp at the end of it, just as I used to feel after listening to Abdul Waheed Khan. To be fair, the aesthetic appeal of Amir Khan's music was greater than that of his mentor, but I could not help feeling that the canvas was too big for my taste and the pre-Raphaelite attention to detail was a bit tiring.

It was not before the early Sixties that I changed my attitude towards his music. By then he also started to cut down the length of his recitals and attempted to give them a structural unity. The approach was not merely cerebral. His love for each and every note that he touched was becoming more and more pronounced. He was obviously growing out of Abdul Waheed Khan's all-pervading influence and the stamp of his own personality was becoming clearer to the discerning listener. Though I had been listening to a lot of Kirana since my childhood, I had finally found my niche in the Agra-Gwalior style. While Gwalior never accepted the long alaap in khayal, I was no stranger to it—thanks to Faiyaz Khan. But what I missed in Amir Khan's music was the middle portion of an authentic traditional khayal presentation, that is, the bahlawa, which gradually transformed into taans and the rhythmic bol-bant and bol-taans to which I was accustomed. He had an elaborate vistar, followed by slow sargams which increased in pace and finally culminated in drut khayal laced with incredibly difficult fast sargams and taans. It is not that the division of laya was not there but the rhythmic variation was missing. When I asked him in later years he told me he never developed a taste for it. *'Meri tabiyat us taraf gayi nahin.'*

Once, in the course of one such discussion, when Vijay Kichlu was present, he stood up and placed his hands on our shoulders. The fingers of his right hand on my shoulder were playing teentaal while the left hand was playing dadra! To say that he was not a layadar would be blasphemous. But he did not revel in layakari in the Gwalior-Agra manner or in the Kirana style of Bhimsen Joshi. What he did in the drut portion of the khayal with sargams is what I would prefer to call layadari. In the vilambit khayal the extremely elongated Jhumra taal inherited from Abdul Waheed Khan was his favourite and he would tolerate nothing except pure theka. As far as I can gather it was the same with Abdul Karim Khan, who got so immersed in sur that anything more than theka would have amounted to interference.

I have a recorded tape of Abdul Waheed Khan's Darbari Kanhra. I put on a record of Amir Khan singing the same raga and matched the key. The similarity was uncanny. Both of them sang the same vilambit khayal *'Gumani jag tajo'* in the same Jhumra taal, the tempo of which remained constant throughout. Both of them did the same kind of slow sargams after the elaborate vistar. Even the tanpuras in both records were tuned to pancham and shuddh nishad, a practice reportedly started by Abdul Karim Khan.

Abdul Waheed Khan did not tolerate murkees in khayal. He used them in ghazals which he himself composed. Amir Khan's murkees were heavier, not the Mewati brand, and their application was appropriate and artistic. When I heard Abdul Waheed Khan he had stopped taking fast taans, and his taans in his salad days (as far as I can gather from many except Mashkoor Ali Khan, the grand-nephew of Waheed Khan) bore no resemblance to Amir Khan's. Abdul Waheed Khan sang antaras whereas Amir Khan very often did not, except when he sang his own compositions, particularly taranas. Finally, Amir Khan's voice had greater depth and appeal. Abdul Waheed Khan was more of a pundit than a performer like Amir Khan, who had a larger following. But neither of them was a crowd-puller like Bade Ghulam Ali or Bhimsen Joshi. They were labelled the 'musician's musicians' and both refused to sing thumris in public.

Oddly enough, Amir Khan never acknowledged his debt to Ustad Abdul Waheed Khan. I had repeatedly asked him about the ustads who had influenced his gayaki. He invariably mentioned Nasiruddin Khan, Rajab Ali Khan and Aman Ali Khan of Bhindibazar. Not once did he mention Abdul Waheed—which is quite remarkable considering that bolalaap or vistar constituted three-fourths of Amir Khan's gayaki and that is palpably borrowed from Abdul Waheed Khan.

I find little resemblance between Rajab Ali's taans and those of Amir Khan, except for the two musicians' propensity for linear and fast sapaat taans. Aman Ali Khan of Bhindibazar was known for a number of beautiful compositions written under the pseudonym of 'Amar', one or two of which Amir Khan made famous, like *'Lagi lagan'* in Hansadhwani. There is little in common in their gayakis. Aman Ali was greatly influenced by Karnatak sargams, faint traces of which are noticeable in some of Amir Khan's recordings. There is little doubt that if there is one ustad to whom Amir Khan is heavily indebted, it is Abdul Waheed Khan. Open denial of this incontrovertible fact cannot but be due to reasons unconnected with music.

What I record here is gleaned from more than one source, the primary one being Mashkoor Ali Khan, currently attached to ITC Sangeet Research Academy. He in his turn had gathered all this from his father Shakoor Khan, the nephew of Abdul Waheed Khan. Mashkoor Ali Khan's father-in-law Niyaz Ahmed and his elder brother Faiyaz Ahmed also provided information. Both of them were related to Abdul Karim and Abdul Waheed Khan and were teaching aspiring musicians from the higher echelons of Bombay and Delhi society for a number of years.

Ustad Abdul Waheed Khan had an intimate association

with a middle-aged tawayef called Jagmagi in Delhi. Her daughter Munnibai, from all accounts, a short comely girl on the plump side, fell for Amir Khan. This was when he was married to the eldest daughter of Ustad Inayet Khan, the famous sitar-player and father of the equally famous Vilayet Khan. In fact, Amir Khan's first major recital at the All India Music Conference at Calcutta, for which Lala Damodar Das Khanna paid him the princely sum of fifty rupees, was on the strength of Amir Khan's exalted family connection. Amir Khan was sold on Abdul Waheed Khan's music and it should not have been difficult for him to take talim from Waheed Khan. After all, as mentioned earlier, Abdul Waheed Khan stayed as a guest in Shahmir Khan's house in Indore for three years.

Either Abdul Waheed Khan was unwilling to accept young Amir Khan as his disciple or the guru-shishya relationship was never consummated. Munnibai, however, found a way. It was in the attached bathroom in which Amir Khan used to hide whenever Abdul Waheed Khan practised or taught Jagmagibai in her house. This went on for well nigh two years. It is further said that Abdul Waheed Khan's suspicion was aroused at some point when he stopped singing antaras of the traditional compositions which are not available outside the Kirana gharana. That is why Amir Khan hardly ever sang antaras of these vilambit khayals which Abdul Waheed Khan had made famous. It is not that Amir Khan was opposed to singing antaras in principle, as some of his admirers claim. That is a ridiculous assumption because Amir Khan's own compositions, especially the taranas, have antaras which Amir Khan sang gaily at every concert.

Abdul Waheed Khan did hear Amir Khan, finally, when the meeting was arranged by Munnibai. Waheed Khan's remarks were, *'Tu to tere baap se bahut achcha ho gaya, tere baap ke to gyarah taraf bhi nahin milte hain* (You have become a much better musician than your father. He can't tune the eleven strings of his sarangi properly even now)!' On hearing this highly talented 'Sunni shagird' Abdul Waheed Khan apparently relented and agreed to teach Amir Khan. Invitations for the gandabandhan ceremony were issued but death overtook Abdul Waheed Khansaheb before the official seal of the Kirana gharana could be obtained by Amir Khan from his mentor.

It is curious that Amir Khan would deny that Abdul Waheed Khan was his ustad, his guru. Amir Khan's shagirds and admirers started calling his gayaki not Kirana but Indore gharana—perhaps with Khansaheb's tacit consent. According to Professor Deodhar, pursuit of the same gayaki and bandishes for three successive generations makes a gharana. Be that as it may, it would be sacrilegious on the part of Amir Khan's progeny and disciples to refuse to admit the truth. Amir Khansaheb's own refusal to do so, according to Mashkoor Ali, was due to private reasons. '*Munni pe bhi Waheed Khan Sahab ne haath phera tha* (Khan Sahab had also seduced Munni)', says Mashkoor. Even if the story is true, the fact of the young daughter of a tawayef allowing her mother's paramour to seduce her need not have stood in the way of a formal acknowledgement of the guru-shishya parampara.

I have a taped recording of a recital of Ustad Amir Khan at a private soiree in Liluah, a suburb of Calcutta. That evening Amir Khan was in his element. He sang Shuddh Kalyan, Darbari and ended with Basant Bahar. It is in this mishra raga that he exceeded the expectations of all his admirers with his taans and sargams. At one stage Khansaheb smiled and looked at Jnan Prakash Ghosh who, among other accomplishments, was a skilful harmonium accompanist. Khansaheb said, 'He has been listening to and playing with me for the last twenty years. It is now that he can make something of what I am doing.' Jnanbabu said, 'Khan Sahab, you never said a truer word. It is a maze, *a golok-dhandha*. I am fortunate that after twenty years, I can now follow you most of the time.'

It is this part of Ustad Amir Khan's music which reflects his amazing virtuosity, and it is entirely his own. There is no resemblance between his taans and sargams and those of any of his contemporaries or his predecessors, although Mashkoor Ali claims that they are not entirely original but are based on the sargams of Kirana sarangi-players, like his father Shakoor Khan partly inherited from Abdul Waheed Khan. Even if that was true, I cannot think of any ustad of the Kirana gharana who could aspire to the height reached by Amir Khan.

Amir Khan's 'Sunni shagirds' are many and not necessarily confined to Bengal. Some of them succeed in giving a pale simulation of the ustad's greatness and mannerisms in the bol-alaap although that often degenerates into the labours of Sisyphus. When it comes to imitating Amir Khan's awesome taans and sargams, the contrast is highly depressing. I wish some of these over-ambitious imitators had the sense to sing within their limitations and not attempt to follow the ustad blindly. They would be well advised to concentrate on other aspects of khayal gayaki which could lend some variety to their colourless recitals. Amir Khan's style, without his personality and innovative genius, can be pretty flat and soporific when adopted by unintelligent imitators.

To sum up my thoughts on Amir Khan and his music, I would place him in the position of the most profound musician of the post-Abdul Karim-Faiyaz Khan era. Comparisons are odious, and sometimes downright foolish, but they are made all the time. People of an earlier generation, whose opinion I can trust, were inclined to place Abdul Karim above him. While I decline to do so on the basis of only the gramophone records of Abdul Karim Khan, I have to believe my elders when they say that the mesmerizing quality of Karim Khan's music was unique. Amir Khan's presentation was better planned and not subjected to impulses, but on his off-days, he, like his mentor Abdul Waheed Khan, could sound dilatory, monotonous and even boring. Amir Khan's judicious use of sargams, both in bada and chhota khayal, prevented him from taking the kind of liberty thát Karim Khan reportedly took with the raga.

Among Amir Khan's contemporaries Bade Ghulam Ali

Khan was much more popular and his music was more colourful, but it lacked Amir Khan's depth, poise and dignity. Bade Ghulam Ali Khan was an extrovert who sang for his audience and took immense pleasure in the dexterity with which he wielded his voice and rhythm. One could use terms like scintillating, exciting and exhilarating about Bade Ghulam Ali but he never moved me the way Faiyaz Khan and Amir Khan sometimes did, especially in their alaaps, the simple principle of architectonics being common to both. After all is said and done, our Hindustani music is raga music and the alaap is the best part of it because it unfolds, interprets and adorns the raga. Taan and sargam lead the listener to a climax, but acrobatics, however breathtaking, without a gradual build-up, leave a void in the mind of the discerning listener.

Amir Khan sang for himself most of the time. Like Abdul Karim Khan's, his music was contemplative or meditative. Except in the drut portion when he switched over to fast sargams and taans with gamak and lahak, which he never forsook, he hardly cared for his audience, a trait which Bhimsen Joshi shares with him. From the very moment he hit the sa with his beautiful, rich, mellow and slightly husky voice, he gave his audience the feeling that he was looking inwards. His penchant for dwelling at length on the mandra and madhya saptak gave depth to his style. This was deliberate. His chronic pharyngitis prevented him from going with an open voice beyond the sa in the upper octave. In the 1940s, when young Amir Khan was living in Delhi, he was given slots of only ten minutes on AIR. I distinctly remember his open and somewhat rugged voice laying emphasis on the akar, which would soar to the pancham in the upper octave. In mature years he fully exploited his deep voice with its rich timbre in the mandra and madhya saptak. He made the most of it in his rendering of the raga Marwa, the like of which I have never heard from anyone else. Chetan Karnani writes in his book:

'When Amir Khan came out with his Marwa, he established a norm which was difficult to transcend. With the suspended tonic, he created an atmosphere of pathos which was indeed haunting. The occasional resolution on the tonic from dha in the lower and re in the middle octave gave a sense of relief from tension. Marwa is a difficult mode: its vaadi and samvaadi komal re and dha are five-and-a-half notes apart instead of the usual four or five and the basic note is sparingly used. The ease and assurance with which Amir Khan rendered it showed the highest level of classicism that he has attained.'[25]

I have heard Ustad Amir Khan devote as many as twenty minutes to the badhat of this raga, from re in the lower octave to the same note in the middle. With a lesser artiste I would have been bored to death. One should, however, mention that with lighter ragas such as the Gara, Barwa, Piloo, Khamaj, Kafi and the Tilak Kamod, which Khansaheb avoided and in which Abdul Karim revelled, this kind of approach would not have been successful. They would not have suited his temperament either.

His love for the lower and middle octaves is not the only reason he did not sing the antara, according to Mashkoor Ali Khan. He had no problem in singing them in the taranas and his taans would touch the gandhar and madhyam in the taar saptak, though not with an open voice. According to Mashkoor Ali, it was Munni Begham who prevented Amir Khan from seeking the unfinished part of the compositions of Hingarang and Sabras, which are not sung outside Kirana and are not available in any of the printed collections, not even in Bhatkhande's *Kramik Pustak Malika*. She would say, 'If you go to any ustad of the Kirana gharana or any of Abdul Waheed Khan's senior shagirds for the antaras, you will have to salaam every member of the gharana.'

Faiyaz Ahmad and Niyaz Ahmad Khan once paid a visit to Amir Khan's flat in Bowbazar Street in Calcutta, when he was living with Munnibai. They arrived in the middle of a huge altercation between the husband and wife, which ended in Amir Khan ordering Munni out of the house. That evening, after a few drinks, Amir Khan reportedly confessed to the Khan brothers, 'It is this *na-murad aurat* (damned undesirable woman), who prevented me from going to Abdul Waheed Khan earlier. *Kasam Khuda ki, mera imaan unhi pe tha* (I swear, in the name of God, my love and loyalty lay with him)'.[26]

I am one of the few who have heard Ustad Abdul Waheed Khan and Amir Khan, the latter extensively, over the years in jalsas, at conferences and in the privacy of my house. Even if the vilambit portion of Amir Khan's khayal, in the words of Vamanrao Deshpande, was 'so close to Waheed Khan's that it sounded like a replica', I would say that the feeling of repose, the high tone of seriousness and the aesthetic appeal which I experienced in Amir Khan's bol-vistar, was not comparable to that of Waheed Khan. To me Amir Khan's version of Waheed Khan's gayaki is a more sophisticated one and qualitatively superior.

Neville Cardus, the famous writer on cricket and music, said somewhere that Nature creates a mould and when her job is finished, she breaks it. Cricketer Alan Kippax used to imitate Victor Trumper right down to his buttoned-down sleeves, his drives and late cuts, but was nowhere near Trumper in performance. Every five or ten years a young talent in Australia, or even our Sachin Tendulkar, is hailed as a new Don Bradman but is not a patch on the great man. This is why there will not be a second Faiyaz Khan, Abdul Karim, Ali Akbar, Ravi Shankar, Vilayet or Amir Khan. There may be new talents, even geniuses, which, of course, I doubt very much in the present musical scene in India, but they will be different. Imitation of a great artiste for a talented beginner is in order, but if his own personality does not make a mark on his musicianship as he attains some degree of maturity, he is not likely to leave his footprints on the sands of time.

It would be unfair to the reader to conclude this chapter on Kirana gharana without mentioning a famous ustad whose un-Kirana-like neglect of vistar and penchant for difficult taans were as well known as his colourful controversial personality. This is Ustad Rajab Ali Khan, court musician of Dewas, a small state about forty kilometers from Indore. I have heard a great deal about Rajab Ali Khan from Nivruttibuwa Sarnaik, who learnt from him after Alladiya Khan was too old to teach him or anybody else. Also, Dr M.R. Gautam, who had got to know Rajab Ali when he was posted at Indore with AIR, told me about him. I would also recommend a highly readable book in Hindi by Amik Hanfi on his guru, Rajab Ali Khan.[27] Yet another source was the late Krishna Rao Mazumdar, a retired civil engineer, who lived in Indore. He was a devoted disciple of the ustad and had a collection of recorded tapes of Rajab Ali Khan's music. It is unfortunate that the electronic age arrived in our country after most of the great ustads of the golden age were gone or were well past their prime.

Buddhadeb Dasgupta, the sarod-player, and I were doing a series of chain programmes in Madhya Pradesh in 1978. When we arrived in Indore, my first port of call was the home of Mushtaq Ali, whom the great Keith Miller called the Errol Flynn of cricket, and whom I had compared to Bade Ghulam Ali Khan in my chapter on Patiala. I missed him but later met him taking his evening walk. For a man in his eighties, he still moved with the panther-like grace for which he was famous on the cricket field. He had barely lost the waistline of his youth, which could have been the envy of the fashionable women who watched him fielding at deep square leg. He was still erect as a ramrod with wide shoulders just as I remembered him in my teens. Only the hair had turned white.

Our second port of call was the house of Krishna Rao Mazumdar, who gave us tea and played a few tapes of his ustad. I was a bit disappointed because obviously the recordings had been done when Rajab Ali must have been in his eighties and was in the process of losing his taans, which were his biggest asset. However, that was partly compensated for when Mr Majumdar played one of his own tapes. When we returned to the hotel Buddhadeb Dasgupta posted a letter to his brother in Bombay[28] in which he wrote, 'Keen as you are on taiyari, difficult and fast sargams and taans, and much as you dote on the ustads of our generation, you would have been surprised to hear the taans of an amateur disciple of Rajab Ali Khan, Krishna Rao Majumdar, whom we met today. I cannot imagine what his ustad must have been like.'

The young do not think much of the older generation and vice versa. This is as true today as it has been through the ages. Lala Amarnath, who was the first Indian to score a century in cricket against D.R. Jardine's MCC Team in 1933, and who later captained India, was asked by a young cricket player, 'Lalaji, one-day cricket has brought about a great change in field placement. Fielding has also become sharper. How would you have tackled the one-day game with its stump-to-stump bowling to a field set to contain the batsmen in your time?'

'There wouldn't have been a problem,' pat came the reply, 'C.K. Naidu and Mushtaq Ali would have opened the batting with me at number three, and the rest of the team could have gone shopping.'

Amarnath's vanity and his prowess at ad libbing have given birth to many stories. In 1946, when India was visiting England, his all-rounder qualities were severely put to the test because of the lack of fast bowlers. Marvellous batsman that he was, the quality and immaculate length of his bowling earned as much praise from English critics. Once, he kept Harold Gimblet, a well-known attacking batsman of Somerset, quiet for an hour by his length bowling. The exasperated batsman walked up to him and asked, 'Tell me, Amarnath, don't you ever bowl a half-volley?'

'Sure I do,' said Lala, 'I bowled a couple in 1942.'

We return to Rajab Ali Khan. When he was fifteen, he was accepted as a disciple by Bande Ali Khan on the recommendation of Sardar Gopal Rao Dighe of Dewas. I have already introduced this famous been-player to the reader but not mentioned his pedigree. He was the son-in-law of Ustad Haddu Khan of Gwalior and the disciple of Nirmal Shah, the grandson of Ustad Niyamat Khan. According to Acharya Vrihaspati, he was the disciple of Bahram Khan and father-in-law of Allabande and Zakiruddin Khan.

When he came to Indore and Dewas, Bande Ali Khan had already crossed sixty. Among his disciples who made names for themselves, the ones prominent were Murad Khan, Abdul Aziz Khan (whose record of vichitra-veena was quite popular in my childhood), Vilayet's grandfather Imdad Khan, the great vocalist Bhaskar Rao Bakhle and Chunnabai, whom Bande Ali Khan married after the death of his first wife. Maharaja Shivajirao Holkar brought him to Indore not only as court musician but as the rajguru. While Bande Ali Khan had received plenty of honours and accolades all his life he never amassed enough means to retire on nor did he care for worldly goods. He had the nature of a fakir and finally settled down in the forest of Shanwarwada where the dargah of Khwaja Syed Hasibuddin Qatal-e-Zarzari Chishti was located.

Amiyanath Sanyal[29] has written in his book that the dhrupad alaap of Allabande and Zakiruddin Khan had meant 'endless boredom' to the average listener, which, of course, Mr Sanyal was not. But even he found it overwhelmingly monotonous sometimes. He changed his views on dhrupad alaapchari when he heard Faiyaz Khan and Bande Ali Khan's been. The latter's music had much greater aesthetic appeal than that of the big names of the Seniya gharana, who, apart from rendering elaborate alaaps, were in the habit of descending to warfare with pakhawaj-players. Bande Ali Khan also sang khayal sometimes and gave talim to sitar-players, which made his position in the then hierarchy of dhrupadiyas and beenkars somewhat dubious. Seniyas called Kirana been 'bhonda' been' while Kirana retaliated by calling the Seniya been 'tansha' been. While the meaning of these terms is not adequately clear, it is obvious that the two gharanas did not hold each other in great esteem.

Rajab Ali Khan's talim from Bande Ali Khan began with dhrupad and been. But this silsila could surely not have encouraged his proclivity for taans. As far as one can deduce, the foundation of Rajab Ali's khayal gayaki was laid by his father Moglu Khan, an ustad of mediocre talent who belonged to the qawaal bachcha tradition. The boy Rajab Ali's precocity had attracted the attention of the ruler of Dewas, who had ordered a regular supply of desi ghee and parathas to Moglu Khan's household for the boy. Those were the days when ghee and almonds were considered an absolute must for the nutrition of every ustad, young or old, removed as they were by a hundred years from the discovery of cholesterol.

Bande Ali Khan, who never could adhere to one place, moved to Poona with his disciples and Chunnabai in 1891. Three years later, he died. Rajab Ali was barely twenty then. Chunnabai decided to take over his talim. There is nothing remarkable in this event. Although it was not customary for male singers to take talim from tawayefs, Chunnabai was a woman of exceptional talent and was fully capable of carrying on the Bande Ali Khan tradition as well as the khayal gayaki, at which she excelled. This is the same Chunnabai, at whose feet Vishnupanth Chhatre and Krishnan Bhat paid obeisance, calling her 'Devi Saraswati'.

Around 1896, Ustad Alladiya Khan became the number one court musician of Kolhapur. He was also a great favourite of Shahu Maharaj, which naturally caused heartburn among lesser musicians of the durbar. One of them was Haider Baksh, the famous sarangi-player, also a disciple of Bande Ali Khan, who had migrated from the Mysore court to Kolhapur. One day, while accompanying Alladiya Khan, he openly said, 'What is this taankari of yours that you are so proud of? I can produce a boy half your age who would perform better after a year or two's talim from me.'

It was only natural that this led to further bad blood between the two. Alladiya Khan is reported to have said, 'There is no one on earth other than my disciples who can produce a single taan of mine unless he is born with the same kind of genius as Bade Mubarak Ali Khan or myself. *Aise sarangiya ke bachche humne bahut dekhe* (I have seen many such inferior sarangiyas).' Haider Baksh left the durbar in a huff and lost no time in rushing off to the post office and requesting the postmaster to send a telegramme in English to Rajab Ali in Poona. Noted by Amik Hanfi in his book, this remarkable message read, 'Come at once (stop). If you are eating come and wash your hands in Kolhapur'.

This strange message from someone he had not been in regular touch with was mystifying, to say the least. Rajab Ali, in fact, was frightened out of his wits. He borrowed some money and proceeded to Kolhapur, with Chunnabai's blessings. When Haider Baksh saw him, all he had to say was, 'There you are. Your talim begins from tonight. In two years you have to be as good as Alladiya Khan—if not better.'

Thus began the rigorous talim in taankari for Rajab Ali. To bring home the taan patterns of Alladiya Khan was not too difficult for a brilliant sarangi accompanist like Haider Baksh. To improve upon them was another matter. Alladiya Khan's taans were based on regular beats. Rajab Ali, in due course, learnt to do aad-kuaad with his taans. He would weave patterns with syncopated movements in clusters of notes of six, five, four and three, which would often go against the rhythm of the tabla only to arrive at the refrain— the mukhda—with a lightning sapaat taan.

Alladiya Khan, one gathers from second-hand sources, never favoured sapaat taans. Linear taans, which can distort the correct portrayal of a raga which, unlike an audav raga, may have a zig-zag movement, would go against the grain of an ustad who started life as a singer of dhrupad. Rajab Ali Khan's fast linear and sapaat taans, Nivruttibuwa swore, were dazzling—the like of which he had never heard before or since. Side by side Rajab Ali built his taans on bols of tabla, which he learnt under his ustad's supervision. He was so obsessed with taans that he almost totally neglected the vistar even later in life when he was acknowledged as a major ustad in those days when Hindustan was not short of them.

My only recollections of Rajab Ali Khan, when he came to sing at Lucknow in 1938—when I was a child—were his drooping moustache and his violent taans. This was the same occasion as when Manji Khan's taankari evoked a lukewarm response from a Lucknow audience consisting predominantly of the landed gentry that was accustomed to the tawayef culture. Oddly enough, Rajab Ali Khan's music was liked not only by the cognoscenti like Thakur Nawab Ali, Rai Rajeshwar Bali, Ratanjankar and his Marris College colleagues, but also the same audience that did not think much of the most brilliant exponent of Alladiya Khan's gayaki. I mention this because, originally, Rajab Ali Khan's taans were based on Alladiya Khan's patterns and Rajab Ali claimed he improved upon them. Mallikarjun Mansoor, however, disagreed with this view. 'Rajab Ali might have started life by imitating Alladiya Khan Sahab's taans,' he told me, 'but he could never go beyond ten per cent of the original'.

Govindrao Tembe, actor, producer of plays and a famous harmonium-player, was a disciple of Alladiya Khan. He has written that Rajab Ali used to listen to Khansaheb from behind closed doors in the Amba Devi temple in Kolhapur.[30] When Alladiya Khan got wind of it, he stopped singing khayal and switched to dhrupad. Barkatulla Khan, the sitar-player and the dada-guru of Mushtaq Ali Khan of Calcutta, was so enchanted by this that he told Alladiya Khan, 'If you go back to dhrupad, Khan Sahab, instead of khayal, of which you are already an acknowledged maestro, I shall give up the sitar and go back to pakhawaj to sit with you in mehfils.'

There is little doubt, according to all known sources, that Rajab Ali, who legitimately belonged to the Kirana school and had sustained talim from Bande Ali Khan and Chunnabai, departed from his gharana tradition of raga vistar and switched to a taan-pradhan gayaki akin to Jaipur's. Even in old age, when his taans almost deserted him, he had little time for raagalaap. When I heard him once in Bombay, he reminded me of the great Wally Hammond against Australia in 1947, when he had nearly lost his agile footwork but would give an occasional glimpse of his past with a flashing cover drive. But unlike Rajab Ali Khan, Hammond eschewed stroke play and concentrated on defence, which stood him in good stead on a sticky Brisbane wicket, when his colleagues were all at sea.

One would assume that Rajab Ali would have acknowledged his debt to Ustad Alladiya Khan. On the contrary, thanks to the seeds of rivalry sown by Haider Baksh, the callow youth started posing as an equal of the venerable ustad by dropping irresponsible comments in mehfils all over Maharashtra where his fame as a taanaiyat was spreading rapidly. All this could not have made Alladiya Khan happy when, as has always been the custom in our world of music, Rajab Ali's boastful remarks were quickly brought to his ear.

The great man retaliated by suggesting to Sahu Maharaj that Rajab Ali's pedigree was doubtful. He had had talim from a sarangi-player and was not fit to hold his place in the durbar. While Islam preaches brotherhood among Muslims, the ustads are no less caste-conscious than their Hindu brethren. Alladiya Khan was proud of his Brahmin ancestry. He was the son of a dhrupadiya and was at the pinnacle of the hierarchy whereas the sarangi-player, who played with tawayefs and ate their 'namak', salt, belonged to the basement. This prejudice has done enormous harm to Hindustani music. Sarangi, which is the closest to the human voice, is possibly the most difficult instrument. It is only because of their association with tawayefs that sarangi-players were looked down upon by ustads, specially the lofty dhrupadiyas. This has been responsible for the gradual dying out of this breed. The harmonium, a bastardized instrument, which can produce neither meends nor shrutis, is replacing the wonderful sarangi today everywhere, including at AIR, which had banned it for years. Rajab Ali Khan, who was a disciple of Bande Ali Khan from whom he had learnt been and dhrupad, therefore had good reason to feel offended. He never forgave Alladiya Khan till his death.

Sahu Maharaj of Kolhapur took the kind of decision able administrators do. He gave letters of introduction to such rulers who were known as connoisseurs and suggested to Rajab Ali Khan to proceed on a long tour. The very first state he visited was Rampur where Nawab Hamid Ali Khan had ruled like an autocrat for forty years. He was known as a great patron whom Pandit Bhatkhande made the chancellor of the Marris Music College and became his disciple, with the intention of collecting precious compositions of dhrupad from Ustad Wazir Khan, his Rajguru. The Nawab of Rampur was an enthusiastic singer of dhrupad himself and had also a collection of rare old manuscripts which were an additional incentive for Bhatkhande to become his shagird.

Hamid Ali was keen on collecting musicians in his durbar in the same manner as he acquired precious jewellery and, if public opinion is to be believed, good-looking women from all walks of life. This was a habit not unknown among rulers of native states in those days. The British political agents, who were entertained lavishly by the potentates, kept their eyes closed most of the time. Unless a heinous crime was committed, like the one by Maharaja of Alwar who, on losing in a game of polo, set fire to his horse after pouring petrol on it, no severe action was ever contemplated by the British government. Everyone knew that dogs and horses are far more precious to the English than the lives of dirty natives.

Maharaj Bhupinder Singh of Patiala, who presided over the chamber of princes and was a keen cricketer, led from the front and scored comfortably over other rulers. He is reputed to have had more than three hundred wives and concubines in his harem. His subjects had complained to the British political agent that the French started their mornings with coffee and rolls, the English with bacon and eggs and His Royal Highness with a virgin for breakfast every morning. Investigations revealed that the allegation was totally baseless. Maharaja Bhupinder Singh was not at all fussy and never confined himself to virgins. In fact, no action was taken against the Maharaja until he is reported to have arranged the abduction of a young woman belonging to the Viceroy's household. The spot where this incident took place is still known as Scandal Point in Simla, the summer capital of British India. Bhupinder Singh, one gathers, was refused entry to Simla for life. He built his own summer capital in nearby Chhail, which boasted of being the highest cricket ground in the world.

All this is by the way. Nawab Hamid Ali was a true connoisseur and the luminaries in his durbar included Bahadur Hussain Khan, Inayet Hussain Khan, young Ahmad Jan Thirakwa and Mushtaq Hussain Khan, beenkar Sadiq Ali Khan (father of Asad Ali), Ajodhya Prasad, the famous pakhawaj player and of course Wazir Khan, the Nawab's ustad[31]. One gathers that Nawabsaheb liked his daily dose of opium. Ustad Faiyaz Khan was once invited from Baroda to give his recital in the Rampur durbar. A few minutes after Faiyaz Khan started, Nawab Hamid Ali Khan opened one eye and asked him the name of the raga. This was surprising as Tilak Kamod was not an uncommon raga.

Faiyaz Khan said, 'Sarkar, this raga is the Tilak Kamod.'

'No, it is not,' retorted Hamid Ali. 'There is no nishad in Tilak Kamod. We never use the note ni in this raag.'

Faiyaz Khan was dumbfounded. Later, Khansaheb's shagirds asked him how he got out of the predicament; did he choose another raga? After all, Tilak Kamod without nishad virtually becomes naked; did the Nawab Sahab not know that?

'*Kuchh nahin hua, Sarkar ka hukum* (Nothing happened, it was His Highness's command)! I went on singing Tilak Kamod minus nishad for another half-an-hour or so and then switched over to another raga,' replied Faiyaz Khan with a smile.

The entrance to such a durbar was not easy for young Rajab Ali. He was pacing up and down before the main gate when he met a young man with a tanpura. The man said, 'I can take you up to Ustad Wazir Khan's residence. He is the

Nawab's ustad. Unless he wishes, it will never be possible for you to see the Nawab—even if you have a letter from your Maharaja. For us, Ustad Wazir Khan is the top boss in Rampur. We show him the same respect as we do to the Diwan, the chief minister. When you meet him, remember to salaam him the proper way, bowing from the waist, and be careful about what you say to him. He is accustomed to courtly manners and utmost respect from his juniors.'

This unsolicited advice irritated Rajab Ali Khan. In his old age he acquired the reputation of being quick-tempered, outspoken and a man of strong likes and dislikes. He was quick to love and quick to fight. One assumes he was no different when he was young. He went inside and offered a plain 'Salaam-alaekum' and sat down without being asked to do so. He picked up the pipe of a hookah which was standing next to his chair, pulled on it a couple of times, found that it was not smoking and threw the pipe on the carpet. The ustad bit his lips and asked, '*Aap ki taareef* (Who might you be)?'

'*Ji*, I am an unworthy disciple of the great beenkar Ustad Bande Ali Khan. They call me Rajab Ali.'

'I see. Is he the one who plays bhonda been?'

'It sounds in his hands infinitely better than your tansha been.'

That would have put an end to Rajab Ali's visit to the durbar, but miraculously, the visit did take place that very evening. The Nawab himself was scheduled to sing. All the courtiers and musicians in Rampur, and their guests, had been invited—which included Rajab Ali Khan. Hamid Ali was a fair exponent of dhrupad and dhamar, but he did not have the same command over sur as he had over taal. But loud praise from the audience with repeated '*Masha-Allahs*', '*Subhan-Allahs*', and '*Marhabas*' more than made up for that deficiency.

The Nawab's recital was preceded by one from a minor ustad from a nearby state. He was a good singer of dhrupad but taal was not his strong point. After he sang a couple of dhrupads, he was asked by the Nawab to sing a dhamar. This calls for layakari which, with a pakhawajee like Ajodhya Prasad, was not easy for even accomplished dhamarees. The unfortunate ustad did his best but soon missed the sam. '*Samhaal ke* (Careful)!' warned Ustad Wazir Khan.

After a couple of aavartans the singer once again went be-taal. '*Laya to dekho bhai* (Look out for the laya),' said the pakhawaj player and Wazir Khan in unison.

The singer stopped, put his palms together and said, '*Laya kaise dekhoon jab Sarkar ko dekh raha hoon* (How can I see the laya when I am looking at the Sarkar)?' Everyone laughed. The Nawab smiled and ordered a large inaam.

In due course Nawab Hamid Ali sat down to sing. After about an hour-and-a-half, he stopped and asked his court musicians, 'Tell me honestly, gentlemen, have you come across such *pucca sureela ustadana gana* before?'

'Never, Huzoor, never!' all said in chorus. 'There is not another singer like you in the whole of Hindustan. It is good fortune for us ustads that Nawab Sahab refrains from singing in public.'

Looking at Rajab Ali Khan, Nawab Hamid Ali said, 'You are from Maharashtra, aren't you? Have you heard such music as mine in any riyasat there?'

'Huzoor,' said Rajab Ali, 'I have been to quite a few states, but none of the rulers can boast of so many guni-jans, so many famous ustads, in their courts, nor have I come across a Raja who can sing like you.'

'Thank you, but that is not the proper answer to my question. Have you ever come across a *kasbi* (knowledgeable), layadar, sureela ustad, who can be my equal?'

All Rajab Ali Khan needed to say was, 'No, never, Your Highness!' Instead he said, 'Since Sarkar is repeatedly asking this question, I am being forced to speak the truth. Any young ustad ka bachcha can sing as well as you can, and possibly more in tune.'

There was complete silence for half a minute. The Nawab got up and said, 'Had you not come from Sahu

Maharaj with his letter, I would have you whipped in public.'
He looked at Wazir Khan, 'Let him be paid three hundred
rupees. He would be well advised not to come within a
hundred miles of Rampur in future.'

Ustad Rajab Ali Khan sang in many durbars, and received
honours galore, including the President's Award in 1954, but
he never sang in Rampur, not even during the reign of Raza
Ali Khan, the successor to the throne.

There are many stories one has heard of this eccentric,
colourful ustad. Once, when invited to sing in Indore by the
Maharaja, he ordered a tonga in Dewas. The driver, in spite
of repeated admonishments from the passenger, kept on using
the whip on the horse. On reaching Indore, Rajab Ali asked
the tongawalla to take him to a sweet shop. He got down and
ordered two seers of jalebi, which he fed the horse himself.
Then he turned to the tongawalla and boxed his ears till he
was red in the face and said, 'Next time you use the whip,
remember this day when your horse and not you who ate the
jalebis.' I am inclined to swear—by Maneka Gandhi—that
such a man could not but be a true artiste.

Rajab Ali Khan was an incorrigible spendthrift. He
would owe money to the sabziwalla, the liquor shop, the meat
shop, his tailor—until some of them stopped supplies. The
moment he earned a big nazrana from a recital, he would
blow it up on expensive attar, good food and drinks for
friends. He was without a single communal bone in his body.
He would carry *tajiyas* in Muharram processions and participate
in the Ram Navami festival with equal zest. After a few
drinks Khansaheb was inclined to pick up quarrels. This
would make him unpopular with friends until he would go to
their homes and beg them to come over to dinner. On one
occasion he was boycotted by some of his friends, one of
whom was getting his daughter married. Rajab Ali gatecrashed
on the wedding that night. His host told him in front of his
guests, 'Sorry, Rajab Ali, you are not invited.'

Rajab Ali Khan asked, 'Where are your shoes? Come out
and show them to me.' When the host stepped out, Rajab

Ali said, 'I am not sure how many of you I had insulted the other evening.' He then picked up the chappals and nagra shoes one by one and placed them on his head and enquired, 'Now tell me, Azmat bhai, am I invited?'

I shall end this chapter with yet another story which reminds me somewhat of the extraordinary love-hate relationship between Ustad Vilayet Khan and his young nephew Rais Khan in the 1970s. Ustad Alladiya Khan had come to Indore as the guru of the princess. He put up with his friend Rambhau Datey. Alladiya Khan was nearly eighty-nine then. Datey persuaded him to send a letter through his driver to Rajab Ali in Dewas. It read as follows:

'Bhai Rajab Ali, both of us are living on borrowed time. I am sending you the car to bring you to Indore. Let us embrace and put an end to our misunderstanding.'

The reply from Rajab Ali said, 'Bhai Alladiya Khan Sahab, we have carefully nourished this enmity for years. I see no reason to kill it just because we are getting old. Let justice be done in the presence of Allah-tala when we are both gone.'

Two years later Ustad Alladiya Khan died. When the news reached Rajab Ali Khan, he wept for days. 'Whom shall I hear and who is going to appreciate my music now that Bhai Alladiya Khan is gone?' he howled like a child. 'I sang only because of him and I have no reason any longer to go on singing.'

For psychologists this remains a textbook case.

8

Bhaskar Rao Bakhle

Pandit Shrikrishna Ratanjankar once told me that every musician, even Abdul Karim Khan and Faiyaz Khan, had his critics, the only exceptions being Bhaskarbuwa Bakhle and Zohrabai. I would have given half of my life's savings to hear them but they were before my time. Zohrabai, at least, has left behind quite a few 78 RPM records. Bhaskarbuwa had none, even though he died in 1922.

Bhaskar Bakhle was born in 1869 in dire poverty in a village called Kathore in the native state of Baroda. He was a bright child with an attractive voice and a lot of talent. Those were the days when talent-spotters from Marathi theatre companies used to look for good-looking young boys who could be groomed into the role of heroines, the pre-requisite being a good voice.

When Bhaskar was not more than fourteen, he managed to get into the Kirloskar Co. which toured the Marathi-speaking states. Marathi Natya Sangeet is entirely raga-based and no play is complete without at least a dozen songs. Bhaskar quickly made his mark as the young wife Kaikeyi of King Dasharatha in the play *Ram-rajya-viyog*. After a few months in Baroda, the company moved to Indore via Dewas and Ujjain. The Marathas love classical music and even famous ustads those days did not consider it below their dignity to be associated with the stage. Bande Ali Khan, the great beenkar, who had moved to Indore as the guru of the Maharaja, happened to see the play *Ram-rajya-viyog* and was so bowled over by Bhaskar's rendering of the song *'Jo mama nayan chakore Indu'*, that he told Nana Panse, his pakhawaj-player, that he wished to meet the boy.

When Bhaskar was brought to him, the great ustad, without any ado, told him, 'Do you want to learn proper music? If you do, I shall be happy to have you as my disciple.' Without waiting for an answer he asked his servant to procure chana and gur from the market and tied a black thread on the boy Bhaskar's wrist.

Young and innocent though the boy was, he realized that it would also mean a guru-dakshina, a token amount of money offered to the guru as obeisance and respect, as was the custom on such an occasion. He joined his hands together and said, 'Ustad, I am very poor. I earn ten rupees a month and I send it all to my parents.'

'Never mind,' said Bande Ali Khan, handing Bhaskar a paisa and a pie, 'Give me the sawa-paisa and that is your guru-dakshina.'

Thus began Bhaskar Bakhle's talim with the song *'Bhor koi milan bhailawa'* in raga Jaunpuri. The boy was talented enough to have picked up quite a few ragas well enough to sing them properly with vistar and simple taans. Till his last day Bhaskar remembered his ustad with gratitude. Once, at a mehfil, he was playing the tanpura rather loudly behind Bande Ali Khan. Ustad turned round and slapped him, saying, 'What do you think these people have come here to listen to—your tanpura or my been?'

Bhaskarbuwa, later in life, would recount this story with a smile, 'Don't think I am an ordinary gawaiya. I have been slapped by one of the greatest ustads of all times in a bharee mehfil!'

Soon after, Bhaskar's voice broke in adolescence and the manager of the theatre gave him notice. He returned home but could not stay there for long, burning as he was with the ambition of becoming an artiste. He made up his mind to go to Baroda and get himself admitted to Maula Baksh's school or learn from Fayez Mohammad Khan, the court musician of

Sir Sayajirao Gaekwad. Fayez Mohammad had learnt from Ghagge Khuda Baksh as well as from Qadir Baksh, father of the great Haddu and Hassu Khan brothers.

To receive lessons from such a musician for a young lad with no ostensible means of livelihood was a bit of a tall order. But for Telang Shastri, the state director of education, who took pity on the boy and recommended him to Ustad Fayez Mohammad Khan, this would not have been possible. Even then the ustad did not take the recommendation seriously. The boy was not from authentic Muslim musician stock. He was a Hindu Brahmin with neither pedigree nor money. His voice had not yet settled down. Bhaskar hardly received any attention from the ustad in whose household he worked as a servant for the first six months. One fine morning Telang Shastri was curious enough to pay a visit to the ustad, who was out. Bhaskar, when questioned about his talim, broke down and told Shastri with tears in his eyes that it was his misfortune that the ustad did not care for him. Shastriji did not take the whole affair too well. His pride and self-importance were hurt. He did not lose any time in informing Fayez Mohammad Khan that he was thinking of awarding the boy a state scholarship and would expect regular progress reports, failing which the matter would go to higher authorities.

Bhaskar Bakhle's proper talim started at last. Bande Ali Khan had taught Bhaskar the rudiments of badhat in the dhrupad style. It helped Fayez Mohammad to give his disciple advanced lessons in nom-tom-alaap along with compositions of the Gwalior and Agra gharanas and their treatment in Gwalior style, with bol-bant and heavy taans. Fayez Mohammad's voice was extremely melodious and his alaapchari was so sweet that Bhaskar Bakhle later in life used to say that it reminded him of alaap on the been by Bande Ali Khan. Khansaheb's style, but for the alaap, was somewhat aggressive, full of bol-bant and gamak taans.

Even in those days when devotion to one's guru was not uncommon, stories about Bhaskar Rao's guru-bhakti had become legendary. One which I heard from Ustad Nissar Hussain Khan, who spent his childhood in Baroda somewhat after Bhaskar Bakhle's time, is worth sharing with the students of music today in case any of them stumble on this passage. When Nissar Hussain Khan reached Baroda, Bhaskar Bakhle was no longer there. Ustad Faiyaz Khan, whose first wife was Fayez Mohammad's daughter, was already the number one court musician and principal of the school of music. His only function there was to come and sing every Sunday morning to the staff and the students while his brother-in-law Atta Hussain and Nissar Hussain's father, Fida Hussain Khan, were left with the job of taking the classes. Although Nissar Hussain Khan had seen Bhaskarbuwa, he had never heard him; but Baroda was full of Bhaskarbuwa's admirers, from whom Nissar Hussain heard this remarkable story.

As was the custom those days, young Bhaskar had to sweep the floors, do the daily shopping, cook the meals and massage the ustad's feet after a tiring day. One morning, Fayez Mohammad called him and said, 'Bhaskar, it is quite some time since I had a meal of beef curry. Here is some money, do get half a seer of good beef and be careful to avoid bones. Do you think you will be able to get it?'

'Ustad's wish is my command,' said Bhaskar and went to the market. For a Maratha Brahmin handling any kind of meat or fish those days was unthinkable, leave alone eating it. Bhaskar had no idea what meat looked like. He had never been to that section of the market. He did not eat even onion and garlic, which he purchased first before going to the meat shop. While he was coming out he met a couple of acquaintances who were surprised to see him emerging from the forbidden section.

'So this is what things have come to,' said one. 'We knew you were a Muslim ustad's disciple, but did not know you shared the same taste for food.'

'No, no,' replied Bhaskar, 'I have never taken meat in my life. The very sight of it is making me sick. But how can I disregard my ustad's wishes? He is more than a father to me.

My real father has been responsible for my birth and no more, but the one who is imparting vidya, learning, to me, my ustad, is more than a father.'

When Bhaskar returned and lit the fire in the oven, Fayez Mohammad said, 'Good, now marinate the meat with a little bit of curd, red chillies and garlic, fry the onions with ghee, and cook the meat on slow fire.' There was no expression on Bhaskar's face when he carried out the orders of his guru. After he was asked to pour water into the concoction and put it on slow fire, the ustad said, 'After a while, when the strong odour of the meat, garlic and onions will slowly turn into the delectable aroma of a proper curry, call me and I will have a look at it.' That afternoon, when Fayez Mohammad sat down to his meal of chappati and curry, he called Bhaskar and said, 'Bhaskar, my son, I was testing your guru-bhakti. I would not ordinarily have committed the sin of asking a Brahmin to cook beef for me. I am praying for you to the Almighty that, like the bad odour of meat, the "badboo" in your music will gradually disappear and will be replaced by the heavenly scent of great music. I am blessing you with all my heart and I am sure you will be at the very top of our profession in the not too distant future.'

After narrating the story, Ustad Nissar Hussain Khan said, 'No one today would realize the extent of devotion and moral strength that was required of a Maratha Brahmin boy to carry out the sacrilegious command of his ustad. The relationship today between a guru and a chela is one of "lena-dena", give and take. Things were different then.'

Earlier in this book I had mentioned that Ustad Naththan Khan of the Agra gharana had reached the pinnacle of fame at about this time. He came to Baroda on an invitation from the Maharaja Sayajirao. His gayaki, especially the way he executed the sthayee of a composition, greatly impressed Bhaskar Bakhle. Of late, Fayez Mohammad also had been feeling that he had little more to offer this fantastically talented shagird of his. It was on his recommendation that Naththan Khan agreed to take Bhaskar on as his disciple.

Here again his experience with yet another ustad was not a happy one in the beginning. The reason was the same as was with Fayez Mohammad Khan, where at least Bhaskar went with a strong recommendation from a high official. There was no need, Ustad Naththan Khan felt, to give the village boy separate talim. He was allowed to be present when Khansaheb gave lessons to his children but not when he was teaching his favourite Abdulla Khan, the most talented of all his offspring. Bhaskar absorbed as much of the general talim as he could merely by listening to Khansaheb and by practising when the ustad left the house.

Soon after, Ustad Naththan Khan went out on a musical tour of several riyasats. At last, fortune once again smiled on Bhaskar Bakhle. Jasia Begham, wife of the ustad and sister of Mehboob Khan (Daras Piya) of Atrauli, was fond of this innocent, poor, hard-working boy. She told Bhaskar, 'Now that the ustad is out for a month or two with Abdulla, you must sit with me everyday and memorize the important bandishes of our gharana. I will teach you whatever Khansaheb has imparted to Abdulla.

This should not come as a surprise to the reader. The begums of most ustads were not without khandaan or pedigree. They had listened to their fathers and uncles since their childhood, and learnt music along with their cooking, although it would have been sinful for any of them to entertain even the thought of singing outside their homes. *Tauba, tauba* (God forbid)! That would have branded them as tawayefs forever. Even in my childhood, but for Acharya Girija Shankar Chakravarty, no one from a respectable family in north India would have sung pucca gana in public. Thanks to him, girls from middle-class Bengali families pioneered the movement initiated by Vishnu Digambar and Bhatkhande in Maharashtra. Otherwise, Brahmo Sangeet, Tagore songs, Shyama Sangeet and Nazrul Geeti were de rigueur. Those who made their mark in classical music in Bengal and UP, the two most advanced states seventy years ago, were Dipali Talukdar (Nag), Bijanbala Ghosh Dastidar, sitarist Renuka

Saha, Jharna Saha, Damyanti Joshi and kathak's Asha Ojha. I remember Asha's dance for one reason. Her father's name was Damri Ojha, a name I had not come across before or since.[1]

A few months after Naththan Khan returned to Bombay, he received an invitation to sing at a conference in Punjab. Abdulla Khan was unwell. The eldest son, Mohammad Khan, for some reason, was unable to accompany Khansaheb. It was Bhaskar Bakhle's turn to play the dual role of porter and tanpura-player. As I have mentioned earlier in this book, very few provincial towns had good hotels big enough to accommodate so many musicians. It was customary for organizers to put up tents near the venue, something which I have witnessed in small towns in UP like Sitapur, Unnao and even Kanpur in my early youth. Next morning, when Khansaheb was out on an invitation to breakfast, Bhaskar sat down to practise in his tent. Slowly, one by one, people gathered outside the tent. Some of them were artistes participating in the festival. They were struck by the extraordinary quality of music emanating from Naththan Khan's tent where the youth, whom everyone thought was Khansaheb's boy-servant, was singing. They went to the organizers of the festival and suggested that the first session that evening begin with the recital of young Bhaskar Bakhle for at least half-an-hour. Khansaheb, of course, was not inclined to entertain the suggestion. The boy had started learning from him only a year ago. He might be talented but he had a long way to go before he could be permitted to give a performance at a music conference, certainly not for another dozen years. However, after a great deal of persuasion from some who had heard Bhaskar that morning, Khansaheb gave his consent.

The evening duly began with Bhaskar Rao's Bhimpalasi after he touched Khansaheb's feet and went onstage. As soon as he started singing, Ustad Naththan Khan sat up and pricked up his ears. This was amazing! Where did the boy get hold of this khaas bandish of his gharana? And the style! It was a carbon copy of Naththan Khan's patented execution of sthayee and antara, which he did usually in an elongated tilwada taal by digging it deep; not like Abdul Waheed Khan's or Amir Khan's treatment of Jhumra. Tilwada is not a taal which should be played so slowly. It is madhya vilambit, or medium-slow, at its best. Naththan Khan's speciality was not only to reduce the tilwada to an extremely slow tempo. His rendering of the sthayee and antara in the bandish did not allow any break or significant pause beyond what was essential to the effect. It called for astounding breath control for which Naththan Khan was famous. Khansaheb could have been knocked down with a feather when he heard Bhaskar that evening. At the end of the recital the young shagird came and touched his feet and confessed that 'Mataji' had no small role in the play towards this amazing phenomenon. Naththan Khan must have realized that the boy was no less talented than Abdulla Khan, and the future of his name and gharana rested on these two.

Years later, Aftab-e-Mausiqui Ustad Faiyaz Khan was singing in the Santa Cruz Music Circle on a Sunday morning. This refers to the period when he was at the height of his powers. After the death of Abdul Karim, he, like the sun (Aftab) extinguished the stars which appear to be less brilliant but not necessarily less beautiful in the eyes of the discerning beholders. Faiyaz Khan started with alaap followed by 'Ye langara turak baat maan' in Lachari Todi. He would arrive at the sam in shuddha gandhar and with an exquisite phirat touching the komal gandhar, would rest on the tonic, the shadaj. Ata Hussain Khan and Latafat Hussain Khan, both my gurus, were playing the tanpura with moist eyes—such was the atmosphere Khansaheb had built up within minutes. Suddenly he stopped and said, 'Hai, isko Bhai Abdulla Khan kya gate the, mai to unka ek zarra bhi nahin hoon (Alas, how wonderfully did bhai Abdulla Khan sing this raga! I am not even a small particle of him).' I am repeating the story for the second time in this book to leave it to the imagination of the reader what Bhaskarbuwa was like.

That would be the perfect ending to the tale of Bhaskar Rao Bakhle. But there is more to his life and career when he grew up into Bhaskarbuwa, one of the all-time great singers of Hindustan. Apart from the stories I have heard from my ustads and seniors in the world of music, I have depended heavily on Govind Rao Tembe and Shaila Datar, both of whom have published authentic biographies of the great man in Marathi.[2]

All was still not well with Bhaskar Rao when he returned to Mumbai with his ustad from Punjab. Naththan Khan was not very prompt in carrying out his noble intention of imparting the khaas talim of his gharana to Bhaskar. Meanwhile, he continued to do the job of a menial in Khansaheb's household. Shopping for the daily meals was his main job, also procuring liquor, since Naththan Khan's moral principles would not let his own children touch the bottles in the shop. One day, the Parsee owner of the liquor shop was curious to know from Bhaskar who the ultimate consumer of those bottles was. When he heard it was an ustad of pucca gana, Naththan Khan, he expressed his desire to hear him.

God knows what he made of it when he came over and heard Khansaheb the following day. He paid a nazrana of three rupees. Bhaskar Rao was livid. Three rupees for listening to the great Ustad Naththan Khan! Bhaskar told his guru he would get the bottles from another shop in future even if it meant walking another couple of miles. Khansaheb said, 'True, the fellow has made a lot of money out of my drinking habits. Let it go. Naththan Khan has received nazrana of thousands from rajas and maharajas. To a sharabwalla, a seller of liquor, music is worth no more than three rupees. Well, I would not have complained if he had left a couple of bottles behind instead of just enough money for a week's shopping of vegetables for the family.'

Another evening, as was his habit, he packed Bhaskar off to the market when he was teaching Darbari Kanhra to his sons. It was an old bandish, possibly a dhrupad turned into khayal in praise of Lord Krishna, which went like this:

'*Kanha ghar aaye janam liye/ Durjan ke desh deshwa bhaktan ke ichcha bhaye*'. By the time the talim was over it was time for dinner. Bhaskar was also back from the bazaar. Khansaheb sent word to his wife to prepare the rotis. Jasiya Begham came out and coolly said to Khansaheb, 'The dinner has not been cooked. The oven will be lit only after the khaas talim is given to my son, Bhaskar, not before.'

The same Bhaskar became Khansaheb's favourite in course of time. He would say, '*Bhaskar mera beta hai; Mohammad, Abdulla aur Vilayet mere aulad hain* (Bhaskar is my son; Mohammad, Abdulla and Vilayet are my offspring).' After Bhaskar Bakhle got married, or possibly even before, he shifted to a one-room flat in a chawl in Girgaon. Khansaheb would arrive there with his bottle and stay till late in the evening, singing and teaching. Once, the owner of the building appeared without notice. While Bhaskar got busy tucking the bottle out of sight, the intrepid Naththan Khan kept on singing. When they finally broke up late in the night, the landlord said, 'I have been praying and performing puja all my life, but it is through your music tonight that I came closest to perceiving Him.'

Soon after this, Naththan Khan, on his death bed, called his children and told them that they should look up to Bhaskar Rao as their elder brother. To Bhaskar he said, 'Take care of my family, especially Vilayet Hussain, my youngest child, whose talim has not been complete. It is in your music that Naththan Khan will continue to live for his admirers. May Allah-tala give you the fame and happiness that you richly deserve.'

Bhaskar Rao Bakhle did all that was expected and more for his guru's family. He built a house in Dharwar and installed Jasiya Begham and her children in it. The major portion of his earnings was handed over every month to her and not to his wife as long as he lived. When Naththan Khan's family visited him in Bombay, he would himself wash their thalis after meals, to prevent embarrassing his wife, a daughter of a Brahmin, who would not ordinarily touch a thali from which a Muslim had eaten. Such was the rigour which bound upper-caste Hindus those days. Vilayet Hussain's talim was completed under Bhaskarbuwa's personal supervision. He was launched by Bhaskarbuwa in Bombay before an assembly of ustads and guni-jan in Vishnu Digambar's Academy on Sandhurst Road. Vilayet Hussain ended up as a vocalist of repute, more perhaps a pundit than a crowd-puller. He is looked upon by musicologists as the bridge between the Agra and Jaipur gharanas.

Naththan Khan had also suggested that after he was gone, Bhaskar should take talim from Alladiya Khan. I have mentioned the close relationship between these two ustads and the esteem in which they held each other. Here also Bhaskar Rao's experience was not an unmixed one. The turning point for the better came after an incident which I have heard of from my ustads. In fact this is a story which is reasonably well known among the senior members of the Agra gharana.

Ustad Alladiya Khan was scheduled to sing in a small township called Basehi, not far from Bombay. A mehfil on a Saturday evening in western India virtually meant a whole night's affair. Serious listeners would turn up at 8.30 after dinner and would leave by the early morning milk train after a concluding Bhairavi thumri. Even now this is the routine followed by various music circles when they engage musicians of repute.

The Basehi mehfil was scheduled to start at nine in the evening. Bhaskar Rao was already there tuning the tanpuras. There was no sign of Alladiya Khan even at 10 pm. People were getting restless. Another hour passed, still no message nor any indication when the Ustad would turn up. The organizers requested Bhaskar Rao to sing until Khansaheb arrived. Bhaskar was not willing. It would be a breach of etiquette to usurp the mehfil which belonged to his ustad. But by 11.30, when some of the assembled audience began to leave and others gave vent to their disappointment in no uncertain manner, Bhaskar Rao was persuaded to begin his recital.

This was exactly the moment when Alladiya Khan chose to enter the hall. The car had let him down. He was in a filthy mood. And what did he see after a tiring journey from Bombay that lasted hours? Here was that young good-for-nothing shagird of Naththan Khan attempting to steal Khansaheb's mehfil! He refused to sing. No amount of persuasion from the organizers, nor entreaties from Bhaskar, made any impression on him. 'I am like your son, Ustad,' pleaded Bhaskar. 'It was to save your izzat that your shagird sat down to sing and that, too, when the situation became most embarrassing for the organizers. It was far from my intention to steal the limelight. Such a thought never entered my head. I have tuned the tanpuras and shall sit behind you. Please, Ustad, do forgive me if I have unwittingly done anything to annoy you.'

Alladiya Khan was adamant, repeating after each entreaty, 'No, you sing, *yeh mehfil ab hamaari nahin* (This mehfil is no longer mine).'

There is a scene somewhere in one of the humorist Kedar Banerjee's books in Bengali where the father loses his temper violently and asks the son to get out of the house. 'I don't want to see your face as long as I live.'

'Neither do I yours,' said the son and walked out. Had Bhaskar Rao been a volatile Bengali, there would have been a first-class scene by then. But he was a poor vegetarian Maratha Brahmin, accustomed to being pushed around all his life. Otherwise the flashpoint would have been reached much earlier. At last, the exasperated Bhaskar Rao stood up and said, 'All right, Ustad, I will sing, and you will never hear the like of it again from any of your shagirds. Don't forget, I am also a shagird of the great Naththan Khan.'

The recital that followed, composed of music from Darbari Kanhra to Bhairavi, was a memorable one not only for the audience but also for Khansaheb. He embraced Bhaskar Rao and proclaimed loudly for everyone to hear, '*Guru milna asaan nahin hai magar aisa chela milna taqdeer ki baat hai* (To find a proper guru is not easy but for a guru to find a disciple such as this one is providential).'

Bhaskarbuwa was taught for a while by Alladiya Khan.
Side by side, he got involved with a theatre company which
was presenting the great Bal Gandharva, the uncrowned king
(or shall we say queen?) of the Marathi stage. His role as a
heroine and his songs, composed and taught by Bhaskar Rao,
made Bal Gandharva a legend in his lifetime. Even Ustad
Faiyaz Khan, whenever he visited Bombay from Baroda,
would take an evening off to go to a play which featured Bal
Gandharva. A sofa was always arranged for him in the front
row. The ladies copied Bal Gandharva's changing hairdo in
female roles. Saris and blouses bore the trademark of Bal
Gandharva. Before the advent of genuine female actresses,
like Gauhar Karnataki, on the Marathi stage, Bal Gandharva
was for years the rage of Maharashtra. Incidentally, Bal
Gandharva was a title, the bearer of which was christened
Narayan Shripad Raj Hans. His second wife, Gauhar Karnataki,
became his partner in business and together they started a
new theatrical enterprise. Both were disciples of Bhaskarbuwa.

Gradually, Bhaskarbuwa's fame spread to Mysore, Bombay
Presidency (which in those days covered present-day
Maharashtra and Gujarat), Hyderabad and particularly to
Punjab and Sindh. Even the Maharaja of Kashmir called him
to Srinagar where he stayed as state guest for a whole month.
In Punjab he made a humble beginning. It was in 1904 that
Vishnu Digambar recommended him to the organizers of the
prestigious Harballabh festival in Jalandhar. Bhaskarbuwa was
booked for a fee of three hundred rupees plus inter-class fare
from Bombay and back. He sang the composition *'Niranjan
kije'* in jhaptaal in Desi Todi in the morning and *'Dinibar dar
nibare ho Shah-e-Jahangir'*, obviously a dhrupad turned at some
stage into a khayal, in raga Shankara in the evening session.
The accompanist on the sarangi was Jhande Khan, who had
regularly played with Punjabi stalwarts such as Aliya-Fattu,
Alladiya Meherban, Bhai Moti and others. At the end of
Bhaskarbuwa's recital, Jhande Khan laid his sarangi down
and said that in his thirty-six years of experience of mehfils
he had never heard such a vocalist. Ustad Bute Khan, in the

Bal Gandharva

audience, stood up and loudly proclaimed that such an artiste would not be born in a hundred years. The organizers, with folded hands, offered the highest fee of one thousand and one rupees and a citation, which bestowed the title of Dev Gandharva on Bhaskar Bakhle. The gold medal which went with it was handed over by him to Vishnu Digambar, his senior, who was also present on the occasion.

I once had a long chat with Pandit Dilip Chandra Vedi, disciple of Bhaskarbuwa and Faiyaz Khan. Most of the incidents mentioned by him were associated with Punjab. The Muslims in Jalandhar, Amritsar and Lahore would invariably ask for the song '*Hazrat Khwaja sang kheliye dhamaar*'. At the end of the recital they would heap flowers at Bhaskarbuwa's feet. The Hindu listeners would touch his feet after he finished with '*Gopal mori karuna*' and ask for his blessings. In those days it was not customary for ladies from respectable Muslim families to go to a mehfil. Dasonga, wife of the famous pakhawaj-player Miyan Malang Khan, would hide herself along with her friends behind blankets and turbans to attend Bhaskarbuwa's recitals. Dasongabibi met him and, with folded hands, said, 'You are a peer, a saint. Please set foot in my house and give us your blessings. No human being can produce the kind of divine music that you gave us.'

Raja Raj Kishan, Diwan of the state of Patiala, once arranged a special soiree for the Maharaja to listen to Bhaskarbuwa. Both Ali Baksh and Fateh Ali Khan were present. Bhaskarbuwa started his recital with '*Phulan ke harwa*' in raga Puriya followed by Kamod. On a request from Ali Baksh Khan, he sang the famous song '*Tu aiso hi Karim Rahim*' in Darbari Kanhra followed by the drut khayal '*Nain se nain milaye rakh to*' in fast ektaal. Ustads of the Patiala gharana are notorious for their indifference to gayakis other than their own. Buwa's recital was punctuated by repeated applause from the seventy-seven-year-old Ali Baksh Khan. '*Subhan Allah!*' he exclaimed. 'These gamak taans are reminiscent of Haddu Khan's. *Masha Allah!* This kind of khanapoori could not have been bettered by Fayez Mohammad Khan himself. This phirat is straight out of Rahmat Khan's. Aren't these taan ka phandas based on those of Bade Mubarak Ali?'

He asked Fateh Ali Khan, 'How did this gawaiya learn all this?' At the end of Buwa's recital Ali Baksh Khan turned to the Maharaja and said, 'Huzoor, people call me a vain person and say that I do not praise any gawaiya. To speak the truth, this pandit is the one person who makes me feel that the authentic khayal gayaki of my buzurgs is still alive. May Allah-tala grant him a lifespan of a hundred years.' Allah Miyan must have been particularly busy when this dua, this boon, was asked for. Buwa did not survive long after his visit to Patiala. He died of leukemia at the age of fifty-three in 1922.

I had asked Pandit Dilip Chandra Vedi what in one word would he say was Bhaskarbuwa's specialty as a musician. He said, '*Khubsurti*, beauty. There was nothing he did which was inaesthetic. He would take a long meend, a heavy glide from the pancham in the upper octave to re in the middle in Chhayanat. It would be like a perfect sweet dish. One spoonful of sugar more or less would have spoiled it. His technique of raga-vistar he got from Bande Ali Khan and Fayez Mohammad. His badhat was like an alaap on the been. But the most important thing about alaapchari or what the khayaliya calls vistar is swar-prayog, the application of notes, and the use of shrutis. Bhaskarbuwa excelled in both. The ati komal oscillating re of Bhairav, the meend from teevra ma to komal dha in Raamkali, the union of dhaivat and nishad in komal rishabh Asavari—these are not easy to attain without a background of dhrupadi gharana to which all four ustads of Bhaskarbuwa belonged. He received the sheer weight of the voice from Fayez Mohammad and Naththan Khan (remember they belonged to the pre-microphone era). Rhythmic variations, bol-bant and taans in the baraabar laya were also the gift of Naththan Khan. Bhaskarbuwa absorbed some of Alladiya Khan's taan patterns and the phirat of Rahmat

Khan. Gwalior gharana produced no greater musician than this eccentric son of Ustad Haddu Khan. Abdul Karim used to imitate him but never could reproduce a single taan of Rahmat Khan. Bhaskarbuwa did it merely by listening to him a few times. And taiyari? What do you hear from the musicians of today who do their harkats with lips kissing the microphone like bloody crooners? Where is the depth in their voice? And the less said about their synthetic gayaki, the better. Let any of them produce a few of the taans of my jawani, my youth, leave alone those of my guru Bhaskarbuwa.'

I asked him, 'Tell me, Vediji, Bhaskarbuwa got the blessings of all his four gurus. But as you say, he copied Rahmat Khan's phirats. Did Rahmat Khan ever hear Bhaskarbuwa?'

'Once in 1921 in Kolhapur, as far as I can remember. Khansaheb, of course, was highly unpredictable. His eccentricity did not follow any pattern. Normally, he never listened to other musicians. I don't know how he came to hear Bhaskarbuwa but I do know that he embraced him with tears in his eyes and said, "This is not Bhaskar Bakhle, he is Khan Sahab Bhaskar Khan from today." This was a great reward for Buwa from one whom he admired so much.'

'Whatever you might say, Panditji, if Buwa were to sing today, he would not have had much of a following unless he could do sargams and taans covering three octaves.'

'Rubbish! Is Bhimsen starving? Is Mallikarjun begging from door to door? Neither of them is addicted to sargams nor do they go up and down three octaves like a monkey. That kind of thing is liked by the Punjabis. I may be one myself but I have not been taught by Punjabi ustads except in the early stage by Uttam Singh, who sang dhrupad and Hari kirtan. Also light Punjabi songs. Anyway, thanks for reminding me. I am talking about the days when Bhaskarbuwa was a great favourite of the Punjabis in Jalandhar, Amritsar and Lahore. There he heard Ashiq Ali, khalifa of Bade Ghulam Ali, who was vain about his fast taans which covered three octaves. He had one of the worst voices I have ever heard but his taankari got him quite a following. Buwa heard Ashiq Ali's boastful remarks, practised hard behind locked doors and at his next concert in Lahore, produced identical taans covering three octaves before Ashiq Ali and his chelas.'

'What about sargams?'

'Sargams!' exclaimed Vediji with a frown. 'We never heard sargams those days from ustads of reputed gharanas like Gwalior, Agra and Jaipur. The paltas and meerkhand in sargams were practised by sarangiwallas and vocalists at home, never meant to be displayed in public recitals. Wrestlers do sit-ups and other exercises to build their bodies, not in the ring before the public. We did not sing grammar those days. When you deliver a lecture, do you have to spell each word? BLA—BLAY, sly fox met a hen, High road to London from *King Reader Part I.* Is that literature? There is a difference between literature and grammar. It is the same with music.'

The strange analogy of Vediji made me laugh. 'But Abdul Karim did sargams, didn't he?' I persisted.

'That is not sargam. That is sheer poetry. Look how he arranged simple notes into beautiful compositions! He was influenced by Karnatak sangeet but he absorbed it and made it his own. He did not sing paltas and hardly ever did fast sargams like a monkey rapidly chewing peanuts, as Faiyaz Khan, my ustad, used to say.'

'Do you mean to say no one ever criticized Bhaskarbuwa?'

'No one. Maybe one or two jealous musicians like Omkarnath, who did not like either of my two ustads Bhaskarbuwa or Faiyaz Khan. But he was served right in the long run. His guru's curse followed him to the end.'

'Really, Panditji? Pray tell us all. Do not leave out any detail, however irrelevant and inconsequential it may sound to you,' I said, echoing the most popular character in English fiction.

'Well, I first heard Omkarnath Thakur in 1916 in Jalandhar. There was no microphone of course. You have heard the kind of fantastic voice he had. It had range, volume and an inbuilt echo. His bhajans, of course, were extremely popular. Acting in Gujrati plays gave him a kind of dramatic sense which in later years degenerated into melodrama. In 1918, at the Lahore conference, he finished his khayal in the morning and embarked on a bhajan in Bhairavi, *'Bhaja Ram charan sukh-daayee'*. His followers were behaving as if an angel had descended on the stage. Their leader, a police inspector, kept on showering currency notes on the stage, obviously from his ill-gotten gains. Seth Daulatram, the well-respected patron, did not like it and asked the police inspector to stop. Omkarnath said aloud, "If my bhajan evokes bhakti in his heart, why do you want to stop him, Sethji?"

'Anyway, all this did not appeal to Bhaskarbuwa who, in the evening started raga Sawani with a song which started with the words *'Akal sab jaane, aur be-akal aap bhayo hai, apni kahat hai kaahu ki na mane* (An intelligent person knows that blowing one's own trumpet turns him into a fool and he stops paying heed to good advice)'. Omkarnath, in the audience, shouted, "Are you making fun of me, Bhaskar Rao?" Seth Daulatram was widely respected. His intervention prevented the incident from degenerating into an ugly brawl.'

'But Panditji, how did all this serve Omkarnath right?'

'I am coming to that. Vishnu Digambar was Omkarnath's guru. A deeply religious man, he looked a bit like a holy person. He had a magnificent voice which could overpower Omkarnath's when he gave support to his guru on the tanpura. He told Omkarnath in the same Lahore conference, "You should be sitting at the tanpura to give me voice support this evening."

Omkarnath hummed and hawed and generally made his reluctance apparent by finally saying, "Guruji, why don't you take someone else? My pitch is higher than yours."

Vishnu Digambarji said, "That hardly matters. You come down by half a note or I shall sing on a key half or even a full note higher." Omkarnath kept quiet but it was obvious that he was not willing. Ultimately Vishnu Digambarji got annoyed and asked, "What is the meaning of all this? Are you not my disciple? Why should any shishya refuse to sit behind his guru?"

"Of course I am your shishya," said Omkarnath. "I am not denying that you have taught me but I do not sing your gayaki, my style is different."

Vishnuji was completely taken aback and asked, "What gayaki is that? Where did you get it? Who gave it to you?"

"God has given it to me. It is the fruit of my tapasya."

"Look here!" Vishnu Digambar was really angry. "I have been watching you for quite some time. I also heard you yesterday. Looks like your inflated ego is getting the better of your music. I have not been miserly in giving you all my vidya and if this is what you have to give me in return, I predict your music will never receive recognition from ustads and the cognoscenti. You may become a popular singer of bhajans but your khayal will not rise to the level of an ustad's silsilewar gayaki."

'As you know,' continued Vediji, 'Omkarnath never again sang the traditional authentic gayaki of Gwalior. It became a vulgar melodrama. Even his taans in his later years were often out of tune. All he got was adulation from Marwaris and those who wanted to back a Hindu singer against Muslim ustads. If Omkarnath were alive today, he would have been the musician royale of the BJP. He played that role perfectly what with his saffron robe, the deerskin on which he sat and the holy Ganges water which was sprinkled on the dais. When Ustad Faiyaz Khan was awarded the title of 'Aftab-e-Mausiqui', Omkarnath assumed the title of 'Poojya Pandit Sangeet Martanda'. Odd, isn't it, to have two suns in the sky?

'Look! A true artiste should keep himself at a distance from flatterers and sycophants. See what has happened to Kumar Gandharva, thanks to his admirers and the media! I know him since 1938 when he held the Calcutta audience spellbound at the age of ten with his bhajans. Lalababu, the secretary of the All India Music Conference announced that Kumar, the boy prodigy, would entertain the audience with kautuk. He went on singing the 78 RPM records of Abdul Karim and Faiyaz Khan, one after another, from memory. The audience laughed and clapped enthusiastically. I went to Lalababu and asked him to stop it. "Why, Vediji?" he asked, "the boy is doing nothing wrong! He is imitating great ustads."

'I said, "All right! If he has to do nakal of great ustads, let him shave off his head, put on a lungi and start from scratch and practise eight hours a day after getting his ganda tied by any of these ustads whose recorded music he has memorised. Do you think Faiyaz Khan and Abdul Karim sang these ragas for two-and-a-half minutes? Can this boy sing Abdul Karim's thumri *'Jamuna ke teer'* for half-an-hour or Faiyaz Khan's Nat Bihag for an hour?"

'All the adulation the boy received at that tender age did nothing except give him a swollen head. There is no doubt he had a touch of genius. He had ended up as a spoilt misguided genius who takes unheard of liberty with established ragas—as if they are his grandfather's property. His style is folk-based. We all know that folk tunes have evolved into a number of ragas but if you have to sing them you should sing them in their accepted sophisticated form. Anyway, his admirers think he is a pathfinder, one who has opened up a new vista in classical music.'

I said, 'True, Panditji, I am reminded of what Acharya Vrihaspati had to say about Kumar Gandharva when someone asked him for his opinion. He said, "I can offer my opinion of musicians but never a paigambar, a prophet."'

Dr M.R. Gautam, a disciple of Dilip Vedi, Ustad Vilayet Hussain Khan and the Dagar brothers had come and sat down to listen to Vediji who was justifiably proud of his shishya who had risen to the position of vice-chancellor of Indira Kala University of Khairagarh after a long stint as head of the vocal music department of Benaras Hindu University. 'If Panditji permits,' said Gautamji, 'I would like to share a story about Pandit Omkarnath and Acharya Vrihaspati. This was in 1959. A seminar was being held in Jaipur where a

special session was devoted to music and its effect on the
human system. Omkarnath started with Naad-Brahma and
the classification of Naad. First was "Baikhari" which our ears
register. Second came "Madhyama" which is the vibration in
our thoughts. "Pashyanti" was the Anaahat-Naad which
yogis hear in deep meditation. Finally, "Parabak" was Naad-
Brahma, which was Brahman, the Supreme Being. After this
preamble, with profuse quotations from the Shastras, he
turned to the impact of music on animals and the human
system.'

'We know about that, don't we?' I interrupted. 'There
have been various experiments abroad with plant life and the
impact of classical music on it. Also on animals. Cows
listening to recorded symphonies of great masters are giving
double the normal quantity of milk. It is the same with
turnips, cauliflowers and horseradish, which grow to twice
their normal size. If pop music is played to them the effect is
exactly the opposite. You get tasteless, shrivelled-up vegetables
not worth eating. Dogs like music. At least Abdul Karim's
Tipu did, not to speak of the terrier on the records of His
Master's Voice gramophone company. So what is new?'

'Right,' said Gautam, 'but Omkarnathji was talking about
the effect of music on the human system, not on cabbages.
The news of a friend's illness reached him, he said. He
promptly arrived with his tanpura and found his friend down
with high fever and a splitting headache. "Not to worry, not
to worry, Omkarnath is here," announced Panditji and sat
down to sing the raga Shree. Miracle of miracles! There was
no sign of fever or headache after an hour of that divine
music. Omkarnathji's friend got up and ate a whole plate of
dahi-vadas!

'There was complete silence for a few seconds in the
seminar, followed by a snigger or two from the back row.
Acharya Vrihaspati was the first to speak. "Amazing!" he
said. "And yet, no raga has been able to cure Pandit
Omkarnathji's arthritic knee in twenty years. *Kyun*, Panditji?"'

When Vediji stopped laughing, I said, 'Sheila Dhar's

erstwhile guru Pandit Prannath is now based in New York. The *Village Voice*, a paper in Greenwich village, had published a long interview with him. Apparently there was no affliction that cannot be cured by music therapy, which is Prannath's specialized field. As far as one could gather, the gandhar of Shuddh Kalyan could reduce blood pressure. The oscillating komal re of Bhairav worked wonders with kidney-related diseases. The two madhyams of raga Kedar, if properly practised, would cure chronic insomnia. Chromatic use of komal and shuddha ni for ten minutes, morning and evening, cleared up coronary arteries. The komal ga of Darbari was the final answer to piles, provided of course, it was used for a quarter of an hour daily in the middle and lower octaves. Any attempt to use it in the higher octave might aggravate the disease. But there was a snag. The tonic, the sa, differed from person to person. Until the right pitch of the patient was located, the music therapy would be useless. Pandit Prannath now has well over fifty disciples, two apartments and three cars. But forgive me, Vediji, for the interruption, I want to know more about Omkarnath and Bhaskarbuwa.'

'Bhaskarbuwa died in 1922,' resumed Vediji. 'Omkarnath's chelas and admirers started saying that he was the leading vocalist now and his music was pure Hindu because, unlike Bhaskarbuwa, Omkarnath never had any talim from a Muslim ustad (as if that omission was something to be proud of). Suddenly, one of them came out with a statement in some paper or the other that Omkarnath's style influenced Bhaskarbuwa. I promptly wrote to Omkarnath saying he should either contradict the assertion or accept a challenge from me to sing a jugalbandi, he in his own style and me in Bhaskarbuwa's. He wrote back that he would contradict it. But he went away to Italy where his recital, I believe, put Mussolini to sleep. Nothing happened to his promise. *'Woh baat phir thandi par gayee* (The controversy died down).'

'But haven't you sung in the same conference with him? Did he try to compete with you?'

'Me? I'm only small fry. But he did not spare my gurus,

especially Faiyaz Khan Sahab. In December of 1934 at the All India Conference of Benaras, we both sang. The gold medal for the best khayal came to me. Thank God, Ustad Faiyaz Khan did not participate in that conference, otherwise the medal, no doubt, would have gone to him.'

'You and Faiyaz Khan must have sung at the same conference at some point. Did you get a medal then?'

'Are you mad? I was like a pigmy before Faiyaz Khan, the Shah-en-shah of khayal. And why khayal alone! He would bring tears to our eyes with his thumris, especially Bhairavi. When he sang dhrupad and dhamar, *lagta tha sirf yehi kaam unhone saari zindagi kiya* (it seemed that is what he had been doing all his life). Oh yes, I remember, it was at the second All Bengal Conference in Calcutta that Khan Sahab bagged the gold medal for khayal, as usual. The medal for thumri was awarded to me. I stayed with R.C. Boral, the well-known patron and raees. He was also the music director of New Theatres. Nitin Bose, Devakibabu, Raichandbabu—all wanted me to act in their films. I had, of course, composed the music for some films in Bombay already. Those days, there was no playback singing. That is how K.L. Saigal got to act in films. I was prevented by Faiyaz Khan Sahab from joining the celebrated New Theatres. "*Is* line *se hat jao* (Move away from this line)," he told me. I was in your city for three-and-a-half years. Calcutta loved me. Kananbala became my disciple. She had a marvellous voice."

'How did you become Ustad Faiyaz Khan's disciple?'

'That was after the death of Bhaskarbuwa. I felt like an orphan. I just could not make up my mind about the future of my career. There was no one whose music inspired me. There would be someone whose vilambit khayal and swar-prayog appealed to me, but not the taans. Again, if I liked the taans and layakari of an ustad, he would not be particularly strong in raga-vistar. Finally, Ismail Khan, the nephew of the well-known sitar-player Barkatullah Khan, advised me. "Vediji," he said to me, "it is hardly likely that you will be bowled over by any ustad after so many years with

Bhaskarbuwa. It would be better if you tried your luck with Faiyaz Khan. To my mind he is the only one who can satisfy you." I went to Baroda. I heard him sing alaap, dhamar and khayal in Hamir. I thanked Providence for solving my problem once and for all.'

'As far as I know,' I said, 'Khansaheb was not a good teacher. He was impatient, especially with those who were slow on the uptake. That is why he would send them either to his cousin Tasadduq Hussain or his brother-in-law Ata Hussain Khan. Ata Hussain was my guru and I know what an excellent teacher he was, although he hardly conquered a mehfil. Sharafat Hussain told me that Faiyaz Khan lost his temper if any of his students could not pick up a taan or a harkat after two or three attempts. The one who bore the brunt of it was Maujood Hussain, who was the naughtiest of the young crowd and also its leader. Once, in sheer exasperation, Khansaheb threw his slippers at him. Maujood caught them in mid-air and disappeared for hours, leaving Khansaheb to walk around barefoot in the house the rest of the day. My other guru, Latafat Khan, would go to Khansaheb and say, "Mamu, please teach me the tarana in Malkauns you sang last night." Faiyaz Khan would make a face, bring out two or three rupees from his purse and give them to him saying, "Go see a film. Just don't bother me. Do you hear me, you idiot?" That would be his reaction each time.'

Vediji laughed. 'That must have been in his later years. A man with brains such as Faiyaz Khan had was not expected to allow his patience to be tested by a slow learner. Bhaskarbuwa could also be impatient and was a hard taskmaster. I found Faiyaz Khan to be one of the kindest and most affectionate men I have come across. He was hardly ever impatient with me or with Ratanjankar, who was my contemporary. It was Shrikrishna's father who went and complained to Khan Sahab against me.'

'Did he really? Why on earth?'

'Yes he did. Ratanjankar's father, an inspector, worked in the police court. I won't say he was a particularly nice man to know. One day he asked me who in my opinion was a greater artiste, Bhaskarbuwa or Faiyaz Khan. I said I would not be able to answer that question. Both of them were my gurus. He had better ask Alladiya Khan who had heard and known both of them well. Ratanjankar's father lost no opportunity in telling Khan Sahab that Dilip Chand thought Bhaskarbuwa was an infinitely better musician than Faiyaz Khan. But Khan Sahab was not the kind of person who paid heed to such nonsense. He was not a small man. I still remember when he made me sing the first time, before tying my ganda. He said, "Do not ever give up Bhaskarbuwa's style which is now well set in your singing. There will never be another singer like Buwa." How many ustads do you think had such a liberal outlook? But people repeatedly carrying tales would have some effect at some point of time even on a man like Faiyaz Khan. One morning, he gave me a taan which I could not reproduce even after three or four attempts. He suddenly said, "One who has suchcha imaan can pick up such a taan without difficulty."

'I said, "If that is what you think, Khan Sahab, you had better not teach a be-imaan like me. I will go back to Bombay tomorrow."

"You say that to your ustad? Do you?"

"'Why not?" I retorted. God has sent me into this world with a mizaj that never lets me compromise on an issue where I know I am not wrong. Anyway, all ended well when Khan Sahab's grandfather Ghulam Abbas Khan said, "What is the matter with Dilip Chand? Why is he not coming for his lessons? You better teach him properly. He is the best among your pupils." Faiyaz Khan's nonagenarian ustad's word was law. My talim started again.'

Vediji heard my first National Programme on AIR and sent word through Inderlal, the sarangi-player who was his disciple, that he would like to see me. It was natural that our conversation would turn to Ustad Faiyaz Khan. With tears in his eyes Vediji said, 'What have I given such a kind and lovable teacher as him? Neither Bhaskarbuwa nor Faiyaz

Khan ever took a rupee from me. Faiyaz Khan Sahab put me up in his house, his begum gave me the choicest food prepared for Khan Sahab. I got his affection and, above all, his vidya. Later in life, when I started earning, I invited Faiyaz Khan and Vilayet Hussain to the Taj hotel in Bombay. Turning to Vilayet Hussain, Khan Sahab said, "It is a good thing that you don't drink but I do not approve of prudery in anyone." To me he said, "Dilip Chand, I know you drink. You may have it in my presence. I am giving you my ijaazat." I had till then never even sat on a chair in his presence. I was always on the floor when he taught me from his cot. How could I drink in his presence? The glass remained untouched on the table.'

That day, Vediji was full of memories of Faiyaz Khan. 'Khan Sahab and I had once gone to see the Vrindavan Gardens in Mysore. There, sitting on the lawn next to a fountain, he started singing '*Vande Nandkumaram*' in Kafi. He sang it for half-an-hour without any accompaniment. His voice had such taseer, he did not need any. When he stopped I said, "Khan Sahab, all the songs which have come from 'Braj-bhoomi'[3] relate to Krishna's Bal-leela, his childhood and the love of gopis and Radha for him. But perhaps you do not know what an astute politician he grew up into. I talked about 'Krishna-charitra' to him, quoting to him from the *Mahabharata* and finally read out from Lokmanya Tilak's commentary on the Geeta for seven days. Khan Sahab was very happy. He said, "*Hamne tumko gaana sikhaaya magar aqal ki baat tumne hame sunaayee* (I have taught you music but you have passed on words of wisdom to me). What did I know of Krishnaji and the Geeta except what I have learnt through folklore and song?"'

I also gathered that Vediji eventually made up with Omkarnath Thakur, the common point between them being their antipathy towards Pandit Bhatkhande and his theories. Their thesis was that the classification of ragas should be based on modulation or change of key. The theory of ten thaats was a weak one. For instance, Bilawal and Khamaj had more or less the same notes. Why should they be separate

thaats? Vediji also could not find any logic behind declaring
Marwa as a separate thaat. How can a *'shadav'* (consisting of
six notes) raga claim to be a thaat? Even if he were to accept
Marwa as a thaat, a raga which belongs to early evening, how
could the early morning raga Lalit belong to Marwa thaat!
According to Bhatkhandeji's time-scale theory, komal re and
shuddh ma denote morning ragas while teevra ma and komal
re belong to the early evening ones. The vivadi swar of
Marwa, an evening raga, is shuddh madhyam. Lalit, on the
other hand, would be absolutely naked if deprived of that
particular note.

And what about Todi, one of the most popular morning
ragas which has a komal re and teevra ma and should
legitimately find its place in the evening? So on and so forth.
Vediji wrote an article on these lines in the *Amrita Bazaar
Patrika* and received words of praise from Omkarnath, who
had settled down in Benaras University in his old age. Vediji
received regular invitations from Omkarnath Thakur to deliver
lectures and was also appointed as external examiner for the
master's degree. Vediji ended our discussion by saying,
'Whatever I told you about Omkarnath's past is true but his
power of analysis and knowledge of Shastriya Sangeet were of
a very high order. And *unki awaaz ka jaadu main bhool nahin
saktaa* (I cannot forget the magic of his voice)."

As I was about to leave, I asked him, 'Tell me, Panditji,
why did you give up singing so early? I don't think I have
heard you since I was in my teens. I remember a mehfil in
Calcutta where you stopped in the middle of a recital and
told the musicians in the audience, *"Jo taan is mehfil mein gale
se niklega woh dobara aaj nahin niklenge* (Any taan I take this
evening will not be repeated)". Such was your repertoire of
taans and your virtuosity. So why did you stop singing?'

'*Kya kahoon Kumar Sahab, ham aiyaashi mein par gaye,*"
replied Vediji, standing up to bid me goodbye. Loosely
translated, what he meant was that he succumbed to bad
habits, not a particularly ambiguous statement which leaves
little doubt about what weaknesses a successful musician
could fall prey to in Dilip Chandra Vedi's halcyon days.[4]

9

Shrikrishna Ratanjankar

My first distinct recollection of Pandit Shrikrishna Ratanjankar was when he sang before Rabindranath Tagore in the house of Professor N.K. Siddhant, a colleague of my father in Lucknow. I was barely eight then—this was March 1935—and had little comprehension of what was happening, though I had heard some of the greatest ustads already on my father's knee. All I remember was that Tagore was not well; he had high fever. Yet, he sat up on the sofa till eleven at night, eyes closed, a majestic Bernini's Moses-like figure with his flowing white beard. When the applause died down he said something to indicate that he liked the Chhayanat immensely, more than the Jayjaiwanti and Paraj that followed, and then proceeded to sing a dhrupad in Natanarayan to the great astonishment of those present, including Pandit Ratanjankar.

Tagore, as I said, was tired and unwell but asked my father to come to his bedroom and we returned home without him. I know now what they discussed because this was the beginning of a correspondence in Bengali between Tagore and my father on music, which was published by Visva-Bharati under the title *Sur-o-Sangati* in 1935.

Tagore's stand, as I find in that book, is a fundamental one. Let us not forget that he had his initiation into classical raga sangeet through Jadu Bhatta, the legendary dhrupad singer of Bengal. So did my father come by khayal and thumri in Lucknow via Radhika Goswami and Mahim

Mukherji's dhrupad in Calcutta. Tagore's contention is: all art has to have clearly demarcated limits born out of proportions—without which art loses its unity. Dhrupad had them, old Bengali songs had them and even bhajans had them. It is only in khayal singing that one has a procession of angas and alankars, which never seem to end and are often repetitive. Why not sing Jayjaiwanti in different chaals based on different compositions? Tagore, who often preferred analogy to logic, asks, 'When your wife dresses to go for dinner in a friend's house, does she wear all her jewellery and all the saris in her wardrobe?'

In case I am misunderstood, Tagore's observations, I hasten to repeat, related to khayal vis-à-vis the kind of music he grew up on, and had little to do with Pandit Ratanjankar's virtuosity in particular. In fact, the best person to give a suitable reply with demonstrations could have been Ratanjankar himself, who could at will develop a raga strictly on the lines of a particular bandish followed by different compositions in the same raga. But the stance Tagore adopted is a pertinent one in relation to khayal and raises a fundamental aesthetic issue. There is little doubt that structural unity in any classical form cannot but be based on the first principles of restraint and proportion. I wonder how Tagore would have reacted to Ustad Abdul Waheed Khan's legendary swar-vistar of Multani for three-and-a-half hours! I do know that he was completely mesmerized by Ustad Faiyaz Khan's Raamkali alaap in Jorasanko, Calcutta, and gave him a nazraana of twenty-one gold sovereigns. Faiyaz Khansaheb also used to recall, not without a hint of fun, how he sang Yaman Kalyan and Yaman in eight different angas to Pandit Bhatkhandeji in Kashmir, something that his illustrious disciple, Ratanjankar, would have been proud of.

To come back to Ratanjankar, whom my father always referred to as an 'ocean of learning'. Of that there is no doubt. Who else had inherited the wisdom and learning of Pandit Bhatkhande, the first Indian to traverse India and systematize north Indian classical music and rescue it from

Pandit Shrikrishna Ratanjankar

the chaotic state of theoretical disorganization in which he found it? But Pandit Ratanjankar did not stop at that. He not only brought his own remarkable analytical powers into play but his experience and talim came from two of the greatest ustads of his time: 'Aftab-e-Mausiqi' Ustad Faiyaz Khan and Ustad Mushtaq Hussain Khan of Rampur. While Ratanjankarji was a disciple of the former, he was greatly influenced by the latter's Gwalior-sahaswan gayaki. Moreover, it is worth mentioning here that Pandit Ratanjankar had his basic talim in Gwalior gayaki from Pandit Anant Manohar Joshi in his young age. In fact, as he confessed to me in his later years, his style was a synthesis of the two.

And what a brilliant synthesis it was! While Annasaheb, as we used to call him, had produced knowledgeable and brilliant disciples like S.C.R. Bhat, Chidananda Nagarkar, K.G. Ginde, Chinmoy Lahiri, V.G. Jog, Dr Sumati Mutatkar and (my old partner in duets) Dinkar Kaikini, why have they not, in their turn, been able to perpetuate this tradition through their disciples with as much success? We of the older generation find this gayaki complete in its aesthetic and intellectual appeal. Why does it not appeal to the present generation? Pandit Bhatkhandeji's dream has certainly come true. No one dares teach music today without the six volumes of his *Kramik Pustak Malika* and the ustads secretly refer to it without admitting it. Classical music has spread widely among the middle classes and is no longer the prerogative of the privileged few, whether for better or for worse is another matter. All this could not have been possible without Pandit Ratanjankar and his boys. But what has happened at the same time to the authenticity of style and the standard of appreciation? What we hear today is not grammatically incorrect. But I suppose, mere knowledge of grammar does not produce literature. It must be the same with music.

What helped Ratanjankar's disciples in becoming established musicians themselves was that their guru was himself an outstanding artiste. Even Balasaheb Poochhwale and C.R. Vyas, who were from a somewhat different stream, though from the same tradition, came under Ratanjankar's spell. His learning and virtuosity had very few equals. I have heard him sing Nayaki Kanhra, Suha, Sughrayi, Shahana and Bahar in one sitting and give each of them its distinct outstanding feature. He would similarly amuse himself by singing ragas close to one another like Poorvi, Pooriya, Saazgiri, Sohini and Hindol, which with lesser musicians would have been a bore, if not disastrous. I have heard him recreate lost ragas like Kaushik Kanhra of Bageshri anga, Deepak and Shuddha Malhar (same notes as in Durga) and hold us spellbound with his blend of artistry and intellectual prowess. It is a great pity that very few, even of my generation, have heard Pandit Shrikrishna Ratanjankar at his best. Years of hard work dedicated to the cause of the Marris Music College, without adequate remuneration, living on indifferent hostel food, away from home and particularly teaching students, male and female, in different keys, had taken its toll of his voice and health. When Keskar became the minister for information and broadcasting at the centre, Annasaheb's luck turned at last, but his voice and form, by then, were things of the past.

In his later years, he would come to Nani Gopalbabu's Bengal Music College, Calcutta, as an examiner. I would make up for my lost youth and spend hours with him in discussion and singing. Also, he would sing at my house every year with varying success before a well-chosen audience. The last time he sang, two of his disciples accompanied him; one was Chinmoy Lahiri and the other Sita Sharan Singh (an old friend of mine from Lucknow who was gifted with a magnificent voice). The tanpuras were tuned to D sharp and Annasaheb's taans in shuddh akar spouted up to pancham in taar saptak with graceful ease, while his two disciples struggled to stand on the upper shadja in imitation of Annasaheb's open-chested voice production.

Glimpses of his glorious past came back that evening, the remarkable control of shrutis, his own specialty, his sargams, which were specially designed to bring out the anatomy of the raga, the playful treatment of the bandish and above all the taans—the like of which I had not heard from him since my youth in Lucknow. He sang Jhinjhoti, Khambawati, Hem-Nat (his own raga and his own composition) and Kafi Kanhra. I could not help feeling that this was perhaps his swan song, so impressive was the recital of the man in his seventies. That evening, I was reminded of what my father said about Pandit Ratanjankar: 'I have heard a good many outstanding musicians in my time but I will walk miles to hear Shrikrishna, wherever he sings.'

At the end of the recital that day, we were all praise. Annasaheb, who did not count excessive modesty as one of his virtues, was quiet for a while and then said to us, 'I am a shagird of Aftab-e-Mausiqi Faiyaz Khan Sahab, the greatest ustad of my time, and a shishya of Bhatkhandeji, the greatest pundit of Hindustan. *Agar kabhi thoda gaa leta hoon to kaun sa kamaal kiya maine* (What is so amazing if I occasionally manage to sing well)?'

Next year he failed to make his annual visit to Calcutta. He was gone forever.

'Look, Shrikrishna is not an ordinary person. He is my disciple all right but in the near future it will be impossible to find a vocalist of his calibre in this country. I have a lot of respect for him.'

—*Ustad Faiyaz Khan*

'Anna Sahab, you are a perfect 'kriya-siddha pandit' (musicologist with divine performing skills). I knew you as a musicologist only. But today you proved that your analytical mind is aided by your remarkable aesthetic sense. Whatever I have absorbed from close association with top-ranking musicians, your music has the same characteristics.'

—*Govind Rao Tembe,
Gayan-pandit of Maharashtra*

'I declare, with all my heart that our generation does not have another guru like him... The truth is, Bombay or

Maharashtra could not assess the qualities of Anna Sahab. They never knew what Ratanjankar was!'

—Pandit Kumar Gandharva

'My span of life, I believe, is nearing its end gradually and I take these new developments as a matter of course. Thank God, He has left me a brilliant pupil in you, and I have little doubt you will satisfy all the hopes I have entertained of you...'

—From the last letter by
Pandit Bhatkhande to Dr Ratanjankar

Notes

2. The Birth of Khayal

1. This view of Mr Mitra seems to be an erroneous one. Dr Wahid Mirza quotes from the third chapter of *Nuh Sipehr* by this poet: 'Indian music, the fire that burns the heart and soul, is superior to the music of any other country. Foreigners, even after a stay of thirty or forty years cannot play a single Indian tune correctly.' In *Qiraan-us-Saadain* the poet asks the reader, 'Why do I love India so passionately? India is my homeland... India is a paradise on earth. India is great, too, because (it is) the land which has a poet and musician like Amir Khusro.'—*Amir Khusro: The Great Indian* by R.K. Das, BPI (India) Pvt. Ltd, New Delhi.

3. Gwalior Gharana

1. Namak-haraam literally means unfaithful to the salt, i.e., he who bites the hand that feeds him.
2. Jagmohan Dalmia, secretary of the Cricket Control Board of India in 1996, is the son-in-law of the same Bhupen Ghosh's brother. On the prestigious occasion of the inauguration of the World Cup at Eden Gardens, Calcutta, viewed by millions on television, he gave us Alisha Chinoy's music, a hot favourite of paan-bidi-wallas.
3. According to Raja Deba Prasad Garg of Mahishadal, Bhaiyya Sahab's mother was a tawayef called Chandrabhaga, the father unquestionably Maharaja Daulat Rao Scindia.
4. Ustad Allarakha, who died at the turn of this century, was the guru and father of the internationally renowned Ustad Zakir Hussain.
5. Trivats contain—a) the usual bols of taranas like na dir tom dir dir tom, which, according to some, are in imitation of instrumental music; b) bols of tabla and/or pakhawaj; and c) usually an antara in Persian or even Sanskrit. If sargams are also added as part of the composition, it is called Chaturang, or a composition having four colours.

4. Patiala and Sahaswan

1. Jgyasa Publications.
2. Popular Prakashan.

3. ibid.
4. ibid.
5. *Here Is Someone I Would Like You To Meet.* Oxford University Press.
6. See chapter 'Birth of the Khayal'.
7. Sampurna ragas use all seven notes in the scale. Yaman has all shuddh notes except the fourth note (sharp madhyam). Bhairav, the morning raga, has an oscillating minor re and dha.

5. Agra Gharana and Ustad Faiyaz Khan

1. *My Life*, by Ustad Alladiya Khan, as told to his grandson Azizuddin Khan, translated with an introduction by Amlan Dasgupta and Urmila Bhirdikar, Thema; Calcutta 2000.
2. Such an attitude at that time was unheard of when ustads preferred to take their knowledge and compositions to their graves rather that teach anyone outside their gharanas—KPM.
3. Modern-day dhrupad singers, especially in Bengal, think saiyams have always been taboo in dhrupad. Faiyaz Khan used sargams in plenty in his fast alaapchari in Jod anga.
4. The discerning student of music may note that Allabande Khan was the grandfather of Moinuddin, Aminuddin, Zahiruddin and Faiyazuddin Dagar. Do we conclude, then, that what they and their descendants sang—and are still singing—is not Dagarbani? Niyamat Khan, his son Dulhe Khan and grandson Haidar Baksh belonged to the Khandarbani tradition.
5. *My Life*, by Ustad Alladiya Khan.
6. *Sangeet Sansmaran* (Sangeet Natak Akademi).
7. Correspondence in Bengali published under the title *Sur-o-Sangati* by Visva-Bharati.
8. *Aesthetics of Agra and Jaipur Traditions*; Popular Prakashan.
9. *On Music and Musicians of Hindoostan* by Ashok D. Ranade; published by Promilla & Co.
10. *Ustad Faiyaz Khan*; Sangeet Natak Akademi.

6. Jaipur Gharana and Ustad Alladiya Khan

1. *My Life* as told to his grandson. Translated by Amlan Dasgupta and Urmila Bhirdikar; Thema.
2. The word 'asthayee' is a corrupt form of the Sanskrit word 'sthayee' which stands for the first stanza of a khayal or dhrupad which dwells on notes in the middle and lower octave while

'antara' covers the upper half of the composition in middle and higher octaves. Usage, however, denotes 'asthayee' as a khayal composition.

3. *Aesthetics of Agra and Jaipur Traditions*; Popular Prakashan.
4. *Here Is Somebody I Would Like You to Meet* by Sheila Dhar; Oxford University Press.
5. ibid.
6. ibid.
7. ibid.
8. ibid.

7. Kirana Gharana

1. Volume III of D.P. Mukherji's collected works in Bengali; Dey's Publishing.
2. *Sudha Sagar Teere* by Suresh Chakrabarty and the author's *Majlis*; Ananda Publishers.
3. *Abdul Karim*; Sangeet Karyalaya; Hathras.
4. '(Why boast of physical beauty and of earthly treasures, for they will crumble to dust. See! The King, who built himself a palace in the city, now lies in eternal sleep in the jungle.)'
5. ibid.
6. See chapter on the Gwalior gharana.
7. Meaning 'one who hails from Baroda', a Maharashtrian custom.
8. Pronounced 'Maanay'.
9. The cuckoo of Kirana.
10. Zariwala ibid.
11. After suffering from Parkinson's disease for six years he passed away on January 31, 2004, at Calcutta.
12. Incense.
13. *Between Two Tanpuras* by Vamanrao H. Deshpande; Popular Prakashan.
14. ibid.
15. Originally meant for mushairas, or poetry reading sessions in Urdu, it means the appropriate appreciative noises and comments made during a recital, a singular feature of soirees of bygone days.
16. See chapter on Gwalior gharana.
17. *Hindusthani Music* by Dr Ashok Ranade; National Book Trust.
18. *Hindusthani Music* by Dr Ashok Ranade; National Book Trust.
19. *Sur-o-Sangati*; Visva-Bharati.
20. Mizaj—an Urdu word which is accepted by the Bengali language

because it is virtually untranslatable. To call it a combination of mood, temperament and style would still be inadequate. So is the word maza. The nearest one can get to it is 'thrill'. To call Abdul Karim a non-gharanedar musician would be factually incorrect. Kirana musicians try to trace the origin of their gharana to Nayak Dhondu and Nayak Bhannu in the sixteenth century. More recently the names of Hingarang (Hussain Ali) and Sabras (Ghulam Maula) of Delhi Court are cited (*Khayal* by Bonnie C. Wade). But there are no big names thereafter among Abdul Karim Khan's ancestors. Also because they played so many instruments, like the sarangi, nakkada, tasha, tabla, etc., like Mirasis, they were perhaps not held in esteem by the conservative ustads.

21. ibid.
22. *Bhramyamaner Dino-panjika* in Bengali.
23. Dada Qalandar Hazrat was a Muslim saint of the Qalandari order, who, like Khwaja Moinuddin Chishti of Ajmer, is venerated all over India.
24. March 13, 2004.
25. *Listening to Hindusthani Music* by Chetan Karnani; Sangam Books.
26. *Imaan* in this context means a combination of love and loyalty, which he is said to have had for Waheed Khan's gayaki.
27. *Ustad Rajab Ali Khan* by Ameek Hanfi; Rajkamal Prakashan.
28. Arabinda Dasgupta, a marine engineer known now as Ustad Dilshad Khan and husband of the well-known singer Parveen Sultana.
29. See chapter on Gwalior gharana.
30. *Alladiya Khan Yanchi Charitra*; a Maharashtra government publication.
31. Ustad Wazir Khan belonged to the dynasty of the legendary Miyan Tansen on his mother's side while his wife belonged to the Seni lineage on her father's. Both Ustad Alauddin Khan and Ustad Hafiz Ali Khan were his disciples. Wazir Khan's place in history is secure as the fountainhead of modern-day instrumental music.

8. Bhaskar Rao Bakhle

1. Damri means a pie, three of which made a paisa and sixty-four paise made a rupee those days. Damri Lal, I found out later, was a common Marwari name.
2. a) i. *Mazha Jeevan Vyasang* by Govindrao Tembe; Govindrao Smarak Samiti. ii. *Majha Jeevan Vihar* by Govindrao Tembe;

Kolhapur Bharat Book Stall. iii. *Bhaskar Guna Gaurav* edited by Vasant Shantaram Desai; Pune Bharat Gayan Samaj. b) *Dev Gandharv* by Shaila Datar; Raj Hans Prakashan.

3. The land of Vrindavan, Mathura, extending right upto Agra.
4. The conversations with Vediji had taken place in Delhi where I spent a lot of time in the 1980s. Some of his thoughts and statements were recorded and are to be found in the archives of the ITC Sangeet Research Academy. Vediji died on November 13, 1992, when he was ninety-one years old.

Glossary

Aandolan—oscillation (L)[1], one type of gamak, a grace consisting of a long amplitude of vibrato just enough to produce a kind of stress and emotional quality in the notes of the raga.

Alankar—(ornament) (L), types of musical ornamentation, decorative scale exercises giving a sense of space and possibilities.

Alaap—conversation, tuning up (L), note by note delineation of a raga bound by slow tempo or laya but not necessarily bound by any rhythmic cycle or taal as in the case of dhrupad alaap.

Amaanat—deposit.

Arohi—ascending (L), a series of notes in ascending order.

Audav—five (L), a raga consisting of five notes or pentatonic scale.

Avarohi—descending (L), a series of notes in descending order.

Bahlawa—recreation, diversion (L), following the vistar further elaboration of the raga using the words of the composition full of meend which traverses through two octaves with increased speed leading to taans. This is a speciality with the vocalists of Gwalior style.

Balai or *malai*—cream of milk.

Bandish—restriction (L), a musical composition. The lyrics are usually composed in Brijbhasha or Bhojpuri dialects of Hindi providing space for musical elaboration. The instrumental compositions are called gat bandish.

Barabar laya—same, even tempo (L), rhythm bound improvisations where one, two, three or even four notes are sung per matra or beat so that the number of the notes is proportional to the number of beats.

Barhat/badhat—orderly development of musical ideas in the form of alaap within the khayal composition.

Begum—respectable, noble lady.

Bhasha anga—literary aspect.

---

[1]Literal meaning

Bol bant—division of words (L), lyrical and melodic lines of a vocal composition rendered in short and various divisions with rhythmic variants.

Bol-taan—word sallies (L), specific melodic figures, note-patterns showing the characteristic phrases of a raga are known as taan. There are sixteen varieties of taans in khayal style. Taans with note sequence rendered with the words or lyrical passages of a composition are bol-taans.

Chaiti—Traditional seasonal songs belonging to Uttar Pradesh sung in the month of Chaitra (March-April). These relate to Radha-Krishna and spring. Ragas like Pahadi, Mand, Piloo enhance the romantic beauty of its Purabia dialect.

Chutkala—witty, humorous proverb or remark (L), a type of composition sung in and around Jaunpur (Uttar Pradesh) during and after Sultan Sharki's rule in the fifteenth century.

Dahi and *khichri*—curd, yoghurt and a preparation of rice mixed with an equal amount of pulses and seasoned with aromatic spices—a common, simple but highly nutritious north Indian combination of food items—not supposed to be a rich diet.

Dana—grain (L), well-defined pearl-like notes enjoined with the help of meend in fast-running taans.

Dhamar—abolish dha—the first powerful beat of almost all the taals (L), a lilting rhythmic cycle with fourteen beats grouped 5-2-3-4 beginning with ka instead of dha and played on the pakhawaj, compositions set to this taal—often sung after a dhrupad; also called Hori-dhamar or pakki Hori. A traditional Holi festival in UP is never celebrated without a dhamar accompanied by a daph. The folk-based dhamars are the origin of classical dhamar.

Dooni and *chaudooni taans*—taans using two or four notes in a cluster per beat as they move.

Drut—fast.

Ektaal—a taal-cycle with twelve beats commonly used by khayal singers.

Fakir—Muslim mendicant, poor.

Farmaan—royal edict, command or mandate.

Fikra—a phrase, also a taunting remark.

Gamak—fragrance (L), essential ten varieties of musical graces or embellishments used in north Indian music, known as dashavidha gamaks.

Gandabandh—a disciple with a sacred thread or amulet around his wrist tied by his master. A symbol of eternal bonding, this indicates that the master has accepted the pupil as a member of his own clan.

Gandhar—the third of the seven musical notes of Indian music.

Gayaki—styles of improvisations in classical vocal music.

Gharanas—family, clan (L), schools of Hindustani music with distinctive voice throw, style of singing and the approach to music. These have names from various towns and cities of India where the originator of the style lived; e.g., Gwalior, Agra, Jaipur, Kirana, Bhindibazar, Rampur, Indore, Sham Chaurasi, Vishnupur, etc. Sons and family members carried the tradition forward. Gradually, the mentor-pupil mode, or the guru-shishya parampara, started welcoming outsiders into its fold.

Ghazal—an amatory sonnet, a popular form of Urdu poetry that is often sung.

Graha—planet (L), the tonic note of a raga.

Halaq taan—a variety of medium-paced taan in which a form of gamak is used to produce a swing.

Harkat—motion (L), refined and lightweight fast-moving embellishments.

Hikka taans—taans interspersed with hiccup-like movements.

Hindu Kayasth—a Hindu sect greatly influenced by Muslim ways and etiquette.

Ilm—education, knowledge (L), musical wisdom.

Jalsa—meeting, festivity, social or musical gathering.

Jhala—fast-paced instrumental improvisation with rhythmic use of the Chikari strings which is supposed to produce the sound of ankle-bells.

Jod—addition, joint (L), the second stage of the alaap when from the slow tempo it moves to the medium pace with the help of rhythmic patterns.

Kajri—black (L), also called kajli, a folk song of Uttar Pradesh sung during the rainy season. Adopted by musicians as a light classical form, it draws upon the tales of Krishna.

Kaku-prayog—a technique of dramatic voice-throw that emphasizes the significant characteristics of a raga.

Kalawant—skilled performing artiste.

Kampa—tremble, shiver (L), oscillation confined usually to one note.

Karnatak—a region of south India (L), a distinctive style of classical music as sung in south India.

Khanapoori—half-hearted formality (L), improvisations within the frame of a composition.

Khatka—doubt (L), a grace (one of the triad—khatka, murkee and gitkiri) with a two-note span giving edge, sharpness and speed to the figure.

Khayal—imagination, whim, meditation (L), the most challenging classical musical form—requires a high order of improvisational skill at several levels and layers of the raga, the range and scope of which covers the whole range of human experience from the mystic to mathematical and intellectual exploration.

Kheer—a popular sweet dish made with thickened milk.

Komal—soft (L), flatter pitch of a note; opposite of teevra—the higher or sharper pitch.

Lakshan geet—a song indicating the main characteristics of the raga in which it is composed.

Larazdar taan—slow-paced intricate heavy taan.

Laya—to merge, fusion (L), tempo of a piece of music; the vilambit, madhya and drut laya indicate slow, medium and fast tempi, respectively.

Layakari—the play of multiples of the three basic layas or tempo. This could be in double, triple and quadruple measures. The aad (1½ matras or beats), kuaad (1¼ beats), biaad (10¼ beats), etc, are known as vikrita-layakari.

Mandra saptak—lower octave.

Marathi Natya Sangeet—the classical based songs and musical score of plays—a genre extremely popular in Maharashtra.

Mazaa—taste, fun, pleasure (L), musical bliss.

Meend—smooth, uninterrupted glide from one note to another connecting them by using shrutis or microtones, one of the most important gamaks.

Mehfil—an assembly, a congregation (L), an intimate musical gathering.

Mridangam—made of clay (L), a two-ended drum used as a classical percussion instrument in Carnatic/Karnatak music.

Mujra—performance of song and dance by professional dancing girls or prostitutes.

Murak—twist, wring.

Murkee—a short sharp twisting figure of two or three notes with high decorative power mostly used in light classical idioms.

Nayika-bhed—different types of heroines (L), *Natyashastra* by Bharat-muni describes all according to their physique, nature and character.

Nazrana—a gift.

Nom tom alaap—an alaap that uses the syllables nom-tom, an abbreviation of the mantra: *Om Hari Ananta Narayana*, to elaborate the raga. Dhrupad singers use this. Some khayal gharanas like Agra also do it.

Numaish—exhibit, show off.

Nyas—a trust, a deposit (L), note on which a musical phrase rests.

Palta—a turn, an exchange, to overrun (L), a figure of notes describing a raga's geometry.

Phanda—loop, trap (L), a twisting short, crisp figure of a few notes taking the shape of a loop within the span of half a matra, or beat.

Phirat—a turn, to turn around (L), meandering taan patterns especially in ragas having a complex gait.

Prakar—variety.

Pujya Pandit—revered master.

Pukar—call, shout (L), singing forcefully, especially in the higher octave, the lyrics/bols to express the emotions/bhava in khayal singing.

Qawaal—musicians who sings qawaali.

Qawaali—originated from the 'qawl'—the mystical Sufi sayings, qawaali was sung by the followers of Khwaja Moinuddin Chishti of Ajmer and became popular in the thirteenth century. Hindustani classical music was used to popularize the words of Sufi saints. While Sufism deeply influenced Indian consciousness through the power of music, the technical elements of classical music along with taans and sargams gave birth to khayal.

Korma and *rotees*—a rich meat preparation and hand-made puffed bread.

Raag-bhava—the underlying emotion of a raga.

Raagdari—the technique and art of raga delineation.

Raaslila—songs describing the Raas (L), Krishna along with Radha, surrounded by gopis or cowherdesses, is said to have performed dance (Raas) on moonlit nights on the banks of the Yamuna.

Rabab—a string instrument without the frets, which is said to be the origin of the sarod.

Raees—noble, affluent person.

Raaganga—the salient features of the raga.

Rekhab—second note of the octave.

Riyaz—practice with devotion.

Sa Re Ga Ma Pa Dha Ni—seven notes of a saptak, called sargam. This solfa in the West includes the first note of the higher saptak as its eighth note and, therefore, is known as an octave.

Sahakaari dhaivat—assisting sixth note of the saptak (L). It is situated in between a major and a minor note.

Sampurna—whole, complete (L), a complete saptak or a raga with seven notes.

Sanskaar—sacraments, purification, reformation, influence of habit-forming exercises.

Sapaat taan—plain taan (L), taan based on the ascending-descending notes of a raga rendered without a break. Also known as shuddh or saral taan.

Shahi tukra—regal piece (L), a rich sweetmeat favourite of the nawabs.

Shastriya Sangeet—classical music.

Sheermal—soft bread.

Shikshaka—teacher, guru.

Shruti—microtone, with an interval smaller than a semitone.

Shuddh akar—pure akar, clear intonation of notes with the help of vowel (aa or a).

Shuddha and *Chhayalag*—pure and tinged (L), pure ragas and ragas with shades of others.

Silsilewar gayaki—singing style following an orderly traditional track.

Soot—threat (L), reverse meend gliding down from the upper to lower note.

Sursingar—a larger and older variety of sarod now on the verge of extinction. This instrument has a special deep tone and dignity that is extremely impressive.

Swarsthaan—place of the swara.

Taar saptak—higher octave.

Taareef—appreciation.

Taseer—effect, influence (L), musical impact on the mind and emotions.

Talim—education, training, teaching (L), process of learning or teaching in the mentor-pupil tradition.

Taluqdar—owner of an estate, a title.

Taan pradhan—based on taans.

Tanpura—a self-effusive drone instrument usually with four strings. Yet this is the basic and the most vital of Hindustani classical musical instruments.

Tap-khayal—a blend of tappa (see Gwalior gharana) and khayal.

Tawayef—professional singing girl, prostitute (L), since the Mughal period, a repository of music, culture and etiquette as noble ladies never sang in public till as late as the twentieth century.

Teentaal—one of the most popular rhythm measures or taal with sixteen beats divided into four equal parts with four matras each. Out of its three accented beats the first is called sam and enjoys the prime position, while the ninth is the unaccented open beat called khali.

Tehai—one-third portion (L), repeating a phrase three times to dramatize the advent of the sam, or the accented first beat of the taal cycle.

Thali—a huge plate meant to serve full courses of lunch and dinner.

Thaat—basic scales from which all the ragas are derived. According to Pandit Vishnu Narayan Bhatkhande, there are ten thaats with the names of the ragas. These are: Bilawal, Kalyan, Khamaj, Kafi, Bhairav, Marwa, Poorvi, Asavari, Todi and Bhairavi.

Theka—the bare structure of the taal played on the tabla with simple bols.

Thumri—originally associated with the ankle-bells, or the dance this idiom later captured, occupied an eminent place in light classical music. Composed in dialects like Brij-bhasha or Bhojpuri the romantic lyrics demand all the skills of a classical musician along with a delicate, emotive appeal obtained by a judicious mix of ragas. The style flourished in Lucknow and Benaras but singers from Punjab popularized it the most.

Tongawalla—driver of a horse-driven cart.

Topee-badal bhai—a 'brother' indicated by an exchange of caps.

Tum—informal, intimate address. *Tu* is even more informal and can be disrespectful while *aap* is a formal, respectful form of address. In polite society in Lucknow, *aap* is de rigeur when used by the wife in public. At least it was, till recent times.

Uttam and *adham*—the best and the worst (L). *Madhyam* means mediocre.

Vilambit—slow-paced (L), slow tempo.

Vistar—elaboration (L), to elaborate the raga while singing the composition, after establishing the tempo, using swaras as vowels or syllables of the lyrics.

Zamindar—landlord.

Sources: 1. *Bharatiya Sangeet Kosh* by Bimalakanta Roychowdhury.

2. *The Penguin Dictionary of Indian Classical Music*, by Raghava R. Menon.

3. *Khayal*, by Bonnie Wade.